SPYING 101:
THE RCMP'S SECRET ACTIVITIES AT CANADIAN UNIVERSITIES, 1917–1997

Spying 101

*The RCMP's Secret Activities at
Canadian Universities,
1917–1997*

STEVE HEWITT

UNIVERSITY OF TORONTO PRESS
Toronto Buffalo London

© University of Toronto Press Incorporated 2002
Toronto Buffalo London

Printed in Canada

ISBN 0-8020-4149-3

Printed on acid-free paper

National Library of Canada Cataloguing in Publication Data

Hewitt, Steve
Spying 101 : the RCMP's secret activities at Canadian universities, 1917–1997

Includes bibliographical references and index.
ISBN 0-8020-4149-3

1. Internal security – Canada – History – 20th century.
2. Intelligence service – Canada – History – 20th century.   3. Royal
Canadian Mounted Police – History.   4. College students – Canada –
Political activity.   5. College teachers – Canada – Political activity.   I. Title.

HV8158.7.R69H49 2002   323.44'82'0971   C2002-901026-8

Parts of this study were previously published as '"Information Believed
True": RCMP Security Intelligence Activities on Canadian University Campuses
and the Controversy Surrounding Them, 1961–1971,' *Canadian Historical
Review* 81, no. 2 (2000): 191–228. Reprinted by permission of
University of Toronto Press Incorporated.

University of Toronto Press acknowledges the financial assistance to its publishing
program of the Canada Council for the Arts and the Ontario Arts Council.

This book has been published with the help of a grant from the Humanities
and Social Sciences Federation of Canada, using funds provided by the
Social Sciences and Humanities Research Council of Canada.

University of Toronto Press acknowledges the financial support for
its publishing activities of the Government of Canada through the
Book Publishing Industry Development Program (BPIDP).

There is only one good, knowledge,
and only one evil, ignorance.

Socrates

The reason there are so few historical certainties is that
so much of history is done in secret.

Bernard Porter
The Origins of the Vigilant State

Contents

Illustrations follow page 144

List of Tables

Preface

This study began on a hot August afternoon in 1994 at the National Archives of Canada while I attempted to avoid doing work on my dissertation. Besides gazing out of the reading room window at the cool waters of the Ottawa River below, I perused the finding aid for Record Group 146, which consists of the records of the Royal Canadian Mounted Police (RCMP) and the Canadian Security Intelligence Service (CSIS). Thanks to earlier requests under the Access to Information Act, the finding aid included several lines indicating that the RCMP, the subject of my dissertation, had collected files on a number of Canadian universities. Curious, I decided to make a request for RCMP material about my home institution, the University of Saskatchewan. The result of my inquiry was a letter informing me that over 2,000 pages of material existed on that topic. I ordered the documents, despite advice to the contrary from some people, and the assurance from others that such records represented simply security clearance investigations. The records stretched from the 1930s to the 1970s, and their contents exceeded my expectations. The wealth of material led me to write an article about the secret activities of the RCMP at my university, which generated a great deal of publicity, including newspaper, radio, and television interviews. Sean Prpick, a CBC radio producer, suggested that looking at RCMP activities at universities in general would make a 'great book.' And so, I began this study.

I write as an outsider to much that is addressed herein. Born in 1966, I was a toddler as confrontations escalated on university campuses in Canada and around the world. Only one of my pre–baby boomer parents attended university, and his degree was in agriculture, obtained in the early 1960s from what was then the Ontario Agricultural College, now the University of Guelph. This was hardly the making of a radical upbringing. My own university experience began in the fall of 1985, a year after the RCMP Security Service rode off into history, or at least switched offices and desks and became the new civilian intelligence agency CSIS.

Although I did not realize it at the time, the research for this project would involve a great deal of police work of my own. I had to develop sources, establish contacts, and search for alternative evidence in the face of censorship carried out in the name of the Access to Information Act. Although the arrival of the act has generally been a positive development for academics, it can be a frustrating experience, especially when the main source for a book consists of RCMP records. Allowing the removal of information relating to persons who are alive or who have been deceased for fewer than twenty years, of details that might be injurious to Canada's national security, and of data on assistance offered by non-Canadian sources, the act can leave gaping holes in documents. Despite the frustrations, the censorship of documents under the provisions of the act requires the participation of fallible human beings. Hence, mistakes are sometimes made, and information is released that would normally be cut. I also sometimes encountered multiple copies of the same document but with different bits excised, which enabled me to reconstruct them by mixing and matching. Material of this type appears in italics throughout the text. I have also attempted to indicate the general nature of the information that has been excised.

Human sources were equally important to this project. My expectation when I started this project was that those who had been on the receiving end of RCMP surveillance, assuming they were aware of being watched in the first place, would be far more willing to speak to me than those who had done the spying. This has not proved to be entirely correct. In fact, I have been surprised at how little cooperation has been forthcoming from those who might have a story to tell. Advertisements in the *Globe and Mail* and letters to various left-wing publications and organizations largely drew a blank. Direct appeals to individuals, including one historian, frequently received no response. On the other hand, after sending out nearly 200 letters, I did find some former RCMP Security Service members who were willing to be interviewed. All told, I had about a 10 per cent response rate to my letters. Several who answered were courteous but expressed an unwillingness to get involved. One respondent was a rather grumpy veteran, apparently upset at having his retirement slumber disturbed, who harangued me over the telephone and then, still not satisfied, contacted my department head to complain. Of those who replied, several opted to do so only by letter, while seven others consented either to be interviewed by me or to provide detailed recollections of their experiences. Some names appear, and others do not. I left this decision completely up to the individual. I am particularly grateful to former Security Service members Peter Marwitz, Donald J. Inch, and 'A' who fielded frequent questions from me. Undoubtedly, they will disagree with many of my conclusions but their contribution made this work much stronger. I invite others with stories to tell or details to fill in to contact me at spying_101@yahoo.ca.

Finally, there is an experiential component to this work. A historian rarely has the opportunity to encounter at first hand what she or he has spent years researching and writing about. This changed for me on 7 June 2000 when two middle-aged men in street clothes rang my doorbell. Opening the door, I was greeted by RCMP Sergeant W.B. (Bill) Cameron and his colleague, both members of the Saskatoon Integrated Intelligence Unit, a joint RCMP–Saskatoon City Police operation. Flashing his badge, Cameron asked if they could ask me a few questions. Sitting in my living room, they proceeded to interrogate me for forty-five minutes about my knowledge (which was not much) on the leak to the *Globe and Mail* of a top-secret document, 'Project Sidewinder,' a joint RCMP-CSIS project that sought to ascertain the extent of the cooperation between Chinese intelligence agencies and triads, as well as the nature of their activities in Canada. (A version of 'Project Sidewinder' is now available on the Internet at: httpı//www.intellnet.org/resources/sidewinder/side002.html.) During the course of our conversation, which was prompted by a now former acquaintance supplying my name to the police, the gravity of the situation was emphasized, with references to possible charges under the Official Secrets Act tossed in for good measure. At one point, Cameron somewhat dismissively made reference to my academic background, adding that 'triads don't play by rules; they kill people.' Ironically, two hours after their visit I was at the unveiling of a recreation of a detachment office of the Royal North-West Mounted Police (the immediate predecessor of the RCMP and the organization that began its intelligence role). In one afternoon I had experienced the entire twentieth-century gamut of Mounted Police history.

Writing a small piece of that twentieth-century history would not have been possible without the assistance of a wide range of agencies. The University of Saskatchewan assisted me with grants, and the Department of History at the same university aided me in numerous ways, including providing me with a research assistant in 1998. The Department of History at Purdue University sponsored me as a visiting scholar, allowing me to complete my research. The Canada Council for the Arts provided me with a generous grant that made this book possible. The *Canadian Historical Review* kindly gave me permission to use parts of my June 2000 article in Chapter 5. The Communist Party of Canada allowed me access to its records. Several university archives and university archivists answered my numerous questions. The Access Section at the National Archives of Canada, specifically Doug Luchak, Pat Milliken, Sarah Gawman, Daniel German, Kim Foreman, Isabelle Tessier, and Marie-France Allenby, worked tirelessly to provide me with access to documents. Equally significant was the work of the Access Section of CSIS, in particular Normand Sirois. At the University of Toronto Press Gerry Hallowell believed in this project from the first and offered his enthusiasm until his retirement. His baton of encouragement was then picked up by Siobhan McMenemy, who finally passed it on to Len Husband.

Then there are the individuals who made this book possible, though, of course, I am responsible for the bad and the good within it. The large number of people who allowed me to interview them or who responded to my letters top the list. Bryce Conrad and Isabelle Ryder kindly put me up (and put up with me) on several research trips to Ottawa. The same generosity was shown by Janelle Wright and Chris Kitzan, both of whom also provided me with feedback on the manuscript. Dorinda Stahl aided by typing up interview transcripts and Curtis Gunn offered research assistance. Several others, including several anonymous reviewers, Paul Axelrod, Kerry Badgley, Dean Beeby, Renée Bergeron, Jim Bronskill, Hamar Foster, Tony Gulig, Greg Kealey, David Knechtel, David MacGregor, David McKnight, Jim Miller, Nigel Moses, Christabelle Sethna, John Starnes, Kent Tricker, Don Wall, Wesley Wark, and Reg Whitaker, gave me access to relevant records or helped with a variety of queries. Daniel Goldstick graciously supplied me with a copy of his Security Service file. Finally, an extra special thank you is due to Bill Waiser, who offered encouragement throughout this project and supplied detailed editorial comments about the manuscript.

Lastly, I would like to thank my family for their love and support. My parents, Richard and Carol, to whom I would like to dedicate this book, my grandparents Ernie and Catherine, and my siblings, Scott and Stacey, all aided in countless ways. My children, Isaac and Flora, inspired me to finish if for no other reason than to enable me to go out and kick a soccer ball more often with them. Then there is Moira Harris, without whose love, support, candidness, occasional irascibility, editing skills, and humour this book would not have been possible. I owe her a great deal.

Abbreviations

ANC	African National Congress
APEC	Asia-Pacific Economic Cooperation
ASIO	Australian Security Intelligence Organization
CAUT	Canadian Association of University Teachers
CBC	Canadian Broadcasting Corporation
CCF	Co-operative Commonwealth Federation
CEGEP	Collège d'Enseignement Général et Professionnel
CIA	Central Intelligence Agency
COINTELPRO	Counter Intelligence Program
Comintern	Communist International
CPC	Communist Party of Canada
CPUSA	Communist Party of the United States of America
CSA	Canadian Student Assembly
CSIS	Canadian Security Intelligence Service
CUCND	Combined Universities Campaign for Nuclear Disarmament
CUS	Canadian Union of Students
CYC	Canadian Youth Congress
EPO	Extra-Parliamentary Opposition
FBI	Federal Bureau of Investigation
FLQ	Front de Libération du Québec
KGB	USSR state security service
LPP	Labour Progressive Party
LSA	League for Socialist Action
MI5	(British) Security Service
MSP	Mouvement Syndical Politique
NDP	New Democratic Party

NFCUS	National Federation of Canadian University Students
NSIS	National Security Investigations Section
PHF	Personal History File
RCMP	Royal Canadian Mounted Police
RNWMP	Royal North-West Mounted Police
SCM	Student Christian Movement
SDS	Students for a Democratic Society
SDU	Students for a Democratic University
SIGINT	(U.S.) Signals Intelligence
SIRC	Security Intelligence Review Committee
SPARG	Security Planning and Research Group
SUPA	Student Union for Peace Action
UGEQ	Union Générale des Étudiants du Québec
VOW	Voice of Women
YCL	Young Communist League
YS	Young Socialists

PART ONE

Spies, Subversives, and (In)Security

1

Introduction

'Youth by nature is radical.'[1] So declared a worried RCMP commissioner, Stuart Taylor Wood, in 1941. His words about the young were part of a considerably longer warning to the Canadian population that, perhaps to their surprise, fascism did not represent the main threat to their liberty. Instead, it was 'the radical who constitutes our most troublesome problem.' By mixing radicalism – and by this Wood meant communism – and youth in the same breath the commissioner revealed an important motive for over half a century of secret RCMP activities at Canadian universities. Across these decades, members of the world's most famous police force ventured onto campuses to collect information, to spy, to observe, to investigate, to interview, to counter subversion, to search for evidence of espionage, to take classes, and to warn.

Mounted policemen performed these tasks largely in secret as part of the development within Canada of the national security state or, as Wesley Wark aptly dubs it, the 'national insecurity state.'[2] In its international context, the intelligence revolution represented a bureaucratic triumph in the form of the file.[3] Tens of millions of intelligence files would be opened in different countries in the twentieth century. In Canada the final report of the McDonald Commission referred to over 800,000 security files on individual Canadians. In 1967, 'D' Branch, the countersubversion branch of the RCMP Security Service, maintained active files on 48,000 individuals and 6,000 organizations. In its final two years of existence, the RCMP Security Service opened new files, including those for security screening purposes, on 134,880 individuals and organizations.[4]

The Canadian paper trail has not gone unstudied. Gregory Kealey has done extensive and groundbreaking investigations on the beginning of the Canadian security state, while Reg Whitaker has produced remarkable work in documenting the post-1945 framework of the Canadian intelligence scene.[5] Nor has this domain been the sole preserve of academics. Journalists, in particular John Sawatsky, have delved into the topic as well.[6] But while at least four journalistic accounts detailing certain activities by the RCMP in the province of Quebec have become widely known, other fertile ground, related to countersubversion operations in particular, remains undeveloped.[7] Canadian scholarship lags behind the groundbreaking work on American domestic security carried out by writers such as Frank J. Donner, Ward Churchill and Jim Vander Wall, Ellen W. Schrecker, and Athan G. Theoharis.[8]

In part, the Canadian gap reflects a problem with documentation. Until the 1980s RCMP security records remained largely unavailable except to 'safe' scholars. The federal Access to Information Act has sparked nothing short of a revolution in the writing of the history of all aspects of twentieth-century RCMP activities. That revolution includes this book, the first to chronicle the history of one aspect of Mounted Police countersubversion work and providing, I hope, a better understanding of one of Canada's most famous and powerful institutions.

Because of their implications for academic freedom and the freedom of speech – two principles that are central to the modern university – the domestic activities of security intelligence agencies are a worthy topic for examination. Police operations connected to universities have always been cloaked with a degree of controversy, a point reinforced by the response to the RCMP's handling of anti–Asia-Pacific Economic Cooperation conference protesters at the University of British Columbia in 1997.[9]

The RCMP and universities both represent fundamental Canadian institutions. The RCMP enforces laws and ensures order in society on behalf of the Canadian state. The university, able to trace its roots back many centuries, performs an equally crucial role. In the nineteenth century and into the early twentieth, the sectarian university cultivated morality and culture within the Canadian elite and among those seeking to join its ranks. In addition, it served as a surrogate parent by preparing students for adulthood, instructing them on how to play their role within the economic, political, and spiritual framework. In the twentieth century, higher education acquired an expanded mandate and became increasingly important. Professional programs developed, and, even more significantly, secularization brought an increased questioning of what had once been dogma.[10]

The university thus represents a fundamental and contradictory duality by both supporting and challenging the status quo. The former is critical to its continuance, since it crafts the next generation of the nation's political, social, and economic elite. As Ralph Miliband observed in the 1960s, universities 'serve ... the state. And not only do they serve it; by so doing, they identify themselves with it, and accept it as legitimate, worthy of support.' This same philosophy, he argued further, is cultivated in the graduates who emerge from universities: 'the pressures towards conformity generated by the university are very strong; and the degree to which universities remain elite institutions tends to foster among many of those who have gained access to them, not least among students from the working classes, a sense of alienation from the subordinate classes and of empathy with the superior classes, which is not conducive to sustained rebelliousness.'[11]

Then came the contradiction. Increasingly in the twentieth century, universities, or more specifically faculty within these institutions, encouraged critical thinking, first towards religion and then the economic system, thereby challenging basic assumptions and values of Western society. Academic freedom, especially once iconoclasts achieved tenure, nourished and protected, to a large extent, their contradictory views.[12]

Both elements of this duality brought the RCMP, which accepted the university (and education in general) as of central importance to Canadian society, onto university campuses. When it came to the notion of higher education as producers of the elite of tomorrow and as supporters of the status quo, the police viewed students as passive recipients of propaganda and inspiration. But the naivety and impressionability of students made them inviting targets to the influence of agitators and others. If students could be corrupted – and societies going back to the time of Socrates have believed that this was possible – then the future of the stability of the state was threatened. In the words of a former police officer, the RCMP's job was to protect universities and students from 'undue influence' on the part of Communists, other radicals, and enemy intelligence agencies.[13] This protective role brought Mounties onto campuses and kept them there for most of the twentieth century.

The second motivation for police involvement, and a reflection of paradoxical societal attitudes towards youth, was that students, radicalized to varying degrees, were themselves active initiators of change and not simply the pawns of others. Wood's comment about the natural radicalism of youth exemplified the contradictory attitudes. Traditionally, energies were either focused within 'legitimate' boundaries established by society and universities or tightly controlled through restrictive social rules.[14] A sense of insecurity about young people underlined the notion of radicalism – youth represented a form of alien identity that could not be trusted. The heyday for the interpretation of youth as challengers of the status quo was in the 1960s and 1970s, and this interpretation led to an expanded police presence in the educational world. With the decline of discontent in the 1970s, the notion of a passive youth, albeit with apathy thrown in, resumed its primary position with state security services on the list of justifications for campus work. Terrorism also became a grounds for investigations on campuses in this decade.

Fearing for students and being fearful of them were both sentiments that were predicated on the idea of a threat.[15] Throughout much of the twentieth century, communism represented the chief danger to state security. For the Mounted Police, the cold war actually began during the concluding years of the First World War. The revelation in 1945 by Igor Gouzenko of the existence of a Soviet spy ring in Canada validated, as far as the RCMP was concerned, the close attention its members had paid to Communist activities. Two main threads inspired the concentration on communism in Canada, and hence the creation of a threat: an internal one based on Canadian conditions, and an external one involving the Soviet Union.

Communism first emerged as a worldwide phenomenon in 1917, when the Bolsheviks seized power in the world's largest nation. Russia became the Soviet Union, and then in 1918 it signed the Brest-Litovsk peace treaty with Germany, effectively abandoning its allies. Worse still for countries such as Canada, which were already experiencing growing discontent in the concluding months of the war, the Russian revolution inspired radicalism on their own home fronts. What was just as important to those who were concerned about Bolshevism was that non–Anglo-Saxons actively participated in such movements: in Canada, Ukrainians, Finns, and Jews represented 80 to 90 per cent of all the members of the Communist Party of Canada (CPC) by the late 1920s. For many people in a government and in institutions, including the Mounted Police, that were rife with prejudice, the ethnic composition of the CPC merely confirmed the equation that 'foreigners' equalled radicals.[16]

Ethnic prejudice aside, the fear of communism was not completely irrational. The menace came not through subversion from within, which was more about the ruling elite's inherent mistrust of workers and ethnic minorities, but from the outside in the form of Soviet espionage, aided and abetted by some members of the CPC. Since the fall of the Soviet

Union in 1991, two forms of archival materials have surfaced to confirm how closely that nation dominated elements within the leadership of Communist parties in other countries: one is records from Soviet archives, including those of the KGB, and the other consists of excerpts from partially decoded Soviet telegrams, intercepted by American Signals Intelligence (SIGINT) in a secret project code-named Venona.[17]

Some aspects of Soviet control, exercised before 1943 by the Communist International (Comintern) and after the Second World War by the International Department of the Communist Party of the Soviet Union, have long been objects of speculation. There were, for example, the famous reversals in the CPC's official policies, like the party's initial support for Canada's involvement in the Second World War before the Soviet Union ordered it to reverse its stand. Rumours abounded in the 1920s and 1930s of 'Moscow Gold,' secret funds funnelled by the Soviet Union into foreign Communist parties. This financial assistance turned out to be more than mere hearsay. In December 1921 the Comintern sent $30,950 U.S. to the Communist Party of the United States of America (CPUSA), $1,100 of which was intended for the CPUSA's sister organization north of the border. In 1926 the CPC received another $1,500 through the same route.[18] As late as the 1970s, the Soviet ambassador to Canada complained about the repeated appearances at the embassy of CPC officials, including party leader William Kashtan, to collect 'US wheat.' Only a year before the collapse of communism in Eastern Europe, Gus Hall, the leader of the CPUSA, wrote a receipt for a $3 million Soviet contribution to his party.[19]

The other part of the control exercised by the Soviet Union involved espionage, with elements of the CPC – and this applies primarily to some within its leadership – working on behalf of the Soviet intelligence community. Again, aspects of this relationship have long been in the public domain, because two rather prominent Canadian Communists, Sam Carr, a senior party official, and Fred Rose, the CPC's only member of Parliament, were convicted of espionage in 1946. What was not publicly known until recently was the extent of the involvement of Communist parties outside the Soviet Union in espionage. Documentary evidence that has become public since 1989 relates primarily to the CPUSA, but with all members of the Comintern tending to follow similar patterns of activity, there is little question of its relevance to the Canadian branch. The Soviet intelligence documents smuggled out by former KGB archivist Vasili Mitrokhin confirm the trend laid bare in the earlier evidence, with a few additional sensational tidbits tossed in for good measure.[20]

The new evidence has proved difficult to refute and has sparked major clashes within the historical community in the United States.[21] In 1930, with Joseph Stalin firmly in control in the Soviet Union, the Comintern instructed parties that 'legal forms of activity must be combined with systematic illegal work.' Later in that year, the message went out that 'all legal Parties are now under the greater responsibility in respect to the creation and strengthening of an illegal apparatus. All of them must immediately undertake measures to have within the legally existing Party committees an illegal directing core.'[22] In the United States, party leader Earl Browder was ordered in 1938 to acquire a short-wave radio so that he could receive coded messages from Moscow.[23] Three years earlier, the Comintern had ordered the CPUSA to select members for training at radio school, including three 'especially reliable and tested, with good American passports, for our chief work.'[24] Other espionage work involved acquiring passports or secretly transporting messages and money. During the 1930s the RCMP investigated CPC attempts to obtain the birth certificates of deceased Canadians, which were used to procure fake passports for Soviet 'illegals,' agents sent to a nation with assumed identities. Another responsibility for some in Communist parties, including that in the United Kingdom, was as 'talent spotters,' charged with either recruiting others for espionage work or handing over the names of potential recruits to Soviet intelligence officers.[25]

Evidence of espionage appears to answer the question of why the RCMP spent over half of the twentieth century monitoring universities. Certainly that is how some former Security Service members remember it. One veteran angrily exclaimed over the telephone that 'the KGB was on university campuses which is why the Security Service went on.'[26] Another condemned

> university professors, whose only knowledge of the period is gleaned from their own research, [who] write with indignation of RCMP 'investigations' conducted at universities, colleges and high schools. During this period when the Cold War was in full swing, and when hostile intelligence services were actively recruiting spies in Canada, anyone whose political views, associates or activities defined them as a possible security threat, was the subject of an investigation, which was merely the inquiries necessary either to clear them of suspicion or to confirm that they were, indeed, a threat.[27]

The editors of *The Secret World of American Communism* echoed these sentiments in the conclusion to their work:

[T]he Communist Party of the United States of America was also a conspiracy financed by a hostile foreign power that recruited members for clandestine work, developed an elaborate underground apparatus, and used that apparatus to collaborate with espionage services of that power. The situation in America in the later 1940s and 1950s was much more complicated than is suggested by the view that a paranoid security apparatus persecuted an idealistic, innocent Communist movement. Although many innocent people were harassed, the secret world of the CPUSA made such excesses possible. Without excusing these excesses, historians need now to take into account the CPUSA's extensive covert activities and collaboration with Soviet intelligence.[28]

There are problems, however, in applying this line of interpretation to the RCMP's interest in universities. The Canadian security state began at the end of the First World War, not its sequel in 1945, and it started collecting extensive information on labour, ethnic, and immigrant organizations and radicals, including some connected with universities, in the 1920s, well before there was any widespread awareness of or concern about Soviet espionage operations. Clearly this work was inspired by something other than a threat of espionage.

Secondly, conclusive evidence has not been provided to demonstrate that assistance to Soviet espionage extended beyond a cadre of party leaders and a few other individuals, many of them loyal Stalinists more than Communists.[29] Missing from Venona and the work of those who celebrate it, argues Victor Navasky, 'is the experience of 99.9 per cent of the million comrades who passed through the CPUSA during the 1930s and early '40s – stay-at-homes who contented themselves with reading ... the *Daily Worker*, demonstrators who sang along with Pete Seeger and social activists who organized trade unions and rent strikes in the North and fought lynching and the poll tax in the South.'[30] Even the secretive behaviour of Communists was not as unambiguous as it appears, but represented more of a complicated chicken-and-egg relationship between Communist parties and domestic intelligence agencies. The use of secrecy by the latter encouraged state repression. In turn, repression stimulated greater secrecy.[31]

Soviet espionage bosses also did not lack intellect. They were well aware, certainly in the aftermath of three celebrated spy scandals in Canada, the United States, and Australia in the 1940s and 1950s, and from their agents who had infiltrated Western intelligence agencies, that Communist parties were under heavy surveillance by intelligence agencies.[32] If a potential agent surfaced in the United States, according to former KGB general Oleg Kalugin, he or she would be ordered to stay clear of the CPUSA because of the risk of being exposed.[33]

Finally, the topic at hand also requires a recognition that records related to espionage should not necessarily be taken as gospel. References to agents often involved exaggeration or wishful thinking on the part of the reporter in an effort to seek career advancement. Double agents and plants, or simply an awareness of the operations of an agent by the opposition, could skew results. In his memoirs, former East German spymaster Markus Wolf recounts the case of a Central Intelligence Agency (CIA) employee who received a promotion based on his recruitment of several East German agents, unaware that they all actually worked for Wolf.[34] Even the much-vaunted Venona is more problematic than its disciples suggest. The third most senior official in the Federal Bureau of Investigation (FBI) admitted in 1956 that because the Venona intercepts were fragmentary, rife with code names that invited guesswork at true identities, and translated into English from Russian, they would not necessarily be allowed as evidence by the American judicial system; even if they were, he cautioned, there was no certainty convictions would occur.[35]

Furthermore, the evidence of Soviet espionage that is specifically connected to Canadian universities is slim. The story of Professor Hugh Hambleton, a long-time Soviet agent arrested while on the faculty at the Université Laval, appeared in the pages of John Barron's *KGB Today* in the early 1980s. Hambleton's valuable intelligence gathering, however, had occurred before his stint in academe.[36] Within the pages of the Mitrokhin Archive is a one-sentence reference to SHEF, a McMaster University professor who was allegedly recruited by the KGB while travelling in Lithuania in 1974. Whether SHEF was in fact an agent for a foreign power or, if he was, what the extent of his activities were remains unknown because CSIS has not been forthcoming about investigations conducted after British intelligence shared with it Mitrokhin's copies of KGB records. An internal CSIS document, heavily censored under the Access to Information Act, implies that by 1975 'most' of the alleged Canadian spies mentioned in the Mitrokhin material were no longer operating, having left to live in other countries or having died. When the cold war officially ends for Western intelligence agencies, then more might be revealed on this matter. Whatever the case, SHEF clearly appears to have been an exception to the rule.[37]

Emphasizing espionage, as it was displayed in the media coverage surrounding the publication of the Mitrokhin Archive, follows a rather comforting 'what they did to us' format and ignores what 'our side' was doing to 'their side' during the cold war.[38] In order to understand why the RCMP maintained a lengthy interest in universities and university-related activities, it is important to note that espionage occupies a secondary role compared to subversion, the founding fear of the security state. This concept emerged in the twentieth century and is closely allied with the era of anti-radicalism in the West.[39] In their contribution to the book *Dissent and the State*, Elizabeth Grace and Colin Leys define subversion as 'legal activities and ideas directed against the existing social, economic and political order (and very seldom against "democracy," as liberal-democratic states are wont to claim).'[40] The *Canadian Oxford Dictionary* describes the meaning of 'subvert' as 'overturn, overthrow, or upset (religion, government, morality, etc.).' No indication as to the means to be employed is supplied.[41] A more applicable definition of subversion from the perspective of the government and the RCMP emanated from the mouth of Minister of Justice Davie Fulton in 1959 when he was pressed during a debate in the House of Commons. 'Communists are so infinitely various or devious or skilful,' he said, 'I should think you would have to have a 500-page book before you could define every one of the methods they might have and therefore every type of organization that should be deemed to be suspect on security grounds. I just do not think we can get a single, over-all, standard definition of what is a subversive or security risk.'[42]

In fact, the RCMP did have a working definition of subversion, as it admitted internally in the 1970s. Anyone or anything at the end of the political spectrum, almost exclusively on the left but with a small smattering on the right, was deemed as inherently subversive and worthy of investigation.[43] It was also an emphasis that ignored the larger social context. Frank Donner labels this security philosophy as 'the agitator-subversion thesis, which denies the relevance of social and economic factors as the cause of unrest.'[44] Instead, the emphasis is on the individual or individuals who initiate discontent where it otherwise would not exist to the same extent if at all.

When it came to subversion, Communists received the great bulk of the police's attention. Mounties monitored almost exclusively individuals and groups connected with the CPC until the 1960s. In that decade, new campus 'threats' under the labels of separatism and the New Left emerged. In both cases, however, the police initially interpreted these movements as disguised efforts at Communist subversion. The new movements, the police argued, included the potential for violence. Yet the

serious incidents of violence on Canadian campuses can be counted on
the fingers of one hand. The most famous, the 'riot' at Sir George
Williams University in Montreal, involved the destruction of property,
not human lives. Context, however, is everything; in the 1960s, student
disruptions, including the occupation of the Simon Fraser University
administration building, must have resembled the final stage of the end
of the universe to those familiar only with a passive student population.
The protesters certainly caught the attention of the RCMP, and their
activities became part of an expanding and unclear interpretation of the
subversion that required investigation. One solicitor general, the RCMP's
immediate political master, admitted after leaving office to being troubled by the broad definitions of subversion that many Security Service
members held: 'It almost included ... any militants who were against the
status quo, sometimes even if it was in a peaceful way.'[45]

Indeed 'militants' were reported on even if they posed no immediate
threat. Long-range fear was 'in,' be in it the 1920s or in the 1970s. In
1977 a Mountie informant, most likely a graduate student in the humanities, attended the Learned Societies conference, an annual Canadian
academic gathering, and sent a warning to his or her handlers: 'The
marxists are very realistic. Over and over again, their leading spokesmen
repeat that they are involved in a very long process, that the hoped-for
revolution will not occur overnight, that it will be a long struggle. But
they are equally clear on their goals: to create a tradition of marxist
academic scholarship in Canada; to get government funding for marxist-
oriented research; to convert their students to marxism; to destroy the
academic credibility of the capitalist social and governmental system ...
[T]heir goals might be called long range ideological subversion.' One of
the informant's superiors scribbled in the margin, 'This is why we have
to be "long term" in orient and accuracy.'[46]

With this in mind, the RCMP focused its attention on protecting
tomorrow's elite. Youth were prone to radicalism, the police believed,
because they were easily impressionable, a shapeless mass that could be
easily moulded by those with strong hands.[47] Enemies of the Canadian
state preyed on these apolitical and, after the 1960s apathetic (from the
perspective of the police) students. Predatory subversives appeared in
several forms. They included radicalized students, who were perhaps
involved in Communist activity. Organizations such as campus clubs
could influence their members or work hard to sway the mass of students; the same was true of campus publications, especially student
newspapers. Outside activists or agitators also posed a problem; they

entered university campuses, often in an endeavour to sway students through presentations and other displays.

The police assumed, however, that it was faculty members who posed the biggest danger, since they had direct access to these vulnerable youth for prolonged periods of time. Academics held positions of prominence, and students had to listen to their words; the young were literally a captive audience. 'For Security, the most threatening thing about the quietly spoken history lecture,' writes Fiona Capp about the situation in Australia, 'was that [the] words carried the weight of the academy ... The "institutional subversive" ... had the potential to wield considerable influence over a captive audience and to subvert the system from within.'[48]

Whatever the source of the threat, the RCMP paternalistically and repeatedly monitored the impact on students.[49] In 1940, for instance, the force's Toronto office cautioned headquarters about historian Frank Underhill's negative influence.[50] In 1948 came a report on the response of an audience at the University of Western Ontario to a controversial speaker: 'The gathering consisted of 40 to 50 physics students, professors and lecturers. The speaker's points of view appeared to have received remarks of displeasure and numerous whispered comments were made. Such remarks as "That's not true" and "I don't believe that," were heard. One of the students claimed to have compiled a list of approx. 20 questions to ask the speaker at the conclusion of the talk but was unable to do so because of the no discussion ruling. The talk, it appeared, was made by one who is well versed in Russian policies and sympathetic with them, a fact that is well known by many of the students.'[51] Then there was the RCMP's shark-like warning in the summer of 1970 that 'subversive' organizations on university campuses 'feed undisturbed upon the student body.'[52]

This belief in the threat to and from youth was not unique to the RCMP; it was just as strongly held in the United States, where J. Edgar Hoover, director of the FBI, described what imperilled America's young people in a 1960 publication, *Communist Target –Youth*:

The successful Communist exploitation and manipulation of youth and student groups throughout the world today are a major challenge which free world forces must meet and defeat. Recent world events clearly reveal that world communism has launched a massive campaign to capture and maneuver youth and student groups ... It has long been a basic tenet of Communist strategy to control for its own evil purposes the explosive force which youth represents. In the relentless struggle for world domination being waged by them, Communists are dedicated to the Leninist principle that 'youth will decide the issue of the entire struggle – both the student youth and, still more, the working-class youth.'[53]

The belief in the vulnerability of youth also reflected attitudes held by the wider Canadian society into the 1960s. In *Making a Middle Class*, Paul Axelrod writes that university authorities 'did not consider students fully formed adults.' Consequently, they interfered with campus publications that they felt were too radical or that in some way challenged societal norms.[54] Doug Owram also comments on similar attitudes in the post–World War Two period in *Born at the Right Time*: 'most students were neither adults in legal terms nor thought of as fully responsible by adult society. Parents sending their children to university expected the institution to take responsibility for more than the education of their children. *In loco parentis*, the universities attempted to regulate the personal as well as academic conduct of students. Such rules encompassed sexual relations, alcohol, swearing, and occasionally even smoking.'[55]

Lacking the ability to regulate student behaviour, the RCMP spied on it to determine the direction of the drift of the student masses. In their coverage, the undercover men and, after 1974, women in scarlet brought to the task the zeal of the employees of a disease control centre: to keep careful watch on any emerging viruses in case they show signs of mutating or spreading. The virus metaphor was even used in a warning in 1940 to the government: 'When a disease spreads until it affects a vital organ it is time for strong remedial action. The virus of Communism, long coursing, almost unopposed, in our social blood-stream has now reached the heart of our educational system as represented by undergraduates and even college professors in several of our leading universities ... Evidence of a Communist "drive" upon our College youth is steadily accumulating. As yet the majority in every student body is loyal to Democracy but it appears to be waging an unequal fight against well organized foreign-controlled disruption and disaffection.'[56] It was up to the Mounties to determine whether what they studied was dormant or infectious. 'The reader should bear in mind that a considerable amount of information has been analysed to arrive at the noted assessment of the general atmosphere [at York University] during the given period,' wrote Corporal J.W. Townsend, a member of the Toronto office of the Security Service, in 1974. 'As a result of monitoring and subsequent recording of areas with no readily identifiable importance to this Service, the reader may feel that our responsibility has been over-extended. I am of the opinion, however, that our interest in seemingly irrelevant issues is valid if we are to be in a position to provide an accurate prognosis of future trends in terms of radical activity and possible disruption to the Institution.'[57] This approach was true not just of the 1960s and 1970s. In fact, what is remarkable about the relationship between the RCMP and universities is the continuity. The Mounted Police began paying attention to Canadian universities during the First World War and carried on until 1984. In that year, the RCMP's Security Service ceased to exist. Although it was reincarnated as a new institution, the Canadian Security Intelligence Service, the RCMP made a reappearance on a campus during the APEC conference in 1997.

There was a consistency to those targeted as well, in that the focus was always on communism. Only in the 1960s did the RCMP grudgingly begin to vary the unwitting participants on their dance card, although the music remained the same. 'Student power,' the New Left, Quebec nationalism, and other social movements gained attention, while the Mounted Police, after initially blaming the unrest on Communist subversion, began to downgrade the potential peril of an increasingly invisible post-Stalinist Communist Party. The same shift was occurring in the United States, the United Kingdom, and Australia. In the United States, William C. Sullivan, a senior FBI official, demoted the CPUSA as a threat, much to the chagrin of an increasingly decrepit J. Edgar Hoover, who had been in the Communist-hunting business as long as the RCMP.[58] What did not change was the idea held by the police that no matter what the form of radicalism practised by individuals or groups, the tactic and goal remained the same: infiltration and subversion.

There was still another element to the police work on campuses and to the efforts at countering subversion in general. Modern police forces and intelligence services are large, elaborate institutions that receive considerable resources from the state. It is never in the interest of these agencies to minimize threats. Instead, exaggeration occurs if for no other reason than to encourage increased funding. Once the RCMP began to pursue subversion, budgets were established, personnel assigned, bureaucracies organized, careers built, and rationalizations developed to defend the past, present, and future. These institutional realities made it difficult to shift the emphasis in other directions.

In making the argument about the importance of the fear of subversion as an explanation for sixty years of police spying on universities, an important caveat must be added. Because of the nature of the Access to Information Act, only a partial documentary record exists. Most of the deletions occur under Section 19, Subsection 1, of the act, which pertains specifically to personal information on individuals who are living or who have been dead for fewer than twenty years. This exemption was extended part-way through this project to include the names of rank-and-file mounted policemen who prepared reports, which is why some of the names of authors appear and some do not. Major deletions also occur under Section 13, Subsection 1, regarding information supplied by other governments or governmental agencies, and under Section 15, Subsection 1. The latter covers anything deemed to be 'injurious' to the national security of Canada or to 'the detection, prevention or suppression of subversive or hostile activities.' This rather broad restriction might include evidence of the use, the lack of use, or the sophistication of technical sources (that is, information obtained by electronic devices) even if the incidents occurred before the Second World War. Such information is deemed sensitive because it could offer an indication to Canada's enemies of the technical capabilities of domestic security agencies; it might also, indirectly, reveal the existence or non-existence of informants.[59] Cumulatively, the deletions tend to relate to the more sensitive international area of counter-espionage. To compensate for the gaps, the widest variety of sources possible, including interviews with some of the participants, were used. Ultimately, however, it must be admitted that this study offers only a strong introduction to the topic, not the final word.

What follows will be an examination of the history of the RCMP's involvement on university campuses. The first section includes this intro-duction as well as an examination of the force's security wing and of its general history, organization, and methods. Section Two addresses the RCMP's activities connected to universities between 1917 and 1960, and Section Three covers the 1960s. The final section explores the period from 1971 to the CSIS era after 1984. Overall, the book's focus will be squarely on the activities and attitudes of the police over eight decades; it is not a history of university radicalism but of police perceptions of and reactions to its manifestations. Nor do I contend that a security service has no place on a university campus. As the 11 September 2001 attacks demonstrate, criminal threats can emerge that are worthy of attention from a policing perspective. The problem lies in what constitutes a threat, what restrictions should govern the work to counter the per-ceived threats, and most important of all, who or what defines the previous two. As will become apparent, Canada's security agencies deter-mined what constituted a threat and what restrictions governed their work for most of the twentieth century. Obviously, they did so within a broad framework created largely in secret by their political masters, who in turn evaded responsibility for what followed. These already large boundaries were flexible enough that they might just as well have been written on water. In following what they believed to be their duty, the RCMP defined targets, designed tactics, and, for the most part, ran its own show. Only after 1975 did this situation change, when the federal government introduced an explicit mandate for the Security Service, but that mandate remained open to broad interpretation by those charged with carrying it out.[60]

The boundaries that did affect the operations of the RCMP were largely imposed by the general public, media, and opposition parties and they assumed the form of a fear of adverse publicity. That an institution dating from the nineteenth century remained concerned not only about its image, but also more importantly about the legitimacy of what it was doing, underlies much of this study. The evidence that is presented clearly supports Wesley Wark's depiction of the RCMP as an insecure institution, despite the bravado and swagger.[61] Yet the RCMP and Canada were not unique. The notion of insecurity is just as applicable to the United States and the FBI, and should records in the United Kingdom ever become available to researchers, undoubtedly a similar pattern will be found there.[62] The commonality of this experience suggests (thankfully) an inherent anxiety for domestic intelligence agencies operating in liberal democracies. Despite the considerable power these agencies had at their disposal, most of the twentieth century was, for them, an age of insecurity.

2

Spying, RCMP-Style: History, Organization, and Tactics

On a fall day in 1917, while the carnage of the First World War continued unabated thousands of miles away in Europe, in Canada S.L. Warrior had an appointment to keep. English-born and a bricklayer and a warehouseman before immigrating to Canada, Warrior had earned his paycheque since 1908 as a mounted policeman.[1] His meeting in Edmonton was at, for him, an unfamiliar location – the University of Alberta, where Cecil Race, the university registrar, wanted to discuss a student with him. One of the first stirrings of a wider relationship that would last for more than sixty years was about to occur.

To examine that relationship properly, it is necessary first to understand what the RCMP was and who its members were. What was the nature of the force's history, especially that of the development of its intelligence role? Who belonged to the security section, and how did its members view the world around them? How were they and their work organized? Finally, how did Mounties do their job?

The example of S.L. Warrior is an appropriate place to start because he was not an ordinary Mountie. As a detective, he exemplified a transformation that was occurring within the Royal North-West Mounted Police. (The designation Royal was added in 1904 and the force would become the Royal Canadian Mounted Police in 1920.) Being a detective meant shedding the famous uniform and working undercover, and it involved surveillance and other activities considered to be un-British. Large-scale security intelligence activities had arrived in Canada.[2]

Prior to the First World War, skills connected to surveillance and spying were not in much demand in Canada. Generally, this type of labour was left to the Dominion Police, a tiny federal agency that was created in 1868 and that was centred in Ottawa. So limited was this organization's resources that it frequently resorted to employing American private detectives to conduct investigations. In the 1860s and 1880s the Dominion Police spied on Fenians who invaded Canada from the United States. As for the North-West Mounted Police, its efforts in surveillance were even more insignificant. In the early twentieth century, it matched wits with the Order of the Midnight Sun, an organization dedicated to the annexation of part of the Yukon to the United States.[3] Temporary threats such as these failed to generate a need for a large-scale permanent security intelligence service.

The First World War changed everything and led to the creation of a new Mounted Police, but the roots of the transformation arose from the pre-1914 era of large-scale immigration to Canada. Many of those who came, especially Eastern Europeans, represented the exact opposite of the Anglo-Canadian norm that was predominant at the turn of the century. Some of the new arrivals also retained an allegiance to countries with which Canada suddenly found itself at war.[4] Now known as 'enemy aliens,' they were viewed with widespread suspicion if not outright hatred, and they were widely considered by the state to be security threats.

Enter the men and boys in scarlet to reassure a nation at war. Under the peculiarities of Canada's system of policing, the Mounted Police, modelled after the Royal Irish Constabulary, a paramilitary colonial police force, was the provincial police force only in Alberta and Saskatchewan, two provinces where by 1914 large numbers of 'aliens' resided. Because the force was predominantly British – in 1914, 79 per cent of members had been born in the United Kingdom – intelligence gathering among non-English speaking minorities proved difficult. Hence the need to recruit members of ethnic communities, not as Mounties but as informants.[5]

With few informants available, regular policemen were occasionally asked to replace their uniforms with civilian clothing and perform the work of detectives. Because of its association with secret police forces, such work was deemed 'un-British,' however, and more likely to occur among police forces on the Continent.[6] Britons and members of the Empire prided themselves on their civil liberties and on the absence of a need for such police tactics. In 1919 a British general who was asked to gather domestic intelligence vehemently protested, saying that his officers 'must act straightforwardly and as Englishmen.'[7] Similar attitudes prevailed in Canada. In 1933 the revelation that a mounted policeman had infiltrated a relief camp in Saskatoon prompted a condemnation from a Regina newspaper: 'Canadian public opinion is strongly against what might be referred to as secret police. The tradition of the country is against it, as also is the British tradition.' As late as the 1960s, when a botched attempt by the Mounted Police to recruit a university student as a source reached the public domain, *Maclean's* magazine decried the incident as being more befitting the tactics of Nazis and Communists. 'We want no part of such patriotism here,' the magazine chided.[8]

Early into the Great War it appeared that the skills of a secret police would not be required, so much so that the informants, or secret agents as the RCMP sometimes called them, recruited at its start were dismissed. European events, however, changed this state of affairs. As casualties mounted overseas, discontent grew on the home front. Two major issues added to the turmoil: a high cost of living made life difficult for ordinary citizens, and the issue of conscription angered French Canadians, workers, and western farmers. It was in this climate that the Mounted Police in 1916 and 1917 began hiring secret agents on the Prairies in order to ascertain the feeling in Eastern European and French Canadian communities towards conscription.[9]

It was also the issue of conscription that drew Detective Sergeant Warrior to the then not quite ten-year-old University of Alberta campus to meet with Cecil Race, the university's registrar. In this instance, it was not conscription in Canada that was at issue, but its American equivalent. A student named Ernest Keller interested the Mounted Police because he had allegedly journeyed north from the United States to avoid military duty. The registrar was only too happy to assist in the investigation, assuring the policeman that Keller was 'a good clean straight lad, and very anxious to get on with his studies.' 'He very seldom leaves the University grounds,' added the official, 'and when he does he invariably goes to the Y.M.C.A. building, and ... never has any visitors.' Not completely convinced, Warrior was given access to Keller's student record. Warrior ended his report by observing, in a pattern that would become a familiar one over the subsequent decades, that Keller 'has not been interviewed and does not know these enquiries have been made.'[10]

The year 1917 was significant to the future of both the Mounted Police and Canada for reasons that went beyond the war in Europe. In October Lenin and the Bolsheviks overthrew the government of Aleksandr Kerensky and seized power in Russia. Within a matter of months Russia concluded peace with Germany and abandoned its allies, including Britain and Canada. The world's first Communist nation had emerged, presenting a clear challenge to capitalism in two ways: it provided an alternative to the status quo and it demonstrated to workers around the world the potential strength of the working class. Senior Bolsheviks, especially Lenin, sought to promote worldwide revolution.[11]

Bolshevism, with its non-British roots, avowed atheism, and appeal to the working class, represented a particularly troublesome problem to the Canadian government, which by 1918 was finding the situation at home increasingly turbulent. It appointed C.H. Cahan, a prominent Conservative, to investigate the roots of Canadian radicalism, and in September he presented a landmark report to the prime minister. Far from finding the popular wartime scapegoats – people of Central European heritage – at the root of the nation's problems, Cahan warned of a fresh menace for the post-war period. 'Russians, Ukrainians and Finns, employed in the mines, factories and other industries' served as the new peril, since they had been 'thoroughly saturated with the Socialistic doctrines which have been proclaimed by the Bolsheviki faction of Russia.'[12]

The significance to the Mounted Police of Cahan's report was dramatic. Under the direction of Newton Rowell, the cabinet minister with responsibility for the force, Commissioner A.B. Perry issued three memoranda in January and February 1919 that effectively created a security intelligence service. First, Perry warned of the growth of left-wing radicalism in Canada, specifically of the increase in the 'pernicious doctrines of Bolshevism.'[13] A second memorandum informed his subordinates that in the battle with radicals, 'one of the most important branches of our work will be that of the detective service and this service must receive your particular attention with the object in view of obtaining all possible information without in any way causing suspicion on the part of interested persons or associations.'[14]

Perry clarified these points in a third memorandum for his junior officers, which was designed to offer 'information and guidance in connection with Secret Service investigations re Bolshevism.' Specifically, he warned of a small group of people 'principally of foreign birth, who have imbibed the real Bolshevist Doctrine of a class war, and they believe in revolution as a method to obtain their ends.' An outline of tactics included the necessity of conducting 'investigations and enquiries ... in such manner as not in any way to arouse suspicion or cause antagonism on the part of such associations or organizations.' Finally, the commissioner indicated that this new intelligence function was a role being performed on behalf of the federal government. The government, he wrote, needed 'the R.N.W.M. Police to keep it ... advised of any developments towards social unrest. It is extremely desirous that such unrest should not be permitted to develop into a menace to good order and public safety.'[15] He also recognized that by making itself useful to the government in every way possible, the force was ensuring its own survival in a period of uncertainty.

In developing a security intelligence service, Canada was certainly not unique. As early as the 1880s, the Special Branch of the Metropolitan Police was formed in Britain to deal with political crime. Prior to the First World War the British military created a formal counter-espionage service. Consisting of nineteen members when the war began, it would be 844 members strong four years later in what had become known as MI5, or the Security Service. Its attention was soon directed at what the British government feared most, domestic subversion. Widespread labour disturbances in 1919, including, in Glasgow, a general strike that was quickly branded a 'Bolshevist rising' by a British cabinet minister, frightened many in elite circles. Even King George V worried about a possible revolution. Throughout the 1920s the fear of Soviet influence in domestic affairs occupied the attention of British intelligence.[16]

An even closer parallel to Canada's situation was occurring south of the border, where a young Justice Department lawyer by the name of John Edgar Hoover was beginning what would become his purpose in life. Hoover had compiled dossiers on enemy aliens during the Great War, but with its conclusion his career was threatened. Post-war unrest saved it. A general strike shut down the city of Seattle in February 1919, and alarmed politicians labelled it an attempt at revolution. By the middle of the year, several hundred strikes were occurring monthly across the United States, and a bombing campaign in April directed at government officials grabbed the attention of Americans everywhere. It was in this climate that Hoover was put in charge of an anti-radical campaign that culminated in a series of raids directed against real and suspected leftists. Immersing himself in Communist writings, the future director of the FBI acquired a lifelong conviction of the danger that Bolshevism represented.[17]

As was the case in the United States and the United Kingdom, chaotic events were also occurring in Canada in 1919. Within a few weeks of Perry's final memorandum directed at creating a security intelligence service, Winnipeg metalworkers walked off the job. Soon thousands of other workers would join them in a general strike. The Canadian government convinced itself that the strike leaders in Winnipeg desired a revolution, despite Mounted Police reports to the contrary, and it brought the full power of the state to bear against the strikers.[18] More than anything, the Winnipeg General Strike convinced the government of

Robert L. Borden of the need for a powerful policing agency with security intelligence capabilities. At a meeting on 5 August 1919, Borden asked Perry to submit options for a new national police force. The commissioner favoured merging the Dominion Police with the RNWMP and drew particular attention, according to official RCMP historians, to 'the dual nature of the force ... Its members were peace officers who could be used instead of the military to maintain order in the streets.'[19] The commissioner's arguments won Borden over, and in February 1920 the RNWMP merged with the Dominion Police to form the Royal Canadian Mounted Police.

Divided into geographic divisions across the country (for example, 'K' Division covered Alberta, 'O' southern Ontario, 'C' Montreal, and 'J' New Brunswick), the new force carried out a dual role for the Canadian state for the next sixty-four years, performing typical policing duties as well as security intelligence work. Nor was there necessarily a separation between the two functions. For most of the inter-war period, and even after 1945 in small centres, Mounties performed both.[20] It was not until the Depression – and a supposed growth of Communist strength – that the RCMP established its first fledgling intelligence wing in its Ottawa headquarters. The Intelligence Section remained part of the Criminal Investigation Branch, reflecting the continuing reality that policemen in the field who investigated radicals were just as likely to do regular policing duties the very next day. From six members in 1939, the intelligence wing rapidly escalated to ninety-eight before the end of the Second World War.[21]

That conflict led into the cold war, which, in turn, sparked a heightened concern about communism and a desire on the part of the state for expanded intelligence capabilities. The momentum continued towards a distinct and separate branch within the RCMP to execute this purpose. Of particular importance was the leadership of George B. McClellan, who would become a commissioner. He received his introduction to the spy business during the Second World War when he headed the intelligence section in Vancouver for three years. In 1947 he became head of the security wing, and during his six-year tenure the Special Branch, as it was then named, finally separated itself from the Criminal Investigation Branch.[22] By the end of the 1940s this intelligence wing had splintered into two distinct bodies: 'B' Branch (counter-espionage) and 'D' Branch (countersubversion). (In the mid 1970s branches were often referred to as 'Ops,' as in Operations.) Over the next twenty-five years several additional branches would develop both at headquarters and at some of the larger RCMP divisions across the country (see Table 2.2). Separate

TABLE 2.1
Heads of Canada's intelligence agency (post–First World War)

Name	Title	Dates
Charles F. Hamilton	Intelligence and liaison officer	1920–33
Arthur Patteson	Intelligence officer	1935
Robson Armitage	Intelligence officer	1935
C.E. Rivett-Carnac*	Officer, Intelligence Section	1935–9
Ernest W. Bavin	Officer, Intelligence Section	1939–41
Alexander Drysdale	Officer, Intelligence Section	1941–4
C.E. Rivett-Carnac*	Officer, Special Section	1944–5
John Leopold	Officer, Special Section	1945–7
George B. McClellan*	Officer, Special Branch	1947–53
Joseph P. Lemieux	Officer, Special Branch	1953–5
Clifford Harvison*	Officer, Special Branch	1955–6
Josaphat J. Brunet	Director, Security Intelligence	1956–7
Kenneth Hall	Director, Security Intelligence	1957–8
Joseph M. Bella	Director, Security Intelligence	1958–61
Joseph R. Bordeleau	Director, Security Intelligence	1961–4
William H. Kelly	Director, Security Intelligence	1964–7
William L. Higgitt*	Director, Security Intelligence	1967–9
Joseph M. Barrette	Director, Security Intelligence	1969–70
John K. Starnes	Director general, Security Service	1970–3
Michael R. Dare	Director general, Security Service	1973–81
J.B. Giroux	Director general, Security Service	1981–4
Ted Finn	Director, CSIS	1984–7
Reid Morden	Director, CSIS	1987–91
Raymond Protti	Director, CSIS	1991–4
Ward Elcock	Director, CSIS	1994–

Source: Jeffrey T. Richelson and Desmond Ball, *The Ties That Bind: Intelligence Cooperation between the UKUSA Countries – the United Kingdom, the United States of America, Canada, Australia and New Zealand* (London 1990), 360, and a letter, Peter Marwitz to the author, 14 February 2000. The persons whose names are followed by asterisks would later become commissioners of the RCMP.

'desks' operated within 'B' and 'D' Branches. In the latter, there were desks for labour, Trotskyism ('Trots'), Maoism, the New Left, and 'alternative societies.'

Who belonged to the intelligence wing of the force? Regular policemen. Almost all joined to be members of the world's most famous constabulary. In the process they signed away several years of their lives to a hierarchical and militaristic institution that demanded unquestioning loyalty and long hours, often in poor working conditions, in return for low pay and no union protection.

TABLE 2.2
Structure of the intelligence service of the RCMP

Name	Function
'A' Branch	Security screening
'B' Branch	Counter-espionage
'C' Branch	Administration
'D' Branch	Countersubversion
'E' Branch	Technical body used to develop plans for installing technical surveillance (known as 'E Special')
'F' Branch	Files
'G' Branch	Quebec separatism
'H' Branch	Chinese espionage
'I' Branch	Watcher service, a non-RCMP surveillance squad used for counter-espionage
'J' Branch	Installation of technical surveillance devices
'K' Branch	Research Branch (also known as Central Research Branch)
'L' Branch	Branch created in early 1970s to deal with all issues relating to informants

Source: John Sawatsky, *Men in the Shadows: The RCMP Security Service* (Toronto 1980), 21–8.

In seeking recruits, some of whom would have duties connected with universities, the force had low educational requirements. As late as the 1960s a new Mountie needed as little as a grade eight education, although grade ten was preferred.[23] This reality opened the force to both criticism and ridicule. *Saturday Night* magazine ran a piece in 1961 entitled, 'Wanted: Intelligence in the RCMP,' which attacked the police's low educational standards. The Canadian Association of University Teachers (CAUT) joined in, arguing that a greater educational sophistication would lead to more discernment when it came to identifying radicalism. Pressed for statistics on the level of university education in his force, Commissioner Cliff Harvison responded in 1963 that he 'didn't have time for all that research.'[24]

Fundamental changes began only in the aftermath of the 1969 Royal Commission on Security, which criticized the Security Service for the lack of higher education among its members. The final report of the McDonald Commission in 1981 filled in some of the numbers Harvison had not provided (see Table 2.3). Despite the larger number of police officers with university degrees, the increase was not sufficient to bring about the broadening of horizons in the force that many people wanted. Police officers who became students at universities were encouraged to follow narrow academic programs in the

TABLE 2.3
RCMP Security Service members with university degrees
(in percentages)

Category	1969	1979
Regular members	5.5	21.4
Civilian members	13.8	26.3
Special constables	0.7	1.6

Source: Royal Commission of Inquiry concerning Certain
Activities of the Royal Canadian Mounted Police, *Second
Report: Freedom and Security under the Law* (Ottawa
1981), 2: 677.

belief that these offered a more practical application to security work.
With the cold war at its height and the emphasis at RCMP headquarters on the ideological crime of subversion, it only seemed natural to
encourage a concentration in political science. One former member
faced ridicule because he selected history and criminology, while
another was told to drop a class in world religions or face having to
pay for it himself.[25] The force also discouraged studies beyond the
Bachelor of Arts level, in part by refusing to assist financially those
who wanted to do graduate work.

A lack of education was clearly not considered an impediment to
police work, especially with its traditional emphasis on brawn over brains.
It did, however, contribute to a climate of anti-intellectualism, which was
of obvious significance to an institution whose duties including university-related investigations, and it promoted simplistic bipolar views of the
world. Moreover, life was often worse for members with a more advanced
education: they faced suspicion and jealousy from their colleagues, especially the older ones, because the possession of a university degree was
viewed within the force as a ticket to promotion.[26]

Educated or not, the policemen who ended up in the Security Service
obtained little or no specialized training for their new careers. Before
1947 nothing at all was offered. Beginning in the 1950s, at the request of
the RCMP, senior Canadian diplomats like Dana Wilgress, former ambassador to the Soviet Union, gave the occasional class on communism.
One member who served in Security Service in this period recalled
classes – more like group seminars – ranging in length from a day to as
long as a week. Occasionally they ended with examinations. Later, in the
1970s, selected instructors in political science from Carleton University
and the University of Ottawa offered special classes on basic political

TABLE 2.4
Disciplines in which Security Service members obtained
degrees (1979)

Discipline	Percentage
Political science	50
History	8
Sociology	7
Psychology	6
Economics and commerce	4
Physical education	2
Public administration	2
Zoology and biology	2
Chemistry	1
Engineering	1
Geology	1
More than one undergraduate discipline	12
Postgraduate studies	4
Total	100

Source: Royal Commission of Inquiry concerning
Certain Activities of the Royal Canadian Mounted
Police, *Second Report: Freedom and Security under
the Law* (Ottawa 1981), 2: 717.

theory. Throughout, rookies were provided with reading lists that emphasized literature about communism, including R. Carew Hunt's *The
Theory and Practice of Communism.*[27]

After the limited training came actual duty. Most new recruits to the
Security Service in the period after 1945 began in 'A' Branch, the body
responsible for conducting security screening of new government
employees. Security screening was monotonous and time-consuming,
reasons why new members were offered such tasks. One, from the
Diefenbaker era, described the work:

In the matter of security screenings, the average member was expected to
complete twenty to twenty-five files each month. The more ambitious
investigators were able to top thirty or more a month. Prior to this period of
fiscal restraint, two members had been assigned to each [motor] vehicle. It
had not been unusual for each member to conduct anywhere from six to
ten enquiries during the course of a normal working day working in
tandem with another member. With the implementation of this new eco-

nomic policy, there were generally four and, on occasion, five men to a vehicle, which meant that one could expect to complete only a single enquiry in the morning and another in the afternoon. Each member was allowed a total of ten minutes to complete his single enquiry and, if he failed to do so, he either had to cut it short or chance having his vehicle leave without him. The 'rule' was that, at the seven-minute mark, the driver would sound the horn of the car once. At the nine-minute mark, the horn would be sounded twice, and at ten minutes, the car would pull away, with or without the investigator. Investigators were allotted two transportation tickets to use in the event they were abandoned by their vehicle.[28]

After spending some time doing background checks, Mounties early in their careers moved on to real investigations. Once out of the office they were generally on their own, although their superiors determined whom or what they would investigate. Often this direction was rather open-ended, as in a broad order to conduct a 'fishing expedition' in order to find out what was happening on a campus. A former Security Service member recounted his and a colleague's experience in the late 1950s or early 1960s in the 'D' Branch:

> This section dealt, primarily, with operational files and related subject files. The unit was controlled by a Senior NCO (Sergeant) who had two Corporals under his command. A new member to the unit was assigned several organizational files that, often, pertained to related areas of focus. Each organizational file had several key individuals, so that a member not only investigated the organization but also kept track of the subjects who made up that organization. As a new target entered the organization, an interim file would be opened until it was determined whether or not he qualified for full file subject status. Once so qualified, a period of intensive investigation followed, which might or might not include varying degrees of surveillance, to obtain as much information about the individual with respect to his allegiances and whether or not he posed a 'threat' in the fullest sense of the word. If that individual became involved, directly or indirectly, with Soviets or those suspected of being particularly close to an intelligence operation, the case could be handed over to 'B' Branch for further study relevant to that area of focus ... [A colleague with responsibility for higher education] was 'on campus' an average of once a week. He would type up the results of his enquiries and pass them back through his NCO who would then distribute them to the individual requisitioners.[29]

Reports proceeded slowly upward through the hierarchy of the RCMP establishment. Once they reached headquarters in Ottawa, 'reader analysts,' usually known simply as 'readers,' pored over all the pages to determine what was of significance and therefore eligible for parcelling out to various other file categories, branches, or desks devoted to specific areas. The official 'Manual of Filing' for the Security Service described the key role of readers in the circulation of information: 'If the Reader digests his reports and correspondence as thoroughly as he should, he must be better equipped than anyone else to decide who and what are of real importance or what may be omitted or destroyed.' The higher a report climbed, the more it shrank, as material was synthesized for digestion by senior administrators and finally their political masters.[30]

Reports had significance beyond their actual content. In a hierarchical organization like the RCMP, some members of the Security Service believed that the secret to advancement, besides improving one's educational qualifications, was to produce a large number of reports. One person witnessed this philosophy first-hand when he served as a 'reader' in Ottawa and received a rather lengthy report regarding the University of Windsor. It was a rehash of previous accounts, something the reader commented on when he passed the report on to his superior. Although the sergeant, who was his superior, did not read the document, he ordered that a letter of praise be sent to the author, in part because tensions generally existed between field investigators and those stationed behind desks at headquarters in Ottawa.

These tensions between mounted policemen run counter to the prevailing memory of camaraderie on the part of veterans. The stressful relationship between the intelligence and the criminal sides of the force is well known, but rivalries also occurred between branches within the Security Service, especially 'B' and 'D,' and between individual Mounties. A member who transferred to the Toronto area in the late 1960s recalls having colleagues who repeatedly displayed a reluctance to share information with him. They sought to defend their territories from an interloper, in order to protect the identities of sources but also apparently out of a fear of having others take credit for their work, which would affect promotions.[31]

Tensions also existed because of the complex nature of what Security Service members did. For instance, legal concerns dogged Mounties during most of the history of the force's intelligence role. As early as 1950, Sergeant W.L. Higgitt, then in charge of the counter-espionage section, warned of the inherent danger in some of their actions to his colleagues:

> It is a matter of real and constant concern to the members of the Counter-Espionage Section of Headquarters Special Branch, that they often have to request, or at least feel they should request, rather unusual courses of action by our field personnel well knowing that by complying with the request the investigators may be seriously jeopardizing their own futures in the force if, through bad luck or human error their operations are discovered by those persons against whom we are directing the investigation. Such discovery could lead to most embarrassing incidents and possibly legal action ... It is to be hoped that some official notice can be taken of this situation and some overall directive laid down for guidance. Again it is stressed that extraordinary measures and methods must be used if we are to effectively cope with extraordinary situations. To some extent the axiom of the 'end justifies the means' is very true in Counter-Espionage operations but the personal risks to the operating members must be recognized before they can be expected to extend themselves in connection with these matters.[32]

Higgitt was alluding to illegal break-ins (often euphemistically referred to as 'surreptitious entries') to collect a wide range of information about targets, including copies of documents or even lists of books, or to plant listening devices by rank-and-file mounted policemen. The extent of these actions cannot be determined but they were far from rare. Such methods would not have been described in reports, and, out of a sense of self-preservation, superiors, bureaucrats, and politicians had no desire to enquire too deeply about how intelligence was gathered.[33]

Although the techniques were the same, the scale of illegal activity undoubtedly did not reach the level practised in the United States in the 1940s and 1950s. There, 'black bag jobs,' a nickname given to break-ins because the tools that were used were carried in black leather bags, had become a regular investigative tactic on the part of Hoover's FBI. In 1956 they reached a new level when the FBI launched the Counter Intelligence Program (COINTELPRO) in an effort to destroy the Communist Party of the United States. It targeted the CPUSA not as a criminal entity but as a political one, hence its recourse to illegal tactics. The FBI actually steered clear of following proper legal practice, because prosecutions meant the exposure of informants within the targeted organizations. It had lost over one hundred people in this way in a variety of trials during the late 1940s.[34]

The RCMP had similar worries. An anti-Communist crackdown was considered in 1951 but was rejected because it would have exposed the force's sources within the CPC. Five years later, in a FBI-style move, 'K' Branch created and distributed a phoney letter from a CPC member that expressed concern about Khrushchev's secret condemnation of Stalin and Stalinism.[35] This type of tactic appears to have been rare. Instead, monitoring and gathering intelligence on the activities of targeted organizations and individuals became the usual activity of Canada's national police. The procedures that were utilized included opening mail, tapping telephones, and planting listening devices.

Before 1954, access to mail had been obtained under the authority of Section 39 of the Defence of Canada Regulations, enacted after the war began in 1939, which gave the government emergency powers. The legislation expired in that year, but RCMP divisions did not stop opening mail, despite not having legal authority. The best-known program, which required the cooperation of Post Office employees, had the code name CATHEDRAL and it had three versions: CATHEDRAL A, to check the name and address on a letter, CATHEDRAL B, to examine the exterior of a letter, including photographing it, and CATHEDRAL C, to open and examine a letter's contents.

Telephone taps were as controversial as opening mail, and had been applied by the Mounted Police since the 1930s. They were relatively easy to carry out since only the cooperation of the telephone company was required. When the emergency powers expired in 1954, the RCMP obtained a legal opinion on the continued use of telephone taps. Known as the Varcoe Opinion after the civil servant who rendered it, the interpretation held that telephone taps were probably legal under Section 11(1) of the Official Secrets Act, which allowed a justice of the peace to authorize the issue of a search warrant and the collection of evidence related to a possible violation of the act. Telephone taps appear to have been used rarely against university targets, and after September 1971 their use on campuses had always to be authorized by the solicitor general. The rejection of a police request for a tap was not unheard of. Solicitor General Warren Allmand refused to allow the RCMP to listen to the telephone conversations of an academic at the Université Laval whom he knew personally and believed to be innocent of any wrongdoing.[36]

'Bugs' were even more problematic. While receiving information from a hidden microphone was in principle not illegal, to plant such a device often required the illegal entrance into premises. Planting bugs also involved considerable resources and planning, and eventually their installation was left to 'J' Branch within the Security Service.[37] Having a regular member or informant wear a 'bodypack' was a simpler way of obtaining information through a microphone.

Whether by means of telephone taps or hidden microphones, electronic surveillance aided the police in the difficult task of discovering the internal workings of organizations. Those targeted were well aware of this, hence the mythic click on the line indicating a telephone was being tapped. Yet for a variety of reasons, including the resources and planning required, microphones and taps appear to have been used rarely at universities. It was often necessary to enter premises to plant a microphone, and should the bug be disovered it created the potential for tremendous negative publicity, an outcome the Security Service feared above all else.[38] Taps, because of the assistance provided by telephone companies, represented much less of a risk than bugs. Their use, however, was more strictly regulated, at least among Security Service members, and they required someone to compile a transcript of what might prove to be hours of irrelevant conversation. Moreover, targets could avoid using the telephone, which, according to the RCMP, was the case among an increasing number of them towards the end of the 1960s.[39]

The belief by some of the people being spied on that this was being done primarily through electronic means was a human response that masked a far more difficult truth: the most valuable information in RCMP reports came from what the police labelled 'human sources.' This terminology was in part an attempt, as Frank Donner notes, to apply a neutral designation to individuals who in the past would have been labelled a variety of unflattering names ranging from 'informer' to 'snitch' and 'stool pigeon.'[40] What is little recognized, however, is that such people were and remain crucial to police and intelligence services.[41] First, they cost less than alternative forms of information collection because they do not require as many resources. Nor do the same legal restrictions apply to their employment. A warrant has never been required to insert an informant into a targeted group or to recruit someone who is already a member. For the RCMP, however, human sources were not all created equal (see Table 2.5).

Why would anyone agree to become a police informant, especially when this frequently involves the betrayal of friendships? In his memoirs, KGB defector Stanislav Levchenko identifies four main types of motives for those who betray their nations: money, ideology, compromise, and ego, which he abbreviated to 'M.I.C.E.' Academics who have studied the question add ingratiation, disgruntlement, and even the simple thrill

TABLE 2.5
Types of sources for RCMP

Type	Description	Payment	Nature of handling
Volunteer	Person who volunteers	Usually none	Infrequent meetings
Undeveloped casual source	Sources who occasionally supplied information; examples on campuses include security officers, secretaries, personnel in a registrar's office	Usually none	Periodic contact after recruitment
Developed casual source	Somewhat permanent sources; an example would be former Parti Québécois cabinet minister Claude Morin	Occasional, especially for expenses	Recruited after considerable planning; the source has a specific RCMP handler who makes frequent contact
Long-term penetration source (sometimes known within the RCMP as a 'secret agent')	The most important sources, described to the McDonald Commission as the 'bread and butter' of security work; either a person already in a targeted organization or someone injected by the RCMP	Paid	Recruited after lengthy profiling and an extensive effort to develop a relationship between the Mounted Police member and the target; extensive handling by Mountie; a strong relationship often forms between the source and the handler

Source: Royal Commission of Inquiry concerning Certain Activities of the Royal Canadian Mounted Police, *Second Report: Freedom and Security under the Law* (Ottawa 1981), 1: 296–7, 300.

derived from trafficking in secrets to the list.[42] Three former Security Service members who handled sources agree that these broad criteria apply but that the picture is even more complex, involving as it often does overlapping motivations. One found that the excitement and intrigue was part of the appeal. Vengeance and nationalism were other factors, depending on the period and the people involved. Many sources, especially those of the casual variety, simply perceived their assistance as that of performing a public good by aiding the police in investigative work.[43] The popularity of the RCMP in some parts of Canada, especially in the west, possibly increased the importance of the last motivation.

Finally, the use of coercion, although especially applicable to criminal investigations, may occasionally play a role.

The competent recruitment of sources resembles an art form. It requires patience, commitment, intelligence, and knowledge of human psychology. Indeed, intelligence services employ psychologists to aid in the recruiting and handling of informants. In Canada, once a potential source was selected, a relationship would be slowly encouraged, during which time the person's suitability was evaluated. Having knowledge of political matters was often important in a source, since he or she frequently had to infiltrate organizations where ideology was paramount. The potential source's stability received special attention, since living a secret life involved considerable pressure; moreover, a source 'gone bad' had the potential to cause considerable embarrassment, a problem that surfaced for the RCMP in the 1960s. After a period of time, a pitch to a person who was deemed suitable was finally made; the offer was not always accepted.[44]

Police officers preferred sources that they had themselves recruited. Those who volunteered to gather intelligence were often viewed with suspicion. When a University of Saskatchewan student walked into the office of his local detachment in 1964 and offered to become a spy, his proposal was not dismissed out of hand but a check was performed on all aspects of his personality. '[Deleted: name] has a very good record among the local Faculty and is anti-Communist,' reported Corporal R.L. Firby. '[He] appears to be a person imbued with his own self importance, fanatically interested in politics and appears sincere; in favour of our Force and enquiries on Campus.' Unfortunately, he added, the potential recruit liked to boast about his contacts with the federal government and the Liberal Party, and the policeman did not entirely trust the man's motives for volunteering. In the end, the RCMP did not recruit the student as a source, though he was encouraged to pass along any pertinent information he came across.[45]

The RCMP had a degree of power over the lives of those who were recruited, although it was less than for sources on the criminal side. 'Remotivation' was often required, and the handler had to be conscious of the possibility of the 'Stockholm syndrome' – in which the captive becomes sympathetic with the captor – occurring between the source and the group that he or she was infiltrating. Money, even if for nothing else than to cover expenses, tightened the relationship and afforded greater control; in extreme cases informants might become dependent on the Mounted Police. A Dalhousie University student who claimed in 1981 to be an informant told a student newspaper that the RCMP paid him as much as $125 a month in the form of salary and expenses for infiltrating a Marxist-Leninist organization. A former police officer noted that the account seemed 'plausible.'[46]

Long-lasting sources developed strong relationships with their handlers in the RCMP, so much so that one former member observed that though he was no longer in contact with his RCMP colleagues he still saw former informants on occasion. To protect their prized suppliers of information, real identities were carefully hidden through the use of coded designations that by the 1970s consisted of the letter of the RCMP division that the source operated in and a number. Early in the same decade, 'L' Branch was established to centralize control of the recruitment and handling of sources.[47]

Human sources of every kind were essential to countersubversion work against university-related targets. Those recruited included campus security staff members, administrative staff – most importantly in the registrar's offices, where access to confidential material could be obtained – faculty members, and students. Members of the latter group were used less frequently because of their transient nature and because they had become decidedly less cooperative by the 1960s. Even so, in the 1970s a young Liberal at the University of Regina who worked part-time at the local RCMP headquarters managed to fashion a secret second career. At one anti-Trudeau demonstration, he handed out Maoist literature on behalf of the Communist Party of Canada (Marxist-Leninist). When confronted by someone who knew his real identity, he fled, carefully dodging behind a pillar to avoid having his picture taken. He later reappeared as a member of the League for Socialist Action, a Trotskyist organization.[48]

Casual sources of information were important and they came from a variety of backgrounds. The head of the Department of Political Science at Carleton University informed a federal government employee at a party in January 1976 of his concern that Vietnamese students at his university had been ordered by the new government in Vietnam to remain in Canada and conduct espionage. The information was quickly relayed to the RCMP.[49]

Whatever the nature of the information or intelligence collected, and regardless of its source, it usually ended up in a file. Opening such an entity, especially on individuals, was far from a precise business. Individuals in contact with an already existing target or in attendance at an event that was in some way deemed subversive might have temporary files

TABLE 2.6
The RCMP's university filing system

File no.	Applied to
D-909	Institutions or organizations in which activity of interest was occurring
D-920s	Temporary category for organizations
D-928	FLQ activities
D-930s	In general, files on individuals
D-931	Individuals of interest who are named in a report but who are not necessarily considered to be subversives
D-933	Individuals of interest; files are opened for two years before a decision is made either to close them or to upgrade them to the D-935 category
D-935	Subversive individuals
D-937	Individuals connected to terrorism
D-938	Informants given numbered code names
D-939	Broadly known as 'character' files, these were for individuals applying for government jobs; D-939-7 were civil servants suspected of being homosexuals
D-944	Organizations, particularly but not exclusively connected to labour
D-945	Communist or Communist-connected organizations
D-950	Publications not necessarily considered to be subversive
D-972	Files with Soviet associations
D-992	Operational intelligence

Sources: Various, including the occasional appearances of specific file references on some of the thousands of pages of records being revealed; 'A' to author, 18 November 1998; Recollections of 'C'.

opened on them while Security Service members investigated who they were and what connection they had to the main focus of the inquiry. By the 1950s three adverse references in a person's dossier would cause that person to be officially designated as a subversive.[50]

Once a decision had been made to start a file on an institution, organization, publication, or individual, headquarters would be asked to supply a file designation. Indeed, headquarters required that a space be left in reports after the name of the target for the insertion of a file number. Later reports would then bear the assigned designation. This filing system predated the cold war, having been developed in 1934.[51] It is normally excised under the Access to Information Act. The categories that were of relevance to the RCMP's university work are given in Table 2.6.

If the file was on an individual, a consecutive number appears to have been applied on the next file that was created. For example, the force designated Leopold Infeld, an academic with suspected Communist leanings, D-935-4385; Charles Boylan, a Communist academic teaching in British Columbia in the 1960s, was D-935-34351; and Mario Bachand, an FLQ member whose file began in the same decade as Boylan's, was D-935-35377.[52]

The file specification for an organization or institution was more complicated. Following the initial D-900 categorization was a number that characterized the particular sector of the file. Number three represented institutions related to education. Next came a letter that denoted geographic location. A file with a Q in it was for all of Canada or for a file at headquarters. Otherwise, the system for the provinces approximated the following pattern: Newfoundland and Prince Edward Island were A, Nova Scotia was B, New Brunswick C, Quebec D, Ontario E, Manitoba F, Saskatchewan G, Alberta H, and British Columbia J. After the geographic location came a number that ranked the target in relation to similar subjects. The University of Waterloo, for example, was D-909-3-E-5, while Waterloo Lutheran University had number D-909-3-E-22. Additional targets at the same institution, for instance the University of Waterloo student association, had the same number as the university, with an additional number tacked on at the end.

Into at least the 1960s the RCMP maintained D-935s in special 'subversive indices.' These involved a five-by-seven card with the individual's name on it and they included evidence, such as information supplied by human sources, on the person's connection to subversion. Staff searched through the cards using the McBee Keysort system, a primitive precomputer filing system that consisted of inserting long rods similar to knitting needles in various holes around the cards. One hole, for example, would represent education. A needle inserted in it allowed for the removal of all of the references to education. The RCMP began using the McBee system on 1 September 1955 and continued with it until the early 1970s, when the first computers arrived. MI5 in the United Kingdom used an almost identical system.[53]

Analysis represented a crucial aspect of RCMP countersubversion operations. To collect information like pack rats had little value if its greater significance could not be ascertained. Indeed, at times the amount of intelligence could be overwhelming, so much so that in 1954 and 1958 the force eliminated files on several hundred individuals and organizations. By the early 1960s the problem had worsened. Raising the standard for a permanent file to six or more subversive references and retiring old files did not prevent some staff at headquarters from doing nothing other than continually reviewing dossiers. A time study at the Sault Ste Marie detachment found that security and intelligence investigators spent 51 per cent of their time on office duties; these consisted of writing reports (62 per cent) and handling mail and files (38 per cent).[54]

The RCMP as a police force was reasonably skilled at going out and getting information. On the other hand, as a poorly educated and unsophisticated security and intelligence service it suffered from analytical deficiencies. George McClellan, the head of the Special Branch, recognized this in 1951 when the RCMP established a research branch, known as 'K' Branch, or Central Research Branch. Eventually, well-educated civilians, like Mark McClung, Don Wall, and Ken Green, served in it.[55] What these men joined was a domestic intelligence system that had been created at the end of the First World War and that had evolved over subsequent decades. It did not, however, function in a void. Threats to the status quo, especially after 1918, justified, at least in the minds of the police and their political bosses, a new intrusive role for the state. Universities were but one location for a widespread search for subversives in the twentieth century, a hunt that had begun well before Igor Gouzenko's defection in 1945.

PART TWO

The Early Years

3

In the Beginning, 1920–1945

The intermixing of fear of radicalism and the Winnipeg General Strike that began in May 1919 produced an offspring nine months later. In February 1920 the new Royal Canadian Mounted Police was created, providing Canada for the first time with a police force that operated from coast to coast to coast. In its functions, the new force was a lot like the old, except in the area of security intelligence, where an expanded and permanent role would develop in the inter-war period. Why the move towards permanence? In addition to the resolve of the Canadian government and the leadership of the RCMP, the Communist Party of Canada (CPC) shared indirect responsibility. Without a perpetual and bona fide threat to the state, the need for a spy agency might have waned as the Great War became a distant memory.

The opposite occurred in the years between the world wars, however. The RCMP's intelligence role persisted as it slowly forged a new role in a new field. At the same time, the CPC appeared on the scene and began to develop as a political entity, providing the RCMP with the task of spying and infiltrating the radical organization.[1] In a sense, the relationship between the two organizations had the appearance of a boxing match, although admittedly the RCMP, with the power of the state behind it, had far greater force behind its punches. In the 1920s, however, there would be several rounds of sparring. Not until the following decade would the RCMP seek a knockout.

Generally, university campuses did not serve as the prime site for the bouts between Mounties and Communists. The notion of a threat is frequently a socially constructed image, and in the inter-war period institutions of higher education ranked far lower than ethnic meeting halls or factory floors as locations of perceived menaces to the state.[2] A revolutionary of this period did not carry textbooks or attend university. In the eyes of the state he – along with its other characteristics, radicalism was gendered male in this era – was far more likely to be carrying a shovel and speaking heavily accented English, if he spoke English at all. This model of radicalism, which encompasses class and ethnicity in addition to gender, largely predominated throughout the inter-war period, and it continued to do so until 1945 when Igor Gouzenko revealed the existence of spy rings that included civil servants and scientists drawn from the Canadian elite, among others.[3]

Nor was it just a simple matter of ethnic minorities and workers appearing to the police to be more radicalized than other segments of the population. Universities were bastions of conservatism, attended mainly by a privileged few. In 1931 no more than 3 per cent of Canadians aged twenty to twenty-four found themselves at institutions of higher education, a rate that was higher than the one in the United Kingdom but significantly lower than in the United States. In Canada 54 per cent of university students came from professional or business families, who represented only 12 per cent for the general population, and 5 per cent had fathers who were unskilled or semi-skilled workers, compared to 37 per cent for Canada as a whole.[4]

So-called agitators recognized the infertility of the university campus, seeing it as a place of privilege and the home of the status quo, and instead for most of the 1920s and 1930s they sought out working-class youth. But the absence of radical activity and even the endemic conservatism in institutions of higher education did not make them completely immune to appeals by radicals. The problem, from the perspective of the authorities, lay with the presence of impressionable young people who could be easily influenced. Thus the police emphasis for most of the inter-war period was on investigating attempts to recruit, influence, and manipulate students.

In many ways, mounted policemen were as different from university students as were Communists. Policing had long been an occupation dominated by, and associated with, the working classes.[5] While the RCMP represented an organization with values that were clearly middle-class, many of its members earned a daily wage that was below even that of an unskilled worker, which is one of the reasons why the force had difficulty recruiting new members in the first three decades of the twentieth century. For an ordinary mounted policeman, or more accurately for his children, university education was out of the question. In 1938 attending university cost a student approximately $500 to $600 per year. The salary for an ordinary man in scarlet in that year would have been roughly $456.[6] For many policemen, higher education was an unattainable objective, which must have generated some resentment towards those who had access to it.

Although they were not necessarily familiar with the university milieu, the police maintained sporadic interest in it throughout the 1920s. Within a month of the birth of the RCMP, for example, its members became concerned about two campuses in western Canada. The spark for this attention was J.S. Woodsworth, a former church minister, a prominent labour activist, and one of those arrested less than a year earlier during the conflict in Winnipeg. In March 1920 he was touring western Canada, speaking publicly about the General Strike. From Edmonton came details at headquarters in Ottawa on Woodsworth's activities, including lectures he gave at the University of Alberta. It was not simply a matter of a policeman supplying information. Citing the case of four University of Saskatchewan professors who had recently been fired, the officer forwarding the report asked Commissioner A.B. Perry whether the University of Alberta's board of governors should be informed of the participation of university employees at Woodsworth's lectures at the campus.[7]

Even more detailed reports flowed in following an unexpected appearance by Woodsworth at the University of Saskatchewan in Saskatoon. After the visitor from Winnipeg addressed an economics class about the radical One Big Union, an unhappy student approached a local newspaper with the story.[8] A subsequent article prompted Detective Sergeant C.T. Hildyard to investigate. An English-born man in scarlet, but not an ordinary one – he had an education from Eton – Hildyard contacted the paper's editor who, in turn, put him in contact with the student. The Mountie interviewed him, finding him to be 'an absolutely reliable youth of about 23 years of age.' The information went into a report on the event, as did the names of the professors who were involved in Woodsworth's presence and the fact that the lecture had been given without the knowledge or approval of the university administration.

Hildyard's main worry was the recurrent RCMP fear of the impact of perceived radicals on the students. In this case, he was reassured by his source: 'While there were quite a few young boys of 17 and 18 years of age present, he did not think that any harm had been done,' although 'he would discuss this address with the rest of his class and find out as to whether any harm had been done or not.'[9]

A surprise, though, awaited the investigating policeman. He discov-

ered that many of the parents of the students did not share his fear about
the persuasive power of Woodsworth's lectures. In fact, several parents,
in telephone calls to the newspaper and in conversations with Hildyard,
stated that 'it was only right that they as students should hear both sides
of the industrial questions of the day, and it was preferable for them to
hear the Radical side under such circumstances than for them to hear
these views from agitators on the street corners or at labour meetings.'
Even the sympathetic newspaper editor who had supplied Hildyard with
the student informant's name turned against him by choosing to run an
editorial entitled 'Liberty of Speech' which asked why the RCMP sought
to investigate lectures at the university. In the face of the indifference to
Woodsworth's speech, the chastened Mountie, in the end, criticized only
the students' lack of choice on whether or not to hear the labour
activist's address – that the students were, in effect, a captive audience.[10]
This was one of the first demonstrations to the police that security
investigations connected to higher education could lead to adverse publicity. It was one thing to spy on a local union meeting; it was quite
another matter to conduct surveillance on a campus. Complete secrecy
had to be a guiding principle in such work, if for no other reason than
the good image of Canada's national police force.

    In addition to the two institutions in the Prairies, Woodsworth drew
police attention to the University of British Columbia during the same
period. This time the social activist was involved in an effort to establish a
labour studies group at the university. The combination of radicalism
and vulnerable youth immediately set off RCMP alarm bells. 'This man
WOODSWORTH, is not only trying to invade the precinct of the University with his doctrines,' warned Detective Staff Sergeant Walter Mundy,
'but is teaching the younger generation the same doctrines in what is
known as the Labor school and Labor College.' He advised contacting
the provincial government in an effort to stop Woodsworth from fulfill-
ing his plans. Seeking more information about events on campus led to
the production of an even more troublesome report from one of what
eventually would be a plethora of RCMP informants. The editor of
Balance, a business paper, was asked by the RCMP to prepare an 'authen-
tic and complete' account of radical activity at the province's main
university. Under the heading, 'Report on the Economic Policies Taught
in the University of British Columbia,' he listed members of the university's Department of Economics and included a clipping from a university
publication inviting students to attend an organizational meeting for a
socialist study group. By March 1921, after further investigations had

been completed, Vancouver headquarters received a more encouraging report from the field. After investigating J.B. Clearihue, the faculty member on the UBC campus who advocated a 'Faculty of Labour,' the RCMP judged him to be their kind of academic: his credentials included lecturing on the 'Evils of Bolshevism' and he was strongly 'in favour of educating the students along loyal and patriotic lines.'[11]

Two years later, the University of British Columbia would again generate police reports, and these reveal the primitive nature of security intelligence activities in Canada at the time: the reliance on not always credible sources, the lack of familiarity with universities, and the evidence of the rampant paranoia and fear of radicalism that had dominated elements of Canadian society since the end of the First World War. The CPC had not yet become the primary concern of the RCMP, which continued to be interested in other forms of radicalism. In March 1923, for instance, a Mounted Police source inside the Socialist Party of Canada warned that it enjoyed widespread support at the university and that one of its members had boasted 'the student body of the U.B.C. was the nucleus of the coming revolution.'[12]

Affecting the perspective of the police was that some opinion makers had an exaggerated notion of the university as a centre of radicalism. The University of British Columbia swirled in controversy after a student newspaper ran a satirical piece on a prominent British citizen. The editorial staff of the *Ubyssey* was forced to resign, but even this was not enough for the *Vancouver Daily World*, which published an editorial condemning the students and advocating a search for those who had misled them down a path of radicalism: 'The epidemic of parlour-Bolshevism at the University must have some contagion centres. There is no smoke without fire. It should be the duty of the Board of Governors and Senate to discover who among the faculty are responsible for the spirit of anti-British sentiment at the University. Then they should see to it that these are made free to offer their services to the Soviet government. They are out of place in a British University.'[13] Its rhetoric would have been shared by at least one member of the RCMP, who clipped the editorial and placed it in the university's recently opened file.

The RCMP's interest in the University of British Columbia in the spring of 1923 represented a trend that would continue, as the concern was not with the university per se but with the activities of individuals and organizations on the campus and with their impact on students. Using the *Ubyssey* as a source, a detective relayed to his superiors that a member of the Socialist Party of Canada was teaching classes in economics. An informant within the party itself warned of the involvement of an academic, whom he called a 'hidden "Red,"' in radical movements and in the manipulation of his students.[14] Three days later, an informant covered a lecture given by a UBC professor at the Workers' Party Hall. Once again, the emphasis was on the harm being done to students: 'there is a big chance of the students of the University becoming imbued with [the radicals'] ideas as their minds are young and susceptible. It is said that about 25% of the students at the U.B.C. are "Red" and this would appear to be fairly borne out at the lectures ... they are given the opportunity to get the W.P. [Workers' Party] view of things. They seem to realise that there is something wrong, but cannot grasp just what it is and, through these lectures, are likely to find someone who will put them right as to what it is.'[15] These and other reports from sources alarmed senior mounted policemen in Vancouver. One contacted Commissioner Cortlandt Starnes in Ottawa to ask whether the university's Board of Governors should be supplied with the name of the faculty member who had addressed radical meetings.[16]

Starnes did not provide the reply his junior officer had sought. Canada's top horseman since April 1923, Starnes was not as completely swept up in the paranoia on the subject of radicalism as some of his colleagues; at least, universities had not become one of his leading priorities. He had assumed office at a time of scarce resources and when the government in power, the Liberals under Mackenzie King, had no great fondness for the RCMP, which they viewed as loyal to the Conservative Party. Starnes would not hear of approaching the UBC Board of Governors: 'I have no objection to hearing of developments of this sort as a matter of news, but there must be absolutely no appearance of any surveillance being exercised by us as regards higher education. Moreover, I do not think it necessary for us to feel perturbed at seeing these young men investigate questions of economics for themselves.'[17] The commissioner had not ruled out coverage of events on campuses, but he did recognize, and events in Saskatoon in 1920 had already proved him correct, that such investigations were performed at considerable risk. The danger came not through breaking laws or regulations, since none existed on these matters at the time, but from adverse publicity for a vulnerable and insecure national police force. The intelligence produced, in other words, did not warrant the risk.

Starnes's response to the RCMP informant demonstrated another reality. The commissioner dismissed the source's information about the professor with a simple, 'I doubt whether he is in a position to speak patronisingly of a member of the teaching staff of the university.'[18] Besides acknowledging the obvious high social standing of university faculty in this era, the commissioner's retort reflected the generally negative view held of informants, even by those who employed them.[19]

The exaggerated accounts of the situation at the University of British Columbia illustrate that much of the security intelligence world remained new to the RCMP. In the panicky aftermath of the First World War, the force and the government cast a wide net over Canadian radicalism. Almost anyone and any group questioning the status quo constituted a threat. A few months after the Winnipeg General Strike, mounted policemen in Alberta charged several Jehovah's Witnesses with possession of restricted literature. One officer reported that only 'nominal fines were imposed as it was plain that these people were not propagandists, but simply religious fanatics.'[20] The attention given to social democrats provides the best example of how the RCMP refined its security intelligence targets during the early 1920s. Woodsworth clearly constituted a leading peril as the 1920s began. By 1925, however, his file, now that he was a member of Parliament, was closed, and Commissioner Starnes ordered a halt to any future investigations on the politician.[21] Politician William Irvine represents an even better illustration of this trend. In 1919 the Mounted Police described him as a 'most dangerous Agitator' and advocated his deportation. Seven years later, Irvine would be rehabilitated in the eyes of the men in scarlet to the point where a senior officer wrote to the commissioner praising speeches by Irvine that 'do much to combat Communism.'[22]

The difference in police attitudes from the beginning of the decade of the 1920s to the middle of it was the result of the arrival of communism in Canada. The Communist Party of Canada came into existence in 1921 in Fred Farley's barn outside Guelph, Ontario. After initially remaining underground using the name of the Workers' Party of Canada, the CPC went public. The RCMP now had a mortal enemy – a revolutionary organization dedicated to the overthrow of capitalism. More than that, however, the CPC of the 1920s represented the opposite of everything the RCMP stood for. It was an atheistic organization whose rank-and-file membership in the 1920s was dominated by people of Finnish, Ukrainian, and Jewish background. Even worse, many of its leaders appeared beholden to a hostile foreign power, the Soviet Union.[23]

As centres of tradition, universities were obviously neither fertile recruiting grounds nor a priority for the newly formed Communist Party. Workers, labour organizations, and ethnic groups garnered Communist attention, and these, in turn, received the attention of the police. While initial appearances by Communists on campuses were not ignored, they occasioned little sense of urgency. One prominent CPC member, Maurice Spector, who would later be expelled from the party, spent part of the 1920s as a student at the University of Toronto. The RCMP inquired as to his status but went no further in investigating his academic career.[24]

Although universities were still not a top priority for Canadian Communists, the consolidation of power by Joseph Stalin in the Soviet Union after 1925 altered their outlook. Under the Comintern, initial, albeit limited, efforts at building bridges with non-Communists, especially among youth and with youth organizations, were attempted.[25] One sign of this new policy, which undoubtedly might have gone unnoticed by the police, appeared in a report from 'No. 30,' the RCMP's top agent in the Communist Party of Canada. To his comrades in the party he was Jack Esselwein, a hound-dog-faced house painter who spoke heavily accented English, a member of the party's Regina branch, and an ultra-committed revolutionary. His police colleagues knew him as John Leopold, and would see him achieve a degree of national fame in the inter-war period unheard of by Eastern European immigrants. In October 1926 Leopold described a meeting that his alter ego and two party members held in Winnipeg with a member of a Soviet trade delegation to Montreal.[26] This individual, whose name was deleted under the Access to Information Act but who likely was Ivan Kulik (or Kulyk), enquired as to the feasibility of starting a club at the University of Manitoba that could be used to disseminate 'working class propaganda' among students. He noted that a similar association, the Labour Research Club, had already been established at McGill University and that it had seventeen members, fifteen of whom were students. Similar clubs were intended at other universities, the trade official added, and he himself was travelling next to the University of Toronto to help create a similar branch there.[27]

The RCMP responded to No. 30's report by investigating existing clubs and warning university administrators about attempts to establish new ones. In the case of the former, it was easier said than done. The force's emphasis on working-class and ethnic activity equalled its lack of sources on campuses. Yet it feared inserting its own undercover members into university organizations, rightly assuming that the newcomers might draw undue attention to themselves. Despite these handicaps, it managed to cover meetings of the McGill club, including one at which Maurice Spector was the guest speaker, and it obtained a list of its members, noting the apparently pertinent fact that these individuals appeared to be predominantly Jewish.[28]

What the Mounties collected about the Labour Research Club at McGill was used in warnings it sent to several university presidents. The senior police officer in Manitoba promised to take the matter up personally with the president of the University of Manitoba at a later date when there would be no chance of the CPC being able to link the information to Leopold.[29] Starnes ordered an officer in Toronto to discreetly contact the president of the University of Toronto, while the commissioner himself wrote to Senator Andrew Haydon, a member of the Queen's University Board of Governors. Echoing his earlier comments about the University of British Columbia, the commissioner played down the threat posed by clubs and by individuals like Spector.

I do not for a moment think it wrong of university students to look into social questions, nor do I suppose that any student who meets Spector will necessarily be converted by him; I should be sorry to see Canadian universities adopt the repressive measures which one occasionally hears of being taken elsewhere. On the other hand, it seems advisable that the university authorities should know what is being attempted. The Communists' purpose in the affair is propaganda and nothing else, and they have visions of getting hold of groups of students, each of whom belongs to some club or society, and in this way spreading their doctrines secretly. The McGill Labour Club is described by them in their jargon as an 'illegal' – that is, underground – society.[30]

The RCMP kept track of the exploits of the McGill Labour Club as long as it existed.

What should be made of the appearance of the Soviet trade official in Winnipeg, an event that certainly surprised the force? It may have been a Comintern initiative, or possibly the man was a Soviet intelligence agent seeking to develop a pool of future recruits, a pattern followed elsewhere in the 1930s. The key point, however, in understanding the RCMP's interest in campuses at this time is that espionage was not an issue. Subversion, through the spreading of propaganda and the sowing of dissension, dominated the police outlook, but in these categories universities remained insignificant. Instead the RCMP sought evidence of covert Soviet influence on overt events – strikes, riots, etc. – much like British intelligence did – it frantically searched for evidence of Soviet involvement in the 1926 General Strike.[31]

As such, there must have been a natural reluctance to examine on-campus activities. After all, any Mountie worth his historic reputation knew that the real threats to order and the status quo came from the lower classes and foreigners, the groups among whom the Communists were most active. And, of course, university professors and students resembled what mounted policemen hoped that their children would be; they were the police's social superiors. Consequently, what occurred on campuses received little attention from the RCMP.

That began to change in the following decade because of internal and external events. In the former category was widespread national unrest, triggered by a worldwide Depression. Unemployment skyrocketed, and some people without jobs roamed the country searching for work, going wherever there was a tiny rumour of opportunity. Others protested the apparent indifference of the federal Conservative government under the leadership of R.B. Bennett. In truth, Bennett and the Conservatives recognized that the pain suffered by many Canadians was real, but they, and the Mounted Police, had trouble accepting the fact that displays of discontent were spontaneous and intricately connected to the larger social context. To them a protest was not simply a random expression of desperation; it was the result of organization, and organization meant agitators. Moreover, there was one group of people whom the Bennett government viewed as synonymous with agitators – Communists. The prime minister's prescription for the menace of communism, one that was shared by the Mounted Police, especially Starnes's successor, J.H. MacBrien, was to use an 'iron heel' in order to stamp it out ruthlessly.[32]

In his diagnosis of the source of the protests, Bennett had a point. Communists often did play a leading role in social protest. Yet the prime minister and others missed a fundamental truth. The CPC did not create unemployment, homelessness, hunger, and hopelessness in Canada; the economic system had done that.[33] It became easier to blame the unrest on Communists, foreigners, and agitators than on the Depression, because the latter course would have involved the government assuming some responsibility for the disaster. Instead, labelling a protest or movement as Communist-inspired became a convenient way of delegitimizing the underlying reason for the protest.

Arresting Communists made the point even more forcibly. In the pre-dawn hours of 11 August 1931, police raids across Ontario rounded up eight Communists, including national party leader Tim Buck. All were charged and eventually convicted under Section 98 of the Criminal Code, a piece of legislation passed in the aftermath of the Winnipeg General Strike and allowing for guilt by association.[34]

The growth of protest and its links to the CPC merely reinforced the pattern of the previous decade, namely that the intermixing of radicalism, ethnicity, and class continued to be perceived by the RCMP as the leading threat to Canadian domestic security. Campuses were still largely left alone. One exception to this rule occurred in 1931, when it appeared that the Mounted Police might have some work to do at McGill University. Public allegations that it was a bastion of communism prompted the Mounted Police in Montreal to label the idea as 'ridiculous.'[35] It was confident in refuting such claims because it had already investigated alleged radical activity at the university, chiefly the operations of the McGill Labour Club and the activities of some of its members, such as David Lewis and Eugene Forsey.[36] No link between the club and the Communist Party had been found. The force, however, did remain in contact with the principal of McGill University, Sir Arthur Currie, for the remainder of the decade. Currie even received congratulations from Commissioner MacBrien for his efforts at throttling communism at his university, although MacBrien lamented that more in general was not being done to control the public pronouncements of certain academics.[37]

That the police did not pay more attention to universities in an era of heightened radicalism across the country reflected the reality that these institutions remained bastions of privilege, where R.B. Bennett could still find a warm welcome. 'Reliable and approved' was how the Mounted Police branded the main student organization, the National Federation of Canadian University Students in the 1930s. It was not just the police that held this view. A visiting student from India was 'appalled' by the absence of political activity among Canadian youths.[38]

The campus environment was different in the United States. With a higher percentage of young people attending universities, it was only natural that a greater number of students would be drawn from segments of society that raised questions about the status quo. Much to the chagrin of American university administrators, students organized strikes and campaigned for a more egalitarian society and against the social ills brought on by the Great Depression. To the annoyance of J. Edgar Hoover and the Federal Bureau of Investigation, Communists played a major role in several student organizations. Historian Robert Cohen argues that in the United States the Communists played a far greater role in the student movement than anywhere else, even the labour movement. One of the most dramatic actions involved a bus trip by a group of students from New York City to Harlan and Bell counties in Kentucky to offer humanitarian assistance to striking miners.

The FBI was certainly aware of these manifestations of student protest.

Throughout the 1930s it collected dossiers on thousands of students, almost all of whom were exercising their rights to freedom of speech and doing so as part of the experience of higher education, something supposedly conducive to the discussion of potentially unpopular ideas. Files existed on two thousand individuals at the University of Chicago alone. In accumulating these records, America's federal police was ably assisted by many university administrators, academics, and students. At Ann Arbor and the University of Michigan, for example, information on the American Student Union (ASU) was supplied to the FBI by a variety of people: 'two confidential sources,' a member of the Ann Arbor Police Department, the chief of police, the secretary to the dean of students, a professor, the university president, and another 'confidential source' in the university's administration, the last furnishing intelligence on an ASU student leader's academic difficulties. Even the reaction of that student's father during a conference with university officials about his son's troubles appeared in the reports.[39]

Such matters seemed of little relevance north of the U.S. border until the mid 1930s. By 1935 Canadian university milieux had started to change, but the student populace was still not radicalized. Students remained largely passive and they were also perceived as such, though the RCMP had by then investigated the occasional organization that questioned the status quo, such as the Student Christian Movement (SCM).[40] What had changed was the Communist Party, which for reasons that lay beyond the Canadian border was now taking an interest in higher education. At the end of the 1920s Stalin had declared war on other elements of the left, specifically social democrats: the Communists would stand alone. In Canada this policy led to the creation of distinct Communist organizations, such as the Workers' Unity League, and the exodus of members, both ordinary and prominent, from the CPC. Cooperation with other left-wing groups was strictly forbidden. Besides splitting the left, Stalin's policy made the RCMP's work much easier, because the identities of 'Reds' seemed clear. Unfortunately for the men in scarlet, the Soviet leader was a fickle tyrant, and in the mid 1930s new orders emanated from the Kremlin. Going it alone was out; forming 'united fronts' with other elements of the left, chiefly the Co-operative Commonwealth Federation (CCF), was the new course. Not surprisingly, the CCF under the leadership of J.S. Woodsworth, who had been harangued as a 'social fascist' by the CPC only months earlier, did all that it could to resist such appeals. A united front also meant that Communists involved themselves in existing organizations, including youth groups, and this made the work of the RCMP, with its fixation on radical activities, increasingly difficult.[41]

Evidence of a shift in the interest Communists were taking in the field of higher education began to filter into RCMP headquarters in Ottawa. In 1936 the Young Communist League (YCL) scrapped its newspaper, the *Young Worker*, in favour of a new more appealing youth, and not openly Communist, publication, the *Advance*.[42] And then, there were the reports from the field. The CPC gained its first official foothold at the University of Toronto when it established a campus club in 1935. A detective corporal joined the initial gathering to hear Tim Buck, recently released from the Kingston Penitentiary, address about forty students. His superiors, in keeping with the RCMP's view of students and universities, received the comforting news that at least half of this number attended merely out of curiosity. More troubling to the police was the attitude of university officials, who seemed blissfully unaware of the new menace on their front steps:

> During this investigation, it was observed that several officials of the University do not make any attempt to disrupt the radical movement in their Houses [deleted], and go out of their way to encourage it. Even such prominent radicals as Tim Buck visit them ... for a discussion on present conditions. At Hart House, the radical element have a library at their disposal, where they can retire and enjoy their reading of Communistic literature without fear of interruption.
>
> ... When it was first announced that Tim Buck would address the opening meeting of this newly formed Communist club, Ontario Government Officials were somewhat perturbed, and [deleted: *J. Burgon Bickersteth*] warden of Hart House, was called to the Parliament Buildings for a discussion on the matter, the result of which was made public, but it is noted that [deleted: *Bickersteth*] is one of the college officials who had Tim Buck visit him in his study, and who looks too lightly upon the radical activities of the boys in his charge.[43]

There are several interesting components to this report. One is the extent of the RCMP's familiarity with the activities of Tim Buck, including his meetings with university officials. Then there is the perception widely held in Canadian society of university students as children. Finally, there is the subtext of the report which equated communism with immorality, specifically illicit sexuality, so that reading Communistic literature took on the status of masturbation or homosexuality, acts also deemed reprehensible in Depression-era Canada. Such discourse had American echoes: J. Edgar Hoover described the route to communism as 'perverted' and compared Communists to drug addicts, while the rhetoric of the state linked the conversion to communism with sexual weakness or degeneracy.[44]

The RCMP's fears that the University of Toronto CPC club might be successful proved unfounded. A report in March 1936 listed the number of Communists on the campus – a number removed under Access to Information, possibly because the figure was quite small – and it added that they were not active. A month later, another Mountie investigated the situation at the University of Toronto and observed that CPC activity was at a 'standstill' and that there was little interest on the part of ordinary students.[45] A concern remained nonetheless on the impact of the CPC's message on the passive student masses.

In the same year as the CPC officially arrived at the University of Toronto, the RCMP became interested in events occurring at an institution in western Canada, the University of Saskatchewan. There the police did not focus on open Communist activity but instead interpreted the questioning of societal norms as a sign of the hidden influence of communism; hence the need for further investigation. The initial target of RCMP attention appears on the surface to have been a rather innocuous one: it was a student newspaper, the *Sheaf*. Student publications were important to mounted policemen investigating radicalism, however, because they were read weekly by large numbers of students. In the hands of persons perceived to be radicals, such an instrument offered an even larger platform to propagate views than did a classroom controlled by an academic. Newspapers also offered insight into the mood of students through interviews, opinion pieces, and letters to the editor, and they provided useful lists of events occurring on campus, such as guest speakers and protest rallies. Policemen investigating university targets read students newspapers extremely closely.

One who did so in 1935 and who was horrified by what he read was Constable M.F.A. Lindsay, who became the fourteenth RCMP commissioner in 1967. He was taking law classes as part of a trial project involving a few Mounties who were selected to further their education.[46] While perusing the *Sheaf*, he encountered unflattering comments about his employer, the Canadian state, and the British Empire.[47] The contentious material included an editorial and a cartoon, the latter depicting a dangling figure with the name Leopold on his sleeve and a bottle of alcohol in his hand. This was John Leopold, the famous Mountie, who had renewed his association with Regina on 1 July 1935 when he was present at the Regina Riot, having arrived prior to the clash with evidence that implicated the leaders of the On to Ottawa Trek, a protest movement of unemployed workers.

The *Sheaf* had first caught the attention of the RCMP in the fall, just before Armistice Day. An editorial accused the British Empire of having 'a record of rapine, savage murder, diplomatic deviltry, cold-blooded bargaining, wholesale stealing, unholy alliances and general aggrandizement unequalled by any other nation in the world's history.'[48] The very British RCMP, whose veterans' organization included among its founding principles in 1919 the promotion of imperialism, was especially offended by anything that cast aspersions on Canada's relationship with its mother country. Lindsay investigated 'the source of the apparent radical activities of a Communist nature' and discovered, contrary to the prevailing stereotype of a radical, that one of the authors was both of 'Anglo-Saxon parentage' and an open Communist. S.T. Wood, who was in charge of the Saskatchewan branch of the RCMP and who would also later be commissioner, sent the offending editorial to the provincial attorney general, depicting it as 'not calculated to imbrue [*sic*] the susceptible minds of the youthful reader with healthy and prideful views of our British Empire, its history, traditions, and institutions.' He ordered that future copies of the publication 'be obtained and forwarded to [his] office as soon as they become available in order that the tendencies of this publication may be followed consecutively.'[49]

As the 1930s continued, the RCMP began to worry far more about what students were doing than what they were writing about. This new concern emanated directly from the Comintern policy of pursuing 'united fronts' with non-Communist interests. To the RCMP, there appeared to be a clear trend to radical activity. At least that was the opinion of John Leopold, who by the end of the 1930s was ensconced in headquarters in Ottawa as the force's expert on communism. He produced a memorandum, 'Communism in Canadian Colleges and Universities,' which was designed to document the pattern of attempts to infiltrate higher education in Canada. The veteran policeman, drawing on his first-hand experience, traced the 'Red' master plan back to the latter half of the 1920s and the establishment of campus labour clubs like the one at McGill. The coordination and extension of such plans, he argued, occurred at the World Congress of Students against War and Fascism in Brussels in December 1934, at which a pledge was made for students around the world to fight against 'militarization in schools.'

The rest of the memorandum outlined the two main forms the Communist assault would take. First, there were the 'radical Professors,' modern-day Socrateses, who because of 'their responsible positions' threatened to have a 'detrimental effect' on the young. A list of individuals working at the University of Toronto, the University of Western Ontario, the University of Alberta, the Université Laval, the Université de Montréal, Upper Canada College, and Brandon College was included. All of the names, with the exception of Frank Underhill's, were removed under the Access to Information Act.[50] The other component of the subversive threat, the police believed, was represented by two student organizations that had appeared in the latter half of the 1930s, the Canadian Youth Congress (CYC) and the Canadian Student Assembly (CSA).

The CYC began in 1936 with members of the Young Communist League playing an important role in its birth. Consisting of a collection of student organizations with a combined membership of at least 400,000, it held annual meetings until 1942 when, thanks to a campaign by the RCMP, it was proscribed under the Defence of Canada Regulations.[51] Throughout the CYC's short life, Mounties kept constant track of the extent of Communist influence within it. The RCMP knew from its informants within the YCL that Tim Buck had secretly helped to draft one of the measures passed at the first meeting in 1936. From these and other sources the RCMP was able to obtain internal documents and produce a list of Communists who attended the 1937 CYC conference, along with a breakdown of the ethnic background of delegates. Despite the evidence, the true extent of Communist influence was another matter. Those in attendance in 1937 passed several conservative resolutions, including one upholding the right to own private property. The initial police analysis was that Communist influence within the CYC was on the wane, but that view was soon replaced by a more sinister interpretation, which was presented to the federal minister of justice, Ernest Lapointe: Communists who continued to pull the strings fooled the other delegates. This stark vision would dominate an RCMP historical assessment of communism and youth in the inter-war period produced in 1948 by a university graduate with a history degree who was hired and placed directly into the force's intelligence branch. This Mounted Police interpretation, according to historian Paul Axelrod, allowed it to continue monitoring organizations like the CYC because they represented a 'clear, present, and continuing danger.'[52]

This approach would become a common response at all levels of the RCMP. Under what can be called the 'RCMP but,' the force never ruled out anyone or anything as a threat, even if evidence and analysis to that effect was available. Much of that attitude had to do with rationalizing continued attention by the police, partly in an effort to justify budgets and the application of resources. After all, if an organization or an individual stops being a threat, then the next obvious question is why should the police attention continue. There was also an even more practical aspect to the 'RCMP but,' especially for those lower down in the hierarchy. One former Security Service member described it as a matter of 'c.y.a.,' that is, 'cover your ass.'[53]

The outbreak of war in September 1939 heightened police concern about some student organizations. There was to be little tolerance for those not fully behind the war effort. The Defence of Canada Regulations provided the federal government with tremendous power to deal with real or imagined opposition to the conflict. The RCMP was in the important position both of drawing up names of those to be interned and then of gathering them up. The tentacles of the state ensnared opponents to the war, including Communists, pacifists, French Canadians, and religious minorities. It also included those on the far right of the Canadian political spectrum, who had been largely ignored by the RCMP for most of the 1930s and whose presence at francophone universities in Quebec continued to be overlooked after the war began.[54]

Joining the CYC in the RCMP's list of enemies in January 1938 was the Canadian Student Assembly, a youth organization formed to oppose conscription. In all contexts, both Canadian and international, controversy accompanies any refusal to fight on behalf of one's country. The pledge by the Oxford University debating society in 1933 not to take up arms on behalf of king and country received worldwide attention. Less well known was a survey of McMaster University students in 1935 in which 62 per cent of male respondents said that in the event of war they would advise a relative either to refuse service or to offer only humanitarian assistance.[55]

War made the issue even more significant. With the CPC opposing Canadian participation in the conflict after the Soviet Union's invasion of Poland, the RCMP had further reason to suspect the motives of anyone or any organization that questioned the war effort. In a time of conflict, the equation was simple: anti-conscription equalled anti-British equalled subversion equalled communism. The negative impact that a CSA plan to conduct a nation-wide student referendum on conscription might have on student recruitment for military service sparked Canada's national police force and its informants into action.[56]

The RCMP launched its new efforts at the University of Toronto, one of the centres of CSA activity. Employing student informants, however, was not without its difficulties; one student who was approached had to write examinations before being able to spy. The RCMP actually conducted a recruiting drive by sending an agent to the campus in search of sources. His first meeting was with a student 'of an old established college fraternity largely consisting of members of old Toronto families and mainly conservative.' This informant also described a sub-source – a student of impeccable background because he was an anti-Communist and had already volunteered to fight in the war – who was prepared to infiltrate any organization on behalf of the RCMP. The recruiter then visited another campus dweller, who was also eager to cooperate because he had been 'horrified' by the radical activities at the University of Toronto. This person had chosen a delegate to attend a CSA meeting in Quebec City in December 1939, and he proceeded to turn over that student's account of the gathering to the police and promised to do the same with future reports.[57]

To monitor CSA activities the RCMP enlisted or used already existing sources at several other universities, including McGill University, where it was a person connected to the student newspaper, the *McGill Daily*, and the University of Western Ontario.[58] One recruit reported that a female member of the CSA had alleged that policemen were watching the organization; an effort to discover how she knew this proved futile. Instead character assassination prevailed. 'From what I can gather,' wrote Superintendent H.R. Gagnon, 'this young woman is quite socially inclined, a member of a Sorority, and one very actively engaged in the social life of the University; one, apparently, who might be suspected of coming to the University for just that purpose.' Nevertheless, she concerned the police enough that they opened a file on her.[59]

Gagnon's comments revealed another reality. The intelligence business was gendered male. The maleness of those who participated influenced their perceptions of society and the way they performed their work.[60] For a woman to be involved in radical activities, or even to be involved in a non-traditional role, there had to be, in the eyes of the police, something not quite right about her. It was no different in other countries. In her study of the Australian Security Intelligence Organization, Fiona Capp notes the male language of reports, including repeated references to 'penetration,' and how it effectively feminized all targets. In the eyes of security services, 'women were either innocent victims,' writes Capp, 'or corrupted collaborators who had succumbed to the spirit of Communism.'[61] The same view applied to women involved in intelligence work. The Kingston office of the RCMP was thoroughly perplexed by a letter in 1963 from a female Queen's University student inquiring about a career in security. 'We are unable to assess this letter at this time,' wrote Constable M.G. Johnston. 'A number of questions come to mind ... Is this a legitimate request? Was she prompted by some one else to write the letter? Is it an attempt to learn something of our operations? In any event it appears to be a peculiar request from a second year female University student, therefore same is being forwarded for record purposes. A check of general and subversive indices here was negative.'[62] The Soviets and Americans held similar attitudes towards gender. The former made derogatory comments over the sexual practices of some of the American women who spied on their behalf, while one of these women, Elizabeth Bentley, was treated just as harshly by the American media and political establishment after her private life became public knowledge.[63]

Reports from sources and regular members in early 1940 reassured the RCMP's leaders support for the CSA was in decline. Superintendent Vernon Kemp observed with pleasure that the University of Toronto student newspaper had ignored the referendum issue. Ignorance, however, was not good enough, especially when students were perceived as a passive and easily influenced mass. Instead, advised a senior Mountie, 'a counter-propaganda' campaign against the CSA, one led by 'competent persons who have the interests of the Universities and the safety of the country at heart,' was necessary.[64] In supporting such a tactic, Kemp touched on several important aspects of the police's view of students and universities:

It is considered ... that some form of education to combat this subversive activity and to instill into the minds of young Canadians the patriotic aspect of War Service in the present struggle, is essential ... Students at Universities accept their leading in so many matters from the Professors that it is not a difficult thing to sway the thought of the students by the utterances of members of the Faculty. Quite irrespective of the effect on the recruiting campaign in Canada, the present student body representing, as they do, the professional men of Canada's next generation, our post-war difficulties would be greatly increased by the school of thought which these Professors can engender on economic matters. Students are very jealous of their standing in the community, and it is submitted that legal action, either through the courts or by way of open police investigation, would result at the present time in swaying many of the thousands of students into an attitude of open sympathy for those against whom action is taken. But delaying such action for a period of two or three months, during which time the student body was educated to think along patriotic lines, would have an entirely different effect. The formation of a student organization whose aims and objects would be citizenship would, it is felt, particularly nullify the effects of the proposed ballot and any other subversive thought which may have been engendered.[65]

The RCMP went so far as to organize a conference in Ottawa among senior officers and government officials. It included one other individual, whose name was deleted under the Access to Information Act, who was connected to the University of Toronto, either as a faculty member or as an administrator, had an intimate knowledge of the university, was trusted by the police, and appeared eager to offer assistance. In addition to recommending an increase in the recruitment of boy scouts and girl guides, this informant suggested that an academic be recruited to observe subversive activities at universities across Canada under the cover of investigating teaching methods. To assist this individual, it was suggested that he or she should be provided with a 'liberal expense account to bear the cost of free entertainment in which tongues are loosened.' Nothing appears to have come of this proposal, although Kemp did make arrangements to address the Canadian Officers' Training Corps at the University of Toronto on the need for cooperation with the police during wartime.[66] Such schemes became meaningless when the CSA died of its own accord in 1940. Before rigor mortis set in, however, the organization would unintentionally lead the men in scarlet to invade the life of a prominent academic.

The RCMP had first noticed Frank Underhill in 1935, but it was not until the beginning of the Second World War that it acquired a deep interest in him.[67] The historian and Great War veteran was a controversial figure because of his public comments, both real and misconstrued, regarding Canada's support for the British Empire and the war effort. A definite pattern suggested itself: Underhill opposed the war and he had connections with the CSA. To the police, the academic became a suspected Communist and the suspicion necessitated further investigation; a January 1940 report lumped him together with a group that included law professor F.R. Scott at McGill University and historian Arthur R.M. Lower at Queen's University, collectively described as 'men of extreme thought, *if not definitely Communist.*'[68] Then, in February 1940 the label took on a more definitive tone. Underhill and several others at the

University of Toronto, whose names were deleted under Access to Information, were officially labelled as 'Reds.' Special Constable Mervyn Black, an important member of the security intelligence staff in Toronto, described Underhill as a 'definite' Communist. Black admitted, however, that proving it would be difficult. It was more a case of guilt by association – Underhill's name apparently appeared in a CPC document and he had had contact with Samuel Levine, labelled as a CPC member by a police informant.[69]

Samuel Levine, a graduate of Cambridge University, where he had been an active Communist, worked at the University of Toronto as a research fellow in the Department of Geophysics. In September 1940 he was arrested under the Defence of Canada Regulations and charged with having in his possession banned Communist literature. Convicted, Levine went to prison for six months. On his release, the RCMP had him sent to an internment camp. Finally freed in October 1941, Levine found that his old job no longer existed. In his history on academic freedom in Canada, Michiel Horn rightly describes this incident as 'doubly sad because it unfolded in the context of a war fought to defend human freedom,' and he singles out the RCMP for special opprobrium.[70]

How and why had Samuel Levine, whose association with Frank Underhill further incriminated the historian in the eyes of the police, caught the RCMP's attention? His case shows that the nature of the interaction between state security and academics is more complex than simply a story of conflict. In fact, some academics have served as assistants or even enablers. Contained within a document about Underhill is a passage missed by the Access to Information censors: 'You will note in para. 6 of the report [the next section was to have been cut but was not] that Sam LEVINE admitted being paid agitator of the C.P. according to Prof. Louden.'[71] Who was 'Prof. Louden'? No one by that last name worked at the University of Toronto during this period. However, the university did employ a Professor Thomas 'Tommy' R. Loudon as its head of the Department of Applied Mechanics in the Faculty of Applied Science and Engineering. Born in Toronto in 1883, Loudon fought as a member of the Royal Canadian Engineers in the First World War. At the University of Toronto, besides being a faculty member, he was active as a lieutenant colonel in the university's branch of the Canadian Officers' Training Corps. Whether Loudon was the 'Prof. Louden' mentioned in the report cannot be said for certain but he certainly had the characteristics of someone who might not be well inclined towards real or suspected Communists. Loudon left the university in March 1940 when the federal government appointed him to lead the school of aeronautical engineering in the British Commonwealth Air Training Plan.[72] Reports to the RCMP from a senior informant at the University of Toronto appear to have ended at roughly the same time.

Because of the information from its various sources at the University of Toronto, the RCMP initially feared that it might be a haven for Communists, thus requiring more detailed inquiries. Reassuringly, it was noted that the 'left wing radical professors' tended to be in history and economics, while faculty in the sciences, medicine, and dentistry occupied the 'conservative' side. Unsurprisingly then, the police increasingly focused on the prominent Underhill, and Vernon Kemp gave orders for a more detailed investigation of him in March 1940. In the course of his memorandum, in language that echoed Capp's point about security agencies feminizing targets, the senior officer alluded to Underhill 'lacking moral courage' and questioned his manhood by saying he 'wept' when previously censured. These characteristics were apparently synonymous with being a Communist. He also noted the need for more information on Underhill's time at Oxford University and issued orders to place Underhill under the surveillance of regular members and of 'contacts' both on and off the University of Toronto campus.[73]

By May 1940 the RCMP was collecting materials on Underhill and two others at his institution as part of the preparation of Personal History Files (PHFs). The system of PHFs had started soon after the birth of the new RCMP in 1920 and were included in the main files on radicals as a way of centralizing important information.[74] Underhill's form was typical of the genre:

Personal History File
Re: Professor Frank H. UNDERHILL, University of Toronto, Toronto, Ont.
Name – Frank H. UNDERHILL
Alias – none known
Nationality – Canadian born
If naturalized – not applicable
When and how arrived in Canada – Canadian born
DESCRIPTION
  Age – 48 years
  Weight – 130 lbs.
  Height – 5 ft. 2 in.
  Build – slim
  Colour of hair – bald – very fair hair at sides
  Colour of eyes – blue
  Glasses (if worn) – no

Complexion – fair
Hair on face – clean shaven
Teeth – good
Nose – regular
Deformities – nil
Marks – nil
Peculiarities – looks down when talking; very high white forehead
Usual dress – inconspicuously, but neatly
Manner – Gentlemanly and polite
Habits: (smokes, drinks, gambles, etc.) – smokes cigarettes and pipe.
    Drinks moderately
Speech – good English
Languages spoken – English and some French
Photo – nil
Married or single – Married, wife Canadian works at St. George's Children's
    school
Family – nil
Present address – 449 Walmer Road, Toronto, Ont. phone Mi 6185
Past and present occupation – Professor of Constitutional and Modern
    History, 1928 – University of Saskatchewan, Saskatoon
Present – University of Toronto
Police record, (if any) – nil
Associations affiliated with – C.C.F. (Research Secretary), League For Social
    Reconstruction
Influence and standing in same – Is somewhat erratic but has a reputation
    as a vitriolic, critical writer and therefore has considerable influence and
    standing.
Intimate associates – [deleted: individual names]
Activities – He is said to be a Canadian Nationalist believing in a Commu-
    nist-Socialist (?) Government without any ties to the British Empire.
General Remarks – UNDERHILL is said to be used as a tool by radicals, but
    is said to be violently anti-Nazi, and to embrace any progressive move-
    ment. Despite his intellect he is said to take people at their face value and
    to be somewhat a fool in this respect. List of files in which this man
    appears – [deleted: file names and numbers].
History, early and recent – UNDERHILL was educated in Canada and won a
    Rhodes scholarship to Oxford ... His radical sentiments have gained him
    some publicity ...[75]

Of course, it was not simply that Underhill was a Communist, or so the
police believed. It followed that he must be propagating his nefarious

beliefs among his pupils, which made him especially dangerous. Kemp advised Ottawa that 'prompt and efficient steps may be taken to eliminate this hazard which is such an insidious method of converting our future professional men into the teachings of Communism.' Although no evidence of Underhill using the classroom to disseminate propaganda existed, one report made reference to him using his time outside of classes to indoctrinate students.[76]

The history professor became even more controversial in the fall of 1940 after newspapers distorted the tone and content of remarks he made at the annual Couchiching Conference. The clamour for his professional scalp escalated.[77] On 17 September, the Ontario attorney general, a representative of the Ontario Provincial Police, other officials, and a member of the RCMP gathered to discuss what to do about him. Because of the lack of concrete evidence, it was decided no action could be taken against him. Underhill, nevertheless, still had to face the wrath of the University of Toronto administration. Days before the issue was to be discussed at the university, a member of the RCMP met with the president, Canon H.J. Cody, venturing the opinion that the historian was 'an extremely bad influence.' According to Cody, Underhill's position was in jeopardy, and he added that he was preparing a negative report for the Board of Governors on the intellectual thorn in the university's side. He did just that, recommending that Underhill be fired, a course of action that ultimately was not followed because of appeals on the professor's behalf from colleagues, students, and political friends.[78]

The RCMP remained interested in Underhill but by 1943 it was reported that his file would be placed on hold until something of interest came up.[79] Indeed, in 1947 an unknown policeman challenged its existence in rather unusual prose: 'I should like to draw your attention to this file on F.H. Underhill in order to counteract to some degree the general impression it gives of his political affiliations and sympathies ... First, Underhill's public utterances at any time could not possibly be construed as Communistic without committing a semantic outrage; to insinuate such is to confess an obtuse inability to distinguish between fabian socialism and communism ... the mere fact that he stands out for individual liberty does not make him any less a socialist. It simply shows him to be an intelligent one.' The only official response to what amounted to a rebuke was a suggestion that Underhill had 'changed his Communistic ideas.'[80]

After resuming its hibernation for several more years, Frank Underhill's file became active again in the 1960s. In December 1964 the RCMP began once more to investigate the academic, who was now seventy-five years old. A neighbour was interviewed about him; his employment file at the Public Service Commission, which at the time employed him as the curator of Laurier House, was examined. His election to the Ottawa executive of the Canadian Political Science Association was reported on. Finally, the fact that he subscribed to the *Marxist Quarterly* as J.T. Underhill, which the RCMP labelled an 'assumed name,' was noted. Why he subscribed under the different name puzzled the Mounties who were investigating him. It was concluded that the subscription itself might be because Underhill had a 'scholarly interest' in the journal.[81] The occasional clipping was added to the dossier until his death in 1971.

The case of Frank Underhill is instructive because it encapsulates several of the important themes in the RCMP's coverage of universities. He initially attracted police attention because of his public pronouncements; it stayed with him because of a belief, albeit based on tenuous evidence, that secretly he was a Communist. That he was targeted demonstrates how an unsophisticated security service could come to believe, with unshakable conviction, that someone who regularly gave expression to unpopular opinions had to be a left-wing revolutionary.

This is not to suggest, as some have, that the RCMP was always unable to distinguish a social democrat from a Communist. In his memoirs, diplomat Escott Reid describes his contact with the RCMP in 1940, during the height of its interest in Underhill. Commissioner S.T. Wood contacted Reid's boss, O.D. Skelton, after a postal censor had reported that the junior bureaucrat was in receipt of a publication from Moscow, but added that Reid had not previously come to police attention for radical activities. Reid mocks the RCMP as incompetent because the only information it held about him apparently came from the *Canadian Who's Who*, thus missing his association with the Student Christian Movement and the Co-operative Commonwealth Federation.[82] In fact, his case demonstrates the exact opposite. Generally, beginning the mid-1920s, the RCMP was able to distinguish between those who sought radical change through revolution and those on the left who were content to bring about reform through the ballot box.[83] The force went after Communists, not social democrats. This point does require a qualification, and Underhill and others, like David Lewis, represent it. Individuals and organizations that challenged the status quo, especially from a left perspective, continued to raise suspicions and to spark investigations.

As was the case with Underhill, RCMP work on campuses went into decline after the initial burst of coverage at universities at the beginning of the war. By June 1941 Communists had either been imprisoned under the Defence of Canada Regulations because of their opposition to Canada's participation in the war or they had gone into hiding to avoid arrest. Then, Germany's invasion of the Soviet Union prompted the CPC to offer enthusiastic support to Canada's participation in the conflict.[84] While not necessarily friends of the Canadian state, Communists were now officially allies. Only a scattering of reports, many of them regarding frivolous matters, appear in files on universities during the remainder of the war. At the University of Toronto, a Mountie investigated a rumour that library books had been found with Communist leaflets inside them. From the head of the University of Western Ontario Canadian Officers' Training Corps came a dire warning that 'subversive activities' were rampant on campus; a police inquiry determined that the 'subversion' involved medical students who signed a petition asking for more time off during exams and that the officer who made the complaint was particularly unpopular with students. In 1943 a mounted policeman covered an address by Tim Buck to the University of Alberta's Political Science Club, while at Queen's a secret agent attended a film forum that involved Professor C.B. Wade, whom the agent concluded was an enthusiastic advocate of Buck. In the same year, the RCMP decided to suspend its file on Communist subversion at the University of Toronto, once considered to be the centre of it, because of a lack of activity.

On a larger scale, another reality was apparent by 1943: the Allies would emerge from the conflict victorious. Planning began for the postwar period. For the RCMP, this meant a reaffirmation in 1944 of which organization remained its top priority. John Leopold, now the assistant intelligence officer in Ottawa, ordered that a national survey on communism in Canada be conducted. Among the categories of activity to be investigated were examples of Communist infiltration into federal, provincial, and municipal services, including education.[85] Even a brutal war against fascism, with Communists as official allies, had not weakened the RCMP's belief in the supremacy of 'Red Menace.' In this, the Mounties raced ahead of many in the general public. Canadians would catch up in the months that followed a fateful stroll by a cipher clerk in the Soviet embassy in Ottawa.

4

Scarlet and Reds on Campus, 1946–1960

On a September night in 1945 in Ottawa, Igor Gouzenko, a cipher clerk at the Soviet embassy, rushed to freedom, liberating himself and his family, as well as many pages of top secret documents. The papers he had hidden in his clothes revealed the existence of a Communist spy ring that operated in the western world and that involved civil servants, scientists, and, most satisfyingly to the RCMP, two senior members of the Communist Party of Canada, Sam Carr and Fred Rose, the latter also being the sole Communist member of the federal Parliament. Gouzenko's revelations marked the symbolic beginning of the second phase of the cold war, a struggle that would dominate democratic and Communist nations alike for over forty-five years.

In the realm of countersubversion, the influence of Gouzenko was great. The documents he brought with him expanded the police definition of who constituted a subversive. Members of the university community – several of those alleged to be spies were graduates of McGill University – now shared a corner with workers and ethnic minorities. At the same time, however, Gouzenko's reinforcement of communism as the most serious threat to the security of the Canadian state ultimately harmed Mounted Police countersubversion operations in two respects, both of which were evident in relation to police work on campuses. First, it left the force unable in the 1960s to appreciate the fundamentally different nature of the challenges to the state that arose in that decade. Secondly, the Gouzenko revelations created a problem that would dog RCMP security work for decades: unclear definitions of what constituted subversion led the RCMP to gather every possible scrap of information about communism at the same time that it suffered from an inability to analyze what it had collected, so much so that an institutional and bureaucratic inertia nearly set in.

The problem was that the Gouzenko documents did not, in the end, offer any simple answers. 'A convinced Communist is a man possessed,' warned the RCMP in a pamphlet issued three years after the spy trials that followed Gouzenko's revelations. 'He is not amenable to argument or persuasion, or even coercion. Society must always be on guard against him, and each citizen must be prepared to combat his ideas wherever they crop up.'[1] Many of those who spied on behalf of the Soviet Union in this era, while acting for ideological reasons, did not fit the police caricature of Communists.[2] The pattern was the same in the United States. Some of the people who were approached by Soviet intelligence agencies to spy on fellow citizens initially did so but then withdrew their services. Others rebuffed attempts at recruitment or, even after being recruited lacked effectiveness because their handlers did not trust them.

That there was espionage carried out with the involvement and assistance of officials of the Communist parties in Canada and the United States cannot be denied. Soviet diplomatic cables obtained through the SIGINT program code-named Venona and recently declassified documents of the former Soviet Union provide undeniable evidence of it.[3] On the other hand, the extent of espionage on behalf of the Soviet Union was never as widespread as was alleged by the West during the cold war. In many ways, espionage had peaked by 1945 and declined as the cold war rhetoric escalated. Indeed, scholar and politician Daniel Patrick Moynihan argues convincingly that the excessive secrecy on the part of the Western world ultimately did more damage than good. Anyone with a radical hue was automatically painted with the brush of disloyalty, with the hunt for spies by Canadians and Americans ultimately becoming, as they had been before the Second World War, searches for subversives.[4]

Witch-hunting ensnared witches and non-witches alike. Julius and Ethel Rosenberg, one involved in espionage and the other most likely not, went to their deaths by electrocution. From making civil defence drills mandatory for everyone to requiring citizens seeking fishing licences to take loyalty oaths lest they poison water supplies, anti-communism and cold war values permeated American society. A previously obscure senator from the generally progressive state of Wisconsin, Joseph McCarthy, contributed a new word to the English language. McCarthyism, however, would not have been possible without what historian Ellen Schrecker calls 'Hooverism.' It was J. Edgar Hoover, a rabid anti-Communist, and the resources of his Federal Bureau of Investigation that funnelled material to those conducting the witch-hunts.[5]

American universities did not escape unscathed. In 1951 the FBI launched the 'Responsibilities Program,' which consisted of the anonymous strategic release of information about people employed in the field of higher education whom Hoover's men had decided were subversives. Several of the faculty members who were subsequently dismissed ended up teaching in Canada.[6]

Moreover, the ideology and practice of anti-communism was widely popular among ordinary Americans. The cold war coincided with a growth in polling, which allowed for new insights into popular opinion. In 1950 the Gallup Poll asked a representative sample of the American population on what 'should be done about members of the Communist Party in the United States in the event we get into a war with Russia?' Nearly 70 per cent favoured internment, imprisonment, deportation, or execution. Only 1 per cent believed nothing should be done because of the protection of free speech under the First Amendment.[7]

The imaginary line dividing the United States from its northern neighbour afforded the latter no special protection from expression of hostility towards cold war enemies. The 1948 victory of the forces of Mao Zedong in China and the role of Communists in the Korean conflict swelled 'better dead than red' sentiments throughout North America. A 1950 Gallup Poll found 70 per cent of Canadians favoured requiring Communists to register with the government while 62 per cent favoured limiting their right to freedom of speech.[8]

Although not on a par with the United States, Canada had its share of rabid anti-Communists. George Drew, the leader of the federal Progressive Conservative Party, publicly led attacks against communism. Another anti-Communist warrior had a career not in politics but in academe. Professor Watson Kirkconnell was a well-respected linguist with a strong dislike for Communists, who laboured tirelessly to warn Canadians of the peril they posed, publicly and privately, to democracy.

In 1949 Kirkconnell, then the president of Acadia University, turned his attention to his nation's institutions of higher education. Writing in *Saturday Night* magazine and relying on an account of a meeting in 1948 of the Labour Progressive Party (LPP), the official name of the CPC after 1943, that he had somehow obtained, the scholar warned Canadians about its plans for higher education. His article consisted largely of quotes from the LPP document, which set out recruitment plans for its clubs at universities. It was the era of the 'united front,' and so these included finding common cause with the Student Christian Movement and the Co-operative Commonwealth Federation (CCF), especially on peace issues, and using the student media and social occasions to enlist new members. Instead of recognizing that the document represented a wish-list of a party struggling to find younger members, Kirkconnell, intoxicated by his anti-communism, exaggerated its implications: 'From the foregoing excerpts from a voluminous document, it is clear that there are militant Communist "nuclei" on the campus at McGill, Toronto, Winnipeg, Saskatoon, Edmonton and Vancouver; that a "peace movement" is this year's front racket, both to help Stalin and to recruit for the Party; and that they have made some inroads into the C.C.F. and the S.C.M. and have conspired in other student organizations.'[9] His views had no monopoly on originality. Three years earlier, a University of Toronto student informed a newspaper that Communists on campus had made unsuccessful attempts to control student and veteran groups on campus.[10] In that same year, the Kellock-Taschereau Commission looking into the Soviet espionage ring in Canada issued its final report, in which it was revealed that several of the people linked to the ring were McGill University graduates. 'As for our universities,' declared a Quebec newspaper at the time, 'it is a matter of common knowledge that for years ... they have been hotbeds of radicalism and centres, not of pure learning but of ideological indoctrination. You send your boy to McGill a Canadian democrat and he graduates an international Communist.'[11] An executive member of the British Columbia Women's Liberal Association echoed these views in 1947 when she warned of the spread of communism in universities. Then there was Solon Low, member for Peace River, who in the House of Commons wondered why so many 'Reds' had found positions at Canadian universities, where 'they find opportunity to undermine the faith of our young people in Canada, in true democracy, and in Christianity.'[12]

There was a degree of truth in all of these warnings, and it was one that the LPP made no secret of. In essence, the party's perception of students differed little from that of the RCMP. Students were a passive audience that the party intended to go after in what the *Canadian Tribune*, the official party newspaper, labelled 'the training ground for bourgeois leadership.' It called for 'vigorous Communist activity on Canadian campuses' in an effort to win students over. The party's success at universities, however, remained marginal. By 1963 internal discussions lamented the absence of young members and immigrants in the party, and a new effort was made to appeal to youths. The central point of that plan was a magazine called *Scan*, an effort to fuse youth culture and student protest with Communist sensibilities. The marginalization of the

LPP only grew in the latter half of the 1960s, when the diverse movement known as the New Left took hold. In the early 1970s the campus club at the University of Toronto had only seven members, while a single member was the party at the University of British Columbia.[13]

Internal LPP information was available to the RCMP through a variety of sources almost at the same time as it was to its own members. Security Service members in the field also supplied details about party activities because, for the first time since the middle of the Second World War, the RCMP began to make forays onto campuses to discover the extent of Communist infiltration. The results confirmed a sparse Communist presence. At the University of Western Ontario in February 1946, for instance, an informant reported through his RCMP handler that the party was having little success finding followers despite the unhappiness of some veterans who had returned to university at the lack of financial assistance from the federal government.[14]

Convinced, as a result of their scant training, of the threatening nature of communism and of the resort by Communists to underhanded tactics, the Mounted Police were clear on the significance of the limited Communist presence on campus: the 'Reds' were there, but they or their subversive activities were hidden, which necessitated greater efforts to catch them. In Edmonton the local security and intelligence office found it indispensable to report on a dispute that led to the expulsion and subsequent reinstatement of a University of Alberta student named Fero F. Zeman. The RCMP found the matter curious, especially since it appeared to be connected to the visit of Dr Lotta Hitschmanova, executive director of the Unitarian Services Committee of Canada and well known to later generations through her USC Canada television commercials. 'Whilst there may not be any subversive activities on the part of either Dr. Lotte Hitchmanova [sic] or Fero F. Zeman,' wrote the commander of security for the RCMP's 'K' Division, 'it would be advisable to have very discreet enquiries made with a view to definitely establishing whether this trouble did arise from "ideological" differences.' During the cold war, the RCMP strongly suspected members of the Unitarian Church of performing the role of 'talent spotters,' tracking down potential recruits for either open or secret membership in the Communist party.[15]

The attitude that no lead should be left unexamined in the search for subversion applied as well to McGill University, which because of its radical reputation remained a favourite RCMP target. The attendance of twenty-three of the university's students at the 1947 World Youth Festival in Prague was deemed worthy of inclusion in the annual report of the

Anti-Communist Section Special Branch, as the countersubversion 'D' Branch was then named. A year later, the Department of External Affairs informed the RCMP that over one hundred Canadian students, including some from McGill and the University of Toronto, had visited Yugoslavia; a list of names was promised.[16] Mounties even followed the summer holiday plans of suspected Communist students: '[deleted: name of source] states that [deleted: names], members of the McGill L.P.P. Club and the National Federation of Labour Youth in Montreal, have stated that they were going to Toronto for a short vacation. [deleted: name of source] also states that [deleted: name] left Montreal at the beginning of September and will return to Montreal for a new term at McGill University [deleted: source] was unable to establish whether [deleted: names] left Montreal for a vacation or for the purpose of attending a L.P.P. school.'[17] Discovering facts like the summer travel plans of suspected Communists or the prominence of LPP members in the Student Labour Club at McGill served a variety of purposes for the police. In immediate terms it represented an attempt to establish whether a person was in fact a Communist or to discover what type of loosely defined subversive activity might be underway. There was, in addition, a long-term significance to these records and this belies the notion that the simple collection of information by intelligence agencies is inherently benign. Twenty years after these reports about the Student Labour Club were filed, the RCMP once more sought information on the nature of the club in this period. Specifically, during a security screening in 1967, a request was placed for an 'assessment' of the club as it had been in 1947. Using old police reports, which in turn were based on newspaper clippings from the *McGill Daily*, the RCMP decided the club had been 'Communist infiltrated' in 1947. What evidence did it have for this label? The president of the club was George Neuspiel, who according to RCMP records was identified as a LPP member in June 1947, and its executive was described in a newspaper article as 'leftist.'[18]

The need to assign labels was another legacy of the Gouzenko defection. One of the RCMP intelligence wing's most important tasks in the aftermath of the revelation of the involvement of Canadian civil servants in spying was security screening of current and future government employees. A cabinet directive in 1948 required that anyone associated with communism in any capacity not be employed in a 'position of trust or upon work of a confidential nature.' Four years later, another cabinet directive expanded that definition to exclude from the public service those who by 'word or actions shows himself to believe in Marxism/

Leninism, or any other ideology which advocates the overthrow of government by force.'[19]

Security screening involved background checks to determine whether a person participated in any potentially subversive activities. For example, if a graduate of McGill University applied for a government job in 1967, the RCMP wanted to know what she or he had been interested in during their student career. Discovering a membership in the Student Labour Club in 1947 made the nature of the club at the time suddenly of interest. Simply having been part of that association twenty years earlier would not preclude employment in sensitive areas, but if it was discovered that the prospective employee also belonged to other organizations deemed subversive or had not been forthcoming about past associations, then the klaxon would begin to sound for the RCMP.

The other reason Mounties were concerned about the operations of the McGill Student Labour Club twenty years earlier is related to security screening in a more complicated fashion. It was linked to the 'Cambridge Five,' the spy ring recruited at Cambridge University in the 1930s. The five – Kim Philby, Donald MacLean, Guy Burgess, Anthony Blunt, and John Cairncross – went on to have prominent careers before their treachery was discovered. Important clues, it was later decided, lay with their Communist beliefs while they were university students. On their recruitment as Soviet agents, they were ordered to distance themselves from expressions of their earlier left-wing leanings. Indeed, Philby took exactly the opposite perspective in order to cover his true allegiance.[20]

The details surrounding the cases of Philby, MacLean, and Burgess were well known by the 1960s. The question for intelligence agencies was how many more Philbys might still be out there. Trying to answer this question was a mounted policeman by the name of Terry Guernsey, who developed the idea of conducting a form of security screening for individuals who had established careers and who, for all intents and purposes, seemed 'virtually untouchable' by intelligence services. Known as Operation Feather Bed, the program, which was conceived in 1958 (after Burgess and MacLean had defected and Philby was under suspicion) but not launched until 1962, consisted of extensive and detailed checks into the careers of important public figures, all in an effort to discover a hint of left-wing radicalism, such as a membership in the CPC or involvement in subversive organizations, or the participation of family members in Communist activities. Guernsey believed that if enough connections could be discovered through a process eventually known as 'link analysis,' then it would be possible to locate a spy or 'agent of influence' on behalf of the Soviet Union. In 1962 a list with the names of sixteen senior federal government employees was sent to the director of security and intelligence for him to consider how to deal with 'the security problems they represent.'[21]

Operation Feather Bed, however, occurred years after Watson Kirkconnell's 1949 pronouncements about Communists at universities. At the time, his words posed a problem for the RCMP, for they appeared to suggest that Canada's national police force had been dozing while a voracious serpent silently coiled itself around the nation's youth. One policeman defined the public reaction in the form of a question: 'if Communist infiltration at the various Universities was so strong, why was there not something done about it?' In fact, Kirkconnell triggered such an intense response that he felt it necessary to offer a McCarthy-like clarification to his earlier claims. In a press release he admitted that only about 2 per cent of university students had any Communist connections. This number coincided with the RCMP's own findings. The force believed that only 150 out of the 5,000 students at the University of Toronto were involved in left-wing activities, and that of this number about fifty (1 per cent) had Communist connections. At McGill University the RCMP estimated that there were seventy 'left-wing sympathizers' out of the 7,000 students, and of that number only thirty appeared to be of 'Communist ideologies' (less than 1 per cent).[22]

Although troublesome, Kirkconnell's warning also aided the RCMP by alerting the general public and university administrators to the presence of Communists on Canadian campuses. In 1949 the RCMP had proclaimed a prescription for throttling communism. Showing no mercy when it came to law enforcement was one means, but another meant having 'a calm but well informed and alert public opinion, capable and quick to detect the Communist Party line in whatever camouflaged form it may take to further its long term plans.'[23]

The attention fostered by Kirkconnell adversely affected the LPP; it complained publicly about harassment and there is evidence of a backlash against the party. The LPP campus club at McGill University was suspended for a time. The names of those who wrote letters to the *McGill Daily* protesting the suspension of the club were forwarded by Constable C.J. Young to headquarters, along with a note that an attempt would be made at the university to expel an LPP member; Young's information about the student undoubtedly came from a source within the registrar's office, a common origin for such details. Several Queen's University students opposed the creation of a model parliament at their institution in order to block Communist political activity.[24] In an editorial, the *Ottawa Journal* severely criticized Carleton College in March 1949 for allowing Tim Buck to be invited to address students:

> College professors are apt to look at a question like this as theoretical rather than practical. They see the world through the eyes of the scholar, are aloof and detached. They may not, for example, realize that in TIM BUCK they have the chief Canadian representative of a deliberate Communist policy that holds over the world the threat of war ...
>
> Such men have not had personal experience with the infiltration of Communists into labour unions. They may not have grasped the significance of the spy revelations in this and other countries. They seem not to understand that every Communist is an enemy of Canada, that the Communist Party is a revolutionary party, that communism is a synonym for treason. Such men are unduly impressed by the suggestion that there should be no bounds on free speech, that in effect in the name of free speech we must permit our boys and girls to hear treason lauded.[25]

Designed to frighten, this rhetoric achieved its goal at Carleton College. In the mid 1950s, after receiving permission from the college's administration to invite a representative of the LPP to speak, several members of the student council appeared at RCMP headquarters to ask that the invitation 'not be misconstrued as a propensity on their part towards Communistic doctrines.' They were sent away without any reassurance. Instead, four constables spied on the meeting at which LPP member Harry Binder spoke. One of them reported, in typical Mountie fashion, that had it not been for a rather forceful denunciation by one of those in attendance, 'the effect upon the students present, numbering approximately 150, might well have been harmful.'[26] The fears expressed by the Carleton students were shared south of the border. The *New York Times* in 1951 found that one-half of 2,500 faculty members at universities who were surveyed felt 'apprehensive' about freedom of speech and that this in turn affected what they said and taught.[27]

The chilly climate in higher education was not a characteristic exclusive to Ottawa. Students at the University of Manitoba also expressed reluctance to have their names publicly linked to a campus peace group out of a concern that it would harm their employment opportunities after graduation. In Vancouver, the University of British Columbia student government voted against allowing a peace council to form on campus because 'it might become a Communist front organization.'

Meanwhile, in the province's legislature the minister of municipal affairs advised his colleagues that Communists had infiltrated the province's educational institutions, including universities, and called for an investigation. An editorial appeared in the *Financial Post* under the heading 'Some Necessary House Cleaning' and the *Ottawa Journal* advocated the firing of Communist faculty members, while the *Vancouver Daily Province* warned its readers that a 'battle is being waged by the Communists for the control of Canada's youth.'[28]

Prompted by Kirkconnell's warning, an Edmonton newspaper published stories that claimed the LPP was losing ground at the University of Alberta. 'It might cheer Dr. Kirkconnell to know the *effect* of his article,' wrote a policeman at the bottom of a report on the stories. Was there cooperation between the RCMP and Kirkconnell? It may very well have fed him information, albeit on a much smaller scale than did J. Edgar Hoover's FBI to anti-Communist activists in the United States. In general, American excesses in the pursuit of communism, especially the anarchical quality to much of it, was a concern to the Canadian government and its institutions, including the RCMP. In Canada, witch-hunting was to be conducted by the state.[29]

As its interest in Edmonton newspaper accounts suggests, the RCMP took a great, immediate interest in the impact of Kirkconnell's article. Divisions across Canada were instructed to report on reactions on campuses to his warning. From the Maritimes arrived the reassurance that at the University of New Brunswick it was insignificant because the 'left-wing element' was small: at this institution, which was populated by conservative students, many of them war veterans, even the Co-operative Commonwealth Federation was banned from campus.[30]

Then there were the people Kirkconnell warned against. Throughout the 1940s and 1950s Mounties opened files on individuals in an effort to ascertain the extent of what they perceived to be Communist subversion in the educational sector. But what did the number of files that were opened represent, and how were they compiled? In 1959 the force used its McBee Keysort filing system to search its 'subversive indices' for the names of teachers, academics, and administrators. Mark McClung, a civilian member of 'K' Branch, received the numbers given in Tables 4.1 and 4.2. As the categories in Table 4.1 illustrate, being an 'inactive' Communist did not end police interest in your career. In fact, it may have done just the opposite, because when a person began to spy on behalf of the Soviet Union he or she was often ordered to sever ties immediately with the Communist party.[31] Some of the members of the force, including one

TABLE 4.1
Distribution of files on subversive educators by province, 1959

Province	Active	Inactive	Total
British Columbia	77	19	96
Alberta	59	12	71
Saskatchewan	17	15	32
Manitoba	20	11	31
Ontario	80	30	110
Quebec	41	17	58
Others	3	5	8
Total	293	109	406

Source: NA, RG 146, Vol. 2782, file 96-A-0045, 'UBC,' pt 4,
Memorandum for Mr McClung, re: 'Subversive Infiltration into
Canadian Education,' 9 March 1959.

TABLE 4.2
Distribution of files on subversive educators by province and educational group, 1959

Type	BC	Alta	Sask.	Man.	Ont.	Que.	Others	Total
Elementary[a]	47	39	22	17	31	8	2	166
High school	15	15	4	3	21	10	0	68
University	15	10	2	2	35	21	5	90
Fine arts	8	1	1	2	12	3	0	27
Administration	3	3	2	1	3	4	1	17
Other	8	3	1	6	8	12	0	38
Total	96	71	32	31	110	58	8	406

[a]Includes elementary and nursery schools
Source: NA, RG 146, vol. 2793, file 98-A-00129, Memorandum for Mr McClung,
9 March 1959.

person who was involved in assembling the data, viewed the 1959 numbers as problematic. He challenged the significance of the statistics from the perspective of someone working in countersubversion:

There is very little indication that these people try to use their positions as a way to spread Communist propaganda. As far as the elementary school teachers are concerned, there would be little point in their trying to initiate their pupils into the mysteries of Marxism, and their only profitable targets might be their fellow teachers. High school and university students, having more political awareness, would offer a better field for propaganda. However, most of these people are no doubt clever enough to realize that parents and school boards would complain if they tried too obviously to put across Communist ideas, or even to slant such subjects as history, economics or political science so as to show Communism in a favourable light. A reading of the files substantiates this theory. A number of people who were quite active in their student days showed considerable slackening off of interest in the Party when they became attached to the teaching staff of a university or college. And some have quite definitely said that they are afraid to become Party members for fear of losing their jobs.[32]

McClung echoed his colleague's comments by observing that while those listed undoubtedly had been or were party members, only 'flimsy' evidence was present to show that they proselytized while on the job. He and his colleague, in effect, challenged an important element of the security state's cold war philosophy, principally in the United States, where Communist teachers faced dismissal. This crucial observation was scrutinized in *Cold War Canada*, where authors Reg Whitaker and Gary Marcuse point out that the RCMP did not demonstrate in the 1950s – indeed they never made an attempt to do so – that Communists in leadership positions in unions caused their organizations to behave differently from others.[33] To the RCMP, the presence of a 'Red' was evidence of that person's influence and, even more, of a concerted, systematic, and organized attempt at subversion.

That philosophy overpowered McClung's cautionary note about the validity of the numbers collected on Communists in education. One of his colleagues perceived a conspiratorial aspect to the Communist presence: 'I feel the teaching Profession is an important one in which they have a specific interest. They have set up their own nursery schools for good reasons. In view of the great number of teachers involved, it may be a good idea to treat the matter in general terms. Youth is their main target – not their interest in P.T.A. groups across the country.'[34] Instead of shelving the statistics, headquarters personnel placed them in a file entitled 'Infiltration of Education Process–Canada–General,' and in individual files for each province four months after compiling them. A version of these statistics would be trotted out again two years later in an effort to sway the government of the day as to the rightfulness of the RCMP presence on university campuses.

McClung, who later quit the RCMP, could not have been surprised by the institutional reaction. When he was interviewed during his retirement in the 1980s, he had only loathing for his former colleagues, especially their intellectual abilities: '[I]n his own mind, [the Mountie] is an omni-competent being. He can go anywhere and do anything at anytime. He can govern the North; he can catch murderers; he can catch dope traffickers; he can do everything. And he does it because of his very special training ... That is one trait. The other trait is a profound anti-intellectualism. He distrusts the thought process, and any person who thinks in a deviant way is a suspect ... The policemen were suspicious of intellectuals. I have seen files in which they would enumerate the books a person would read.'[35]

Who were the subjects of the files? A few names have been liberated from the restrictions of the Access to Information Act. Leopold Infeld, a theoretical physicist at the University of Toronto, was one. Polish by birth, he had emigrated to the United States before moving to Canada in 1938. He first came to the attention of the RCMP in 1942 when he served on the sponsoring committee of an organization advocating an end to the wartime ban on the CPC. He also co-founded, with Professor Barker Fairley of the University of Toronto, the Canadian-Soviet Friendship Society and they later were both active in an effort on behalf of those arrested as a result of Gouzenko's revelations.[36]

The intermittent coverage of Infeld's activities continued after the war. What the RCMP lacked, however, was definite evidence that the academic held forbidden beliefs. In 1948, after covering a speech he gave in Montreal, a member of the force reported that 'Dr. Enfeld [sic] apparently is a firm believer in democracy and he does not advocate or approve of the Communist system.' Several policemen covered the meeting because it dealt with the sensitive topic of atomic energy and because Infeld, according to the same report, 'is known to have been closely connected with Albert EINSTEIN who recently granted his support to [deleted: *Henry Wallace's*] candidature in the forthcoming American elections.'[37]

Interest in Infeld paralleled increases in tensions in Canada as a result of the cold war. Of particular significance to state security were Infeld's ties to both the scientific community and his native Poland, which by 1948 was Communist. In July 1949 John Leopold reported that Infeld had made a trip to his native country and he included a copy of the professor's passport application. He recommended that 'discreet enquiries' be conducted to discover the reason for, and the length of, his trip to Poland. Conservative leader George Drew later raised the matter in the House of Commons, implying that Infeld was engaged in treasonous activity. At the time of that cold warrior's comments, the physicist and his family had returned to Poland as part of a sabbatical; with the growing hullabaloo back in their adopted country, including threats and surveillance by Mounties, they elected to remain in Eastern Europe.[38]

Thanks to the assistance of the Department of External Affairs, the RCMP was able to continue monitoring Infeld's activities, even after he had chosen to remain in Poland. A summary of information on him was included in a special appendix of a report issued in 1956 by the Joint Intelligence Bureau, a special intelligence committee involving the Canadian military, the Department of External Affairs, and intelligence officials, which circulated not only in Ottawa but also in Washington, having been sent to the Central Intelligence Agency. Its sources included W.S. Karpinski, 'different informers from University of Toronto circles,' and internal research. In order to obtain further intelligence, the report suggested that an approach be made to one of Infeld's former colleagues at the University of Edinburgh.[39]

Details continued to trickle in about Infeld in the 1960s. John Starnes, the future head of the Security Service but then an under-secretary of state for external affairs in 1960, forwarded to the RCMP a letter by the Canadian ambassador to Poland describing a meeting he had had with Infeld during a social occasion. The exile himself re-entered the Canadian psyche when newspapers took up his complaint that his children had been unfairly stripped of their Canadian citizenship because they had been out of the country too long.[40]

Why the strange and continuing interest in a University of Toronto academic who had apparently left Canada for good? Although it was not stated directly, the RCMP was attempting to determine whether there was something more to Infeld's activities during his time in Canada. Was he in fact a loyal Communist or even an agent who fled out of fear of exposure or because his mission was complete? Or was he a victim of zealous anti-Communists? Evidence existed to support both positions depending on the preconceptions that were brought to bear. That he left Canada for good demonstrates the impact of the harassment he endured. On the other hand, those convinced that there was something more to Infeld's time in Canada could point to the propaganda role he performed for the Communist side during the cold war. In 1952, for example, he published an article in a Communist newspaper denying Soviet responsibility for the 1940 Katyn Forest massacre of Polish military officers.[41]

The other academic publicly embroiled in controversy, communism, and the RCMP in this period was Professor George Hunter, a biochemist at the University of Alberta. On 30 June 1949 the university dismissed him because, it claimed, he had on more than one occasion injected his personal views on communism into his teaching. Hunter's firing certainly interested the RCMP. The force had first noticed him in 1939 when he addressed a meeting of the Edmonton branch of the Young Communist League. Initially, the Mounties did not believe him to be a Communist, but that changed dramatically in 1940 when a police student taking Hunter's class reported on his professor's approach to teaching chemistry:

2. This, his concluding lecture, was not upon the subject matter of the course but rather was a philosophical discourse upon the relationship between Science and Religion and Modern Concepts of Living. The general trend of thought throughout the lecture was anti-Christian and pro-Marxlsm.

3. Dr. HUNTER commenced by stating that he was not here to preach but to teach ... [and that] the society in which we live today will not permit us to think for ourselves but feeds us only that propaganda which they think we should hear. These are the capitalists ...

7. He lauded Russia and the great strides made by Communism, stating that he realized that what he was saying would have brought upon him the condemnation of our society in normal times, and now would expose him to the rigours of persecution by war-bound authorities.

8. On various occasions during the past year, Dr. HUNTER has spoken along these lines, but today more than previously he distrubed [sic] his students, raiding [sic] the ire of many, but still receiving an interested and attentive listening from others.

The force supplied the deputy attorney general of Alberta and the university's president with the details of Hunter's behaviour.[42]

When Hunter made another attempt at proselytizing in 1949, the university responded by firing him. Whether the RCMP played a role in his dismissal is unknown; a report on the firing affirmed that, as usual, the police were 'undesirous of becoming involved in any dispute of this nature.' Certainly it had no doubt that the right decision had been made by the university. In the months leading up to the professor's dismissal, police officers reviewed his file in the hope of ascertaining Hunter's political affiliation. At the beginning of June 1949 an informant named the chemistry professor, two other academics, and the wife of a member of the Zoology Department as 'closed club' members, RCMP slang for secret Communists. 'K' Division in Edmonton reiterated to Ottawa that

Hunter at no time had any involvement with the National Research Council, an obvious reference to the scientists caught up in the Gouzenko affair. As for Hunter, his days of being followed by the RCMP ended shortly after his dismissal: he packed up and moved to the United Kingdom to teach. Undoubtedly, the important information in his file, along with photos for identification purposes, was shipped off by the RCMP to MI5, its British cousin and ally in the war against subversion.[43]

Both Hunter and Infeld were suspected Communists. Harry Ferns, an active Communist while at Cambridge University in the late 1930s, found his academic career blocked because of his early political activity. In 1949 Royal Roads College, an academic institution affiliated with the Department of National Defence, offered Ferns a position; it revoked it after discovering his past. Now unemployed, Ferns left Canada for a job in England.[44] Ironically, the same college later hired historian William Rodney, who worked as a civilian analyst with the Security Service in the 1950s.

For others in education who were openly Communist, the Mounties deployed a near-blanket coverage. One was Stanley Ryerson, an historian who would later have a career at the Université du Québec à Montréal. Wherever he went, the RCMP was sure to follow. The London, Ontario, detachment of the RCMP seemed to have the giddiness of those waiting for a prizefight to start when it reported that Ryerson had been invited to address a fourth-year University of Western Ontario economics class about the writings of Karl Marx. Apparently with first-hand knowledge, a mounted policeman added that the students would keep Ryerson's focus on the assigned topic. After the talk, he enthusiastically scored the encounter as a victory for the students, who 'felt that Ryerson failed to show that Karl Marx was anything but inconsistent in his writings.'[45]

Openly Communist students received the same extensive attention. The style of this approach is evident in an excerpt from the file of Stephen Endicott, son of the controversial Reverend James Endicott, who had his university years and subsequent life profiled in detail.

Employment: Teacher [deleted: *Stephen Endicott*]
In 1947 [deleted: *Endicott*] was elected Chairman of the L.P.P. University of Toronto Club, replacing [deleted: name] He continued in this post during 1948.
   Doubts as to the connection between the L.P.P. University Club and the National Party organization were dispelled by an interview [deleted: with *Endicott*] which was printed in the February 1947 issue of the 'The Varsity.'

He stated that: 'Membership in the Labour Progressive Party Club is of particular meaning in that there is a direct affiliation with the national Labor-Progressive Party' ...

During [deleted: year] [deleted: *Endicott*] was a member of the N.F.L.Y. [National Federation of Labour Youth] Beaver Brigade which went to Eastern European countries. Upon his return to Canada, [deleted: *Endicott*] had great praise of the Communist countries in Eastern Europe and contempt for the Marshall Plan.

[deleted] the L.P.P. University of Toronto Club did not want all Party members to attend a Campus Club meeting because the Party did not want the public to know all the members.

After graduating from the University of Toronto [deleted: *Endicott*] was appointed as the Provincial Organizer of N.F.L.Y. in B.C. He continued in this capacity during 1950 and 1951. In 1952, he was elected Provincial Secretary of the organization. [deleted] In recognition of his activities in the N.F.L.Y., [deleted: *Endicott*] was appointed as the Canadian representative to the World Federation of Democratic Youth (W.D.F.Y.) (Communist international front) and took up residence with his wife in Budapest. He held this position from 1952 to 1954.

Returning to Canada on May 1, 1954, he became National Secretary of N.F.L.Y. During the next few years, he continued to be active in the N.F.L.Y. and the L.P.P., but in early 1957, he was released from his position as the National Secretary of N.F.L.Y. [deleted: *Endicott*] has not been employed in a full-time position in the Communist movement since 1957 although he continued to attend meetings of the L.P.P. and other Communist organizations. However, he has been much less active since he gave up his position with N.F.L.Y. [deleted] It is reported that he teaches [deleted: name of school subject] to Grades 10, 11 and 12.

There are indications that [deleted: *Endicott*] became disillusioned with the Party as a result of the revelations of the 20th Congress. However, investigation and surveillance indicates that he has now returned to the Party fold and that he has been a member of a C.P. of C. Closed Club in Toronto since 1960. [deleted].

The information on the internal workings of the University of Toronto LPP club that Endicott belonged to was supplied by a 'reliable contact,' who undoubtedly belonged to the club. As for Endicott, he was aware of the RCMP's attention, which also took the form of harassment as he tried to pursue his career, first at a high school and then at York University.[46]

Communists like Endicott who were open about their commitment interested the police not for their own sake but because of the possibility that they influenced others or might reveal the identities of those who kept their party affiliation a secret. All RCMP campus work, therefore, was geared toward ascertaining the true extent of communism, and hence the real level of subversive activity, at universities. The problem was that spying on individuals did not necessarily supply the insights the police craved. A more effective way of determining what headway Communists might be making on campus lay, or so the RCMP believed, in the field of student politics.

By the 1940s mock parliamentary elections were a tradition at universities across the country. Each year, students voted for candidates representing a variety of Canada's existing political parties. To the RCMP, these elections afforded the LPP a degree of legitimacy that it might otherwise not have. Election results were also useful indicators of the level of support for Communists among society's vulnerable youth. A rise in the number of votes over the previous year was something to be alarmed about, while a decline represented a failure for the Communists. It was also possible that party members felt protected in identifying their affiliation through the anonymity of the secret ballot, thus providing a more accurate gauge of support on campuses across the country.[47]

Alarm among Mounties over such rituals was particularly strong at the University of Alberta after the Second World War. Policemen were instructed to gather information about Finlay MacKenzie, the LPP candidate in the 1947 mock election campaign. An encouraging report informed headquarters that while the LPP had won two seats in the election, it garnered only 4 per cent of the total votes cast, or less than 2 per cent of the total eligible university votes.[48]

In the election nine years later, the same office in Edmonton took great pains to analyze the results, even providing a detailed breakdown by polling station. The police emphasized that students treated the entire matter with 'levity,' especially to explain why forty-seven medical students voted for Communists. That, however, was still not sufficient for headquarters. 'Discounting the Medical vote,' wrote Inspector N.O. Jones from Ottawa, 'we are wondering if [deleted: name of the Mountie or informant] would possibly determine which, of the balance, are serious votes. We could presume that the Arts and Education votes are representative, but Engineers (9 [votes]) and those at the Students Union Building (6) are an unknown factor.'[49]

Similar reports reached headquarters from other divisions. At the

University of Manitoba it was recorded that most of the LPP votes came from the Faculty of Arts, which the RCMP suspected harboured those most likely to be Communists. As late as 1960 the RCMP remained interested in mock elections at the University of Toronto, and it monitored LPP campus club leader Daniel Goldstick's efforts and the subsequent assumption by him and three of his colleagues of seats in the model parliament.[50]

Police investigations extended from the pretend world of mock parliamentary politics to the real world of student government and the wider world of student life. University elections were followed closely in an effort to ferret out overt or covert Communist power grabs.[51] Campus clubs, especially those suspected of being infiltrated or controlled by Communists, like the 'Carl [sic] Marx' club at the University of Alberta, also generated attention. In dealing with student associations like the Student Christian Movement and the Co-operative Commonwealth Federation the police interest was not in the groups themselves but in whether or not they might be infiltrated by Communists. The appearance of activity that might be in some way similar to a CPC agenda was sufficient to raise suspicions. Sponsoring a debate entitled 'Is the United States a Warmongering Nation?' at the University of Saskatchewan led to the campus SCM club being monitored. A joint protest by the University of British Columbia branches of the SCM and CCF against the shipments of weapons to Kuomintang China was secretly observed by the police. This type of behaviour indicated to the police that hidden manipulation was at work. The notion that clear-headed individuals might hold such views, independent of being secretly or openly swayed by Communists or Communist sympathizers, does not appear to have been considered by those doing the investigating.[52]

Finally, there were campus organizations that had no apparent ties to the left, communism, or Communists but that were investigated because of rumours, innuendo, or police stupidity, or because of make-work efforts. The latter possibility is an issue rarely addressed and yet it is a valid explanation for some of the RCMP's involvement with universities. Having a security intelligence service necessitates it having something to do, if for no other reason than to justify its existence, including its assigned resources. In other words, having a security service dedicated to ferreting out subversion will inevitably lead to it discovering subversion. With the RCMP, this principle was made worse by its imprecise mandate and by the fact that its members were scattered across the country and had few targets. Even the smallest Canadian towns in this period, places like North Battleford and Kirkland Lake, had at least one RCMP member who performed security intelligence work. In smaller locales that had institutions of higher education, these were the most obvious places, especially to a poorly educated policeman, to find subversive ideas being bantered about.

In Wynyard, Saskatchewan, the force warned headquarters that Communists had infiltrated the town's little theatre, an organization affiliated with the University of Saskatchewan's Extension Division. 'It will be of interest to see to what extent the Communists will use this group to further their aims and activities,' remarked the local commanding officer. Perhaps somewhere in the National Archives of Canada or in CSIS headquarters resides a file that answers his query.[53]

In 1957 a Mounted Policeman at 'A' Division, in opening an envelope found an advertisement for a public lecture, 'In Defence of Rationalism,' to be held at Carleton College in Ottawa. If not already evidence enough that something improper was afoot, the sender had scribbled helpfully on it with red ink: 'ATTENTION! They are Communists! It is just a cover title. They are lecturing on communism.' Instead of dismissing the message as the work of a crank, the RCMP proceeded to undertake a surveillance of the talk. The report that followed demonstrates the intellectual limitations of those wearing scarlet uniforms and the danger in such people covering academic activities. The investigation consisted of a regular member and of an informant attending the lecture. Indeed, Constable G.E. Land, who filed the report, was grateful for the attendance of his secret colleague, since the talk 'was far beyond the comprehension of the average layman, and were it not for the assistance of a reliable source, also in attendance, the writer would have found it impossible to evaluate the lecture to any degree.' Only one report was produced on the 'In Defence of Rationalism' series of lectures, because, in a burst of honesty, Land admitted the 'futility of further attendance ... by anyone lacking the necessary higher educational background.' Even the source said he would not attend subsequent lectures.[54]

In Edmonton the local RCMP decided that an important centre of subversion was the Philosophical Society, a group that included several faculty members in its ranks and met frequently on campus to discuss, not surprisingly, philosophical issues. At a 1952 gathering, Constable R.C. Francis sat in on a review by Anthony Mardiros, a philosopher at the university, of the plight of Australian Aborigines. After making a note of those in attendance whom he personally knew to 'entertain pro-Communist views,' the policeman settled down to listen to the speaker. A précis was offered to his superiors, and Francis emphasized Mardiros's view that under the present system nothing would change. Being a good police officer, he remained for the question period. Questions after a talk were crucial, according to the security mindset, because they demonstrated how well the audience had received the speaker's message. At the University of Alberta on a chilly day in February 1952, the Mounted Police constable decided that Mardiros's answers were not specific enough and provided little 'satisfaction' to the crowd.[55]

Six years later, it was Ottawa's turn to request more information on the apparently still threatening Philosophical Society. This time, headquarters asked for a list of the society's objectives, the subjects discussed at meetings, and the extent to which it had been 'infiltrated' by subversives. The request came in response to a report that had listed Mardiros along with Henry Kreisel, H.B. Collier, Esther Milner, and W.J. Eccles as composing the leadership of the society. The following January a Mountie found a notice on a university bulletin board advertising the society's next meeting, to be chaired by Mel Hurtig and featuring chemistry professor Harry Gunning, a person the RCMP believed to be sympathetic to subversion.

Hurtig, a future star of the Canadian publishing scene, became embroiled in the investigation of the Philosophical Society. In his memoirs he recounts having been approached while on board an airplane by a Security Service member for information about Mardiros, who was an acquaintance. He also mentions a meeting with another Security Service member, who said that microphones were in place at the University of Alberta. Refusing to cooperate, Hurtig instead criticized such intrusions into the lives of Canadians.[56]

Overall, these investigations uncovered little in the way of Communist activity. The 1949–50 annual report for the intelligence branch mentions only limited LPP activity at four universities. The story differed little in the 1950s, an era of general conservatism at Canada's institutions of higher education. The hunt continued nonetheless. In October 1950 at the University of British Columbia, for instance, the RCMP discovered that students attended university primarily to learn, not to participate in radical activity.[57]

Watson Kirkconnell tried his best to provide the RCMP with more work by creating controversy once again in 1953, when he told a McMaster University commencement audience that a Communist cell under the control of local 'party bosses' operated at the university and that any 'Communist robots' on faculty should automatically be dismissed. Privately, local Mounties discounted his message, but headquarters was assured once again that investigations would go on. The only potential problem they turned up at the university was an attempt to sell Communist literature. These sales, a police officer stated, were unwelcome by the vast majority of students, but a few believed that they needed information in order to make an informed choice about whether or not to reject communism.[58]

It was a similar story at the University of Western Ontario, where local Mounties reported as late as 1958 that subversive activity seemed to be virtually non-existent. One possible contradiction, at least in the minds of the police, was that students in London voted in favour of a student exchange with the Soviet Union. Having Soviet students at the university, let alone a Russian studies program, caused alarm. The local Mountie opined, however, that this did not represent subversion but the opposite, since the students voting in favour of the exchange believed that knowledge was the best way to combat communism. How the exchange arose in the first place, however, intrigued the RCMP, which investigated the university's branch of the National Federation of Canadian University Students in order to discover who initiated the invitation.[59]

Then there was the search for signs of subversion at Canada's largest university. Besides coverage of elections to the mock parliament, the RCMP at the University of Toronto became interested in the university library and the student newspaper, the *Varsity*. It was thanks to the growing bureaucracy of the Canadian security state during the cold war, of which the RCMP represented but one part of a machine that included other federal departments and even the Post Office, that the library came to the attention of the police. Indeed, the Post Office greatly aided police efforts to track the activities of alleged subversives, and particularly significant was the postal customs section, which supplied the police with the names of those in receipt of 'subversive' publications. The University of Toronto Library and the warden of Hart House appeared among the list of organizations and individuals forwarded to the force because they had received 'For People's Peace, for People's Democracy,' Communist material shipped through Romania.[60]

The attention paid to the *Varsity* was not just for its content. Perusing the paper, an eagle-eyed policeman noticed that many of the advertisements were for businesses that handled 'subversive' material. Then there was the content. Setting off alarms was a special issue in January 1953 devoted to civil liberties and carrying articles decrying the treatment of Aboriginals and criticizing Quebec's draconian Padlock Law – 'all the present day subtle issues of the L.P.P.' An investigation on campus uncov-

ered the names of the three editorial members who had assembled the
issue. The fact that university president Sidney Smith and other officials
were upset by the publication also received comment, although how the
RCMP obtained this information was not made clear.[61]

In the latter half of the 1950s, LPP manifestations on campuses
concerned the police far less than did the impact of LPP activities on
students off-campus, chiefly in the form of the burgeoning Canadian
peace movement. The threat of nuclear weapons, tensions between the
superpowers, the death of Stalin, and the Korean War all sparked discussions on peace. The Canadian Peace Congress, founded in 1949, was
affiliated to the World Peace Council. Although the Canadian Peace
Congress was not officially a Communist organization, members of the
LPP played an important role in it and critics reviled it as a Soviet front.
The RCMP's focus invariably fell on the Reverend James Endicott, its
leader and a controversial figure because of his support for the Chinese
Communists and his accusations that the United States was using biological weapons in Korea.[62]

Stalin's demise in 1953 was especially pivotal for the cause of peace.
His successor, Nikita Khrushchev, produced a contradictory mixture of
bellicose posturing and of talk of reconciliation. Yet, in Canada the
promotion of peaceful accommodation between the superpowers greatly
concerned the RCMP. In 1955 Assistant Commissioner Cliff Harvison
warned in a memorandum that an increase in activities by peace groups
secretly manipulated by Communists could reduce anti-Soviet sentiments
among the Canadian public, making the RCMP's counter-intelligence
activities more difficult.[63] Moreover, Canada's national police feared that
messages of peace might be especially appealing to university students,
who might some day influence Canadian policy. Headquarters ordered
'D' Division in Manitoba to discover who might have been the author
using only initials when he or she wrote letters on peace issues to the
student paper, the *Manitoban*. Erring on the side of caution, it wanted
the list to include all individuals who might have such 'inclinations.'[64]
An obvious target for surveillance was any peace conference that included James Endicott, and one was to occur at the University of Toronto
in February 1958 when the Student Conference on Problems of Disarmament and Peace convened. Following the usual pattern, two mounted
policemen infiltrated the crowd and soothingly remarked in their report
on the absence of politics from the meeting, with the exception of
Endicott's participation.[65]

While talking was sufficient for some peace activists, others, some of whom had previously been involved with the Canadian Peace Congress, selected a more aggressive approach. The Combined Universities Campaign for Nuclear Disarmament (CUCND) was formed in November 1959, and a month later its members held a silent vigil at the War Memorial in Ottawa; they gathered again the following December, a few days before Christmas.[66] Already in July 1960, forty-one university students from Toronto, Montreal, and Ottawa had gathered in North Bay, Ontario, to picket a military base containing Bomarc missiles, nuclear-equipped weapons designed to take down Soviet bombers; the RCMP was secretly in attendance.[67]

Although no one recognized it at the time, the peace demonstrations marked the symbolic start of a new era. Over the previous decades the Mounted Police had watched quiet campuses populated by impressionable students. The biggest threat to the status quo, in their view, came from preying Communists. All of this, however, was about to change. All the while having to battle both a new type of student and a new kind of university, the RCMP would find its previously secret activities facing widespread publicity, scrutiny, and criticism for the first time in its history. A tumultuous period for Canadian society, and especially for one of its most famous institutions, was about to commence.

PART THREE
The 1960s

5

Controversy and Contravention

'That little girl got excited and it is very easy to alter the facts,' explained Inspector J.F. Berlinguette. The Mountie sat across a table from two Université Laval students, Hélène Senecal and Edward Smith, and repeatedly told them that a colleague of theirs, Jacqueline Cyr, did not know what she was talking about. Cyr had claimed that a mounted policeman had asked her for information about Senecal and Smith, authors of anti–nuclear weapons material that had appeared in a Laval student newspaper in April 1961, and that he had questioned her about the Laval branch of the Combined Universities Campaign for Nuclear Disarmament, to which they belonged.[1]

Jacqueline Cyr had refused to help, and instead she informed Senecal and Smith of his visit. They went to the local RCMP detachment and met with Berlinguette, who denied the allegation that he was spying on them and tried to discredit Cyr. In doing so, he inadvertently revealed that the police knew Smith was an American citizen. Offering no apologies and arguing that investigations by the RCMP of the Communist infiltration of a wide range of non-Communist organizations were legitimate, the officer ended the meeting. The Montreal newspaper *La Presse* eventually ran a story about the incident, which was then raised by the Opposition in the House of Commons.[2] A corner of the veil covering RCMP campus work had been lifted, since for the first time in its history the force's countersubversion operations received public scrutiny.[3]

It was no coincidence that the controversy involved the peace movement. The cold war, especially the nuclear arms race, remained hot. President John F. Kennedy had in 1960 hammered the sinister-looking Richard Nixon over an imaginary missile advantage that the Soviet Union enjoyed over its capitalist adversary. The gap, in reality, existed in the opposite direction, something that the American government was, thanks to its improved intelligence estimates, aware of. For this and a variety of other reasons, the peace movement was perceived as an important strategic avenue for the Soviet Union and a potential threat to American policy.[4]

The RCMP had long spied on the Communist-dominated Canadian Peace Congress, the Canadian branch of the World Peace Council. The CUCND was a different matter. It had its roots in the Campaign for Nuclear Disarmament, which had begun in the United Kingdom in 1958; it brought together a diverse group of people, including some like historian E.P. Thompson who had left the Communist Party of Great Britain over its authoritarian bent and who were looking to generate a new left. In the case of the CUCND, it was neither organized by the Communists nor a party front, as RCMP commissioner Cliff Harvison admitted to the minister of justice in 1961. Nevertheless, in Harvison's view, 'Communists are very quick to seize on the lead provided by such organizations to further their own objectives.'[5]

Perceived Communist infiltration and influence behind the scenes became the rationale for police to investigate peace groups like the CUCND, the Voice of Women (VOW), and the Canadian Committee for the Control of Radiation Hazards (CCCRH). Whatever the presence of Communists or the extent of their influence in the peace movement, the principles of those who belonged to it were nevertheless at odds with the cold war policies of Canada and the United States. The movement thus loomed as a threat, especially since it appeared to be having an impact at odds with official policy. Between 1958 and 1962 the number of Canadians favouring a ban on U.S. nuclear tests grew to nearly 50 per cent. In 1961 the CCCRH presented Prime Minister John Diefenbaker with a petition containing 141,000 signatures rejecting the presence of nuclear weapons in Canada.[6]

Enter the RCMP. Since the end of the First World War, its members had performed security investigations in almost complete secrecy. The incident at the Université Laval changed that. The report of a similar approach to an Ottawa student fuelled the political furore. Beating down attacks from the Opposition, Minister of Justice Davie Fulton, the force's boss, publicly stood by his men.[7] Privately, it was a different story. He verbally ordered a halt to investigations on campuses, although the Conservative politician allowed the RCMP to continue receiving intelligence from already established sources. RCMP headquarters dispatched a letter to its divisions instructing them to suspend 'all investigations connected with Communist penetration of universities and colleges ... pending an analysis of our requirements.' In this letter, the second paragraph provided individual divisions with the leeway to continue these activities, albeit through the careful avoidance of any publicity: 'This should not be interpreted as meaning that we have waived our interest in Communist activities within educational institutions ... It should be made clear that no action of any kind which could result in public discussion or complaints to the Minister is to be undertaken until the review.'[8]

Spying continued on some campuses. At Queen's University, for example, an RCMP source in the executive of the National Federation of Canadian University Students (NFCUS) relayed information on the group's internal business and reported on the visit of two Russian students it had invited.[9] As if to comfort his handlers, the source added that an American student, the vice-president of the National Student Association, an organization secretly funded at the time by the Central Intelligence Agency,[10] outperformed the Russians when he addressed the crowd in English, French, and Russian. A year later, the RCMP followed a Soviet diplomat who travelled from Ottawa to the same university to address the World University Service of Canada. The surveillance was so complete that the Mounties even searched the men's washroom the diplomat had used at a gas station. In the end, they concluded he was there simply on a propaganda mission, one that failed because the student audience seemed unresponsive to his speech.[11]

Although it continued to cover some campuses, the RCMP did attempt to adjust its operations to conform to the new political reality. Simultaneously, it also sought to reverse Fulton's order, turning to its research wing, 'K' Branch, staffed with civilians, to compile a report designed to explain to the government why it was necessary to investigate groups and individuals at Canadian universities. The opening paragraph of the August 1961 document that was prepared, 'The Communist Program for Control of Youth and Intellectuals,' reflected the tone it projected throughout:

> All countries of the world are keenly aware of the importance of youth, and of the education of youth, as a vital part of a nation's survival. To the international Communist movement, the younger generation has a much more significant role. It must be trained to destroy the state structure of its own nation and to assume the leadership in the new socialist society. The youth who cannot take so bold a step may join the ranks of fellow-travellers,

'abettors,' to assist the devoted revolutionaries. Those who are perplexed by
the political, economic and military problems of the day must be
'neutralized,' so that they will not join forces against the Communist cause.
Youth, then, and a nation's intellectuals, are prime targets in the Communist offensive. It is precisely at universities where this group may be approached most easily and most successfully.

According to the report, communism on campuses posed three potential threats. First, future leaders could be transformed into Communists.
Then there was the threat that actual espionage would be conducted by
Canadians on behalf of the Soviet Union.[12] 'It can be no mere coincidence,' argued the report's author or authors, 'that many of the individuals involved in the [Gouzenko] trials were McGill graduates.' Although
they presented no evidence that those tried had been subverted at
McGill, there undoubtedly was an awareness of how the newly exposed
members of the Cambridge Five had been converted to communism
while at university.[13] Finally, the document's authors warned that Communists on campuses could subvert student organizations and make
them potential threats to civil order through riots or other demonstrations. For evidence of this potential menace, the RCMP cited the demonstration in 1960 in San Francisco against the House Un-American Activities
Committee. This protest, which foreshadowed what was to come later in
the 1960s, so troubled FBI director J. Edgar Hoover that he had his men
produce a special study, *Communist Target – Youth; Communist Infiltration
and Agitation Tactics*, the title of which the 1961 RCMP document
echoed.[14]

The author or authors of the Canadian report even resorted to presenting a revised and updated version of Mark McClung's 1959 'flimsy'
statistics to back their warning of the 'Red' threat to education (see
Table 5.1).[15]

Despite the emphasis on Communists on campuses, it was admitted in
the report that only three actual Communist organizations operated at
universities. The Mounties sought to monitor instead the extent of Communist involvement in other groups such as the CUCND, the Student
Christian Movement, the Fair Play for Cuba Committee, the Afro-Asian
Studies Group at Sir George Williams University, and even the generic
category of 'film societies.'[16] As usual, no effort was expended to explain
how Communist involvement in such organizations imperilled Canadian
security.

Private reassurances by the RCMP of the legitimacy of its work, did

TABLE 5.1
Alleged Communists on Canadian campuses

	University students	University professors	Total
Total active suspects	114	48	162
Total inactive suspects	43	42	85
Total suspects	157	90	247

Source: NA, RG 146, Vol. 5008, file 97-A-0076, pt 2, 'The Communist Program for Control of Youth and Intellectuals,' attachment, n.d.

little, not surprisingly, to dispel public criticism of these activities. They did not even convince Fulton to rescind his June 1961 order.[17] Except for efforts by the Canadian Association of University Teachers (CAUT) on the issue, including resolutions encouraging its members not to assist in intelligence gathering, and frequent letters to the minister of justice asking for meetings, the issue remained dormant for over a year. Then, in September 1962 a New Democratic Youth newsletter published a lengthy interview with a person who claimed to have been asked by the RCMP to spy on the CUCND. Three months later the matter was again raised in the House of Commons, with Donald Fleming, Fulton's successor, facing questions from New Democratic Party members.[18]

The reappearance of the issue triggered a response from the increasingly embattled head of the RCMP. 'It would be less significant if it represented only a genuine interest among law-abiding citizens for the preservation of human rights,' Cliff Harvison wrote to Fleming. '[H]owever this is not the case.' Harvison, whose career stretched back to the 1920s, chose to interpret the attacks as part of a deliberate strategy by Communists to discredit their chief opponent.[19] Despite the bravado, he seemed unsure of what his troops were up to at universities, and so he sought more information. Headquarters ordered the relevant intelligence officers at RCMP divisions across Canada to comment, not on the extent of police activity on campuses but on the more sensitive and potentially explosive issue of the recruitment of informants on campuses. By early January 1963 the results had arrived in Ottawa. Appearing as an exercise in damage control, the divisional feedback focused on discussions of attempts to recruit campus sources that had gone wrong and that might be used as ammunition against the RCMP. References were also made to attempts to obtain information on the political beliefs of students on campuses. Superintendent N.O. Jones of 'O' Division, which covered southern Ontario, was 'unaware at the moment of any instances where University students have been directly interviewed regarding subversive activity within the Campus insofar as this Division (Toronto SIB) is concerned.' The trend continued down the line. In Edmonton, Inspector J. Dean found 'no reason to anticipate any embarrassing publicity through these approaches and interviews.' He assured headquarters that even investigations on campuses of people with subversive backgrounds were done 'only to obtain biographical data or confirm employment or attendance,' not to find information about their political beliefs. The officer in charge of what passed for the Security Service in Newfoundland added a different twist: 'It might be of interest to note that insofar as our relations with the University at St. John's is concerned, the situation is somewhat reversed ... it will be noted that this force was approached by Educational leaders in an attempt to gain information on prospective and currently employed members of the faculty.'[20]

Even before the reappearance of the issue in the House of Commons, the Diefenbaker government had grown tired of it, willingly ceding control to the police. In June 1962 Fulton's executive assistant, Lowell Murray, described CAUT's requests for meetings as a 'bit tedious' and reiterated his boss's desire not to meet with its representatives. He asked the police to draft a reply to a letter from the organization. Donald Fleming also had little time for CAUT's concerns. 'Farfetched' was his description of charges that RCMP investigations on university campuses imperilled academic freedom.[21] In his autobiography, he made it clear that he both supported and was fully aware of domestic security intelligence operations: 'It is poppycock to picture this as introducing the "police state"; rather, it is intended to defeat the machinations of those whose methods for suppressing freedom always include the police state. I have seen the records they keep on individuals, including Members of Parliament. If they failed to keep one on me I should feel slighted.'[22]

The government, with a cabinet minister as sympathetic to the RCMP as Fleming, felt no hesitation in accepting its assurances about its operations. Fleming, for instance, did not appear surprised when the force supplied him with the wording of a CAUT resolution opposing investigations on campuses that had been obtained by an informant within the organization. Indeed, he had personally intervened with Harvison to put in a good word on behalf of Dr Irvine I. Glass, a member of the Institute of Aerophysics at the University of Toronto, who a mutual friend had suggested might have seen promotions blocked because of adverse security references from the RCMP.[23]

The police, in fact, directed the government's defence of the activities of the police. In December 1962 NDP member of Parliament Thomas Berger placed a question on the order paper regarding RCMP activities on university campuses. The government forwarded it to Harvison for a reply. He and his staff supplied Fleming with a response that was carefully constructed, right down to the verb tense:

I refer to Question No. 1,234 ... asking if members of the R.C.M.P. are engaged in interviewing students and faculty members at Canadian universities about their respective political views and activities.

2. The answer to ... the question has been given in its present form on the basis that members of the R.C.M.P. are not concerned with the political views of students or faculty members. Where inquiries are made at universities, it is either for the purpose of security screening or to ascertain what subversive activities are being carried out.

3. In preparing the answer to ... Mr. Berger's question, we have differentiated between investigations into subversive activities and the political views and activities in general, as implied by the question.

On the same day as Harvison's letter, the minister of justice's parliamentary secretary rose in the House of Commons to reply to Berger's question: 'Members of the R.C.M.P. are not engaged in interviewing students and faculty members at Canadian universities about the political views and political activities of other students and faculty members.'[24]

Neither carefully nor poorly crafted answers ended the controversy. The executive of CAUT continued its pressure, as did the NFCUS and the media.[25] The force was well aware of its critics, since divisions forwarded to headquarters relevant newspaper stories when they were published. An inventory of detractors was compiled, listing various groups that denounced the Mounted Police and that seemed to be supported by the NDP. From the perspective of the police, the *Kingston Whig-Standard* was a particularly annoying adversary. The RCMP's Kingston office studied the newspaper's editorials over several months and found them to be leftist in nature and distasteful. Constable M.G. Johnston identified the paper's editor as the culprit and suggested that he was under the influence of Queen's University historian Arthur Lower, a long-time critic of the RCMP.[26]

It was also in late 1962 that members of the force first took a direct interest in the activities of CAUT, including investigating the politics of several of its members, especially Stewart Reid, the executive secretary, in an unsuccessful effort to discover earlier subversive activities. Headquarters in Ottawa later ordered the preparation of political assessments of CAUT's executive members, specifically on their attitudes towards campus security investigations and on whether they could be influenced easily. J. Percy Smith, a University of Saskatchewan professor and Reid's successor at CAUT, particularly concerned the Mounted Police after it discovered that he had several adverse references in his file. Even articles from the *CAUT Bulletin* ended up at headquarters to serve as examples of 'propaganda, it's [*sic*] dissemination and build-up.'[27]

In an effort to slow the momentum of the force's critics, Harvison became directly involved by granting an interview to the Canadian University Press. His intervention essentially gave away the game, that countersubversion was the dominant reason for the RCMP's secret activities on campuses since the end of the First World War and that it was of the type exposed at the Université Laval in 1961. Repeating many of the themes expressed in internal police documents, he explained that RCMP activity on university campuses was about discovering Communist subversion. It was not the open 'Reds' at universities who concerned his men, he noted, since their agendas were well known, but the '"underground" agents who are not known as Communists.' Later in the interview, Harvison contradicted himself when he expressed a decades-old RCMP perception of students: 'University students are naturally curious. At this age one finds a great deal of idealism and a strong sense of social morality. There are certain abuses in our system which the student may think communism will cure, if he gets only one side of the picture.'[28]

Harvison intended to diminish the controversy with his newspaper interview; instead his words fuelled it. Critics like Arthur Lower, himself the subject of an RCMP file, argued that the commissioner had contradicted what the government had been telling the House of Commons and Canadians. Perhaps fearing that the government's resolve might weaken, the RCMP continued to warn privately about Communist subversion on university campuses. Deputy Commissioner George McClellan forwarded to Fleming an article from *Newsweek* that showed how universities in Venezuela had become sanctuaries for that country's Communists.[29]

Another attempt to control media coverage of RCMP activities proved equally disastrous. Harvison and the RCMP cooperated with Sidney Katz and *Maclean's* in the writing of an article on the force's role in spying. The journalist conducted extensive interviews with Harvison and with J.W. Bordeleau, the head of the Security Service, and he even had access to the security intelligence offices at RCMP headquarters. The end product, however, was clearly not what the force had anticipated. In fact, Harvison was furious with the article because of several errors in it and of its portrayal of the Security Service as unsophisticated and out of control. Even worse, the story raised once again the issue of security investigations at universities.[30]

What did change in 1963 was the federal government: as a result of elections in April, the Conservatives went out and the Liberals, under Lester Pearson, came in. Pearson, perhaps because of the Herbert Norman affair, in which the Canadian ambassador to Egypt committed suicide after repeated American allegations that he was a Soviet agent, appeared more interested than Diefenbaker had been in a compromise between the RCMP and CAUT, its main critic. Yet concern about security investigations of higher education had not disappeared. At the University of Alberta, a debate on the issue was organized by the CUCND. An invitation to participate was sent to the RCMP, which declined formally; instead a policeman secretly attended and filed a report on the gathering.[31]

CAUT's lobbying culminated in a meeting in November 1963 bringing together the various parties, including NFCUS and the prime minister. It achieved an informal agreement, often known as the Pearson-Laskin Accord, whose meaning, however, varied radically with each participant, mainly because there was no shared understanding of what exactly the Mounties were doing on campuses in the first place. To CAUT the agreement represented an end to sweeping security investigations on university campuses, with the exception of security screenings that involved background checks for those seeking government employment. The RCMP saw it as a continuation of the restriction on recruiting sources on university campuses that had been in place since Fulton's 1961 order. NFCUS received an official assurance that the force could not carry out 'general surveillance of university campuses' but that it would continue to investigate 'espionage or subversive activities' at educational institutions if 'definite indications' existed that they were occurring.[32]

The notion that the 1963 meeting had accomplished anything of substance was a mirage. Neither the RCMP nor the government was pressed to define subversion or what constituted 'definite indications' of its existence. Opposition New Democrats had previously raised such matters publicly: Thomas Berger in December had made it clear that to him an act of subversion should be clearly spelled out in the Criminal

Code, and party leader Tommy Douglas had added that the government evaded the issue through rhetorical twists and turns.[33]

Nor was there awareness on the part of the force's detractors that subversion had long been its justification for university investigations, including the ones that had brought the issue to the attention of the general public in the first place, despite strong indications to that effect from the commissioner. At a meeting of the Security Panel, the government's interdepartmental body that dealt with security intelligence matters, Norman Robertson, the under-secretary of state for external affairs, dismissed critics of police activities on campus as 'uninformed.'[34]

Then, there was the word 'general' in the agreement. The RCMP said it would not conduct 'general surveillance,' but mounted policemen, despite some public and media notions to the contrary, had never done this; they had always targeted particular individuals and organizations. Headquarters reiterated to its own members its promise not to conduct 'general security surveillance of university campuses.' Moreover, even in the one area where the police had appeared to concede ground, the recruitment of on-campus sources, a loophole had been provided. George McClellan, who had succeeded Harvison as commissioner at the end of October 1963, repeatedly maintained the right of his men to accept information from 'volunteer' sources on campuses.[35] This would prove to be an important qualification.

Some of the real subtext of the agreement was apparent immediately after the November 1963 meeting. After the CAUT and NFCUS representatives had left the room, McClellan, according to one of those present, turned to Pearson and said: 'Mr. Prime Minister, I am sure there are some things you would rather not know about.' To which Pearson, looking squarely at McClellan, replied: 'I am not at all sure of that.' Pearson, despite his apparent concern, did not pursue the matter. On the subject of how information was acquired, his government would rely entirely on the RCMP to police itself. The agreement reached at the meeting was not legally binding and the prime minister never raised it with his cabinet.[36]

The issue of security investigations and universities did not completely vanish from public attention after the CAUT-RCMP agreement. Rumours of Mounties roaming on university campuses continued to appear, mainly in the student press. In a sense this critical scrutiny – and even the occasional mockery, such as a cartoon portraying mounted policemen as uneducated thugs – of a powerful state institution, coupled with the growing anti–nuclear weapons movement, signalled a change in the student population, which was more willing to challenge authority. The Canadian University Press led the charge by surveying the attitudes of members of parliament towards police investigations on campuses. One of those who participated in the survey, Robert Thompson, the leader of the Social Credit Party, kept a copy of his answers, in which he supported police surveillance, and he forwarded these along with the questionnaire to McClellan. 'Thompson's views are well stated,' the commissioner wrote in the margin.[37]

Slowly, however, interest in the issue waned. In 1967 a representative of CAUT testified to the Royal Commission on Security that not a single complaint about RCMP on-campus surveillance had been received from its members since the November 1963 meeting. Later, the McDonald Commission, in relying on RCMP policy records instead of operational ones, inaccurately interpreted the silence of critics and police grumbling about restrictions on their work as signs that security investigations on campuses had stopped. Allegations in February 1967 by the president of the Canadian Union of Students that the RCMP was questioning students who attended conferences in Communist nations received scant editorial attention in newspapers, and the solicitor general of the day defended what was a regular police practice.[38]

Ironically, public interest in the issue declined at the same time that RCMP activity on university campuses escalated. Many Canadian campuses were, like universities elsewhere, becoming centres of protest and radical activity. The era of the New Left and of movements such as 'Red Power' and 'Black Power' was at hand. The RCMP monitored manifestations of them at universities on the assumption that they represented organized subversion and, in some cases, the threat of politically motivated violence. The problem for the force was that its presence on campuses would be controversial, and there was also the matter of grappling with the boundaries established in 1961 and 1963. What practical implications did these factors have for the men on the beat?

'It didn't fucking matter,' recalled one former Security Service member who served in the Toronto area. 'If we wanted the information, we'd get it.' Another veteran from the 1960s had a similar response when asked about the impact of the 1963 CAUT-RCMP agreement: 'Nothing. We just had to be a little more careful. Not be obvious.' A third recalled a colleague being ordered by his superiors to continue work on campuses but with an accompanying warning that should he be caught his employers would disavow any knowledge of his activities.[39] The documentary evidence supports their recollections. While reports related to universi-

ties declined between 1961 and 1963, the numbers increased during the
remainder of the decade.

Intelligence work requires information. The real significance of the
1963 agreement for the RCMP was that it continued Fulton's restriction
on recruiting campus informants. Some divisions compensated by turning to alternative sources of information. They did not have to look far.
In the 1960s a growing number of mounted policemen began to take
university courses as part-time or full-time students, and they represented readily accessible sources on what was happening on campuses.
Even if fellow students were aware of their presence, the policemen
could accurately claim their right to be on campus. Using RCMP students was risky, however, and headquarters had forbidden it as early as
1959 because of allegations in Montreal newspapers that Mounties were
spying on their fellow students.[40]

An incident at Queen's University demonstrated the inherent danger
in using police students for intelligence work. Constable M.J. Spooner, a
full-time student, was used for surveillance duties in November 1962
because he had 'no classes during this period.' Rumours of this appeared in the *Kingston Whig-Standard*, creating the potential for considerable negative publicity, something the Security Service was eager to
avoid. Despite the fact that he was violating official policy, the officer in
charge of the security intelligence wing of 'A' Division defended Spooner.[41]

The practice continued elsewhere. 'On the 5th November 1968,
[deleted: name of the RCMP officer] of this branch advised the writer
of being an extension student at YORK UNIVERSITY'S ATKINSON
COLLEGE and is enrolled in Political Science 241,' Constable Terry
Beckett reported. His colleague supplied information on the student
make-up of the class, the course content, and an assessment of the two
instructors. Beckett concluded his report with a comment on the useful-
ness of such sources: 'As several members of this Force are attending
classes at YORK UNIVERSITY, they will be approached at the end of
each academic year to give an assessment of the course instructor and to
determine if the particular course has been subjected to any degree of
Marxist orientation. It is felt such a course of action will contribute to an
assessment of the left wing's influence and activities within the classroom, and in addition may serve as a means of pin-pointing academics
who are moderate in their views with an appreciation of the responsibilities of this Force.'[42] While the last sentence was an obvious reference to
potential recruits as sources, the entire passage reflected a widening
definition of campus radicalism.

Another Mountie who was a student at York University in the fall of 1968 observed that his instructor in a natural sciences class permitted the recording of his lectures, while other instructors in more politically oriented courses objected to the practice because the tapes might be used against them. 'It is interesting to note his obvious awareness of the political involvement of some of the staff at York and also that he should make reference to this matter.' At the University of Saskatchewan it was Constable Robert D. Laing, a member of the criminal side of the force but also a law student (he would later serve as a Saskatchewan provincial court justice and from 1989 to 1990 was the president of the Federation of Law Societies of Canada). He offered his colleagues in the Security Service information about Communist involvement in the campus branch of the CCF and later the NDP youth organization and the names of two potential informants. The Security Service initially worried that Laing was being set up and that his involvement violated RCMP policy. The trepidation disappeared three years later when Laing supplied information about the campus branch of the League for Socialist Action, a Trotskyist organization.[43]

At Sir George Williams University in Montreal, Corporal J.J.L. Jodoin took the RCMP student's role to a new level. In December 1968, after he was no longer registered in the Faculty of Arts and Sciences, he wrote a lengthy assessment of radical activity at the school. Included in it were detailed assessments of the departments he was most familiar with, history and political science, the former being especially controversial because of the presence of Eugene Genovese, an American historian who had lost his job in his home country over his opposition to the Vietnam War. Jodoin warned his readers at the beginning of his report that he had been ostracized by other students and that 'leftist' academics had 'doctored' their lectures for his consumption. 'When discussing with students,' he complained, 'I could not even ask subtle questions without raising suspicions. A few times when I did ask discreet questions to moderate students, I usually received evasive or non-committal answers.' Jodoin was right in lowering the expectations of his readers. His assessment, as someone familiar with the situation observed, offered little that was not readily available from contemporary newspaper accounts.[44]

Although the report contained nothing new, in his conclusion Jodoin advocated an increased use of other Mounties as students for insight into campus events, suggesting that they should be interviewed for their insights and that they should be requested to write an intelligence summary of the situation at their campuses upon the completion of their studies. Another policeman wrote a similar assessment based on his experiences as a student at Waterloo Lutheran University in the 1969–70 academic year.[45]

RCMP students were also used as sources of information at the University of Windsor and the Université de Montréal. At the latter, seven Security Service members in 1969 took a special night class in sociology that explored the roots of the world-wide protest movements. After completing the course, each one wrote an evaluation that included assessments of the class, descriptions of the students, comments on the politics of the instructors, and observations on the personal hygiene of those in attendance. One policeman, unhappy with the entire experience, asked to be compensated for its cost. Even RCMP students not directly used as sources supplied their divisional intelligence offices with pamphlets, posters, and other material connected to on-campus radical activities or were asked to identify photographs of student 'file subjects' who took part in demonstrations.[46]

Officially, headquarters in Ottawa did not approve of the use of Mounted Police students as sources; neither did it acknowledge that members of the force were being used in this way.[47] Because divisions submitted reports to Ottawa, there must have been an awareness at headquarters that some RCMP students were collecting intelligence while taking classes. It was apparently a case of being thankful for receiving the information but of not asking questions about how it was obtained.[48] (The same philosophy applied to the federal government.) Some policemen grew increasingly frustrated about the formal restrictions as the 1960s wore on. One officer wrote a memorandum in which he complained about the contradiction between the increasing pressure from headquarters in Ottawa (which was itself pressed by the federal government) for information about campus unrest while restrictions remained in place on the methods that could be employed. A colleague wrote 'You better believe it,' in support. The memorandum concluded with the recommendation that the federal government be requested to change the policy. The assistant director of the Security Service concurred, but his superior, Leonard Higgitt, dismissed the idea, arguing that the RCMP was not unduly affected by the policy and that, in any case, the student power movement was not necessarily subversive.[49]

Thus the force continued to search for alternative sources of information and for ways of skirting the supposed restrictions. Among them were other police forces. In Toronto, members of the RCMP accompanied city police officers on a raid against a New Left target on at least one occasion. The Mounties took photographs of membership lists and seized copies of literature during the search. The Security Service also had special relationships with police forces across Canada.[50]

Moreover, departments of the federal government, especially the Department of National Defence, came to the assistance of the RCMP. One way the RCMP avoided on-campus entanglements was to obtain information from the Canadian military, which operated its own domestic intelligence agency. The military had bases in several cities with universities, and this allowed the two organizations to swap information on campus organizations.[51]

In April 1968 Leslie James Bennett of the Security Service was approached by Lieutenant-Colonel A.J. Laidler of the military's Directorate of Security concerning the two institutions' 'mutual interest in activities on university campus.' The force responded with a memorandum giving details on Communist 'penetration' of higher education.[52] Two years later, the RCMP and the Canadian military exchanged information regarding the activities of radicals at the University of Western Ontario in London. Essentially, the Mounted Police provided the other with a shopping list of radical organizations it was interested in and it added some advice:

> To assist your investigator, we would appreciate receiving information in relation to the foregoing organizations, developed along the following lines:
> 1. Dates and locations of meetings.
> 2. Number and identification of persons attending meetings, particularly at the executive level.
> 3. Identification of members.
> 4. Identification of supporters and sympathizers.
> 5. Planned activities and attempted goals.
> 6. Sources of financial support.
> Any additional information that could be developed which would establish links and liaison between these organizations would also be very beneficial.[53]

In addition, the military used its Special Investigation Unit to spy on campus protests, including some that occurred at Bishop's University in Lennoxville, Quebec, in February 1970.[54]

The Departments of External Affairs, Manpower and Immigration, and National Revenue were also involved in this interdepartmental relationship. The first employed its facilities and resources at home and abroad to collect information on the movement of alleged radicals, at the same time that it operated a liaison program designed to foster better relations with academe. Occasionally material relating to the latter role – an example is a note that the University of Guelph had established an Asian Studies program, and another is a copy of a letter sent by a McGill University official regarding some of the university's international students – ended up in the RCMP's possession. In 1969 a report on a tour of western Canadian universities by a Department of External Affairs official was sent to the force; it was not found to be useful, although an officer expressed gratitude that the 'author realizes the ideological hostility that prevails throughout the university community.'[55]

The Department of Manpower and Immigration proved an equally useful ally to the RCMP by providing it with passport and immigration information, which allowed the police to trace the movements of suspects and to have access to personal information supplied on the passport applications. The Department of National Revenue supplied the force with confidential tax-related information on individuals and organizations.[56]

These other branches of the Canadian state also offered aid in the highly contentious area of recruitment of sources on campuses. The Joint Intelligence Bureau carried out its own investigations of a visit by Soviet scientists to the University of Toronto. Not included in the bureau's final report was information considered to be of special interest to the men in scarlet, namely assessments of several University of Toronto scientists, particularly on how cooperative they appeared to be in supplying information to the authorities.[57]

These alternative suppliers of information helped compensate for the apparent absence of police sources on campuses. This was the one area where Fulton's 1961 order and the 1963 understanding appear to have had an impact, although another factor was at play. Mounties hesitated to approach individuals on campuses not just because of the official policy but just as much because of the fear of exposure and of negative publicity of the kind that had plagued it at the beginning of the decade. In October 1968 it admitted that it did not have a single long-term source in the more radical elements of the student movement.[58]

Accordingly, intricate, as well as less than intricate, schemes were developed to circumvent the restrictions on recruitment. The most complex, and one identified in full by the McDonald Commission, was described internally in 1967 by the then head of the Security Service,

Assistant Commissioner Leonard Higgitt. The 1963 agreement with CAUT
had allowed the RCMP to retain the privilege of accepting 'volunteer'
information from human sources on campuses. Moreover, the right to
conduct official investigations as part of a security screening process of
prospective government employees was protected in the agreement. The
police had been performing this work for the government since the late
1940s; students and others seeking sensitive civil service employment
were all screened. This process also provided mounted policemen with
an excuse to gather other information.

In a 29 November 1967 directive, Higgitt pointed out that security
screenings could be used to obtain 'volunteered' information and thereby
circumvent government restrictions. 'It is felt that with tact and diplo-
macy,' he wrote, 'we could achieve our objectives, or a good portion of
them, without transgressing the assurances we have provided to the
government.' He specifically cited the example of an unnamed institution where two veteran Security Service members handled both security
screenings and subversion investigations. Through their screening interviews they were able to compile a list of faculties considered particularly
vulnerable to radical activity. Next, they listed the names of professors
not already in the RCMP's 'subversive indices,' and then decided to
make an effort to interview them. Higgitt carefully explained the next
step:

> Additional faculty heads and assistants, even though they were not specifi-
> cally mentioned on the PHFs [Personal History Forms], were requested to
> provide character references on former students seeking sensitive govern-
> ment employment. As part of the character study the professor was rou-
> tinely invited to comment on the person's loyalty and patriotism ...
>
> Following each interview the investigator committed the salient points
> thereof to paper in a book which was maintained for the express purpose of
> compiling data on faculty members of the university concerned ... Special
> attention was devoted to his willingness, or lack of same, to cooperate with
> the investigator, his general attitude towards the force and what sentiments
> he displayed, verbally or otherwise, to our presence on the campus.

He described a process whereby the policeman slowly developed a personal relationship with his potential source. Frequent meetings, often
over lunch or coffee, occurred. All the while, the academic was being
appraised for his or her receptivity to a direct approach. Eventually the
topic of communism was raised, as were events connected to the cold

war. Finally, the policeman broached the subject of RCMP investigations on university campuses. Through the reaction to all of these topics he developed a clear impression about the suitability of approaching his new friend with a proposition. Often making an offer proved unnecessary:

> When the foregoing plan had been pursued over an extended period of time, some rather pleasant developments took place. The most significant of these was in the number of professors, etc., who eventually offered their full cooperation on all matters of interest to us. Many, without prompting on our part, volunteered, or at least chose to discuss, the activities and political views of a number of their colleagues. It was evident that they would have spoken to us sooner but did not know anyone connected with the Security Service and would not take it upon themselves, for obvious reasons, to call our offices 'blind.' Once an association had been developed some individuals actually called us to pass on pieces of information of potential interest ... This willingness to cooperate was displayed in varying degrees and in a variety of ways, however, of immense importance to us was that a workable liaison had been established ... The essential point in this type of operation is that no attempt of any kind is made to solicit an individual's cooperation. What we are doing, in effect, is making ourselves known and available to the profession should any of its members have occasion, and the desire, to speak to us. Once this desire is expressed we would be grossly negligent in our duties if we refused to listen to the person.[59]

Unfortunately for the head of the Security Service, the McDonald Commission did not view this activity as benignly; it reprimanded Higgitt for 'improper' behaviour.[60]

Through his memorandum, Higgitt encouraged circumvention of the one prohibition to its activities that the RCMP interpreted as restrictive. By taking such a cautious approach to recruitment the force also lowered the risk of its efforts backfiring and of being exposed in the media or in Parliament. A risk remained, nevertheless. 'It should be remembered,' warned an officer, 'that one unfortunate incident, no matter where in Canada it may occur, would negate all our efforts throughout the country, not to mention the public furore which would most certainly follow.'[61]

From the police perspective, administrators represented another key category of volunteer sources, since they appeared to have an unambiguous motive for assisting the police: the maintenance of order on a campus. Twice in the latter half of 1968 senior administrators at McGill University invited Superintendent L.R. Parent to meet with them about the New Left. In between those meetings, he and Inspector Donald Cobb received an invitation from officials at Sir George Williams University; they left that meeting with the belief that a 'useful relationship' was developing. These events were apparently not unusual. The McDonald Commission reported that in 1968 and 1969 the Security Service met with the presidents and senior administrators of several major Canadian universities at the request of the institutions.[62] But not all of the interaction with the police was initiated or encouraged by administrators. At a Christmas party at Simon Fraser University in the chaotic latter half of the 1960s, a Security Service official approached its president, Kenneth Strand, and stated that the two enjoyed mutual interests on campus. Strand refused to bite. At the University of Regina a failed attempt by the Security Service to influence a hiring decision nonetheless afforded it the opportunity of demonstrating to an administrator that it might be to their mutual benefit to share information. In many cases, however, the RCMP discovered that administrators envisioned only a one-way street when it came to cooperating with the police – they wanted information from the Mounties but were horrified when the same was sought in return.[63]

Even worse, some university administrations had turned against the RCMP by the end of the 1960s. One resource it had previously used freely to gather information not only about those seeking employment with the government but also about active targets was the files in offices of university registrars. These records yielded valuable information about students, including addresses, marital status, and employment status. In 1969 the Mounties suddenly found themselves facing new restrictions at the University of Alberta when they tried to examine student records. For legal reasons, the officers were required to produce a form demonstrating that the student in question had given her or his consent to have the records accessed. This rule applied to security screenings. 'However,' assured the local Security Service member, 'in our case, we are checking files in the interest of national security, with the permission of [deleted: name of university employee] and nothing has changed our position at the U. of A. We will continue to have access to whatever information they can supply us from their records.' The Université de Montréal also began requiring written permission to access student records.[64] These restrictions angered the RCMP, which increasingly felt boxed in as pressure from the federal government for campus information increased. One Mountie in Ottawa expressed annoyance with an administrator or CAUT executive member (the person's name was removed under Access to Information provisions) who failed 'to fully understand that along with academic freedom there must be a sense of responsibility to the country as a whole. Just because the security authorities make enquiries about an individual does not necessarily mean that they are threatening his academic freedom. But should the individual take advantage of this "freedom" to the detriment of the country as a whole, we are sure that the first people who would be blamed for his actions would be the security authorities for not having taken enough interest in the individual.'[65]

In this same vein, Queen's University proved again to be particularly troublesome for the RCMP in two matters. The first involved a doctoral candidate named Charles Edwards who, unlike most other activists at the time, was a student in the sciences. He had been a leading radical at Queen's since the late 1960s, at one point even becoming the leader of the main campus student organization. In the course of a security clearance investigation on campus in October 1969, the name of Edwards came up in a conversation between a police officer and Professor R.H. Clark. Whether it was Clark or the policeman who raised it made a difference; if it was the former, then it was volunteered information. The alternative violated the restrictions placed on campus investigations. Each side, the university and the RCMP, blamed the other for raising the student's name. The head of Queen's, John Deutsch, complained to the solicitor general and demanded that a mounted policeman appear before a Queen's committee. The RCMP refused.[66] The refusal appeared to have resolved the matter. However, a miscommunication led Sergeant B.L. Campbell to attend a meeting of the Queen's University Senate Committee on Grievance, Discipline, and Related Matters. Campbell's appearance was on condition that he would not discuss intelligence matters. At one point he was asked what planning and studies his employer had done with respect to the possibility of violence occurring on the campus. He did not have an answer, instructing the questioner to contact the commissioner of the RCMP instead. Two weeks later, the chair of the committee did just that.

The RCMP tied itself in knots as it sought ways to answer the question without revealing the extent of its work on campuses or its considerable supply of detailed reports on the campus-related problems of the late 1960s. The reply for Leonard Higgitt, now the commissioner, went through several drafts before the best form of prevarication was agreed upon: 'We have not undertaken the kind of research that I am sure you had in mind. Our major concern in these matters insofar as it has any bearing on universities is the maintenance of law and order where universities are within areas where the [RCMP] have the primary law enforcement responsibility. As you can appreciate there are very few of these, thus the initial responsibility for the maintenance of law and order in these matters rests with police forces other than the [RCMP].'[67] The following year the Queen's University Senate passed a motion restricting RCMP activities on its campus, including requiring investigating officers to be accompanied by a faculty-student advisor.[68]

This increasingly difficult climate for the RCMP necessitated the development of elaborate machinations to ensure a steady flow of good intelligence. Intricate planning, however, was not necessarily needed to recruit volunteer sources. One former Security Service member who had been active at universities in the Toronto area remembered that it was simply a matter of phrasing. Even if the information had been solicited by a mounted policeman, it would be recorded as having been volunteered and therefore still within the self-enforced rules. The RCMP officer who was in charge of informants in April 1970 confessed that imprecise records were kept relating to the development of casual sources on campuses and that, in any case, 'if a man was recruited in contravention of direct policy it is very unlikely the details will be reported to us.'[69] The police officer filing the report thus created the framework in which his work would be viewed.

Throughout the tumultuous 1960s a convenient mythology developed within the Security Service and in certain other quarters according to which the Mounties were being hampered in carrying out their work, not because they were prevented from recruiting sources but because they were forbidden to set foot on campuses. 'One positive step toward combating revolutionaries,' pontificated journalist Peter Worthington in a *Toronto Telegram* column, 'would be to remove the immunity that gives our universities a status comparable to that of diplomatic foreign missions, as far as RCMP security forces are concerned.' Worthington's piece, which was forwarded to headquarters in Ottawa, echoed internal RCMP documents and may have contained material deliberately planted by the Security Service to sway public opinion, a tactic in use at the time. The burst of student radicalism between 1968 and 1970 encouraged such rhetoric, which was based on the faulty assumption that the growth of unrest was fuelled by a lack of awareness of it. The erroneous notion that the university had become a sanctuary beyond the reach of the police was also raised in the final report of the Royal Commission on Security in 1969.[70] As campus protests grew, the federal government and its agencies increasingly sought relevant information from the RCMP. The leaders of the force greeted a request from the Department of External Affairs for information about a student protest against the president of Trent University with a reminder of the obstacles that it faced:

> In view of the restrictions placed upon us in connection with campus inquiries, we have very little intelligence concerning Trent University. As you are no doubt aware, these restrictions resulted from pressure placed upon the Government by the Canadian Association of University Teachers in [1963] and have seriously restricted our capabilities in this field. Our campus investigations have since been limited to:
> (1) The security screening of individuals requiring access to classified data;
> (2) Personal security briefings for persons travelling to Iron Curtain countries;
> (3) [deleted: *Inquiries through sources in recognized subversive organizations.*][71]

With tensions escalating in Quebec at the end of the 1960s, the federal government increasingly desired intelligence on the situation there. Like those in command of the RCMP, it was willing to overlook the fact that some operations were being carried out on campuses. In November 1969 Don Wall, the secretary of the Security Panel, contacted Higgitt's successor as head of the Security Service and supplied him with the name of a prominent employee of a Quebec university whom Marc Lalonde, then within the Prime Minister's Office, said would make a useful source. Wall, too, was reminded of the restrictions placed on RCMP activities on university campuses: 'Mr. Wall agreed that we should be very careful in carrying out investigations on the campus but he felt that the Government would not likely criticize the force for such activities if same were conducted in the Province of Quebec where the present situation certainly justifies our intervention, etc. It was suggested that the Government would probably not tolerate our intrusion on campuses situated in provinces other than Quebec.'[72] Clearly perceptions differed as to what the RCMP was prevented from doing at universities. Wall had supplied the force with the name of a potential informant on a campus, something its leaders believed they had been officially prohibited from doing since 1961. When these limitations were mentioned to Wall, he proceeded to talk, not about the recruitment of the informant but about investigations in general. In commenting on the relationships between the federal government and the RCMP on the subject of universities, the McDonald Commission accurately described the lack of communication between the two parties. In fact, real or pretended ignorance provided politicians with convenient grounds for denying responsibility in the event of a scandal.[73]

The constraints on RCMP activities on university campuses would again become a public matter because of events in Quebec in 1970. In June 'K' Branch had prepared 'Academe and Subversion,' a paper whose purpose was to persuade the government to remove the restrictions. The document contained the untruth that the RCMP did not use Mounties who were students to collect information and the even bigger canard that all RCMP on-campus investigations of subversive activities had been halted in 1961. A clearer indication of the reality of police involvement in universities lay in the section in which the paper emphasized that change was needed. It called for the Mounted Police to have the freedom to infiltrate subversive organizations on campuses: 'It is one thing to know, [deleted: *through "off-campus," casual or other source*]s, that a particular subversive organization exists "on campus"; it is quite another to know what transpires at its meetings. This can only be obtained through penetration of the organization.'[74]

The report, designed to lead to a change in official policy, reiterated the RCMP's difficulties. Increasingly pressured by the government for information about the rising tide of radicalism and separatism, the force found its most important avenue to information, namely the use of infiltration sources, blocked:

With the passage of time [deleted: *many of the sources it did have within institutions have disappeared owing to faculty transfers, retirement and graduation. The effect over nine years, of course, has been cumulative and to rebuild an adequate network of sources will take time. Despite vigorous efforts by the Security Service to develop reliable sources outside educational institutions as such, the results have been disappointing. Moreover, casual sources, for a variety of reasons, have often proved to be not very useful.*] Much of their information is limited to biographical and historical material and some of it is inaccurate.

4. The inadequacies of the existing situation can best be illustrated by mentioning that during the peak of unrest at educational institutions in 1968–69 ... [deleted: *the Security Service had one active source in the entire radical student movement, and even he was only in the process of development.*] It is understandable, therefore, that while the Security Service has gained con-

siderable insight into the nature and extent of revolutionary activities at educational institutions, it lacks any in-depth knowledge.[75]

Finally, in December 1970, after nearly a decade of complaints, controversy, and contravention, and in the immediate aftermath of the FLQ crisis, the issue of RCMP investigations on campuses reached the federal cabinet. Members of the Security Service carefully studied government pronouncements to see if a policy shift was in the works. Pierre Trudeau's opinions were extremely important to this analysis. On 8 December 1970 journalist Mike Wallace interviewed Trudeau on the television program *Sixty Minutes*, following which the Security Service had a transcript prepared. Trudeau sent out a signal that the constraints were about to be lifted, warning that if people on campuses aided terrorism of the kind that the FLQ represented, then the freedoms of universities would have to be curtailed. On 23 December the cabinet, believing that the RCMP had ended investigations on campuses in 1963 and that this 'immunity' aided terrorism, lifted the restrictions.[76]

Confusion on the issue ensued. John Starnes, director-general of the Security Service at the time, recounts that this was 'genuine and understandable,' because 'Ministers and officials simply did not know how best to deal with the complex problems.'[77] It also reflected a deliberate strategy. The federal government, especially Minister of Justice John Turner, had no desire to inform CAUT of the policy shift or to reopen the controversy.[78] The lifting of the supposed restrictions remained a secret, however, not only from Canada's leading academic association but also from some rank-and-file mounted policemen. 'We would appreciate receiving some official correspondence with regard to ... the present policies regarding inquiries on campus,' requested the Security Service office in Sudbury after a member had read an article about a policy change in the *Sudbury Star*. Assistant Commissioner L.R. Parent did not have a lot of sympathy for the confusion of his colleagues: 'I think that our personnel generally make too much of our alleged difficulties on campus. Usually if members can [deleted] there is no problem other than the odd S.O.B.'[79] Before arriving in Ottawa, Parent had been with the Security Service in Montreal. In that position he would have been well aware of the extent of RCMP intelligence gathering on university campuses.

In September 1971, only a few months after lifting restrictions on RCMP activity on campus, the Trudeau government, through the office of Solicitor General Jean-Pierre Goyer, reinstated the 1963 agreement.

Why the flip-flop occurred has been the subject of some speculation. One theory suggests that the Trudeau government might have been concerned about police investigations infringing on academic freedoms. The cabinet record from September 1971 reveals the opposite. Canada's political leaders had finally realized that the 1963 understanding was irrelevant. John Turner even felt it necessary to ask what constituted 'general surveillance.' Both Trudeau and Goyer pointed out that such work had never occurred; the real problem, they said, was that the RCMP continued to follow Fulton's 1961 order restricting the recruitment of campus informants. The cabinet rescinded that order and restored the 1963 understanding with CAUT. According to Goyer, the change was 'satisfactory' to both the RCMP commissioner and the head of the Security Service.[80]

When it came to campus work, the RCMP's hands were not completely freed, however. The cabinet, at Goyer's insistence, added modifications that forbade the RCMP from using technical means and paid informants at universities without the explicit permission of the solicitor general. The fact that these sources of information were not being used or used infrequently (in 1972 there were only five paid informants and no telephone taps and bugs) received no comment.[81] For some members of the Mounted Police, conversely, the solicitor general's unexpected amendment provoked anger. O.M. Davey, a civilian Security Service member recruited by John Starnes, wrote a memorandum suggesting ways of circumventing the new policy. These included going over the solicitor general's head to Prime Minister Trudeau, ignoring the policy completely, or attempting to convince Goyer that the policy was being complied with when it was not.[82] John Starnes did not accept these recommendations and instead sent a reassuring message to his troops: 'A first reading' of the memorandum on the new policy 'may give you the impression that the effect of this new directive is to make little difference in the restrictions ... which have existed since 1963 ... Accordingly, I wish to emphasize that the directive does not mean that the Security Service will abandon its interest in subversive or espionage activities which occur within the confines of Canadian colleges or universities. On the contrary, now that there is a well-defined channel by which we can acquire complete authority for our presence on the campuses, I expect Division Security Service officers to intensify or maintain, as the situation warrants, our coverage of the university milieu.'[83]

As Starnes suggested, the status quo had not returned. Instead, what the RCMP had always been doing was now made easier, and previous grey-area activities now had official legitimacy. By rescinding Fulton's 1961 order and excluding the use of unpaid sources from requiring his approval, Goyer effectively cleared the way for the recruitment of sources on campuses without the fear of government retribution. His successor as solicitor general, Warren Allmand, could not recall approving the use of any paid sources on campus.[84]

The decade-long battle ended with only a partial victory for the RCMP, since by the time it was achieved the battleground had shifted dramatically. Because of the New Left and, ironically enough, of the growing number of Mounties with university education, the Security Service became increasingly sophisticated in its approach to countersubversion. Such changes, of course, do not occur in a night or even a fortnight. The appearance of the New Left in the 1960s dramatically affected intelligence services throughout the Western world. The RCMP was no exception. Whether it recognized it or not, its simple red-and-white world composed of passive students and preying Communists had ended.

6

From the Old Left to the New Left

On 6 October 1961, forty-three members of the Université Laval chapter of the Combined Universities Campaign for Nuclear Disarmament (CUCND), fortified only with homemade placards, set off on a bus for Ottawa to participate with other university students in a Thanksgiving weekend demonstration. Among their numbers was a man clutching a camera, who proved to be particularly enthusiastic, taking frequent pictures of the protesters, especially the leaders. The same person displayed an equal zeal for collecting the CUCND's literature. His efforts had a secret purpose, however. The photographs he took and the pamphlets he collected ended up not in a scrapbook but in the hands of the RCMP's Quebec City detachment – the very same unit that only six months earlier had botched the recruitment of an informant, thereby launching a decade of negative publicity and controversy. The campus informant offered his employers additional aid by identifying some of those whom he had photographed. Individuals in the pictures were marked with letters to speed their identification and to allow for the proper placement of the images in the huge network of police files.[1]

For the RCMP, the targeting of the CUCND had a special significance beyond the place it occupied in the peace movement. It and its 1964 successor, the Student Union for Peace Action (SUPA), represented a symbolic bridge across the 1960s, linking the old adversarial world familiar to the RCMP with the new.[2] A decade that had started as a battle against a major enemy, communism, and a lesser one, Trotskyism, ended with the RCMP facing a fractured array of adversaries, ranging from the polymorphous New Left to Red Power, Black Power, Maoists, and Quebec separatists, along with Communists and Trotskyists as before.[3] In the process, the traditional police view of students as passive and easily influenced would for the first time be fundamentally challenged by the realization that many young people were radical entities unto themselves. Finally, it was not just police attitudes that had changed by the 1960s. The impact of a higher level of education among its own members, as well as the arrival of new opponents, inspired the countersubversion branch of the RCMP Security Service to transform itself, at least in part.

When the decade began there was little to suggest that the pattern of the past would change. The RCMP pursued its traditional Communist foe in whatever form it was perceived to have taken, including fronts and in attempts to infiltrate non-Communist organizations. Commissioner Leonard Higgitt explained the nature of this threat:

> It is not suggested that universities, per se, are involved in conspiratorial activities directed against our democratic system. However, it is an irrefutable fact that they do exert considerable influence on sociological issues of the day and are, therefore ripe targets for communist infiltration and manipulation. You will undoubtedly agree that a person who privately harbours Communist sympathies and who gains an influential position in a select faculty on a university, can contribute immeasurably to the Communist cause. The value of such a person to the movement is obvious as is our corresponding security responsibilities.[4]

Careful watch was kept on any manifestation of communism on campuses in the early 1960s. An advertisement in the University of Western Ontario *Gazette* inviting interested parties to form a Communist club was of concern until the event failed to materialize. At McMaster University a member of 'B' Branch, the counter-espionage wing of the RCMP, lent a hand to his countersubversion colleagues, offering material he had accumulated in investigations at that institution. Not far to the northeast, the Mounties followed the activities of the University of Toronto branch of the Student Christian Movement, although the force was unable to decide 'whether the SCM motivation is purely academic rather than of an ulterior nature in which we may be interested.' Young Communist League work connected to the NDP and the peace movement interested the police at the University of Alberta.[5]

Because the University of British Columbia appeared to have more subversives than other universities it received a proportionately greater share of the attention of the RCMP. Of particular concern was Professor James Foulks of the Department of Pharmacology, because he appeared to be employing measures to counter surveillance. These included parking his car farther from Communist Party of Canada (CPC) meetings than anyone else, and glancing about before leaving his car and entering meeting places. He was one of sixty-four faculty members at his university, out of a total of approximately 1400, on whom the RCMP held files in 1964; it held only 'references' on another twenty-three. It was not necessary to be an open member of the Communist Party to be targeted, but only four people fit this category. In an effort to discover radical trends at the university, the Vancouver office of the Mounted Police supplied headquarters in Ottawa with a crude correlation that listed departments and the percentage of subversives in them.[6]

It was not just University of British Columbia faculty members who concerned the police. Fifty-four students had their own D-935 file label, indicating that they were subversives. They were concentrated in the Faculties of Education and of Arts and Sciences, prompting the reporting officer to see the choice of teaching as a profession as a deliberate plot: 'No doubt a number of the students currently studying Arts and Science will also go into the teaching profession. [deleted] we feel that this gives a fairly accurate picture of the future education potential and influence available to the Communist Party and its related front groups.' Superintendent M.W. Jones, in charge of the security intelligence wing of British Columbia's 'E' Division, added a note of caution to this potential threat, pointing out that the students in the D-935 category represented only .5 per cent of the overall student population at the university.[7]

During the cold war such cautionary logic was rare. Instead a deterministic philosophy drove the RCMP, and the pattern at the University of British Columbia was replicated elsewhere with the RCMP looking for enemies wherever they could be found, including the private homes of non-Communists. In 1963 Cedric Cox, an NDP member of the British Columbia provincial legislature, hosted a farewell garden party for the Cuban ambassador to Canada. Naturally, the gathering drew the attention of the police. The officer who reported noted that most of those in attendance belonged to the NDP or were Trotskyists. In addition, he observed, in an openly disapproving tone, several people from the university 'of the "Beatnik" type – bearded men and females wearing slim-jims and similar type of clothing inappropriate for a function of this kind,' who socialized with the others.[8]

The police also searched for subversion in radio and television. The Canadian Broadcasting Corporation's habit of allowing alleged subversives from universities on the air throughout the 1960s perturbed the RCMP. It was decided that a place to watch was the CBC's Public Affairs Department, which had, according to an RCMP source, 'the reputation within the Corporation of being particularly vague, wooly [*sic*] and psuedo intellectual.'[9]

Occasionally the general public aided the hunt. An anonymous letter to the Vancouver detachment in 1962 warned that the Asian and Slavic Departments at UBC were centres of Communist activity. 'No need to go to the field,' wrote a Mountie at the bottom of the letter, 'INFO is already on files.' As usual, much of the detail came from police informants, one of whom was among eleven faculty members and twenty-nine students who attended an Asian Studies departmental meeting.[10]

University departments with connections to the Communist bloc were special targets. Academics in these departments often travelled to Communist countries, creating the possibility of their recruitment as agents through a variety of enticements or the threat of blackmail.[11] Then there was the prospect, which again reflected a crude understanding by police of academe and the continuing emphasis that was placed on subversive threats, of programs consisting of the study of Communist countries being, in fact, programs designed to promote communism to impressionable students. Thus the RCMP investigated the Russian Studies Department at the University of Western Ontario, as well as a seminar series on Asian affairs at Sir George Williams University, after which the Mounted Police collected copies of papers that were presented and newspaper clippings of what was said. At Brock University, where the RCMP spied on several members of the Germanic and Slavic Studies Program, the department's habit of showing German and Russian films was deemed worthy of mention.[12]

As with the Brock University example, the examination of these programs really meant investigating the academics behind them, since it was they who had the potential to influence impressionable students. The most obvious individuals to draw the attention of the police were those who were openly Communist. Over four decades, RCMP members chronicled the public, political, and academic, and even the private life of one of these, University of Toronto philosophy professor Daniel Goldstick. He first came to the attention of the Mounted Police at the age of fifteen, and his subsequent life, first as a student, including a stint at Oxford University, and then as an academic – where he was 'ideally suited for the subtle influencing of young and enquiring minds,' was the police description of one of his classes – received documentation in his file.

Comments about his character were also made. As with all suspected subversives, his file was updated yearly for his current address, telephone number, employment status, and other pertinent information. The investigations even continued for years after the RCMP had labelled Goldstick, who was an open Communist, an independent thinker and someone who did not blindly adhere to the party line.[13]

Greater police effort was expended to discover those who secretly harboured 'Red' tendencies, but the evidence unearthed to establish such connections was frequently tenuous. At Laurentian University in June 1961 a source, most likely a disgruntled colleague, provided the names of five potential Communists. After doing background checks on them, the only evidence of radicalism appeared to be membership in CAUT, public criticism of an anti-Communist television program, and frequent clashes with the university's administration. Special note was made that the men were not from Sudbury, as well as the fact that one of them was active in the NDP. The report was cross-referenced to 'Communist Activities in Political Parties, Ontario.'[14]

Nor was it necessary to be a Communist to have a file created with one's name on it. Simply being associated with a cause championed by the CPC was sufficient to raise suspicion. A lecturer in Spanish at York University was reported on after she repeatedly spoke at a Fair Play for Cuba meeting. Journalists Pierre Berton and Peter Gzowski had files opened on them, or reports added to already existing ones, the former after he chaired a meeting of an anti-Apartheid organization, and the latter after he appeared at the University of Toronto to criticize the quality of Canadian universities. Academics who consistently took a radical line or criticized the police also faced investigation for possible ties to the CPC. University of Toronto law professor Bora Laskin, president of CAUT in 1964–5 and a future chief justice of the Supreme Court of Canada, and C.B. Macpherson, a University of Toronto professor of political economy, had dossiers opened on them or material added to already existing ones.[15]

Investigating the manifestations of communism and the activities of its adherents was the only world the Security Service had ever known. That path, however, involved following a fading star. As a result of the anticommunism of the cold war, the authoritarian nature of the party's leadership, and the party's split over the Hungarian Revolution and Khrushchev's verbal assault on Stalin, the CPC's membership had shrunk to between 1,500 and 3,000 by the early 1960s, and those who remained tended to be the older members. Increasingly, the party attempted, in an echo of its 'united front' strategy of the past, to ally itself with non-Communist organizations such as the Voice of Women in order to create a more influential profile for itself, thereby providing the Mounties with grounds for spying on these organizations.[16]

Because of the blanket coverage of the activities of the CPC, the Mounted Police was well aware of its difficulties. After the annual meeting of the Vancouver branch of the party in 1962, for example, headquarters in Ottawa received a breakdown of those in attendance by gender, age range, average number of years in the party, membership in outside organizations, and occupation. Internal party documents, including personal letters, came into the possession of investigating Mounties in an almost miraculous fashion.[17]

Because of their training, which emphasized Communist perfidy, and limited sophistication, members of the Security Service had trouble believing the evidence of the CPC's decline. Slowly, however, a transformation in the thinking and approach to countering subversion took place. The growing presence on campuses in the early 1960s of the old adversaries of the Communists, the Trotskyists, suggested a changing environment among radicals. The RCMP infiltrated the Young Socialist Alliance, which the League for Socialist Action launched in 1964, with numerous sources, who offered intimate details on the activities of the two organizations, including their members and plans. A long-term RCMP source, who was code-named A358 because 'A' Division in Ottawa recruited him, infiltrated the Trotskyist movement at Trent University in the early 1970s.[18]

In a similar vein, the RCMP spied on a variety of Maoist groups from the 1960s to the 1980s. Its investigations began with the Internationalists, which was founded in 1963 by Hardial Bains, a graduate student in microbiology at the University of British Columbia and which initially brought together students and faculty from Bains's university and later from Simon Fraser University. By the end of the 1960s a related front organization, the Canadian Communist Movement, had formed student groups at a number of institutions. In assessing Maoist and Trotskyist organizations, the Security Service sought information on a wide range of subjects, including publications, printing facilities, party-owned bookstores, executive members, and affiliations. Finally, the police attempted to ascertain the 'adverse' effect of radical organizations on surrounding communities, in particular the potential for politically motivated violence.[19]

The Maoist and Trotskyist campus groups were merely the beginning.

A sign of how quickly and how complex the radical map would soon become was this somewhat plaintive and abbreviation-ridden clarification on the part of a mounted policeman in 1969:

2. There appears to be some confusion regarding the Toronto Student Movement [deleted: file number]. The T.S.M. as formed by [deleted: name] and other left-wing radicals at the University of Toronto [deleted: file number] in September 1968 is not the T.S.M. which is the local students arm of the Canadian Communist Movement (Marxist-Leninist), the Canadian Internationalists, Canada [deleted: file number] and their Canadian Student Movement.
3. T.S.M. is very active on U. of T. campus and has penetrated the Students' Administrative Council at the executive level. The C.S.M.'s T.S.M. appears to exist in name only with the membership drawn from the rank-and-file of the C.S.M. young people.
4. [deleted: name] has complained in the recent past that the C.S.M. are confusing the left and have really confused the student element by employing his T.S.M. for their own organization.
5. We have not opened a file on the C.S.M.'s T.S.M. for this reason, and the fact that C.C.M. is utilizing their general membership to many of their various groups.
6. Now, however, [deleted] T.S.M. has split into two groups: the New Left Caucus (NLC) and the Worker-Student Alliance (WSA), so we will likely hear less about this T.S.M. [deleted: file number].
7. Also, the McMaster Student Movement [deleted: file number] is not part of the C.S.M. but is aligned with the Canadian Party of Labour.
8. More confusion arises with the York Student Movement [deleted: file number], formerly the York Sunday Movement. This group is also aligned with the C.P.L. and the old T.S.M. and is definitely not part of the C.S.M.
9. It is becoming increasingly more difficult to distinguish the difference in these above groups, however, the C.C.M. sponsored organizations send out a rabid pro-Chinese line, while the others tend to promote violent revolutionary ideology.
10. In short, the Y.S.M. and the M.S.M. are both C.P.L. influenced and the remainder of the 'Student Movements' are probably inspired by the C.S.M.[20]

Something bigger than abbreviations was underway. Although it represented diverse beliefs, a movement called the New Left emerged in the 1960s. With a name designed to distinguish it from the traditional, and to many a staid and authoritarian radical left, it brought forth strong challenges to political systems and institutions, including universities, and, in the process, became associated with the worldwide movement of youth discontent and protest that helped characterize the era.

Several factors explain its emergence. A massive demographic shift was one cause. By 1964 the first wave of the baby boom (a coherent single entity demographically although clearly divided along the lines of class, race and ethnicity, region, etc.[21]) began to arrive on campuses. At every stage in their lives, baby boomers changed the society around them by sheer force of numbers. With the end of war and the return of veterans, the birth rate had shot up and it remained high throughout the 1950s. Because so many children entered the educational system at the same time, they brought about adjustments within elementary and high schools through the absolute weight of their numbers. It would be no different for universities, but the change to these traditionally stuffy institutions in the 1960s would be more dramatic.

Why? In the history he wrote of his generation, Doug Owram argues that the booming economy of the 1960s absorbed the demographic boom of the post-war period. Universities, however, had greater difficulty in adjusting as the student population grew from 163,143 undergraduates in 1960 to 475,548 ten years later. Despite the appearance of several new educational institutions in the 1960s, overcrowding (both the University of British Columbia and Simon Fraser University reached record enrolment levels in 1968, a key year of protests) and a concomitant strain on resources fed the discontent of students and faculty alike. A great deal of the energy was focused on democratizing universities, perceived by many as elitist institutions that were interested mainly in catering to the wealthy and powerful and that were unresponsive to the needs of students whom they continued to treat like children.[22]

The decade that had preceded the new era provided a strong incentive for change. For many young people, the cold war–dominated 1950s was a bland period when the emphasis, especially in popular culture and education, was on conformity in all aspects of life, including sexual roles and political beliefs. In American state discourse, radicalism was equated with sexual weakness or degeneracy, and one of the manifestations of that discourse, McCarthyism, had ruined countless lives. A strong backlash against orthodoxies was inevitable.[23]

The so-called Old Left in North America and Europe did not escape the reaction, though it was more against institutionalized parties than the principles of communism. Many of the first wave of New Lefters, people like British historian E.P. Thompson, an early contributor to the influential academic journal *New Left Review*, left their respective Communist parties in response to Stalinist-style leaderships and to the events of 1956, when the Soviet Union invaded Hungary and Nikita Khrushchev denounced Joseph Stalin.[24]

For the younger people who were part of the second wave within the New Left, the work of a group of political theorists encouraged a sense of disillusionment. At the top of the list was Karl Marx, whose work many turned to – in the process proudly calling themselves Marxists – as an antidote to the rigidity of institutionalized Communist parties. The scholarship of C. Wright Mills and Herbert Marcuse, among others, inspired many more in fashioning their critiques of the society they lived in.[25]

Finally, there were the social factors that were at play in fashioning the new movements, an area that the Mounted Police, in its pursuit of individual agitators, never really understood. Growing up with the threat of extinction through nuclear war deeply affected young people, many of whom in both Canada and the United States moved into radical politics through the peace movement. The increasingly unpopular role of the United States in the Vietnam War, as well as the African-American struggle for civil rights also influenced Canadian campuses, through both media coverage and the presence of American students and faculty, some of whom lived in Canada as a means of escaping military service. Indeed some people would later criticize the American-driven agenda of elements of the Canadian New Left.[26]

Part of the unpopularity of the Vietnam War, however, was related also to rising opposition to American hegemony around the world but especially in Canada. Philosopher George Grant's *Lament for a Nation*, which argued that the battle for the control of Canada had already been lost to the United States and to American values, captured the interest of young people who were concerned about their country's future. In a sense they represented a third wave of the New Left, and in the latter half of the 1960s they would be particularly active in organizations like the Canadian Liberation Movement that worked to Canadianize universities.[27]

These factors and others inspired a remarkable decade. Hints of what was underway surfaced as early as 1960, when American students played a prominent role in demonstrations against the House Un-American Activities Committee in San Francisco. J. Edgar Hoover, who linked the protests to the Communist Party of the United States of America and who used right-wing American organizations like the Young Americans for Freedom to spread his gospel, missed the message. Then, in 1962 came Tom Hayden's 'Port Huron Declaration,' official word that a fresh age had arrived. By the end of the 1960s Jerry Farber had published *The Student as Nigger*. Students for a Democratic Society in the United States, which had grown from three hundred faithful members in 1961 to as many as 100,000 seven years later, was fracturing and spawning the Weather Underground, a group that would launch a bombing campaign in the 1970s. Finally, and most significant of all, movements along racial and gender lines, including Black and Red Power groups and feminists, had arisen to render a new critique of both society and the radicalism that had preceded them.[28]

In Canada the trends were similar, albeit delayed and modified. *Our Generation against Nuclear War*, originally published as part of the influential SUPA, became a forum for New Left thought, and by the end of the decade had shortened it name to *Our Generation*. It was edited by Dimitrios Roussopoulos, who had been head of the CUCND in 1961, and it included contributions from prominent members of the Canadian New Left, like Simon Fraser University student Jim Harding. The Security Service began subscribing in 1968.[29]

How did members of the Security Service react to the arrival of the New Left and the protests associated with it? Initially they did not realize that anything had changed, even as evidence grew that something different was underway. A mounted policeman covering an anti–Vietnam War teach-in at Carleton University in October 1965, besides observing the presence of several 'dark-skinned people,' labelled the gathering as supportive of communism. His superior was a little more discerning: 'Communists and pro-communist elements in Ottawa tried on numerous occasions to exercise more influence in the preparations for and conduct of the Teach-in with very limited success,' wrote Inspector G.E. Witherden to the commissioner. Instead of seeing the possibility that a new epoch had been launched, Witherden continued, however, with a traditional RCMP 'red-and-white' worldview. 'I believe these two events [the other was a Quaker peace conference] proved a useful example of what a few Communists can do if given free rein in arranging such events which involved public issues.'[30]

As the sixties progressed and the unrest increased, the RCMP reaction reflected its history, training, and perception of youth. Accordingly, a constant effort was made to discover Communist causes behind problems, even when the corroboration, as contained for example in a June 1966 report on the Student Union for Peace Action, suggested a more complicated picture.

S.U.P.A. is a loosely controlled organization comprising several groups doing different things in various cities. Each group is a unit in itself and, while they hold some allegiance to the whole they are not bound by any executive control. The projects which these groups attempt are usually in the line of social improvement such as equality for Negroes and Indians. They are known also to do such things as campaigning for the installation of traffic stop signs, etc. ...

2. [deleted] the members of S.U.P.A. can be divided into three basic types: a) 'The rich kid,' rebelling against his parents and society, often is dirty and unshaven. His only desire is to rebell [*sic*], and he needs to be shown the direction. b) Emotionally immature, they are mixed up and do not know what they want out of life. c) These people are comparatively intelligent, mature people who see injustices in our country and in the world. They are sincerely interested in improving our society. [deleted]

4. [deleted] it would be very difficult for Trotskyists or Communists to gain control of S.U.P.A. [deleted] since it lacks central direction, any organization trying to subvert S.U.P.A. would be required to infiltrate each individual group.[31]

It would be difficult to gain control of SUPA but not impossible from the standpoint of the police, and so the spying continued. A University of British Columbia petition condemning U.S. involvement in Vietnam was labelled by a Mountie as trickery by a 'group of dedicated leftists.' The policeman, after underlining the names of faculty members that the RCMP had interest in, including George Woodcock, a strong critic of the New Left youth protest and Walter Young, a political scientist, informed headquarters that 'the true majority of the U.B.C. Faculty is unorganized and silent as ever.'[32]

Elements within the RCMP continued into the late 1960s and early 1970s to interpret campus unrest as the handiwork of professional Communists, a point of view caused in part by the fact that former Communists were active in some of the new social movements. In 1968, for example, a police analysis entitled 'Communist Threat to Universities' had recourse to the 1948 report on the LPP, the same one used by Watson Kirkconnell, to support the notion that Communist manipulation caused campus unrest.[33]

The finest example of this traditional RCMP genre was, however, a document entitled 'Communist Activity among Youth Particularly in the Educational Field,' apparently prepared in 1967 for the Royal Commission on Security, the final report of which in 1969 criticized restrictions on police investigations on campuses. The RCMP submission took first an international perspective in an attempt to show a deterministic drift to the unrest. Then came a discussion on Communist activity at Canadian universities in the 1960s. It was noted that the Young Communist League of Canada operated clubs on several university campuses. 'However,' warned the report, 'the C.P. of C. and the Y.C.L.C. do not always operate openly, or disclose their true colours. In the past they have chosen to operate from within other campus clubs which are not recognized as being Communist, and which have many legitimate members who are not Communists.' At Carleton University, it added, a 'closed club member' had started an anti–nuclear war group. The efforts on the part of the YCLC to organize high school students were also commented on, as was the involvement of other organizations in this initial effort, such as the New Democratic Youth. Finally, the report noted the parallel efforts by Trotskyists, who practised 'entryism' in an effort to infiltrate and affect the activities of other organizations. The report's conclusion, which even raised the spectre of Quebec nationalism, reiterated decades-long themes, while serving as a justification for eternal vigilance:

> One might argue that these Communist, Trotskyist, and radical separatist groups, represent a very small percentage of the students who attend our educational institutions, and an even smaller percentage of Canadian youth as a whole, and of course this is true. However, I do not think that the Young Communist League of Canada or the Young Socialist Alliance can be looked upon as ordinary groups on campus, comparable to other campus political groups. These two organizations ... are integral parts of much larger, well organized international networks, which are dedicated to the overthrow of our system of democratic government, and their sole purpose for being on campus is to promote the aims of their parent bodies, the Communist Party of Canada and League for Socialist Action. Their small size is not really relevant, for what they lack in numbers they make up in organization and dedication to their task. [34]

The Security Service was in no way unique in how it reacted to the growing expressions of unrest on university campuses. In the United States the FBI largely determined the domestic security response to the New Left and campus disturbances; its approach was decided by the whims of J. Edgar Hoover.

In 1965 the FBI began a close investigation of the American New Left in an effort to discover its Communist base. Hoover ordered the FBI to prepare a memorandum for the administration of President Lyndon Johnson, one that would emphasize the Communist role in the movement. Three years later, after the 1968 student occupation of Columbia University, the FBI launched its Counter Intelligence Program against the New Left. Among the tactics it used were strategic leaks to the media in an effort to discredit its enemies. It also encouraged local police forces to arrest members of the New Left on drug charges whenever and wherever possible. While Hoover's dictates were dogma, others within the Bureau recognized the limitations of his approach. His right-hand man, William Sullivan, the designer of COINTELPRO, admitted to a journalist in the early 1970s that communism was not a part of the protests on American campuses.[35]

By 1967 the embattled administration of President Johnson had grown impatient in finding the links between international communism and the dissent enveloping university campuses. Instead of turning to the FBI, which was in the process of scaling back investigations on campuses because of negative publicity similar to what the RCMP had experienced in 1961, the Johnson administration sought the assistance of the Central Intelligence Agency. One result was a report entitled 'Restless Youth.' Defining the New Left as 'an amalgam of disparate, amorphous local groups of uncertain or changing leadership and eclectic programs,' this well reasoned and original document demonstrated the extent of the CIA's sophistication and complexity in comparison to its poorly educated Canadian intelligence cousins.

Presented to Johnson in 1968, 'Restless Youth' was an attempt to answer an important question: why was student unrest occurring worldwide? Student movements in several countries, although interestingly enough not in Canada, were examined in an analytical fashion with historical context, both distant and immediate, thrown in. The report's author or authors noted two interrelated trends in the international tendency towards student unrest: 'neo-Marxist social criticism,' influenced by scholars such as C. Wright Mills and Herbert Marcuse, and student activism, which had its roots in problems related to universities. Both, argued the report, 'co-existed in a mutual search for a meaningful program, a lever for overturning social structures.'[36]

Like the FBI, the CIA was unable to discover Communist links to the protest: 'There is no convincing evidence of control, manipulation, sponsorship, or significant financial support of student dissidents by any international Communist authority,' the authors noted. They added that while Communist nations could take some pleasure in what was happening in the West, eventually they would face similar discontent among their own young people.[37] The project did not end there. In fact, the CIA expanded it during the Nixon administration, in part because Hoover was growing increasingly reluctant to use the FBI for illegal activities. Labelled Operation CHAOS, it continued until 1974, in the process creating files on 10,000 individuals and 100 organizations, and a computerized database of 300,000 names.[38]

British intelligence echoed the American view. At a late 1960s Commonwealth Security Conference, MI5 attributed the international protests to contradictions within capitalism, not Communist machinations:

One of the contradictions of advanced capitalist societies is becoming increasingly clear. Modern economies require enormous organisations employing thousands of people. An increasing number of these need advanced education just to operate the technology, lay the investment plans, handle the governments and prepare the consumers for the ever more complicated expensive and controversial products of the scientific age. Yet this whole 'system,' as they call it, is less than acceptable to a significant minority of younger people being subjected to the higher education which the system itself demands. The roots of much of the anxiety, insecurity, frustration and confusion in the young seem to lie in the pace of social change and the sheer speed of technological advance ... Those who resist it see it as a conspiracy against idealism in society and identity in themselves. The protest is made not so much against their parents as against the system which governs their parents' lives and threatens to engulf themselves.[39]

Closer to the RCMP's perspective on campus unrest was that of the Australian Security Intelligence Organization (ASIO). While realizing that the social and international context was necessary for understanding what was happening at universities, in analyzing the New Left ASIO still perceived the Communists as trying, largely unsuccessfully, to steer the unrest. Whether it controlled the unrest was immaterial, the agency ultimately concluded, since the Soviet Union would seek to take advantage of it.[40]

Institutional behemoth that it was, the RCMP changed slowly. Nevertheless, the force's institutional perception of the New Left did perceptibly begin to shift. Also under reassessment was its approach towards the unrest. A restructuring that represented an analytical revolution within the RCMP was about to occur, in part because those who had had personal experience at universities began to look at old problems in a different way. Increasingly, complex analysis that employed ideas and concepts from political science, sociology, and history, among others, was being directed at what was occurring on campus. Yet the RCMP was to open its eyes only part-way. Even though it eventually recognized that the New Left in Canada was not an appendage of the CPC, the final objectives of both, it believed, were the same: an organized and coherent attempt to infiltrate and subvert government and public institutions.

This partially new perspective on the New Left did not materialize quickly. In fact, differing interpretations overlapped within the force into the 1970s. Those espousing a new perspective appear to have been younger and better educated members of 'D' Branch. One such individual was Constable Terry Beckett. While stationed in Toronto, the University of Windsor graduate wrote his own analysis of what was happening with young people. Relying almost exclusively on open sources and existing scholarship, Beckett attempted to place the University of Toronto situation within the international context. Emphasizing the ability of a few activists and agitators to control and to inspire a largely 'apathetic majority' of students, Beckett zeroed in on the background of those in leadership roles. In making this emphasis, the young Mountie displayed the impact university training was having on the Security Service. A study of student activism at the University of Toronto by sociologist Kenneth Walker and a publication by the Center for Higher Education at the University of California, Berkeley, were his two principal sources. The former found, through a survey, that two-thirds of the students at the institution had not participated in protests. The latter examined individual activists and found that they came from left-wing, upper-middle-class, and secularized families and that they were of above-average intelligence.[41]

In the end Beckett's novel report reiterated familiar themes. First, it emphasized the Communist role in the dissent. Communists or Trotskyists had organized 90 per cent of anti–Vietnam War demonstrations, according to Beckett. He then added the traditional RCMP nugget – an interpretation already rejected by the CIA – on how 'Contemporary Communist emphasis in connections with campus activity has been in two main areas: recruiting of students, or obtaining them as sympathizers to prepare the groundwork for the penetration of key sectors of society; the second is encouraging students to participate in demonstrations which are exploited for propaganda purposes and to condition students for future mass demonstrations.'[42]

There was also the usual RCMP way of explaining unrest, that of blaming it on outsiders. 'Most unrest on Canadian campuses has been initiated by radical immigrant professors from the United Kingdom or the United States,' he wrote. This interpretation, promulgated by an instrument of the Canadian state, was nothing if not traditional. It was far easier to blame unrest on outsiders and agitators than it was to address the issues behind the discontent. As in the past, the second part of this approach was to recommend the loosening of deportation laws in order to remove those perceived as troublemakers. The RCMP put pressure on the Department of Manpower and Immigration, invoking worst-case scenarios that even the Department of External Affairs found excessive, to tighten the rules that allowed international students and scholars to enter Canada. A comment by one officer, 'Since the subject has indicated that he intends to form a Communist Club on the Campus of Western Ontario, I wonder what his status is in this country,' said it all.[43]

Clearly, non-Canadians did play a role in protests at the Canadian universities, but emphasizing their participation glossed over deeper societal discontent among youth in Canada and elsewhere in the world. Martin Loney, as one of the 'foreign agitators' that the RCMP had in mind, points out that outsiders had little to do with efforts at Simon Fraser University to rename it Louis Riel University. In fact, many of the most prominent students involved in the Simon Fraser University protests came from Saskatchewan.[44]

While the presence at universities of those from abroad troubled the Security Service, it was, ironically enough, bothered just as much by those who criticized foreign, chiefly American, influence on the world of Canadian higher education and on society in general. Beginning in the 1960s and continuing into the following decade, a movement to Canadianize universities regularly raised the issue of the national background of faculty members. As a result, it had its activities monitored by the RCMP. In one example, Constable J.D. Moodie attended a teach-in at the University of Alberta in November 1969 and spied on the activities of one of the leading figures in the Canadianization effort, Robin Mathews. American influence on Canadian foreign policy was also a matter of concern to many people, particularly those in academe, and the University League for Social Reform was one of the groups campaigning to have the Canadian government withdraw from NATO and NORAD. There was even support for withdrawal in the federal cabinet. In 1969, two months after the matter was discussed in cabinet, the Department of External Affairs asked the RCMP to investigate the League out of concern over its influence.[45]

Then there was the Waffle, a movement within the NDP that was trying to push the party further left. The Security Service was interested in this faction, believing that subversives were using it as means to infiltrate the NDP. Accordingly, Mounties investigated manifestations of the Waffle, such as meetings of the New Democratic Youth, which was strongly pro-Waffle, both on and off the campuses.[46] Occasionally the coverage went further. On 6 March 1970 a police informant attended the 'Americanization of Canada Teach-In' at the University of Toronto, an event sponsored by the campus NDP club and the Waffle movement. He or she was not impressed, reporting on the growing factionalism within the New Left: 'several more teach-ins of this type would really scatter any semblance of cohesion left within the "New Left."' A non-RCMP member also in attendance took issue with this interpretation, calling it 'short-sighted.' Instead, in his opinion the teach-in demonstrated the 'planned evolution of anti-Americanism follow[ing] the communist general plan for gaining support through the "popular front of progressive forces."' He added: 'There is little doubt that the Waffle Movement will help polarize public opinion on the independence issue ... In a relatively short space of time Canadians will choose between continentalism and political alliances favouring Canadian independence from the U.S. The building of this alliance is already in progress by the Waffle Group within the New Democratic Party.'[47]

With growing frequency, the Security Service, as an institution, began to believe that a new form of subversion was at work, though with the same tactics as previous models. Terry Beckett had warned headquarters that radicals would increasingly focus their attention on university-related issues, such as tuition or housing, not in an effort to improve conditions for the burgeoning student population but as a means of radicalizing the student majority.[48]

Interpreting a wider range of activities as representing subversion, the Security Service now extended its investigations in this direction. If someone spoke out, especially at a smaller institution where protests were a rare occasion, it was certain to garner police attention. The police obtained a subscription to *Advise and Dissent*, a publication of the University of Calgary's faculty association, which they hoped would provide 'insight ... [into] the most vociferous faculty members.' In October 1970 a Security Service member attended a conference on Marxism at the University of Waterloo. Smelling 'socialistic views' and noting the presence of 'quite a few "well-versed" Marxists' and of a commentator with a 'noticeable British accent,' he added that several RCMP targets were in attendance. Then there was *Heresy*, a satirical and radical newsletter with a tiny circulation put out by two Queen's University students. A copy ended up in RCMP files after a member of the force took it off a university bulletin board. The Security Service awaited a second issue, but it never circulated: the master copy was stolen from the printer.[49]

Fishing expeditions for new subversives were not undertaken uniformly across the country. The English-language universities in Atlantic Canada generally received little attention, because little radical activity took place there. The Security Service dismissed a demonstration by members of an Acadia University branch of Students for a Democratic Society (SDS) as not falling in a 'true radical area.' At Dalhousie University the Mounties employed a broader definition of radical activity: reports were made on student organizations doing charitable work in Latin America, striving for better student housing, and working to improve social problems in Halifax.[50]

Nor was chasing university-based subversion solely a campus sport. A typical example where it went beyond the campus occurred in 1966 in Saskatoon where Vanguard Tours, a group of activists travelling across the country to discuss the guerrilla struggle in Venezuela, was followed around town by a team of Mounties. When Rae Murphy, a CPC executive member, flew into Windsor for a visit to the university campus in 1968, Mounties followed him in from the airport. At Prince Albert in October 1968 a member of the University of Saskatchewan's Student Representative Council spoke on issues of concern to students at the Saskatchewan Federation of Labour's annual convention; in attendance was a Security Service source, who depicted the speech as being 'of a low-key nature [which] did not make any demands or threats of student revolution.' In Charlottetown, Premier Alex Campbell and two of his cabinet ministers ordered the force to carry out a surveillance of a student protest over tuition hikes in January 1970; the off-campus demonstration, which was covered by six plainclothes officers and thirty-six uniformed members waiting in reserve, ended with the occupation of the minister of education's office. Reflecting the cultural divide, one policeman emphasized the students' apparent lack of civility when they 'grossly insulted' the cabinet minister with 'profane and filthy language.'[51]

In addition to Terry Beckett's work, another analysis (perhaps also by Beckett) of the changing nature of Security Service appeared in the fall of 1968. It attempted to connect disturbances at Simon Fraser University with broader societal trends. 'It has been said wisely and proved sadly,' wrote the author in an unusually creative opening to a widely circulated document in the RCMP and among government departments, 'that "organized minorities always defeat unaroused majorities."' The piece raised the same points as had the earlier study by Beckett: the overrepresentation of non-Canadian faculty and students ('the Che GUEVARAS of our society') in protests at several universities and the escalation of confrontation by students, with a prediction that it would grow in the coming year.[52] The report went even further in finding evidence of Communist machinations behind protests, including a visit to Cuba by Gerry Sperling, an academic at Simon Fraser University, and the presence at the university of Maurice Halperin, who in 1953 fled the United States after being called to testify before the Senate Internal Security Subcommittee regarding allegations of espionage. Based on these factors, combined with the possible conclusion of the Vietnam War, the report concluded that the Soviet Union might be targeting American involvement in Latin America as a new source of anti-American protest. Simon Fraser University, because of its geographic location and 'extreme liberalism and free-thinking,' would serve as a Soviet 'listening post' with students 'under the supervision of these professors ... innocently ... drawn into the type of research by being given special research assignments.'[53]

Another sign of the evolving interpretation of the New Left by police appeared in January 1969. Senior officers in the RCMP and government bureaucrats received a copy of 'New Left (Student Power), Canada,' a special paper prepared by the Security Service and the first real recognition by those at the top that things had changed. But breaking out of the decades old mind-set remained difficult: after warning campus unrest would increase and noting that the security agencies of Canada's allies saw the 'New Left as an integral part of the security threat,' the writer of the report observed that there was 'evidence of links with International Communism.' Such an explanation, besides being largely inaccurate, confirmed the RCMP's close relationship with the FBI, which under the domination of Hoover continued stubbornly to subscribe to that perspective.[54]

There was now, however, a different interpretation of the CPC's role in the unrest. No longer were Communists considered to be the masterminds behind the disturbances. Instead they sat poised, according to the paper, to take advantage of any disorder. Also original, and a further manifestation of the impact of higher education on the outlook of the RCMP, was the historical context that was provided on the development of the New Left, which it traced first in the Civil Rights movement in the

United States and then in the activities of the Student Union for Peace Action in Canada. Some of those prominently involved in the latter were later in the Company of Young Canadians, a program started by the government of Prime Minister Lester Pearson. The significance of the creation of the Students for a Democratic University, the Canadian equivalent of the American Students for a Democratic Society, was mentioned, along with the shift leftward of the Canadian Union of Students, especially after that group's August 1968 meeting in Guelph, Ontario, which the Security Service infiltrated with at least one informant.[55] Together, the breadth of interpretation and the evidence marshalled reflected an increasing and systematic sophistication on the part of the Mounties in the Security Service. It extended into how the force organized its countersubversion operations, specifically in the form of a new weapon to battle nation-wide radicalism.

Inspiring the change was a growing sense that the New Left and the protests on campuses represented developments intrinsically different from those of the past, both in the part played by Communists and in the behaviour of youth. A June 1969 report remarked on the fact that other groups on the political left were overshadowing the CPC and that 'the left wing element is dividing.'[56]

There was a practical aspect to the new police approach. The tendency to hoard information, evident in the 1950s, had continued into the 1960s. Drowning in a sea of reports, all with red margins, the RCMP expanded resources simply to sift constantly through files in an effort to determine their relevance.[57] Increasing unrest on campuses only made the situation worse. As a solution, 'D' Branch gave birth to the Key Sectors program in 1967. The rationale behind the plan was straightforward: 'In view of recent developments within the subversive movement in Canada, it is apparent that "D" Branch investigative procedures must also undergo considerable change and adjustments to cope with this situation.' While elements of the program started in February 1967 when an effort was undertaken to discover Communist 'penetration' in the Ontario educational sector, the official program was only unveiled later that year.[58]

Key Sectors began with the mission of investigating the extent of subversive infiltration in three significant areas of Canadian society: the government at the federal, provincial, and municipal levels, including the armed forces and police; the media, specifically private and public television and radio, and print; and education, namely universities, high schools, elementary schools, school boards, and parent-teacher associations. The plan considered libraries to be in the 'Mass Media' grouping, although in one instance a target working for a library at an educational institution was placed in two categories.[59] The larger divisions, such as those that included Toronto and Montreal, had their own Key Sectors personnel. They and other 'D' Branch colleagues funnelled relevant material to headquarters in Ottawa, where Key Sectors readers examined it and passed it on to an analytical team of six to nine members, who then evaluated the trends.[60] Overall, the program had three aims: '1) to determine quantitatively the extent of penetration into vital sectors of society by all persons of interest to us ... 2) to assess (qualitatively) what threat if any was represented by that penetration and 3) to attempt to counter or at least contain that threat.'[61]

While this new effort was a recognition that the New Left was not the same as the Security Service's old Communist foe, the assumption remained that the tactics of the two were similar, that they represented an organized, concerted, and persistent effort to 'penetrate' 'vital sectors' of Canadian society.

Although the three areas that made up the Key Sectors program were officially of equal importance, education was clearly foremost, since it produced individuals who migrated to the other two categories. The ambitious program involved the creation of a new centralized filing system in order to increase the awareness of current threats to security. Under the new arrangement, education files were divided by province. All Security Service files developed by Key Sectors in Alberta, for example, would be placed in 'Education–Alberta.' Major reports were then copied to 'Education–Canada–General.' Those employed in education who were deemed subversives had their files placed in 'Education–List of Persons Employed–Alberta.'

One of the first tasks of the Key Sectors program was to centralize files on alleged subversives working in education. Officially, students were excluded from the list because of their transient nature, but in practice, much to the annoyance of headquarters, that exclusion did not occur.[62] Key Sectors sought long-term institutional subversives, chiefly among the ranks of academics.

All divisions received instructions to compile lists of employees in all three categories who had had at some time a file opened on them by the force. Simply having a file was enough; no evidence that the person was using his or her position to advance a particular agenda was required. In the case of the government section, the list was to include individuals whom the government had hired despite an 'adverse' assessment given

by the Security Service. In the educational section, the criterion was
employees with active files. University and faculty directories served as a
useful guide for following employees from year to year. The lists were to
be comprehensive, although divisions in Ontario discarded the names of
janitors, carpenters, and those in similar occupations 'because of their
obvious lack of influence.'[63]

Under Key Sectors, the characteristics attributed to subversives were
expanded to include the categories 'CP of C member, suspected Trotskyist,
self-admitted marxist, black nationalist, student agitator, anarchist, red
power advocate, or an associate of communists.' Only those with permanent files were eligible for inclusion, and in their cases personal information, such as address and employment and subversive status, had to be
updated on an annual basis. Divisions then dispatched their lists to
headquarters in Ottawa, which quickly discovered that information on
several of the names was fifteen years out of date.[64]

The number of files on university-connected individuals grew under
Key Sectors beyond anything that had come before. In 1969, for example, the Security Service held active files on 357 individuals working in
Ontario alone. Manitoba, with roughly a tenth of its eastern neighbour's
population, had twenty-nine names.[65] The number of names of people,
all of which were deleted under Access to Information provisions, varied
at different universities depending on the size and nature of the institution. A small, conservative establishment like Waterloo Lutheran University (later Wilfrid Laurier University) did not have a single name on the
1969 list.[66] The University of Toronto occupied the opposite end of the
spectrum, and its list, organized by academic department, covered thirteen and a half pages. Even a lengthy document like this one involved
some narrowing down. The Toronto names did not include people with
only one reference, so that not all the faculty members who were involved in an organization like the Faculty Committee to End the War in
Vietnam ended up immortalized on the list, only those who 'displayed
more than a casual interest in the field.'[67]

The Key Sectors program differed from previous approaches in its
second goal, that of 'qualitative' analysis. This principle certainly applied
to individuals: 'One of the keys to the eventual success of this program is
the concept of character analysis or personality evaluation to be applied
particularly to persons like the "state of mind" Communist, the Marxist,
or the person whose stand and service to the Communist cause has
attracted our attention.'[68] Besides coordinating and consolidating files
and, in effect, creating a hierarchy of alleged subversives, Key Sectors

launched a campaign to recruit more informants in the three areas. One of the people heavily involved in the planning was Sub Inspector Donald Cobb, later to be charged and convicted for his role in authorizing the 1972 break-in against the Agence de Presse Libre du Québec. The operation for developing sources, he cautioned, would take three to four years; only then would a critical mass of informants be reached.[69]

It was not only the introduction of the Key Sectors program that represented at least a partial alteration by the countersubversion wing of the Security Service. By 1969 'D' Branch, or 'D' Ops as it would soon be called, sought to be more analytical about what had occurred and what was likely to occur in the future, in particular regarding organizations, institutions, and protests. The occupation of the administration building at Simon Fraser University in 1968 and a similar occupation of the administration building at Sir George Williams University in 1969, the latter ending in vandalism, pushed 'D' Ops in a new direction. Both had taken the Security Service by surprise and seemed to indicate the limitations of their intelligence-gathering methods. In response, it introduced a system to assess threats. Organizations and institutions were to be subjected to the same type of scrutiny that a Security Service member applied, for example, to a notice from *Here and Now*, a daily summary of events at the University of Toronto. Beside announcements for meetings of the Women's Liberation Movement and the New Left Caucus, he wrote: 'How many attended? What [decisions] were made? Were they considered? By whom? What effect? Assess threat? What consequence for us now? Future?' Next to an ad for 'Dial a Commie,' which consisted of a telephone number for a recording with information on protests and radical meetings, the unidentified Mountie scribbled: 'What response? What effect?'[70]

The occupations at the two universities in Burnaby and Montreal sparked the RCMP into action and heightened within it the sense of impending doom. Headquarters reminded its Security Service to turn over information on approaching demonstrations to the criminal side of the force and other police forces. In Saskatoon and Edmonton, the local Security Service offices reported on preparations by the city police forces for the eventuality of dealing with campus riots. There was even a fear for the safety of uniformed members conducting job fairs at universities: a warning went out to recruiters that they should consult with local security members before appearing on campus.[71]

Almost in military fashion, headquarters instructed divisions in May 1969 to monitor carefully the 'planning, organization, manifestation,

execution and effects of manifestations pertaining to the educational
sector.' The following questions were to be answered: the names of the
leading organizers and their capabilities, organizations expected to be
involved in unrest, at which educational institutions protests might occur, dominant issues, the nature of the protests, including whether they
might involve occupations or violence, any foreign influence connected
to the unrest, and, again in keeping with RCMP tradition, the public
response to previous protests.[72] 'F' Division in Saskatchewan, for instance, reported on the main currents of unrest at the province's two
main educational institutions, the University of Saskatchewan and Regina
College. It included a list of people, both students and faculty, and
organizations, such as the Students for a Democratic University, that
were likely to be the sources of disorder on campus. The section on the
more radical Regina campus contained assessments on individual
faculty members:

> [deleted: name]: The leading activist both as an organizer of students and
> the radical left faculty. Has a strong influence over both. His effectiveness
> would be overwhelming should an occasion arise.
> [deleted: name]: Close associate [deleted: name]. Considered that he will be
> a leading activist should trouble result. Will probably be effective with the
> radical left students.
> [deleted: name]: A leading figure in the New Left. Has influence over
> students as a lecturer and from living and social contact. Would probably
> have good effect over the radical left students.[73]

This pattern of investigations was consistent across the country. In Nova
Scotia the New Democratic Youth was submitted as the group most likely
to be involved in protests. From Halifax came a warning that Dalhousie
University, 'one of the most conservative universities in Canada,' might
face a 'militant occupation,' although no evidence of foreign influence
was discovered. For Ottawa-area universities, the politically explosive issues
that were cited were greater student representation in university decision-
making and issues surrounding the Vietnam War. As in Nova Scotia, the
role of non-Canadians was non-existent. The author of an assessment on
educational institutions in the Hamilton region threw in some sarcasm in
his assessment, predicting that the fall of 1969 would see 'the usual "peaceful" demonstrations.' He made special note of Mohawk College, where
nothing untoward was heard from the 'work oriented' students. In British
Columbia mention was made of activities, as expected, at Simon Fraser

University and the University of British Columbia, but the RCMP's concern extended to the colleges, in particular Vancouver City College and the College of New Caledonia in Prince George. The latter was scheduled to open in the fall of 1969 and it intended to employ Charles Boylan, a CPC member who was prominent in the party's campaign to attract more young people – and who was a Security Service target.

In Toronto the Security Service singled out about two hundred 'known activists,' as well as the '"hippie" element' in Yorkville, a centre of the counter-culture in the city, and many of those who resided at Rochdale, a communal apartment building. The policeman warned that at the University of Toronto 'the increasing lack of imposed discipline, the breakup in formalized educational structure with greater student participation cannot but help extend greater freedoms to the activists. This is true both in time to organize and in freedom of access to the general student body by the activists.'[74]

The new and improved analytical approach continued into 1970 and was increasingly directed at Canada's largest and most important higher educational institution, the University of Toronto. Reflecting the shift from the traditional threat of the machinations of Communists to the untraditional one of the New Left, the RCMP worried about the infiltration of existing institutions and organizations by radicals, including the 'highjacking' of student governments.[75]

Detailed analytical work required considerable time and effort. On 6 October 1970 Superintendent Murray Chisholm ordered the Research ('K') Branch to undertake a study of the University of Toronto Students' Administrative Council and, in the process, answer several questions:

(1) What is the designated role of the SAC (include terms of reference, if available).
(2) To what extent has the SAC been infiltrated by student radicals and subversives, potentially subversive individuals and/or organizations.
(3) To what extent, if any, has the SAC been manipulated as a result of the infiltration noted in (2) above (compare the support given to subversive or potentially subversive endeavours as opposed to non-subversive endeavours and determine if this support is in contradiction to the terms of reference indicated in (1) above. [deleted]
(4) The effect of the overall operation of the University resulting from SAC manipulation.

Chisholm wanted the material to be available for a broad report being prepared for the Joint Intelligence Committee, an interdepartmental group that dealt with intelligence matters, on security threats to Canada. It was to provide information that could be disseminated to other government departments. The task eventually fell into the lap of Sergeant Don Roller, who had been in the Security Service since 1959. He represented the transformation that had occurred within the Security Service in the 1960s and the reality that higher education was helping with the development of more accomplished police officers who, in turn, could direct their new analytical skills at university-related targets. While stationed with the Security Service in Vancouver in the 1960s, Roller had taken night classes, and then he had become a full-time student, graduating, as many did, with a Bachelor of Arts in political science. In October 1970 he found himself with the task of writing a report about the central student government body at the University of Toronto. After perusing the existing files, Roller requested six weeks to produce a first draft. Ken Green, a civilian holdover from the days of Mark McClung and head of the Research Branch, gave him a deadline of 18 December 1970.[76]

What Roller produced would become the model for the RCMP approach to universities in the 1970s. A lengthy report, it included a table of contents and a list of sources, and it offered predictions of the future climate at the University of Toronto. It also provided brief comments about a wide range of campus groups, including the Edmund Burke Society, a far-right campus organization started in 1967 by University of Toronto student Paul Fromm.[77]

In the end, Roller's document downplayed the threat of 'subversive penetration' by the Students' Administrative Council, pointing out the trend, as witnessed and reported upon elsewhere by the end of the 1960s, of a fracturing of the radical left. He raised the cyclical nature to SAC's radicalism – it was strongly dependent on election results, which revolved around the atmosphere on campus at the time of the vote.[78]

By 1970 the contrast between the university environment the force monitored and analyzed with the one that had existed a decade earlier could not have been more stark. The earlier period seemed almost quaint, as Mounties chased down 'Reds' in a largely homogenous campus scene. A day in September 1970 demonstrated the extent of the change. A plainclothes policeman attended, at the start of term, 'Day One of the New University of Toronto' and gathered pamphlets from a wide variety of groups. Apparently unsure of what the top threat to society would be, his collection included material from a gay rights group, the Varsity Christian Fellowship, and the Campus Crusade for Christ.[79]

A. Bowen Perry, commissioner of the Mounted Police from 1900 to 1923 and the father of the Mounties' intelligence role.

The Annual
Bolshewheatie
Parade

is scheduled to march as soon as your new wheat sprouts. The tender green shoots of growing grain will be at the mercy of this horde of hungry raiders—unless you break up the march with GOPHERCIDE.

NOW is the time to rid your fields of Gophers; before the new wheat comes up; before any damage can be done.

Gophercide

Gets the Gophers Every Time

GOPHERCIDE is Strychnine, without strychnine's bitter taste. It is strychnine that dissolves in warm water without the use of acids or vinegar. In other words, GOPHERCIDE has all the deadliness of strychnine, without any of the disadvantages of ordinary strychnine.

A package of GOPHERCIDE, dissolved in half a gallon of warm water, will poison a gallon of wheat; this wheat will kill about 400 gophers, because gophers like the taste of it and will eat it eagerly.

Go after the Gophers NOW. Get GOPHERCIDE—soak the wheat in it and sprinkle the poisoned grain in and around the holes. Never mind the weather: rain doesn't affect GOPHERCIDE.

National Drug and Chemical Company of Canada, Limited

MONTREAL, WINNIPEG, REGINA, SASKATOON, CALGARY, EDMONTON, NELSON, VANCOUVER, VICTORIA and EASTERN BRANCHES.

Chemical Analysis of Manufactured Poisons reported by Andrews and Cruickshank, analytical and consulting chemists to the Deputy Minister of Agriculture, Regina, showed Gophercide contains ten times the quantity of Strychnine of all other preparations examined.

Subversion invades advertising: a 1920 advertisement for gopher poison.

This February 1936 cartoon from the University of Saskatchewan student newspaper, *The Sheaf*, triggered a police investigation of the newspaper. The dangling figure in the drawing is Mountie John Leopold.

S.T. Wood, commissioner of the RCMP from 1938 to 1951.

"O" Div. Ref. ███████ (C.P. Activity in the Universit
of Toronto - Toronto, Ont.)

To - N.C.O. I/C Hamilton Det.
FORWARDED, for your information.

███████ Your attention is directed to ███████
of para. 4. Is anything known of Prof. Herbert
NORMAN at Hamilton? It would seem as though there
were some substantial reason to account for his reluctance to return to McMaster. You will note
also that members of his family are alleged to
belong to the intellectual group of the Party.

3.   Will you please make discreet enquiries
regarding Prof. NORMAN'S record at McMaster
and you will appreciate, of course, that it is
imperative that any enquiries made should be made
to appear as purely impersonal as it is not desired
that our interest in the professor's activities be
disclosed.

4.   Similar enquiries should be made regarding the activities of members of his family.

                    (F. W. Schutz) Inspr.,
Toronto   I/C C.I.B.
21-2-40
MB/WB.

D.D. 16-3-40.

The Commissioner:
         FORWARDED, for your information.

2.   Please note S/Cst. Black's remarks in
para. 5 herein.

3.   You will note also in para. 6 of the
report ███████ Sam LEVINE ███████
███████ C.P. according to Prof. Louden. Please refer
in this connection to file re: "Sam LEVINE,"
"O" Div. T945-1/2. H.Q. D.945-3-E.12 ███████

4.   Further report will be submitted as
per diary date above.

                    (V.A.M. Kemp) Supt.,
Toronto ███████   Comdg. "O" Div.
21-2-40
MB/WB.   26-2-40

An RCMP document pertaining to Samuel Levine that was marked up under
the Access to Information Act.

ROYAL CANADIAN MOUNTED POLICE
Intelligence Br. Toronto.

Ref. No.

Place. Toronto, Ont.

Date. August 13, 19

Personal History File

Re: Professor Frank H. UNDERHILL,

University of Toronto, Toronto, Ont.

Name—   Frank H. UNDERHILL,

Alias—   none known.

Nationality—   Canadian born.

If naturalized—   not applicable.

When and how arrived in Canada—   Canadian born.

DESCRIPTION—
Age—	48 yrs.
Weight—	130 lbs.
Height—	5 ft. 2 in.
Build—	slim.
Colour of hair—	bald - very fair hair at sides.
Colour of eyes—	blue.
Glasses (if worn)—	nd.
Complexion—	fair.
Hair on face—	clean shaven.
Teeth—	good.
Nose—	regular.
Deformities—	nil.
Marks—	nil.
Peculiarities—	looks down when talking; very high white forehead.
Usual dress—	inconspicuously, but neatly.

Manner—   Gentlemanly and polite.

Habits: (smokes, drinks, gambles, etc.,)—   smokes cigarettes and pipe. Drinks moderately.

Speech—   good English.

Languages spoken—   English and some French.

Photo—   nil.

Married or single—   Married, wife Canadian works at St. George's Children' school.

Family—   nil.

Home address—

Present address—   449 Walmer Road, Toronto, Ont. phone MI 6185.

Former address—

Historian Frank Underhill's 1940 RCMP Personal History File.

Senior members of the RCMP's intelligence operations at a 1944 conference in Ottawa. Then Commissioner S.T. Wood is in the first row sixth from the left. Two future commissioners, Cliff Harvison and George McClellan, are side by side in the middle of the second row starting fourth from the left. Intelligence officer John Leopold reveals his shortcomings at the right end of the middle row.

Crowd gathered in front of the Montreal courthouse where the Soviet spy ring trials occurred, March 1946.

RCMP Inspector Terry Guernsey, who played an important role in the evolution of the Security Service.

TRAINING

Recruits are posted to a Training Division, either at Regina, Saskatchewan or Rockcliffe, Ontario, where they undergo an extensive course of study which lasts for not less than eight months. The course is divided into two parts with examinations at the end of each. Instructions are given in Law, investigation methods, report writing, typing, swimming, first aid, and many other subjects considered necessary to fit a man for a career in the Force. Mounted drill and equitation (care and management of horses), also forms part of a recruit's curriculum.

When posted to Divisions in the field recruits are placed under the supervision of experienced Officers and N.C.O.'s until such time as they have gained sufficient experience and practical knowledge to work by themselves. Many years of experience is required before a member can be termed an efficient policeman.

ITEMS OF INTEREST

The initial period of enlistment is for FIVE years, the first year of which is probationary. Upon completion of the first term of service a member may re-enlist for a further period of from one to five years at a time, with the Commissioner's approval.

Members are not permitted to marry until they have served for 5 years and are 23 years of age. They must have cash or convertible assets in the amount of $1,200 at the time of applying for permission to marry.

While in training a deduction of $1.70 per day is made from a recruit's salary for board and room. Thereafter, where meals and board are provided, the deduction is 40c each meal and 50c a day for lodging.

Married members, not residing in Government owned or rented quarters, receive a Married Accommodation Allowance of $25.00 per month.

BASIC QUALIFICATIONS

Applicants must comply with the following:

Single;

British subject or Canadian Citizen, resident in Canada;

Between 18 and 30 years of age;

Grade 8 education. (Grade 10 or higher preferred);

Height not less than 5' 8" and not more than 6' 5" in bare feet;

Maximum weight allowances:
5' 8" to 5'10" — 185 lbs.
5'10" to 6' — 200 lbs.
6' to 6'5" — 210 lbs.

Chest measurements at full inspiration and expiration must total 70", with a minimum expansion of 2 inches;

Physically fit with good muscular development;

Exemplary character;

Speak, read and write either the English or French language.

Edmond Cloutier, C.M.G., O.A., D.S.P.
Queen's Printer and Controller of Stationery
Ottawa, 1958

Serve Canada
WITH THE
ROYAL CANADIAN MOUNTED POLICE

THE ROYAL CANADIAN MOUNTED POLICE | MAKE YOUR CAREER IN THE R.C.M.P.

1958 RCMP recruitment brochure.

Combined Universities Campaign for Nuclear Disarmament protest march in
Ottawa, December 1959.

Combined Universities Campaign for Nuclear Disarmament members on Parliament Hill on the 1961 Thanksgiving weekend. This photograph was taken by an RCMP informant operating out of Université Laval. His shadow is visible at the bottom of the page. The RCMP added the number and letter for identification purposes.

Another Mounted Police informant photograph of Combined Universities Campaign for Nuclear Disarmament demonstrators in Ottawa, Thanksgiving 1961. Again, the RCMP added numbers for identification purposes.

André Marsan of the Security Service with a camera around his neck is featured
on the front page of a Quebec newspaper in November 1963 after the federal
government denied the RCMP took photos at peace rallies.

THE CLASS OF 1984

Duncan Macpherson's 7 December 1962 *Toronto Star* cartoon during the height of the controversy over Mounted Police security investigations on campus.

Cartoon mocking the RCMP from the Carleton University student newspaper,
25 January 1963.

1965 student protest outside the United States consulate in Montreal.

C 237
REV. 1-4-66

1098

OTHER FILE REFERENCES: REF. AUTRES DOSSIERS:	DIVISION "O"	DATE 28 Oct 68	RCMP FILE REFERENCES: REF. DOSSIERS GRC:
	SUB-DIVISION - SOUS-DIVISION		
	DETACHMENT-DÉTACHEMENT Toronto S.I.B.		

RE:
OBJET:

Daniel Jeffrey GOLDSTICK
Toronto, Ontario.

JDL.
Sgt.

INFORMATION

1.   On 6 Oct 68 Danny GOLDSTICK was photographed as he left the Central Committee Plenum in Toronto.

2.   The following amendments are submitted for Forms C215:

QUE. 3:   ADD: (TO) Sept., 1968
            ADD: 43 MacKenzie Ave., Toronto, Ontario - Sept., 1968
QUE. 4:   ADD: University of Toronto - Toronto - Philosophy
            Professor - Sept., 1968.
QUE. 16:   DELETE: 1962
            ADD: 1968

INVESTIGATOR'S COMMENTS

3.   Prints of the subject's most recent photograph are attached. The negative is being retained on reel at this point.

S.U.I.

D.D. 15-7-69

The Commissioner, Ottawa

        Information believed true.

2.   Please find two photos attached.

3.   The necessary amendments have been made to our copy of the subject's Form C-215.

S.U.I.

TORONTO
31-10-68

C. S. Hogg
(C.S. Hogg) Supt.
Officer i/c. S.I.B.

Reviewed

NOV 20 1968

S - I RECORDS.

NOV 4 1968

12.11.6

RCMP report from 1968 describing surveillance of Professor Daniel Goldstick.

CEGEP student protest march in Montreal, 1968.

Student occupation of the University of British Columbia faculty club,
25 October 1968.

An RCMP surveillance photograph of Mario Bachand, March 1969.

Jean-Pierre Goyer, whose directives while solicitor general had a major impact on RCMP campus investigations.

THE NEW LEFT

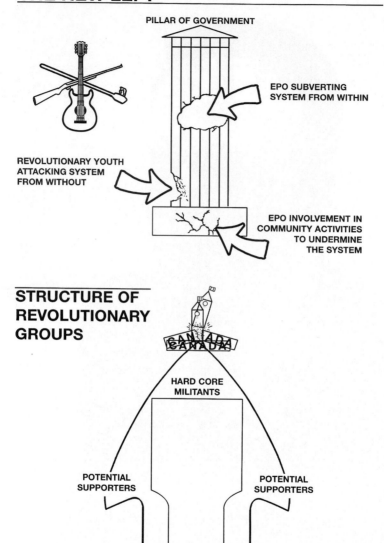

Slides from a September 1971 RCMP presentation on security threats to Canada given to Pierre Trudeau and senior cabinet ministers and bureaucrats.

TRIBULATIONS OF THE GENERATION GAP

New recruit : Peace, man ... like which of you cats do I rap with?

Drill Corporal : There there, Sergeant Major, take it easy. It must be a prairie heat mirage. Let's keep our cool and it'll go away.

Cartoon from the RCMP Quarterly (January 1972) poking fun at the generational gap within the force. Increasing numbers of Mounties began attending universities in the 1960s and 1970s.

John Starnes, (left) head of the Security Service from 1970 to 1973, with Maurice Nadon, former RCMP commissioner, at the Keable Commission hearings, 1978.

John Starnes, a civilian appointed director-general of the Security Service by Prime Minister Pierre Trudeau in the fall of 1969, was well aware that a different game was afoot. In July 1970 the Interdepartmental Committee on Law and Order met to discuss the future. In a lengthy letter to the committee, later hailed by Trudeau as a 'damn good piece of work,' Starnes offered a dire portrait of what was to come, especially from increasingly discontented young people.[80] Citing the example of student protests in France in May 1968, he warned that the problem was not that most students were radicalized or even disillusioned, but instead that they were apathetic. The impressionable and passive student of old remained, albeit in a more indifferent mode:

> The real revolutionaries amongst them are tiny minorities and would quickly find themselves isolated if they were unable to win the support of the less severely disaffected on particular issues. There seems to be a real danger that hard-core revolutionaries increasingly can win support from a larger body of disaffected Canadians and create conditions of anarchy and violence in many parts of the country. Their strategy appears to be to promote direct confrontation with authority in any form over issues generally formulated in the shape of unreasonable demands in order to trick authority into using force against them. The use of force is represented as oppression and large numbers of the confused and mildly disaffected are won over to sympathy with the revolutionaries.

The solution, he added, came not just from the police, but also from the wider society where reforms were needed to win over youth.[81] The events on Canadian campuses between 1968 and 1970 inspired Starnes's worried analysis. American-style protest had apparently arrived in Canada.

7

The Crisis Years, 1968–1970

For the Montreal office of the RCMP Security Service, Christmas 1970 arrived four days late. It came in the form of a rather pleasant gift: the 958-page student directory of the Université de Montréal, containing personal information – address, telephone number, citizenship, the type of degree being sought, and other details – on 16,000 students. Unlike most Christmas gifts, this one had to be returned to its 'originator,' a person with access to sensitive material at the university. The Mounties were not left empty-handed, however. They microfilmed the directory and kept a copy at headquarters as a reference tool.[1]

Campus events after 1968 explain why the Security Service reached the point where it was microfilming student records over the Christmas break. Elements of the New Left seemed to hold sway at many universities and in the nation's main student organization and university press service. The Black Power movement had arrived in Canada and its advocates were linked to a major act of vandalism at Sir George Williams University that shocked Canada. The possibility of a 'Red Power' movement sparked typewriters at RCMP offices into action. Most significant of all, Quebec had apparently narrowly escaped a complete meltdown into anarchy in October 1970. The variety of new threats represented a period of crisis for both Canada and the Security Service, out of which each would emerge partially transformed. In the case of the Security Service, by the end of the 1960s there finally was recognition that the turmoil of the period was not the responsibility of the Communist Party of Canada. Nonetheless, the police blamed the problems on outsiders and chose to believe that the tactics and goals of these new radicals, be they Aboriginal activists or Quebec separatists, were the same as those of Communists, who still remained a threat to security.

Circumstances in the United States loomed in the background of campus disturbances in Canada. Nearly three weeks after an assassin's bullet ended the life of Martin Luther King Jr in April 1968, Columbia University students, under the banner of the Students for a Democratic Society, occupied several university buildings to protest the construction of a gymnasium in a New York City park and the university's involvement in research for Vietnam War–related industries. Among the spaces taken over by the occupiers was the office of the university president, where they helped themselves to his cigars and liquor. The audacity of the protest shocked the American elite. J. Edgar Hoover, angered by the flouting of authority, ordered the FBI's Counter Intelligence Program to attack the New Left. The New York Police, with little sympathy for the students, concluded the peaceful occupation after eight days, arresting nearly 700 people and injuring 100, including some faculty members who intervened to stop the brutality. The students left in their wake only minor acts of vandalism.[2]

The example had been set, however. A similar occupation occurred at Simon Fraser University later the same year. There was some irony that it should be the site of the beginning of this period of turmoil in institutions of higher education in Canada. One of Canada's newest universities, it was a symbol of Canada's burgeoning post–Second World War affluence. The university, which one Mountie called the most 'far out' in Canada, had been the subject of Security Service attention since shortly after it opened in 1965. The RCMP's specialist on the Burnaby institution was Corporal W.G. Rohr, who through the use of human and other sources gathered intelligence on the activities of those who were deemed subversive at the university.[3] It was certainly a different form of radicalism than any the force had ever before encountered. Protests over the construction of a gasoline station on the campus, the passing of a motion to rename the institution Louis Riel University, and a call to change the name of the highway adjacent to the university to Ho Chi Minh Trail, all ended up as clippings or reports in the institution's burgeoning file. Other events, such as an attempt to unionize teaching assistants, graduate students, and faculty in 1967, were spied on by undercover Mounties and informants.[4]

The Mounties did not believe that it was just the presence of 'radicals' that fostered an environment of protest. 'New and liberal approaches to the teaching concept,' such as tutorials, encouraged the 'radical penetration' of Simon Fraser University. Marxist faculty members sought to have more like themselves hired, the Security Service warned in a June

1968 report that later served as a brief sent to a variety of government departments and to the attorney general of British Columbia. They controlled faculty hirings, recruited like-minded graduate students, and brought in friendly speakers. The hotbed of radicals was the Political Science, Sociology, and Anthropology Department, or PSA for short; the police had active files on half of its faculty members.[5]

As usual, the word from the field emphasized the 'foreign' content involved in the radical scene at the university, which convinced one important government official of the need for action. On 12 August 1968 Art Butroid, a civil servant in the Department of Manpower and Immigration, contacted the Security Service to express his concern about academics from abroad who 'are offered employment at Simon Fraser University and are later adversely reported on.' He asked for a special paper on subversive activity at the university in order 'to strengthen an individual case when we seek Ministerial approval to refuse undesirable persons seeking entry to Canada or applying for landed status.' After receiving an analysis from the RCMP, he wrote back to praise it, adding that it had inspired a memorandum advocating a tightening of the policy allowing academics and students into Canada before a thorough security screening had occurred. This pleased senior Mounties. 'It is to be hoped that Art Butroid's concern will have it's [sic] effect higher up!' wrote Assistant Director of Security Intelligence J.M. Barrette. In the 1970s the Canadian government succeeded in restricting the entrance from abroad of several academics with reputations as radicals.[6]

The situation at Simon Fraser University became increasingly serious in the fall of 1968. On 21 November dozens of students occupied the administration building.[7] This unexpected move triggered frantic messages from officers in British Columbia to headquarters in Ottawa. The type of tactics employed, on the other hand, did not surprise the police. Mounties had already met with Simon Fraser University president Kenneth Strand to discuss methods for ensuring the safety of university records. Later, they were perturbed to learn that the university had adopted none of the safety measures that had been considered.[8]

When the occupation was underway, both the security and criminal sides of the RCMP at Burnaby, which had the RCMP as its city force, kept in close communication with Strand. Over a hundred Mounties readied themselves to storm the administration building, an option that seemed increasingly inevitable by the second day of the occupation, after Strand indicated that he would not negotiate with the occupiers. At a meeting with the police authorities, he requested that the building be cleared unless students left of their own accord, and the force opted for 3 the next morning, on the 22nd, as the opportune time. Then the president changed his mind. All the while the troops waited.[9]

Eventually Strand again supplied the green light for ending the occupation but the attorney general of British Columbia intervened to suggest that every possible alternative, including suspending the students, be taken before proceeding with the use of force. Strand, however, said that he could not count on the support of the university senate. Thus the RCMP prepared to act in the early morning hours of 23 November. Using building plans, a strategy was drawn up in preparation for moving units into place to take back the building. Water and telephone lines were cut. The Burnaby Fire Department brought in equipment to deal with emergencies. At 2:25 a.m. Kenneth Strand, his voice crackling through a bullhorn, told the occupiers they had thirty minutes to leave the building or face arrest and forcible removal.

When the deadline arrived, some of occupiers exited and were photographed by the RCMP Identification Section. One of the first to exit, an officer carefully noted, was Martin Loney, the president of the student council and the person considered to be the top student radical on campus. When it was clear that all those who were going to leave voluntarily had done so, members of the Burnaby RCMP detachment, who had been ordered by their commander to remove side arms, batons, and other weapons and to put on cloth caps and belts, went in. The well-planned operation proved a strong contrast to the mayhem at Columbia: 114 occupiers were arrested and the invasion ended peacefully.[10]

Despite its non-violent conclusion, the attack on authority and the apparent application of American-style tactics placed the affair in a unique police category. Accustomed to students who were apparently passive, the force now encountered a group who behaved in a disrespectful and apparently anarchic fashion. Although rather tame when placed in a broader historical context, the occupation was, at the time, considered to be anything but. Two former Mounties, one of whom had been involved with 'E' Division, remembered it as a 'riot.'[11]

A broader cultural divide was at work when it came to relations between the police and universities. As always, it was about educational levels and social class. However, the differences extended to a fundamental clash of cultures. Mounted policemen served in a hierarchical institution in which discipline was the ultimate ideal. Even plain-clothes members had their appearance governed by strict dress codes, although those who were undercover were allowed to wear casual clothes. The only appropriate facial hair was a moustache. Clearly, there was a degree of envy in the derogatory comments made by individual policeman about the appearance and actions of students. Students enjoyed a freedom in their lifestyles that Mounties could never enjoy. Members of the force who attended universities in the 1960s and 1970s noticed the difference. One felt as if he had had 'scabs' removed from his eyes. Another was struck by the freewheeling environment that university students enjoyed.[12]

The RCMP retained an interest in Simon Fraser University after the conclusion of the occupation, especially when tensions escalated again in 1969 over an effort by the PSA Department to make its administration more egalitarian. Eventually nine members of the department were suspended, some had their jobs terminated, and the department was broken up. The tough line pleased the RCMP, which continued to follow the situation, going so far as to record carefully the names of outside faculty members who wrote letters to the campus newspaper in support of the PSA members.[13]

While the Simon Fraser University occupation represented a turning point for university protest in Canada, circumstances in February 1969 at Sir George Williams University in Montreal suggested that a new era had arrived. The university, later to merge with Loyola College to form Concordia University, had for some time its share of problems, many of them connected to issues of race. Many students from Caribbean nations studied at Sir George in this era of heightened awareness of racism because of the civil rights campaign in the United States. The issue in January 1969 was a charge of racism that was made by a student against a member of the Biology Department. After considerable pressure over a number of months, the university administration finally agreed to a special hearing on the matter. Before the meeting could begin on 29 January, a large number of students, many of them angered by what they interpreted as an administrative cover-up of the actions of a racist professor, disrupted it, and then proceeded to occupy the faculty club and the university's computer centre.[14] They remained there until 11 February, when a rumour of an impending police intervention spread. The rumour became a self-fulfilling prophecy when students began vandalizing a cafeteria, causing the Montreal police to intercede. Those occupying the computer centre proceeded to throw computer records out of windows and someone started a fire. By the time police cleared the building and arrested ninety-one people (in one of its reports on the destruction of the computer centre the force did a careful breakdown of those arrested by race, origin, age, and gender), close to $2 million in damage had been done.

As was the case at Simon Fraser University, the RCMP had no advance knowledge, but it did have someone on the ground when the occupation occurred. It is not known who the informant was, but he or she was allowed to enter the Computer Centre, a privilege that the anonymous individual noted was accorded only to Blacks and to Whites who were 'extreme radicals.' The source supplied general information and even relayed an overheard conversation. Inspector Donald Cobb was pleased with the result and asked permission from headquarters in Ottawa to use Mounties who were students in this fashion.[15]

In general, however, the RCMP's intelligence about events at Sir George Williams University was poor because of a combination of factors: the restrictions on carrying out activities on campuses, specifically the recruitment of sources; a fear of having the activities at universities exposed in the media; and the predominance of Whites in the force, which made the investigation of Black student groups difficult. The latter factor led the Security Service to borrow an informer, Warren Hart, an African American, from the FBI.[16] Until his arrival at Sir George Williams University, the RCMP had had to rely on information from only the one source, whose view of the occupation reinforced its view of student radicalism in the 1960s: 'The end result of mass student unrest and agitation will terminate in a communist dictatorship of the proletariat that will be more fascist than even that of the Nazi regime in Germany during World War II. [deleted] the infiltration of Sir George Williams is pre-planned and is an example of what is happening in Universities throughout North America.'[17]

The vandalism of the computer centre was to prove useful to the authorities for dealing with student radicalism. It, like the occupation in British Columbia, shocked many Canadians and drove politicians to demand in the House of Commons that those who were arrested and who did not have Canadian citizenship be summarily deported. It also led to calls on the government of Pierre Trudeau to investigate the causes of the problems of Sir George Williams University and of the unrest in general. The prime minister, apparently with his fingers crossed, replied that such a study was not within federal jurisdiction.[18] For the RCMP and others, the mayhem in Montreal confirmed that radicals did indeed pose a threat to the Canadian system; it was also another tool in the force's campaign to have the government change the rules governing security investigations on campuses.

However, there was another aspect to what happened in Montreal and Burnaby that troubled the RCMP and that skewed its perception of the nature of campus unrest. It saw a conspiracy in the connections that existed between the occupations and American radicals. Mark Rudd, the leader of the occupation at Columbia, and Jerry Rubin, one of the 'Chicago Seven,' had both visited the University of British Columbia in the weeks preceding the occupation at its neighbours. Rubin, who was closely followed by three Mounties, even led an occupation of the UBC faculty club.[19] The RCMP warned the federal cabinet of collusion between 'activists [at Simon Fraser University] and unidentified individuals in Chicago,' leading to the 'coordination of campus unrest on a North American scale.'[20]

Sir George Williams University, and the spectre of Black nationalism that it raised, presented the most troubling example of all to the force of the possibility of growing American influence on Canadian radicalism. According to the final report of the McDonald Commission, the Security Service did not take an interest in 'racial groups' until June 1969, when Commissioner Leonard Higgitt warned the federal government that American militants were sneaking across the border and helping to establish urban guerrilla camps.[21] In fact, several reports and investigations on the topic had been filed months before the incidents in Montreal. In early October 1968 the Security Service at 'C' Division reported on a upcoming conference, sponsored by the Sir George Williams University Caribbean Society, of Montreal-area Black organizations. A suggestion was made, although not acted upon, to approach a Department of Labour employee who was scheduled to speak at the conference to obtain information on 'Black Power elements' in attendance.[22] Two months later, at the University of Manitoba, an RCMP officer attended a lecture by Paul Boutelle, a follower of Malcolm X and a member of the Socialist Workers Party. Boutelle's talk was, noted the police reporter, 'as expected, very critical of our present system of Government and favourable towards the Socialist philosophy.'[23] Also spied on, because of the involvement of 'Black Power activists,' were a rally and a teach-in at Dalhousie University and at St Francis Xavier University respectively.'[24]

On the day the occupation at Sir George Williams University began, the Montreal office of the Security Service, under the leadership of Donald Cobb, began forwarding information to Ottawa about the alleged involvement there of the Black Power movement. The following excerpts from a lengthy report represented for headquarters the first detailed look at this apparently new phenomenon. The attitudes expressed in the memorandum reflect a narrow interpretation of a broader social movement, a certain amount of racial stereotyping, and fear, insecurity, and paranoia about the changing nature of protest.

General Conditions and Subversive Activities amongst Negroes – Province of Quebec

1. The term 'Black Power' has appeared to a number of people as being an organization of Negroes bent on determining for themselves a new society within the world. 'Black Power' is a motto, constituting the entire movement, radical and non-radical, militant and non-violent. 'Black Power' pertains to the entire Negroe [sic] situation. It is an attempt through varying methods to introduce the Negroe people to their identity. The means of attaining these goals are of interest to us and the following is intended to briefly outline the subversive elements within the Black movement.

2. The current situation amongst Blacks in this area has gained in momentum and popularity during last year. Militancy appears to be the vogue to both White and Black radicals alike. In response to the militant policies as set out by the Black Power advocates it is attracting a large number of followers. The exponents of violence find a great deal of freedom of expression in this country and as such many are being attracted here. Perhaps the key factor in the Black Power movement in Montreal is the Universities and predominant among them is Sir George Williams University ...

University

11. Sir George Williams University as stated before is at present the key point in the militant attitudes. The Caribbean Student Society of this University was during the early part of the present semester the main body of militant and radical Negroes at this College. This society has since been relegated to a social organ although it still retains its militant membership ...

12. At present the key body at the University is the Black Students' Association [deleted: file number]. There are a number of minor persons who appear to have adopted militant attitudes [deleted: names].

13. The Black Student Association has organized a Black Studies program in an attempt to educate Black students with their heritage. The program is extremely similar to that as commenced at Berkeley University under the direction of Eldridge CLEAVER [deleted: D-935 file number]. This union in the past has been extremely active in student strikes and violence at Universities in the United States. Black students and Black professors at Sir George who are of a militant mind have been noted at demonstrations in this area.

14. At this time it is felt that it should be definitely stated that the Black

Panther Party [deleted: file number] here in Montreal is quite powerful. It is believed that they are the guiding light for the militants and have direct connections with the United States. It is also felt that the Black Panther Party has a tie with other violent groups especially in the separatist field. Again it should be pointed out that this organization is able to find its greatest following at Sir George Williams University [deleted: D-909-3-D file number].

15. The militants at Sir George Williams University have adopted shock troop tactics and have put them to extremely good use. The use of gross obscenities, mockery and insults are the main instruments with which they attempt to force White persons to commit acts or say something that might be construed as Racist. They appeal to other University students in speeches by adopting methods used by Eldridge CLEAVER.

16. The Black Student Union is believed to be organized by the militants in conjunction with present student movements as organized by the Internationalists [deleted: file number]. The Black Student Union has become strong in a number of Universities in the United States and has found support in the Third World Liberation Front [deleted: file number]. The Internationalists have supported the militant Blacks in all moves at Sir George Williams University and it is believed that the Black Student Union and the Black Panther Party are strongly influenced and activated by the Internationalists. It is believed that the principles of both factions appeal to one another. It is also believed that during 1969, demonstrations, student strikes and the possibility of riots will occur under prompting of the Internationalists action in accordance with the Black militants.

17. Although there are fairly recent organizations on the subversive scene in this area, the militant Black Power advocates and the Internationalists are indeed the most active. Their effect is being felt throughout the Canadian Universities and unfortunately their popularity is growing steadily at an amazing rate. It is my firm belief that the Internationalists and ... the Black Power organs ... constitute an extreme threat to the national security and their influence in our educational institutions is presently being felt with strong consequences. If able to break down the educational area of our society within the following generation the Nation's Government could be destroyed [deleted]. It is anticipated that in 1969, the organizations noted in this report will gain movement and power, increasing their areas of concentration. The present situation at Sir George Williams University as reported on file [deleted: number] is a valid indication of progress within the Black Power movement. Similar radical incidents are expected in the future.[25]

Greater attention was paid towards manifestations of Black Power after the Montreal occupation. When one of the occupation's leaders, Rosie Douglas, spoke at the University of Calgary, he began, according to the Mountie in attendance, by asking if any members of the RCMP or CIA were present. The Kitchener unit of the Security Service informed headquarters in March 1969 of the creation of a West Indian Club at the University of Guelph. Engaging in the stereotype of the 'militant Black,' the recorder noted that the new club had a 'potential coloured member-ship of 107,' because that was 'the number of coloured students attending the University of Guelph.' A list of leading University of Guelph Black 'militants' was helpfully included in the dispatch.[26]

The definition of Black Power that was employed often appeared rather free and loose and took in any expression of a desire to address racism in Canadian society. The efforts of Owen Ball, a Black student at the University of Windsor, represented one such example. Ball had published several stories in the campus newspaper on problems related to racial prejudice in Canadian society, and it was duly noted in July 1969 by the local RCMP contingent, which also pledged to continue investigating his efforts. Another target at the University of Windsor was Howard McCurdy, a professor of biology and later (1967–8) president of CAUT and a federal NDP member of Parliament. He had first come to the attention of the Security Service in 1966 when he was nominated to a provincial academic body. An informant linked McCurdy with CAUT and with 'a Negro Windsor group interested in Civil Rights' that had two Communists in attendance at one of its meetings. As part of their investigative fishing expedition on McCurdy, the police paid attention to the fact that he had chaired a federation of Canadian Black organizations, was involved with CAUT, and had made an address at Sir George Williams University sponsored by the Caribbean Students' Society.'[27]

The concern about McCurdy's activities could not compare to how the police felt about the Black Panther Party. In November 1969 three of its members, including Fred Hampton, who less than three weeks later would be shot to death in his bed by Chicago city police, came to Canada to speak to students at the University of Alberta and the Saskatoon and Regina campuses of the University of Saskatchewan. Mounties secretly shadowed every stage of their visit. The telephone numbers the men called were obtained from the telephone company and an undercover member of the Mounted Police who wore a body pack recorded the speeches they made 'for seditious purposes' at the Regina Educational Auditorium and the Regina Labour Temple. The recording was part of a scheme to find a justification for deporting the men that failed. Nevertheless, it was while they were in Regina that the Security Service discovered from a casual source that two of the Black Panthers were travelling under false names. The RCMP in Regina quickly telexed this information to their colleagues in Edmonton, where the Panthers had gone; they were quickly expelled from Canada.[28]

The fear of Black Power was based to some extent on real and imagined links between the Black Panthers and Quebec separatists. The RCMP barn-burning incident in the 1970s that became a source of embarrassment for the force was an attempt to prevent a meeting between members of the Front de Libération du Québec and the Black Panther Party.[29] There was, however, another connection at the time that equally worried the Mounted Police. This one was between proponents of Black Power in Canada and the United States and Native Indian advocates of Red Power. As in the case of Black Power, the force was especially concerned about concatenation between organizations such as the American Indian Movement in the United States and sympathetic groups in Canada. Assistant Commissioner William Kelly articulated these fears before the House of Commons Justice Committee in May 1969. After being asked for evidence about links between the groups, Kelly admitted: 'We have a feeling but no particular proof.'[30] According to the final report of the McDonald Commission, the RCMP did not take an interest in Red Power until 1973,[31] but this timeline is four years too late. The interest of the Security Service in Red Power and Native activists began in 1969. As happened with Black Power, a lengthy memorandum that occasionally invoked stereotypes was prepared, and it was based in part on information supplied by a senior Mountie who had attended a human rights conference where Aboriginal rights had been discussed:

In recent months we have been faced with growing unrest amongst the Canadian Indian and Metis population across Canada. In an age of revolutionary change, public attention has been focused on the plight of our native Indian population. With the drastic civil rights turmoil amongst the negro population in the United States and with similar unrest in other parts of the world, Canadian Indians have come to realize that aside from achieving equal rights and better living conditions through established Canadian Government Departments and agencies, other avenues such as pressure groups and demonstrations, both violent and non-violent, have proven more successful in forcing a change in government policies.

2. Early in 1953 our attention was drawn to the formation of a new provincial political party in British Columbia ... the Indian Independent Party ... [deleted] ...

5. [deleted: name] while addressing a Saskatchewan provincial committee meeting of the Communist Party of Canada pointed out that the Indian population is beginning to organize and protest against their inequalities. He states that the Indian problem must receive support and action by the Communist Party. He disclosed that contact had been made with an Indian representative ... The militant Students for a Democratic University (SDU) at the University of Alberta immediately passed a resolution to investigate the case and a fund raising campaign on campus was set up for their defence ... Representation has also been made to start a defence fund at the University of British Columbia ...

22. In December 1968 it was learned that Dr. Howard [deleted: *Adams*], previously mentioned, is attempting to form a new organization amongst the Metis and Indians of Saskatchewan fashioned after the B.P.P. [Black Panther Party] in the U.S. [deleted: Adams has] already been successful in organizing an association or group amongst Indian high school students in Saskatoon ... He hopes to influence the adult Indian population through the youth and according to him he already has the students aroused and they are preparing to take 'explosive action' ...

36. On December 1st, 2nd and 3rd, 1968 Supt. G.C. CUNNINGHAM represented our Force at an International Year for Human Rights conference held in Ottawa where he sat in on a seminar on 'Aboriginal Rights.' As pointed out by Supt. CUNNINGHAM in his summary of that conference, the Indians are aroused and our Force will no doubt become involved in any Indian uprisings which might occur.

37. In [*sic*] appears that our uniformed members throughout Canada will be faced with continual confrontations between themselves and treaty Indians. Many such confrontations will no doubt be staged by extremists for the purpose of gaining public sympathy and support for the Indian cause. The Communist Party of Canada may see this as an area where they can successfully destroy the R.C.M. Police image. It is, therefore, important that our detachment personnel realize their dealings with treaty Indians will be scrutinized by the local press and television and that discretion and tact will be of decided importance during the coming summer months.[32]

By this time a report displaying a nebulous definition of radicalism had already been filed, under the heading 'Red Power–Canada,' on a seminar held at Lakehead University to discuss the Trudeau government's proposals for reforming the Indian Act.[33] Much of the attention given by the RCMP to the Red Power movement in Canada, however, was in Saskatchewan, a province with a large Aboriginal population. Here the local men in scarlet opened a file on the Métis Society of Saskatchewan and sent warnings of dire consequences for the future to headquarters: 'the current situation amongst the Indian and Metis peoples [is] remaining very tense and highly explosive. *Red Power advocates* [deleted: names] are gaining more and more influence in the various native organizations and communities. These people, many of whom are university students and/or graduates, represent the future leaders, particularly those who have entered the field of education. It is their intentions, apparently, to return to their reserves as teachers and as a result, would have a great influence on the population as a whole and particularly on the young and impressionable students.'[34]

Constable J.S. Rae, responsible for spying on a speech at the University of Saskatchewan on the poor conditions of the Native People in northern Saskatchewan, found himself journeying from simply reporting information to trying to refute an argument. 'The talk about people starving in La Loche is unjustified. Hunting and fishing in the area is good and food is plentiful; enough so that when these people receive their welfare cheques they spend the money on liquor. As an example, if a person receives a $90 cheque, he will charter a plane from La Loche to Buffalo Narrows for $60 and return with $30 worth of liquor.'[35]

The RCMP's interest in Red and Black Power movements reflected two realities: a growing concern with the possibility of violence and the belief that the growth in the likelihood of violence occurring was connected, directly and indirectly, to problems in the United States. Through watching television, Canadians knew well the chaos and violence in the streets of their southern neighbour: political assassinations and riots in cities such as the one in Los Angeles where thirty-four people died in August 1965. Violence, nevertheless, did not end at the border. Quebec had been the scene of several bombings during the 1960s, many of them connected to the cause of Quebec independence. The occasional bomb exploded on university campuses as well. One at Loyola College in Montreal in 1968 caused $150,000 in damage, and explosive devices also rattled the campuses of the University of British Columbia and the University of Waterloo in 1968. Despite monitoring campuses, the men in scarlet had no idea who the culprits were; indeed, in the case of the University of British Columbia they inquired as to whether 'student activists or fellow travellers' might be responsible.[36] Mounted Policemen clearly believed that things could get much worse; the United States was evidence of that.

In its institutional thinking, the Security Service increasingly attempted to interpret Canadian developments in a broader international context and it encouraged the government to do likewise. This shift reflected the influence of the New Left and a realization that youth unrest in Canada represented a manifestation of an international phenomenon. In a July 1970 letter to Deputy Minister of Justice D.S. Maxwell, John Starnes encouraged the federal government to view the problems related to unrest on all Canadian fronts 'from a continental standpoint.' 'This would involve,' he advised, 'among other things, [deleted: *an appreciation of the implications for Canada of a breakdown of law and order in the U.S.A.*] and the drawing up of plans to cope with the many different contingencies which could arise in such an event.'[37]

Starnes's words reflected the interconnection he believed existed between events in Canada and the United States. Implicit as well in his message was the close affiliation between those whose job it was to deal with domestic subversion, namely the intelligence services in the two countries. Under Section 15(1) of the Access to Information Act, material related to this relationship can be excised. Despite these deletions, evidence of the close association remains. When Noam Chomsky spoke to academics in Montreal in May 1967 and Jane Fonda addressed students at the University of Windsor in February 1971, the Security Service was there. Beyond the traditional RCMP mantra of determining what impact the speakers had on the audience, the presence of Fonda and Chomsky was of far greater interest to the FBI or CIA or both than to their northern equivalent.[38]

The affinity between Canadian and U.S. intelligence agencies began in the 1930s when Commissioner J.H. MacBrien met with J. Edgar Hoover in Washington. During the Second World War each organization stationed a liaison in the office of the other. It was in the years after 1945, however, that the ties were officially cemented as part of a grand alliance of the intelligence agencies of the United States, the United Kingdom, Canada, Australia, and New Zealand. Part of the agreement involved the sharing of signals intelligence gathered electronically, but there also was strong cooperation on other fronts.

The closest collaboration was in counter-espionage, especially between the CIA and 'B' Branch of the force. The countersubversion relationship between the FBI and 'D' Branch was also important, and information, especially on individuals, was frequently exchanged. Indeed, one of the few things Canada could offer the Americans was intelligence on Canadian citizens and other nationals, in particular Americans, residing on Canadian soil.[39]

The alliance with the FBI, according to one former Security Service member, was primarily a matter of sharing intelligence on individuals and groups. Hoover's troops pursued details on individuals travelling to the United States, especially if there was an indication that they might be in contact with groups such as the Black Panthers or Students for a Democratic Society. In April 1965 the RCMP opened files on two University of Saskatchewan students who had formed a group in sympathy with the American Student Non-Violent Coordinating Committee. Inspector L.R. Parent noted that the information 'may be of interest to the U.S. authorities.'[40]

Then, of course, there were the activities of Americans in Canada. Their participation in the anti–Vietnam War movement greatly interested the FBI and elucidates the RCMP's dedication to investigating this largely campus-based movement against a war in which Canada had no official involvement. A report was filed in 1967 on efforts at the Universities of Waterloo and Toronto to assist war resisters, although the Mountie who wrote it added the number of individuals in these support groups was small. A few months later the force acquired a transcript of a CBC Radio *Ideas* program that dealt with the Americans who had come to Canada to escape the Vietnam War. Another officer assembled a list of American war resisters in southern Ontario who were 'employed in positions which at some time may be of influence.'[41]

More extensive was the coverage given by the RCMP of the university-based anti–Vietnam War movement. Something as simple as signing an anti-war petition at the University of British Columbia led to a person's inclusion on a list of people whom the RCMP believed were politically naive or lacked a proper 'understanding of the Communist conspiracy.' Individuals involved in organizing anti-war efforts or who simply appeared on mailing lists of campus anti-war organizations had files opened on them. Debates and teach-ins represented another favourite target of undercover men. Corporal E.A.E. LaFontaine of the Toronto office sat in on a debate at York University on April Fool's Day 1967 over whether Canada should become involved in the war. Besides recording the presence of specific individuals at the gathering and the lack of the 'typical beatnik/peacenik set' he added, in the familiar phrasing, that students would not be adversely influenced by the experience. A September 1970 anti-war conference at the University of Toronto was another target.

Among the speakers was a young member of Parliament and future NDP leader, Ed Broadbent, whose name in the report that was filed is followed by the traditional blank space indicating a file number was removed under the Access to Information Act provisions. The RCMP was, in addition, interested in the movements of Vietnamese who came to Canada, so that when three members of the Vietnamese Liberation Front visited Toronto in the winter of 1969 the RCMP obtained their itinerary and followed them around the city, including onto the campus of the University of Toronto, where they met the Reverend Eilert Frerichs of the Student Christian Movement.[42]

The end destination for some of the material accumulated on the anti-war movement and other radical manifestations in Canada was clearly American intelligence agencies. In February 1967 the director of security intelligence, William Kelly, forwarded a lengthy analysis to the RCMP's liaison officer in Washington and to Moss Innes, the long-time FBI representative in Ottawa. The document contained a general description of campus-related radicalism, especially at York University and the University of Toronto. It also referred to parallels with events on American campuses, and it warned that the growing opposition at universities to the Vietnam War was part of an effort to influence Canadian government policy on the conflict. Headquarters in Ottawa also passed other general reports on the anti-war and anti-nuclear movements in Canada to both the FBI and CIA.[43]

In addition to Black and Red Power and to other cross-border student radical movements, another reason why the Security Service sought to see problems in a continental and even international perspective was Quebec nationalism, another of the phenomena of the 1960s. More than any other part of Canada, Quebec was experiencing dramatic and occasionally turbulent change in the 1960s. The province began to express more forcefully its unique voice within the country, and some people in the province began to campaign actively, both peacefully and violently, for its independence. In 1968 Pierre Vallières published *Nègres blancs d'Amérique*, a polemic in which he argued that only through violent revolution would Quebec free itself from English Canada's colonial subjugation.[44]

As with the other elements of concern in the 1960s, the burst of nationalist expression in Quebec in all of its forms was new and foreign to the RCMP. The advocacy of terrorism was part of the novelty, and both the police and its political masters were frequently unwilling to differentiate between those who sought the independence of Quebec through peaceful means and the groups and individuals who advocated and employed violence. Both wanted to break up Canada; only their methods differed. The Security Service initially tried to explain the new phenomenon in the same way as it had the New Left – by placing the expression of nationalism within its traditional 'Red'-and-white framework. Reference was made in its analyses to Communist 'penetration' of and 'influence' in the FLQ.[45]

Already by April 1963 the Security Service had several members of the FLQ under surveillance. The organization had begun a bombing campaign that was aimed at destroying traditional symbols of Canada's British roots. Some of the bombers had university connections. One, a Université de Montréal student, claimed that he had stored dynamite in a locker at his university. More famous was Mario Bachand, active in the FLQ for most of the 1960s and later assassinated by persons unknown in Paris in 1971. Bachand was a part-time university student in his early FLQ days. Another cell composed of faculty and students was later active at the Université du Québec à Montréal. [46]

Whether the majority of students supported FLQ tactics is another question. Carole de Vault, an informer for the Montreal police and herself a student at the time, recalled widespread support for the FLQ manifesto and equivocal positions on violence, but that was during the tense period of October 1970. Certainly large numbers of young Québécois did lean in some way towards separatism. This posed a problem for the force. How could it, a predominantly English-speaking institution, one in which a member had once boasted to the solicitor general that the Mounties were 'a WASP organization, and ... proud of it,' distinguish between a small number of terrorists and a much larger numbers of peaceful separatists? The answer is that it generally could not, and it rarely even tried. Nor, for that matter, did the federal government desire it to do so. In this era, everyone was dumped into the same pot. In the Key Sectors program there was a single category: 'French Canadian Separatism–Terrorism.'[47]

In the fall of 1967 the Security Panel convened to discuss the issue of separatism and what could be done about it. Separatism, Prime Minister Lester Pearson declared, should be considered by the Security Service as a threat comparable to communism. The point was reiterated at a meeting of Pierre Trudeau's Cabinet Committee on Security and Intelligence in December 1968, at which the RCMP advocated an extensive program to develop human sources in order to ferret out necessary information.[48]

Perhaps reflecting better intelligence, the Force had already begun to move away from viewing separatism as Communist-inspired. A report on the Communist Party of Quebec described its claim that it had recruited 100 young separatists to communism as exaggerated, contending that while many separatists professed to be socialists most were not 'Reds.' If they were separatists or suspected separatists they were, nevertheless, worthy of reports. The appearance of Laurier LaPierre and René Lévesque at a University of Windsor teach-in on French Canada was recorded, as was a speech by Jacques Parizeau at McGill University in the early 1970s.[49]

Analyses on separatist activity in educational institutions was also beginning to reach Ottawa from the Security Service in Quebec. In a response to queries from headquarters that was sent immediately after the 1968 Saint-Jean-Baptiste Day riot, headquarters, in Montreal prepared a detailed examination of protest by youths in the province. While noting the potential for violence, the document's author dismissed fears that there might be some in the immediate future. The report ended with the names of organizations that were most active in stirring up young people, among them the Union Générale des Étudiants du Québec (UGEQ), the main student organizations at the Université Laval and the Université de Montréal, and the Company of Young Canadians, which at one time included Mario Bachand in its ranks. Near the bottom were the Civil Liberties Union, described as 'traditionally anti-establishment,' motorcycle and 'muscle' gangs, and separatist Pierre Bourgault's Rassemblement pour l'Indépendance Nationale (RIN), the entity behind the 1968 riot.[50]

Quebec was not alone when it came to expressions of nationalism. At the Université de Moncton in New Brunswick, outbursts of Acadian nationalism appeared frequently in the latter half of the 1960s. As usual, the RCMP was there to spy on the activists. In this case, however, the force and the federal government sought evidence of the role that French nationals might have played in fomenting trouble. In *The Gaullist Attack on Canada, 1967–1997*, J.F. Bosher argues strongly that elements within the French government made a concerted effort to promote separatism in Canada.[51] In the Moncton example, *coopérants*, French teachers sent abroad in lieu of military service, involved themselves in the production of the Acadian newspaper *L'Évangeline*. The Department of External Affairs was certainly interested in French involvement in Acadian nationalist activity. After a boycott of classes and the occupation of a building in the fall of 1968, E.R. Rettie, the under-secretary of external affairs, supplied information on the alleged participation of a

French *coopérant* in the disturbances. The bureaucrat also mentioned the actions of a professor from France who allegedly met with engineering students to obtain the plans for the university's electrical plant in preparation for its future takeover. Although on the surface a seemingly fanciful account, Mounties in the Moncton area were ordered to make careful inquiries through an informant in the university's administration. After an investigation, the answer was that no French role at the Université de Moncton could be discovered. The only outside involvement seemed to be that of students from Quebec and of members of the CBC who had been forewarned about the occupation. As for the French professor and his dastardly plans for the university power plant, it was part of a scholarly assignment.[52]

The issue, nevertheless, did not disappear. In September the head of the Security Service, after receiving information from Inspector Donald Cobb of its Montreal office, encouraged Rettie and other government officials to authorize a systematic study of the presence of French nationals in Canada as part of the *coopérant* program. What Cobb desired from External Affairs was a complete list of them, including relevant background information. The RCMP then intended to check the names against its indexes on subversives.[53] Whether the department ever produced the names is unclear, but in the 1970s the Security Service established a special group charged with investigating 'foreign interference' in Canada, although those involved in it nicknamed it the French Interference Unit.[54]

Despite the RCMP's concerns about the situation in New Brunswick, Quebec educational institutions remained its centre of action on the separatist front. In the spring of 1969, 'Opération McGill,' a protest aimed at turning McGill University into a Francophone institution, emerged as a threat to public order. Once again, Mario Bachand played a leading role. Details of the protest were known weeks in advance: at a large meeting in the offices of UGEQ, Bachand called for an occupation of McGill on 28 March 1969, and then swore everyone to secrecy. Not surprisingly, word of what was coming spread. As members of the Security Service would later note in an assessment of 'Opération McGill,' they had been 'amply forewarned' about what was going to occur. Surveillance of the preparations continued, a fact discovered by the march's organizers when they happened upon a group of Mounties and Montreal police secretly filming the proceedings of one organizational gathering.[55]

By the day of the march, the police forces were ready and McGill

University prepared for a siege. Two hundred and seventy-five security guards locked and reinforced doors and windows. Searchlights and cameras were strategically placed. Twenty-six police cars cruised the area. Besides the numerous city police in uniform, one hundred Security Service members mingled with the crowd. A reserve force of Montreal city police and Mounties was held back in case of emergency, but their services were not needed that day, which ended with forty-one arrests and eighteen seeking medical treatment for a variety of injuries.[56]

Following the failed occupation, the Security Service accelerated its collection of information related to separatist activity in the Quebec educational sector. Occasionally there was a hysterical quality to the reports that arrived at headquarters, such as this warning from a Francophone Mountie about the manipulation of students in classrooms:

[A] large number of professors at Lionel Groulx C.E.G.E.P. and Secondary School, Ste. Therese [sic] de Blainville, as well as professors in most of universities, C.E.G.E.P.s and important colleges of the Province of Quebec are socialist and separatist in ideology. [deleted: source or sources repor]t these professors are promoting Marxism, Separatism, Communism and other subversive ideology while given [sic] their respective courses. [deleted] would incriminate two (2) professors of the Lionel Groulx Secondary School and prove that they have endoctrinated [sic] and encouraged their students to Socialism and Separatism.[57]

The Collèges d'Enseignement Général et Professionnel (CEGEPs) were post-secondary institutions started by the Quebec government in September 1967. Although initially they were quiet on the security front, student protest at CEGEPs escalated in the fall of 1968. Part of the problem, a member of the RCMP admitted, was a lack of job opportunities for baby boomers and of access to universities for graduates of the system. But, according to the same policeman, subversive infiltration was underway at these institutions, including by means of student newspapers, which 'radicals' had taken over and were using as platforms to 'encourage student contestations [protests]' and to 'take [an] anti-Administration stand.' Even worse, their editors 'often tried to ridicule Christian religion, Occidental Democracy, as well as American and Canadian politicians.'[58]

More worrisome than challenges to authority were the actions of the Mouvement Syndical Politique (MSP). This organization, established in March 1969 by Université de Montréal philosophy students, allegedly acting under the influence of the ubiquitous Mario Bachand, brought together remnants of UGEQ after it dissolved and was dedicated to achieving Quebec independence through whatever means necessary. In December 1969, through information that was undoubtedly supplied by informants on site, the force reported to Ottawa that the MSP, although consisting of no more than 100 members in the entire province, had developed 'cells' at thirteen CEGEPS and that more were expected to be formed (see Table 7.1). In June 1970 the RCMP supplied the federal government with the results of a more detailed survey, based on its extensive files, on subversive activity in Quebec educational institutions.

2. A recent statistical examination of the Security Service files of persons having Separatist/terrorist sympathies or affiliations is most revealing of the extent to which such persons have gained a strong position within the educational system in Quebec. A tabulation of the files according to occupations showed the following results:

(a) Of the some [deleted: *2600*] persons whose files were examined, those known to be in education and related occupation constituted approximately [deleted: *25%*].

(b) Students comprise [deleted: *39%*] of this [deleted: *25%*].

(c) Although not conclusive, a correlation analysis of the 'no occupation known' group of files indicated that the percentage of persons involved in education could be revised upwards from [deleted: *25%*] to [deleted: *30%*] of the total files examined.

(d) Of those from the teaching professions a majority are at secondary and post-secondary level. Some have very senior positions.[59]

Most significant of all in the RCMP's 'separatist-terrorist' field were Quebec's French-language universities, and among them the Université de Montréal was investigated for separatists twice in 1969 and again in 1970. As had been done in the past with suspected Communists and members of the New Left, mounted policemen examined each department in order 'to establish the degree of infiltration by subversive elements' for an August 1969 report. Getting a clean bill of health were the Rehabilitation School and the departments and faculties of Art History, Psychology Guidance, Educational Psychology, and Nursing. Demonstrating the rather imprecise quality to the entire enterprise, a definitive assessment for the Radiology and Psychology departments could not be given, since the RCMP was unsure whether 'Jean Doe' assessed as a

TABLE 7.1
Alleged Mouvement Syndical Politique activity at CEGEPs, 1969

CEGEP	Comment by RCMP
Ahuntsic	Very active, approximately 10 members
Chicoutimi	Cell probably
François-Xavier-Garneau	Control the students' publication *Praxis*
Jonquière	[No comment]
Limoilou	Where they control the student publication
Rimouski	[No comment]
Rivière-du-Loup	[No comment]
Rouyn	[No comment]
Sherbrooke	A maximum of 40 students sympathizers at that point
Édouard-Montpetit	There is no M.S.P. cell at that point but liaison is maintained with the M.S.P.
Sainte-Foy	M.S.P. is apparently in control of publication *Animation*
Trois-Rivières	M.S.P. cell active but with little influence
Vieux-Montréal	M.S.P. cell active. There is unrest among students and a climate of tension [name deleted] and her associates are active at that point
Maisonneuve	There is no M.S.P. cell at that point due to some dissatisfaction amongst students; one is likely to develop
Shawinigan	No M.S.P. cell yet but the action committee is very active and students are generally dissatisfied
Saint-Hyacinthe	No M.S.P. cell yet but a CYC action group is very active and attempts will probably be made to [make an MSP cell at] one that point
Saint-Jean	M.S.P. cell being formed

Source: NA, RG 146, vol. 2731, file 96-A-00045, pt 8, Superintendent L.R. Parent to Inspector G. Begalki, 19 Dec 1969; vol. 2728, file 96-A-00045, pt 6, Report of Inspector D.G. Cobb, re: 'Mouvement Syndical Politique,' 16 December 1969.

separatist was also 'Jean Doe' the psychologist. Departments in which individual faculty members whom the RCMP had labelled as separatist worked were Modern Languages, Biochemistry, Surgery, Medicine, Experimental Surgery (there was a file on at least one out of the four department members), Microbiology and Immunology, Obstetrics Gynaecology, Pathology (on one of the thirty-three members), Paediatrics (on two or three individuals out of forty-three), Physiology (on two to four names out of the eighteen members), Psychiatry (a large number of names out of the thirty-one members), Radiology (the force was unable to determine whether the members of the department were the same as those appearing on its list of separatists), Dietetics and Nutrition (one out of the thirty-two members), Technology, Pharmacy, Philosophy, Medieval Studies, and Biological Sciences. This survey was updated again in August 1970 when the university's new staff directory, an invaluable police reference tool, appeared.[60]

Two months later, the October Crisis erupted. The War Measures Act was invoked by the government, a move the RCMP had counselled against and which, Reg Whitaker convincingly argues, the Trudeau government employed more to intimidate those leaning towards separatism than to combat the FLQ. Two separate FLQ cells through two different kidnappings had plunged Canada into chaos. Another cell, the Viger cell, included Robert Comeau, a professor of history at the Université du Québec à Montréal, and three students; one of the students eventually became a police informant.[61]

As the term cell suggests, the number of people prepared to utilize violence to achieve Quebec independence was small. On the other hand, those who openly desired an independent Quebec represented a far larger portion of the population, creating confusion for a security institution that had shown an unwillingness to distinguish between the two groups. In the confusion of 1970, the RCMP expanded its coverage of the Quebec educational establishment – hence the reason for 'borrowing' the Université de Montréal student database – and it continued the trend of mixing together separatists and terrorists, with dashes of the New Left and the old standard subversives tossed in for good measure:

> Separatist influence in the student milieu and academic environment in Quebec has been enormous, with extreme Quebec nationalism and New Left rhetoric providing a cohesive ideological position for the Separatist groups which strongly appeals to student activists ... The Separatist movement undoubtedly gained additional support in 1968, with the introduction of the [CEGEP] ... In short, the CEGEPs were an ideal breeding ground for subversive elements in the Separatist movement, and served to replenish radical ranks at the university level.
>
> The campuses of the French-language universities in Quebec and, in particular, the University of Montreal ... have become hotbeds of Separatism and some use has undoubtedly been made of them by terrorist

elements, e.g., for the distribution of subversive literature ... Moreover, Security Service files indicate that in 1969 some forty members of the U of M faculty and administration had Separatist/terrorist sympathies. Some FLQ cell activity is presumably continuing at the U of M.[62]

The force was also worried about the reaction on English-speaking campuses across the country to the imposition of the War Measures Act. Emergency reports flooded into RCMP headquarters in Ottawa from local Security Service offices and some Mounties ventured into class-rooms and lecture theatres to gather information. At Waterloo Lutheran University, a member of the force described how two Maoists praised the FLQ during a psychology class. Another member attended a University of Waterloo talk about events in Quebec that was given by a history graduate student. Here the message back to headquarters was satisfac-tory: students had attended because they were curious. During the same period, a University of New Brunswick political scientist noticed an unfamiliar face in the second-to-last row in his classroom. At one point during a lecture he turned to the student and asked him to produce his university identification card. Instead the 'student' rapidly exited the classroom and another policeman later confirmed to the academic that RCMP members were sent into classrooms during this time. The moni-toring may also have extended to technological measures. The *Globe and Mail* claimed, in part based on the testimony of a former member of the the University of Ottawa campus security force, that in October 1970 the RCMP and Canadian military planted a bug in the ceiling of a room used by academics and students.[63]

The generally satisfying message coming from the campuses outside of Quebec in the aftermath of the War Measures Act and October Crisis was in contrast to the vision of the apocalyptic Canadian university world that appeared in 'Academe and Subversion,' the Security Service's December 1970 briefing paper for the federal cabinet. The month itself was signifi-cant, as the decade of 'love' and 'chaos' had but a few days left to run. A transformed and more professional Security Service emerged from this era, with increasingly well-educated members. It was also moving for-ward in new directions. The federal government had given it clear orders to take care of the threat of separatism in Quebec. The govern-ment had also accurately hinted to the media and to Parliament that it was about to lift the restrictions on campus work by Mounties.

As 'Academe and Subversion' conveys, the leaders of the RCMP be-lieved that they had a clear idea of the threats to be encountered in the decade that was about to begin. They helpfully supplied the Trudeau cabinet with an 'enemies list' at universities, which included the Canadian University Press and its 'extremely radical' executive, as well as the Canadian Union of Students (CUS), because its executive 'members maintained links with international Communist front organizations and during national meetings in 1968 CUS adopted a militant, revolutionary position with respect to issues such as student power and Vietnam.' Then there was the New Left, which subscribed to a 'theology [that was] ... Marxist-oriented with nihilistic overtones.' According to the Security Service, its 'apostles' included 'Dr. Jon ALEXANDER, professor of Political Science at Carleton University, who was involved in setting up Pestalozzi College which is to be used as a headquarters for student radicals and possibly the FLQ in the Ottawa area; Jennifer PENNY, a former student, now editor of the Canadian University Press which has replaced the Canadian Union of Students as co-ordinator of radical student activities; and David FRANK and Bob PARKINS, editors of *Varsity Press*, University of Toronto, who are using it to propound revolutionary views.'[64]

Finally, the Communist Party of Canada appeared on the 1970 list of university-based headaches. Although the Security Service had come to recognize during the decade that communism had nothing to do with much of the social unrest underway and that it no longer carried much weight with students, the Mounties had not forgotten their old nemesis. After all, they noted, 390 actual and 'suspected' CPC members continued to be employed at Canadian universities.[65] There remained a certain reassurance in having a familiar subversive enemy, as the 1970s would prove.

PART FOUR

From the RCMP to CSIS

8

'Moving from Campus to Community,' 1971–1984

Members of the Cabinet Committee on Security and Intelligence, including Prime Minister Pierre Trudeau, Director-General John Starnes, and other senior Mounties, politicians, and bureaucrats gathered on Parliament Hill on 24 September 1971 to watch the Security Service's preview of the world of radicalism to come. The projector hummed and coughed out slides of thirty-six portraits of menaces to the nation. The RCMP believed that the 1970s would make the 60s look like the 50s, and the slide show did nothing to counter this. 'The Threat to Security from Violence Prone Revolutionary Elements in Canada' presented a shopping-list approach in its recapitulation of the forces threatening Canada's national security. The crudely drawn slides yielded a visual representation of the dangers. One depicted a bomb burrowing its way out from underneath the Parliament Buildings. Another showed the pillars of government being subverted from within.[1] All were deeply symbolic of how the RCMP perceived subversion, including that spawned by universities.

Essentially, the police argued, the virus that had infected campuses in the latter half of the 1960s was now in the process of spreading to the wider society. Moving 'from campus to community' became a recurrent concept and phrase in police reports of the 1970s. Leading the migration were self-confessed 'Typhoid Marys,' members of the New Left who, having graduated, now looked to spread their message of revolution and radicalism to the society outside the universities. Playing the role of doctor, the RCMP offered first a diagnosis and then the cure that the government was demanding.[2]

Ironically, just as the Security Service was gearing up, with the federal government's encouragement, for an aggressive campaign against allegedly subversive and potentially violent groups, these same groups were dropping all plans for preparing the revolution and were being abandoned by their members.[3] Radicalism was in decline in Canadian society in the early 1970s, especially on university campuses. The country was entering hard economic times, and for both students and faculty the future, one that previously had been assured by a booming economy, suddenly seemed threatened. While it is an exaggeration to say that the radicals of the 1960s, who had been in a minority among the university population in the first place, had jettisoned their values by the 1970s, it is true that many had begun to rethink the path they were following. Efforts by the state against manifestation of protest also played a role in curtailing it. The slaying of four anti-war protesters at Kent State University in May 1970 demonstrated the potential price to be paid for dissent, while behind the scenes the FBI and other police forces conducted campaigns to destroy those considered to be enemies of the state.[4]

Part of the trend towards quieter campuses reflected the impact of a growing public backlash against campus radicals and radicalism that had begun in Canada in the latter half of the 1960s and that picked up steam after the occupation at Simon Fraser University and the vandalism at Sir George Williams University. Noted surgeon Wilder Penfield, a member of the board of governors at McGill University, slammed student radicalism in a speech to the Canadian Club in Montreal. Journalist Duart Farquharson wrote a series of articles condemning university disturbances that were published as 'Confrontation on Campus'; the RCMP liked the collection so much that it sent it to American intelligence as part of an exchange of papers on student protest in their respective countries. Travelling even further in the escalating anti-radical rhetoric, *Toronto Telegram* columnist McKenzie Porter labelled restless students as 'man-sized children' who should 'be suitably punished for any show of idleness, impertinence or defiance.'[5]

A similar counter-attack was underway on campuses. In the fall of 1968 a nursing student running on an anti-protest platform easily defeated radical Stan Persky for the position of student president at the University of British Columbia. The Canadian Union of Students, representing only eight universities by 1969 after criticism from the right and to a lesser degree from the left, dissolved.[6] University administrations displayed an increasing determination to stand up to protesters, as the University of Toronto did when students disrupted the appearance of Edward Banfield, an American academic who had been invited to give a guest lecture. The protesters faced widespread condemnation and were expelled, but the Security Service secretly applauded their efforts: '[T]hings couldn't look rosier. The SDS [Students for a Democratic Society] is now in disrepute with the faculty, the administration and the students. It might be banned from campus; it certainly is going to be in for indirect harassment from faculty members. The administration is now under heavy pressure from the academic community to ensure measures preventing future occurrences of the type as the "Banfield Incident." Thus, other radical groups on campus may likely be placed under direct pressure.'[7]

Spies on campuses confirmed the decline in support for radical movements.[8] Demonstrating the growing impact of a higher level of education among the Mounted Police and the growing sophistication of the Security Service, individual policemen went beyond simply reporting the trend to trying to explain it. In fact, they seemed fascinated by the conundrum of youth, among whom radicalism had appeared to arrive so suddenly and who were now returning to an apparently passive mode. One Mountie dismissed the weak efforts for a protest by York University students as a sign that most of them came from an upper middle-class background and therefore did not desire the destruction of their privileges.[9] Another, a faculty member who was an informant at the University of Waterloo, cited an increased consensus among students, the poor economy, and general apathy as contributing factors to the changing atmosphere. He added that in the eyes of faculty, ignorance and passiveness were generally bliss: 'Several members of local Arts departments have commented that the past year has been both a pleasure and one of concern for on the one hand while students generally are more polite, work harder, are better groomed and more manageable there is concern that students are becoming less and less involved, outraged or interested in significant political or ethical issues in the world beyond the University.'[10] At the University of Toronto, explained a policeman from personal experience, the academic discipline of the student was often a factor: apathy and right-wing politics had traditionally ruled in the sciences and in engineering, while police targets had usually come from the humanities. Because of the economic downturn, there were fewer radicals, while at the faculty level those of a more radical hue found their activities countered by their colleagues. Nostalgia for the conformity of the 1950s was another important factor, according to the same officer, who cited the popularity of the movie *American Graffiti* and the television show *Happy Days*. Still another policeman echoed Richard M. Nixon in saying that the 'silent majority' of students was expressing its opposition to the era of radicalism.[11]

Despite the recognition by many Mounties, especially rank-and-file members who were responsible for universities, that campuses were increasingly conservative and quiet places, the force did not stop spying on them. Often it trotted out its famous 'but,' as in 'things are not happening today, but there is always tomorrow.' That view demonstrated that the old notion of a passive student body at risk of manipulation by radicals remained.

Perhaps influenced by history classes at university, one officer chose to place the new climate into a broader historical context. Pointing to bursts of revolutionary fervour in Europe in 1848 and 1870, he argued that unrest was cyclical, the last high point having been in the 1960s. 'The wave is in a trough, and there is a period of quiet again and re-study. However, that does not mean the wave could not be blown up by the winds of an issue.'[12]

One Mountie suggested that it was the Russian Revolution that provided the proper historical comparison. He criticized the Security Service's emphasis on 'the "Great Man" theory of history,' which led the agency to believe that 'these individuals and their organizations have the power to act arbitrarily as causal agents in the flow of events and can precipitate social change regardless of the circumstances in which they find themselves.' On the other hand, he warned that just because 'would-be Lenins' had not materialized did not mean that the environment was not conducive to revolution; after all, Lenin had not made the revolution in Russia. 'If we are to obtain any credibility with the government that we serve, it will be necessary for all of our members to appreciate that our primary focus of attention should be situations and issues.'[13]

In a report in 1975 about Concordia University, Corporal C.E.G. Savard turned to more immediate history when he reminded his superiors 'that the facility [sic] members who played a larger role in the computer incident that transpired on the 11-2-69 are still teaching at Sir George.' He noted that 'D' Branch continued to infiltrate groups of interest to the Security Service.[14] A similar rationale was presented in a 1976 report about the University of Toronto, in which Corporal J.G.L. Toews quoted a campus source to explain that the increasing calm on the campus was likely the cover for nefarious activities:

The (radical) faculty, aware of an increasingly stringent financial situation, in effect went underground as they concentrated on winning converts, gaining academic status and tenure, and planning for the future. The key leftist activity (strategy) is no longer to challenge the university government system but to gain a foothold within it and assist fellow radicals to gain corresponding positions of influence ... The members are fewer, to be sure, but the committed radicals who remain are more mature, cautious, have better philosophical grounding, positions of some permanence, ability to influence students and most of all the ability to lie low, plan and then mobilize when given issues arise.[15]

The desire of the force to remain on campuses reflected deeper factors. For instance, there was the reality of turf wars. The burst of radicalism at the end of the 1960s had led to a restructuring of the Security Service to make it more effective in dealing with it. Having erected these mechanisms, tearing them down proved difficult and this was one of the issues that engendered internal debate. Key Sectors, a revolutionary attempt at change within the Security Service, was one centre of discussion. Originally designed to identify the infiltration of areas such as education, media, and government, to offer analyses regarding threats and to provide methods for countering them, it created too much information and too little evaluation, the traditional problem with RCMP programs. The first of the three Key Sectors goals, and the one that represented familiar territory for the RCMP, that of identifying areas of infiltration, dominated. In November 1971 a seminar was held in Ottawa bringing together relevant personnel. Perhaps reflecting the era, the gathering discussed the concept of countersubversion itself, including what constituted a 'threat,' as well as whether RCMP Security Service members should work to impede societal change and, if they did so, whether they were doing so as 'ultra-reactionaries, arch defenders of the status quo?'[16]

A decision was eventually made to implement the second phase of the Key Sectors program, which consisted of a qualitative examination of files. Lacking the resources to go through all of the more than two thousand dossiers on individuals, it was decided to reduce the number by 95 per cent. Divisions were ordered to separate the most threatening 5 per cent of targets from the remainder. Some Security Service offices, like the one in Kamloops, which dealt with Okanagan and Cariboo Colleges, could not find anyone to put on their list.[17]

In the end, 114 files of individuals for the period from 1971 to 1973 received special attention. Of these, fifty-nine worked in education but only twenty-six or twenty-seven individuals represented, in the opinion of the Security Service, a continuing threat (see Table 8.1). Members of the Key Sectors program also produced a chart listing the groups that were targeted at universities, all of them English-language institutions except for Moncton, and identified which ones they felt represented significant threats (see Table 8.2). The results compiled in it reinforced the message from the rank-and-file who covered universities and directly contradicted the exaggerated rhetoric of the September 1971 Parliament Hill meeting. There was 'no apparent organized threat within the Canadian academic community at the present time,' was how Key Sectors put it.[18]

Recognizing the decline in campus unrest was one thing, accepting it and adjusting to it something else entirely. The Security Service was the equivalent of an institutional elephant. For decades it had been charging in one direction, towards communism. Suddenly, in the 1960s new challenges emerged and it slowly began to redirect itself. By the 1970s it had shifted to a new path, but by that time the reason for the shift in momentum had disappeared. Again, however, changing bearings proved difficult. Budgets and personnel had been allotted, rationales for new emphases developed, and a parallel reality created.

In the case of its coverage of campuses, the RCMP began a new style of reporting with a report in March 1972 by Corporal E.W. (Win) Wilmore about Trent University. It, and a similarly structured report about the University of Manitoba, were praised and funnelled up through the Security Service hierarchy all the way to John Starnes.[19] The style would quickly be adopted and applied to all of Canada's major universities. It consisted of an annual or semi-annual comprehensive report about each institution of higher education. Relying primarily on open sources – an important one was campus newspapers and the force kept files on them, with political labels ranging from 'moderately radical' for the University of Toronto *Varsity* to 'Maoist' for the *McGill Daily* and 'Trotskyist' for the University of Guelph *Ontarion* – the reports sketched out a brief history of the institutions and included general information about the student population.[20] The heart of the record was a lengthy depiction of the subversive elements on each campus along with other aspects that were thought possibly destined to cause the RCMP problems in the future. The reports usually ended with a prediction of what the Security Service might face on the campus in the coming year.

Some did not adjust effectively to the new style. The first comprehensive report on the University of Toronto was ridiculed by Key Sectors personnel in Ottawa, who called its conclusion 'sheer B.S.'[21] Subsequent

TABLE 8.1
Details on the persons in education who remained of interest to the Security Services after 1973

	A. By institution	
	Persons deemed to be 'major protagonists' by the RCMP	Persons considered as 'requiring additional enquiries, or of continuing interest' to the RCMP
Day Care Centre, Toronto		1
McGill University	2	
McMaster University	1	
Ontario Institute for Studies in Education	1	
Richmond Hill School		1
Ryerson Polytechnical Institute		1
Simon Fraser University		1
University of Alberta		1
University of Calgary		1
University of Guelph		1
University of Saskatchewan (Regina campus)	1	2
University of Saskatchewan (Saskatoon campus)	1	1
University of Toronto		5
University of Waterloo		2
University of Winnipeg		2
York University		2
Total	6[a]	21
	B. By nationality	
Canadian	15	
American	9	
British	1	
Argentinian	1	

Source: CSIS, access request 117-1998-71, The Findings of the Key Sectors Program, 1971–3, April 1974.
[a]This figure conflicts with other RCMP accounts that list this number at five.

reports about the University of Toronto would make up for the short-comings of the first. They became increasingly detailed and comprehensive, so much so that the 1974 version ran over one hundred pages and included a table of contents, an index, and footnotes. It was praised by those who first read it (subsequent readers were encouraged to skim

TABLE 8.2
Targeted groups at Canadian Universities, 1971–3

University	CPC ML	YS	CPC	Waffle	Gays	CLM	BSU
Alberta	X	X	X				
Brandon							
Brock		X		X			
Calgary	X		X	X	X		
Dalhousie	X						
Guelph		X	X	X		X	X
McGill	S	X		X			X
McMaster	X	X		X			
Manitoba	X						
Moncton							
Regina	X	X		X			
Saskatchewan	X				X	X	
Sir George Williams	X						X
Toronto	S	S	X	S		S	S
Victoria		X					
Waterloo		X			S	X	
Western Ontario				X			
Winnipeg							
York		X	X	X		X	X

Note: Significant threat (S); limited threat (X).

Abbreviations:

ASA	African Students Association	CPC Univ.	Communist Party of Canada Universities
BSU	Black Students Union		
CLM	Canadian Liberation Movement	CPL	Canadian Party of Labour
CPC	Communist Party of Canada	CSS	Committee for Socialist Studies
CPCML	Communist Party of Canada (Maxist-Leninist) (Maoist)	Fem.	Feminist groups

Source: CSIS, Access request 117-1998-71, 'Key Sectors: The Findings of the Key Sectors Program, 1971–73,' April 1974, 3–5, Appendix C.

through much of it), and it represented a new trend in Security Service reporting, which was labelled Divisional Intelligence Profiles.

The view the report provided of a year at University of Toronto, like others in the genre, offered a little of the old and some that was new. The usual suspects, namely Communists, roamed the campus and were seeking, according to the Mountie scribbler, to have more Marxist-related courses taught. A senior administrator who was also a member of the Communist Party of Canada was suspected of using her position to find

LSA	SDS	NDY	CPL	CSS	WIS	WG	JDL	Fem.	ASA	CPC Univ.	Sep.
X											
					X						
					X						
X											
											X
		X									
		X						X			
							X				
	X		X	S		S					
										X	
	S										
	X										
		X									

Gays	Gay and lesbian groups	
JDL	Jewish Defence League	
LSA	League for Socialist Action (Trotskyist)	
NDY	New Democratic Youth	
SDS	Students for a Democratic Society	

Sep.	Separatist groups	
Waffle	New Democratic Party Waffle Movement	
WG	Western Guard	
WIS	West Indian Students	
YS	Young Socialists (Trotskyist)	

recruits. The Graduate Student Union was considered to be Communist-controlled because of the involvement of a party member in the organization's leadership.

The unique aspect of the report was that it sought targets outside of the radical left, the RCMP's traditional snooping grounds. An entire section was devoted to such right-wing groups as Campus Alternative, which had been established at the University of Toronto in November 1973, and the more extremist Western Guard, a white supremacist group.

The latter and another group with a similar philosophy, the National Socialist White People's Party, received brief references saying that they enjoyed no support on campus.

The comprehensive report even ventured to cover other campus organizations and outside events considered to have had an impact on university life. Under the heading of 'Native Extremism,' it referred to growing opposition on the campus to the James Bay hydroelectric project in northern Quebec. The RCMP author also described the activities of the Black Students Union and the Gay Alliance toward Equality. Finally, some religious groups received mention. On the left there was the Student Christian Movement, while the Reverend Sun Myung Moon's Unification Church occupied the right. Recognizing that support for many of these entities was not significant, the force justified continuing its coverage because 'they have drawn away support from the radical groups as both appeal to the same type of individual, that is individuals who are disoriented from society and seek the comfort of simplist [sic] solutions to problems.'

The report also found space to comment on individual faculty members and departments, including Mathematics and Political Economy. Mathematics received police attention 'because unlike other physical sciences Mathematics ... is more akin to philosophy as it is an abstract subject. This means it is open to a more individualistic interpretation and accordingly attracts a more free thinking and unconventional individual.' Political Economy was there because some of its faculty members had become 'celebrities in their own right' and therefore had the ability to influence students and the general public. Also included were the Faculties of Social Work and of Library Science, the latter because of the presence of activists seeking unionization. The Advisory Bureau, set up to aid students, received a reference because of its work connected to the movement for freer access to abortions.

The document ended with a projection on what the climate on campus for the following year might be. Things were expected to be quiet, especially in those areas of concern to the federal government. Then came the usual 'but,' which in this case consisted of a warning that if a high level of inflation continued to trouble the Canadian economy, it might fuel 'political extremism.' The author's superiors, in sending the report upwards, added praise and emphasized the clear indication that radical students and faculty members were increasingly isolated by their peers, a positive finding, in the minds of the RCMP.[22]

Such was the approach taken by Security Service personnel across

Canada. Annual and semi-annual reports on larger universities were filed for several years in the 1970s. Assessments of universities or educational sectors with little history of unrest died quickly. Alberta exemplified the quiet side. In 1973 headquarters received a description from the local division of the educational sector in the province, which included not only the province's three universities but also its 'lesser institutions' – community colleges and organizations like the Federation of Alberta Faculty Association. Little of substance was found for the report. For the University of Lethbridge, the report, besides recording that the force held files on about 10 per cent of the faculty members (seventeen out of 151) and giving their ethnic backgrounds, forwarded gossip, namely stories about 'wild drinking and sex parties' in the co-educational residence having alienated the large Mormon population in the area, as intelligence.[23]

The same principle applied to other Prairie universities, those in Atlantic Canada, and smaller institutions in British Columbia and Ontario. Little of substance could be found, and reports invariably concluded with the authors making almost boastful cries – and perhaps laments – about the conservative nature of campuses in their areas. At Brock University a list of names of potentially subversive faculty was forwarded to headquarters, but only one name on the list was considered worthy of further examination.[24]

More attention was directed at universities that had been the sites of extensive protest in the 1960s. The results of student elections at Simon Fraser University, for example, were reported on, as was a paper entitled 'A Geographer's View of China.' Mordecai Briemberg, one of the fired PSA Department members at the university, continued to have his activities and those who worked on his behalf spied on even after he left the university. In fact, on this issue the coverage went all the way to the door of NDP premier Dave Barrett. Writing to Robin Bourne, the head of the Security Planning and Research Group, a new body created in the Department of the Solicitor General to offer more analysis regarding intelligence issues, Superintendent L.R. Parent described how 'a late evening visit by [deleted] to premier Dave BARRETT accomplished nothing' on behalf of the fired faculty members. Whom the Mounted Police were following and how it knew that the visit to the premier failed in its goals are interesting unanswered questions. Certainly the force, through its Key Sectors program, followed political developments, especially efforts by radicals at infiltrating the NDP. In his letter to Bourne, Parent included details of a meeting provincial minister of education

Eileen Dailly had with academic representatives and of a letter she received from some Simon Fraser University faculty members.[25]

Regardless of the institution, the recurring message by the middle of the 1970s was clear: there was little in the way of campus countersubversion work for the Security Service to perform. A lengthy annual report about York University concluded that while the situation there was troubled, it was 'from a social point of view, not from a Security Service point of view.'[26] Conversely, the Security Service's Kitchener office, which in 1973 held active files on ninety people at the area's three universities,[27] warned, in a ludicrous and expansive fashion, of the continuing threat of subversion to the wider society:

> In general we have adopted a laisser-faire [sic] approach to the marxist-leninist groups. Cities like Kitchener and Waterloo form the backbone of the Canadian society. If a city such as Kitchener or Waterloo is converted to maoism then the rest of the country will fall. This did not happen nor is it likely to happen. The marxist-leninists by and large used a soft sell approach, on radio, at rallies, and at open meetings. They did not convert. Even with the widespread economic woes and discontentment with the present federal and provincial governments, the people, the 'average citizen' is not streaking to join the ranks of the maoists. People here, the blue collar workers see them for what they are. Certain bus drivers and postal workers during their respective strikes, spoke on the marxist-leninist radio program – out of naiveté on the one hand and out of a desire to publicize their plight. These speakers did not get involved with the maoist rhetoric but simply expressed their union's position.[28]

Before the 1970s, the concept that societal factors and not agitators might be the cause of unrest had not been recognized by the RCMP, because the latter required the intervention of state security services while the former did not. Now there was an increasing understanding that the world was rather more complex. In a 1971 trial project initiated by its newly formed Special Operations Group to understand better the state of Canada's youth, the Security Service even went beyond surveillance and clipping newspaper articles to initiating dialogue with members of the '"counter-culture" ... opposed to established authority.' Over several months, members of the Security Service met openly with some young people in an effort to understand better the reasons for their discontent. John Starnes informed Solicitor General Jean-Pierre Goyer of the project and described it as reasonably successful, especially after some Security Service members managed to dissociate themselves from their crime-fighting brethren. Starnes went so far as to suggest that the Security Service might have a role to play in serving as a mediator between the regular police and disaffected youth.[29]

By the time of the so-called dialogue, however, campus protests of the kind frequent in the 1960s had largely disappeared. Rather than admit that it now lacked purpose, the Security Service found alternative duties, both at and away from campuses. On campuses, it began to look at different groups, and in the 1970s international issues, including international terrorism, a new phenomenon in this decade, seemed increasingly relevant to it for campus-based surveillance. On the question of the Middle East, for example, members of the RCMP feared the potential for conflict between Jewish and Arab university groups, and thus investigations on both were initiated. The fact that other left-wing targets of the Security Service openly supported or expressed sympathy for the Arab cause and that left-wingers often belonged to Jewish organizations also contributed to the RCMP's concerns.

With the exception of visits by controversial figures, such as that by Rabbi Meir Kahane, the founder of the Jewish Defence League, who spoke at Montreal-area universities in 1971, the force focused on campus groups. At McMaster University in 1970, McMaster Hillel, a Jewish student organization, had a file opened on it, and reports were filed on Jewish student organizations at Simon Fraser University, the University of Manitoba, and at the University of British Columbia. One target in British Columbia was the thirty-member Jewish Liberation Project, described by the reporting policeman as Zionist and socialist, although he added that the latter was 'spelled with a small "s" and in no way does the JLP support the Communist ideologies, whether Marxist, Leninist or Maoist.' By 1974 'D' Ops would have a Jewish desk to house relevant information, including reports about the McGill Zionist Students' Association.[30]

Also in 1974, the RCMP's countersubversion branch established an Arab desk to handle incoming reports that differed in style little from those collected about Jewish organizations or other university-related subjects. A meeting of the Middle East Anti-Imperialist Coalition at Sir George Williams University had its low turnout noted, especially the fact that most of those who turned out were there 'to kill the time.' A similar message was conveyed in a report about a banquet in Montreal at which the Iraqi ambassador spoke. Through inside knowledge the force knew that attendance was less than was hoped and that the organizers lost $200 on the venture. Another informant described the contents of speeches given at a McGill forum on the situation in the Middle East.[31] At the University of Alberta the focus was on the Arab Students Association because Constable A.D. Napier believed it was one of the leading sources of potential disorder on campus.[32]

The international directions of the Security Service's coverage of campuses in the 1970s extended beyond the Middle East. 'D' Ops organized a special desk to handle targets connected to Latin America, in particular Chile, where in 1973 the democratically elected government was overthrown in part through the machinations of the United States government and its CIA. A Canadian 'double standard' had long been applied to such events: opposition to left-wing dictatorships was generally seen as legitimate; the same was not true of opponents to right-wing equivalents.[33] The RCMP viewed efforts on the part of groups like the Latin American Working Group and Oxfam to influence federal policy regarding countries where human rights abuses were a regular occurrence as illegitimate for two reasons. First, they were conducted outside of Parliament, and secondly, the efforts often coincided with Soviet foreign policy goals in the areas in question. The fact that extra-parliamentary efforts by corporations to influence government policy occurred all the time seemed irrelevant to Canada's security agency.[34]

Another hot international topic on and off campuses in the 1970s was Northern Ireland. With the escalation of the conflict there in the early 1970s, any discussion on the topic was bound to draw RCMP attention, although, at least in part, the interest was in aid of British intelligence. Sean Kenny, a representative of the Irish Republican Army, made a tour of campuses in November 1971. His movements were reported on, and he was assigned file D937-9314.[35]

In the case of the African National Congress (ANC) and the anti-apartheid movement, it was a matter of the friend of my enemy is my enemy. The ANC's connections to the Soviet Union and its willingness to use violence automatically set off alarm bells and made the Security Service suspicious of any activities associated with it. In turn, Canadian universities were centres of the anti-apartheid movement. At Carleton University, the South African ambassador was assaulted when he appeared on campus to defend his country's regime. Support for the anti-apartheid movement extended to Parliament Hill. In January 1982, NDP member of Parliament Dan Heaps hosted a seventieth-anniversary party on behalf of the ANC, an event reported on by the Mounted Police. Besides noting the presence of Communist Party of Canada members and representatives from Eastern Bloc nations, the investigating officer warned that the presence of the gathering on Parliament Hill could be construed by the South African embassy as a sign of sympathy for the ANC.[36]

Despite their wider view of the world, the Mounted Police did not ignore those they perceived to be campus radicals. Thus in the 1970s the Committee for Socialist Studies came under scrutiny, as did Marxist study groups at Carleton University and Laurentian University. Even the venerable Canadian Political Science Association had investigators at its meetings. Often the reports displayed either the continuing intellectual shortcomings of some members of the Security Service or a strong effort by the members to ingratiate themselves with their superiors by telling them what they wanted to hear.[37]

Of equal significance in the 1970s were connections between campuses and the outside world, and it was not just the Security Service that worried about the danger of these links. One of the myths about the RCMP that developed as a result of the 'dirty tricks' era was that the criminal and the security sides existed in two separate worlds. In fact, the opposite was frequently the case. All members of the RCMP followed the same training, and in smaller centres there continued to be a great deal of shared work into the 1970s, when finally the Security Service, as a result of older Communists dying off, began a program of crashing files and closing offices. Superintendent L.G. Pantry, in charge of 'L' Division, which covered Prince Edward Island and included all the members there of the RCMP, felt it necessary to send advice to the commissioner about security threats and solutions:

Re: Trade Unions – Canada
3. With the exception of the National Farmers Union, a known militant group, [deleted] we have found all other unions to be fairly well managed. Most certainly in their executive level, they have been most co-operative and they do not promote violence. However, there are elements in the rank and file that are totally undisciplined. In certain cases they disobeyed their leaders and indeed in some instances were prepared to split the union.
4. In my opinion outside influences are being exerted on the rank and file and particularly those of the uneducated classes. I feel there is a profound influence on this type by so called educationalists and half baked intellectuals.[38]

Faculty unionization at Anglophone and Francophone universities across Canada appeared to suggest that Pantry's 'half baked intellectuals' were exerting their influence elsewhere. Unionization did not necessarily equal strikes, as the Security Service member with responsibility for the University of Toronto observed when he dismissed the potential for a labour disturbance because the university's faculty association was 'firmly controlled by essentially conservative people who are supporting unionism as a regrettable last resort.'[39]

The link between campuses and communities was relevant beyond the labour sector. The interpretation by the Mounted Police of efforts at social change had a cynical underpinning to it. Day care advocates who occupied a building at the University of Toronto in the early 1970s did so not out of conviction, the Security Service contended, but to promote subversion. The same principle applied to people who were involved in movements to liberate women. 'There is still a small vocal minority who are attempting to use women's liberation as a means to radically alter society,' warned the author of the composite report on the University of Toronto in 1972 and 1973, while from Vancouver came the observation that the Vancouver Women's Caucus had 'a definite extreme left and political radical undercurrent.'[40] Activism among women reflected, at least in part, the impact of academe on the outside world in the form of the emergence of the so-called second wave of feminism.[41] Mounties disapproved of such movements, not simply because they perceived them as politically subversive but also because they challenged traditional gender barriers, including those within the force itself, which women were able to begin joining only in 1974. Proponents of feminism suffered in the opinion of one policeman from an 'armageddon complex,' as the increasingly conservative campuses inspired a desperate search for potentially explosive issues to exploit.[42]

The RCMP's investigations of women's groups continued throughout the decade, and in the process it blurred distinctions between on-campus and off-campus radicalism. The mixture of reports prepared was telling, as they ranged from the Women's International Terrorist Conspiracy from Hell (WITCH) and the Phantom Purple Penis Avengers, the latter having disrupted a Miss Teen-Age BC Beauty Pageant, to an abortion rights group at the University of Saskatchewan and a women's conference at Montreal in January 1973. The latter, open only to women, was covered by a female source – the RCMP followed the pattern of the FBI in the United States, which either recruited from within women's groups or had women infiltrate from outside.[43] As late as 1982 members of the Kitchener office of the Security Service spied on a gathering in Guelph to commemorate International Women's Day. Unfortunately for the Mounties who were present, there was not sufficient light to allow for photographs to be taken of the members of the Communist Party of Canada (Marxist-Leninist) in attendance.[44]

The same formula applied to the Security Service's interest in other areas that had both an on- and off-campus presence. Gay rights' groups, like the University of Guelph Homophile Association, the University of Saskatchewan Gay Student Alliance, Vancouver's Gay Liberation Front, and the Gay Liberation Group at McMaster University, are cases in point. The RCMP spied on the latter, even though the force admitted, in an internal communication, that it was not being used as a 'front by any subversive organization.'[45]

Then there was the make-work nature to some of what the Security Service did in an era when the number of protests was dwindling. Concern about government grants going to subversive groups led to a report from Hamilton on some McMaster University students who received a grant to put on the plays of Bertolt Brecht. At the same institution came the threatening news that the McMaster Library was scheduled to establish an archive of material related to Canadian radicalism. A promise was made to keep headquarters updated on its acquisitions.[46]

As in previous decades, the Security Service cooperated with other government departments. In May 1977 Major Tom Haney of the Police and Security Liaison Section of the Department of National Defence contacted the Security Service to request information about Project Ploughshares, a newly formed peace organization at the University of Waterloo. Major Haney wanted to know if this pacifist group posed a threat to the Canadian Armed Forces and if it had the potential to 'subvert' members of the military. Headquarters in Ottawa passed it on to the Kitchener-Waterloo branch of the Security Service, which quickly determined that Project Ploughshares did not pose any more of a threat to the Canadian military than did other pacifist groups. The military officer was informed of this discovery, along with the reassurance that the Project Ploughshares would continue to be 'monitored.'[47]

National unity continued to draw the attention of the RCMP. Its coverage ranged from simply adding information to the files on prominent Québécois, including René Lévesque, Eric Kierans, and singer Pauline Julien, to attempting to discover whether there was any FLQ activity at Quebec universities and CEGEPS in 1971. The RCMP also noted the support for the FLQ on the part of a member of the Romance Languages Department at the University of Alberta, monitored a speech at McGill University by the lawyer of the FLQ, Robert Lemieux, obtained passport information from Washington, DC. regarding a member in Maine of the Franco-American Resource Opportunity Group who visited the Université de Moncton in 1972, and filed a report on a conference at the University of Manitoba under the caption 'Subversive Separatist Activities amongst French Canadians.'[48]

That the Security Service seemed increasingly interested not just in what was happening off campuses, but also in justifying its continued presence on campuses confirms even more how the university environment had shifted since the 1960s. However, the tactics of the Security Service had changed as well. In fact, at the very time that all aspects of radical activity were in decline, which the RCMP itself acknowledged, it launched its most determined effort to destroy its opponents. The Security Service had far less experience than the FBI's Counter Intelligence Program (COINTELPRO) with going beyond investigating subversive targets to attacking them. An underlying tension within the RCMP Security Service made the temptation to move to action understandable. The force was a police organization that conducted investigations, accumulated evidence, made arrests, and frequently had the satisfaction of seeing a conviction, but the Security Service was different. Those who came to it from police training quickly noted that difference. Unable to discuss what they did with outsiders or even with many of their colleagues, members of the Security Service also had no conclusion to their work. A member could theoretically spend an entire career following Communist leader Tim Buck, only to retire and have the file passed on to someone else; this person would have known the intimate details of Buck's life without being able to act on that information. The opportunity to strike back, to counter those who in their mind posed serious threats to the state, must have been irresistible for some in the Service. Superintendent Murray Chisholm testified at the McDonald Commission that aggressive tactics appeared necessary because the law offered no means to combat violence until after it had actually occurred.[49]

The tension, combined with the charged environment of the latter half of the 1960s, radicalized elements within the Security Service. In testimony to the McDonald Commission, those involved in planning operations of disruption cited among other motivating factors the Sir George Williams University computer centre incident, connections that apparently existed between American and Canadian radicals, and the appearance of Jerry Rubin at the University of British Columbia in Then came the October Crisis and the use of violence by the FLQ, as well as the encouragement given by the federal government to the RCMP to launch countermeasures, including break-ins and an alleged assassination, that have been well publicized in recent publications.[51]

Less studied has been what the Security Service did against targets that were not 'separatist-terrorist.' An obvious tactic resorted to by the RCMP, and one used with frequency by the FBI against the New Left, was to report infractions like drug use to colleagues on the criminal side as a means of eliminating an opponent.[52]

The RCMP planned a series of disruptive operations under three different code names, Tent Peg, Oddball, and Checkmate, all under the ultimate authority of Murray Chisholm, with another officer, Ron Yaworksi, playing a significant role. (Tent Peg was set up in 1969 but did not apparently move beyond the planning stage.) In the summer of 1970 the Special Operations Group was formed to discuss the tactics and methodology of these operations. According to Chisholm, 'disruptive measures were aimed at the organizations, to create confusion within their ranks, discrediting their leadership and/or their programs, all with the purpose of turning their attention and energies inward as much as possible, rather than outward to the community.' Oddball existed from April 1971 to September 1972, and it was followed by Checkmate from September 1972 to December 1973.[53]

The Special Operations Group consisted of four members at headquarters who conducted brainstorming sessions to come up with proposals for the 'neutralization' of certain groups and individuals. These were passed on to field offices, where more concrete recommendations would be developed and forwarded to senior officers such as Chisholm for authorization. One person who was involved in planning operations insists that they were not illegal but certainly often open to question from a point of view of ethics.[54]

Nearly a year and a half after the October 1970 crisis, junior officers and rank-and-file members also faced mounting pressure to take more dramatic measures against a variety of targets. In March 1972 John Starnes met with his senior colleagues and ordered all members of the Security Service to be 'more vigorous in their approach to disruptive activity' through the employment of 'well conceived operations.' Nor, he added, should Mounties be bothered by 'reticence' in performing such duties; a person who resisted carrying them out would have to be prepared to face the consequences in the form of disciplinary action or a transfer.[55]

The countermeasures carried out in this period, which were condemned by the McDonald Commission chiefly because they aimed to combat a general, imprecise threat of violence, included the filing of a false income tax return in the name of a targeted individual, the theft of a letter, the use of threatening phone calls, the manipulation of the media to disseminate detrimental information about groups and individuals, and anonymous phone calls designed to cause discontent within organizations. In one case, Security Service members distributed an anonymous letter containing attacks on the character of a candidate for the leadership of the Young Socialists, a Trotskyist organization that the RCMP knew posed no immediate threat of violence.[56]

Trotskyist and Maoist groups were among the targets, one of the latter being selected to receive special attention in a bid to destabilize it and promote dissension within its ranks. In September 1972 two new categories of targets were established. The first applied to organizations that constituted a 'violent revolutionary threat,' including elements of the New Left, and the second, which also featured New Left groups, were those seeking to 'infiltrate or penetrate existing groups or institutions for the purpose of promoting dissident or subversive influence aimed ultimately at promoting revolutionary activity.'

The RCMP's notion of what constituted groups and individuals seeking in a concerted way to 'penetrate' the 'key sectors' of Canadian society changed in the 1970s because of the growing conservatism at universities, combined with the 'campus to community' concept, the radicalization of the Security Service, and a mixture of make-work justifications and of pressure from above. These led the RCMP to take quite remarkable steps against two largely illusory targets, the Praxis Corporation and what it termed 'Extra-Parliamentary Opposition' (EPO).

Formed in 1968 as a research body for issues connected to such social problems as poverty, the Praxis Corporation enjoyed strong ties to the academic community. In the spring of 1969 E.R. Rettie, an under-secretary of state for external affairs, contacted the RCMP for information about it; Professor Stephen Clarkson at the University of Toronto had asked him to assign a research assistant to Praxis. Rettie wanted to avoid associating the Department of External Affairs 'with individuals who are active in "New Left" movements and who are connected in some definite way with the more violent and politically oriented manifestations of the fascist left evident in student/faculty dissent described in the briefs you have sent us recently.' Assistant Commissioner Len Higgitt was happy to comply, and forwarded the information on board members that the force had in file to External Affairs. The favour did not come without a price. Remarking on the difficulty the Security Service had in compiling information on university targets, the assistant commissioner asked External Affairs to assign a research fellow to Praxis so that the RCMP could use that individual to gather details about the organization.[57]

Whether such an appointment was made is not known. However, the Security Service's interest in Praxis Corporation, especially its connections to government employees and the Extra-Parliamentary Opposition, only grew.[58] In December 1970 a mysterious fire occurred at 373 Huron Street in Toronto, where Praxis Corporation, the Women's Liberation Movement, and Hogtown Press were located. Who started the fire remains a mystery. What is known is that the files of Praxis Corporation ended up in the possession of the Toronto office of the Security Service, arriving apparently on 23 February 1971 after an anonymous telephone call indicating where the material could be found. By April, Canada's spies had sorted through the documents for material of interest, which they then forwarded to Ottawa with the recommendation that the stolen pages be used for a detailed analysis of Praxis. One was produced by Sergent W. Ormshaw the following June.[59]

How the RCMP came into possession of stolen documents became a matter of public and political interest six years later when the Opposition in the House of Commons used the question to hammer away at the government. The *Toronto Sun* had no doubt that the RCMP was not only the author of the deed but also was fully justified in having carried it out. For others who were more concerned about civil liberties, the Praxis controversy, along with another revelation from the same period, were signs that an inquiry into the operations of the men and women in scarlet was overdue.[60]

The other matter that emerged at the same time as the stolen Praxis files was the RCMP's attempt to curtail an imaginary New Left movement known as the Extra-Parliamentary Opposition. The concept was first put forward in a Canadian context in a 1969 issue of *Our Generation*, a publication which had at one time been connected with the peace movement but which had evolved into a voice of the New Left in Canada. The article, by Dimitrios J. Roussopoulos, advocated the creation of an extra-parliamentary opposition to produce a critical mass prepared for revolution. He made it clear, however, that it would not be 'a formal organization but rather a *critical concept or a political term of reference.*'[61]

The RCMP chose to interpret the words differently. Nurtured to identify organized Communist attempts to infiltrate government, the notion of an extra-parliamentary opposition appeared to fit well with the belief that was prevailing among the police in the 1970s that radicalism was extending from universities to the surrounding world. When student radicals graduated, they continued their efforts to undermine the state, now from the inside instead of from the outside. The Praxis Corporation played a role in blinkering police perceptions. The fact that two prominent members of the organization, Gerry Hunnius and Howard Buchbinder, apparently had ties with this opposition seemed, to the police, to confirm that a cross-fertilization in the memberships of radical organizations was underway. Hunnius was of particular interest to the Security Service, especially since he had been born in Estonia. He had come to its attention in 1957 when he attended the World Festival of Youth in Moscow, and his activities over the next twenty years were recorded in detail and were still of interest to CSIS as late as 1986. The résumé of his radical activities made him into a synthesis of the ideal national security threat in the post-1945 era. He belonged to the Unitarian Church, the Combined Universities Campaign for Nuclear Disarmament, the Canadian Committee for the Control of Radiation Hazards, the Waffle Movement, and other New Left organizations, and he served on the editorial board of *Our Generation*. It was the latter that convinced several policemen that a large effort at subversion was taking place and that the prey included all levels of government.[62]

The concerns of the police soon became the concerns of the politicians. In May 1971 John Starnes forwarded to his boss, Solicitor General Jean-Pierre Goyer, a thirty-two-page report entitled 'The Changing Nature of the Threat from the New Left – Extra-Parliamentary Opposition, Penetration of Government' that had been months in the crafting. It contained the names of twenty-one government employees, several of them former campus activists, who intended, according to the RCMP, to steer government grants and sensitive government information to fellow radicals. In turn, Goyer, acting on the advice of Robin Bourne, the head of the Security Planning and Research Group in the Solicitor General's Department, sent several of his cabinet colleagues the names, along with a letter informing them that employees within the federal government 'appear to have as their aim the destruction of the existing political and social structure in Canada ... Of more concern, however, is the presence within certain government departments and agencies, particularly [the Canadian Mortgage and Housing Corporation], of a small group of former campus revolutionaries.'[63] Dealing with those named went far beyond a briefing. Several were dismissed or their contracts were not renewed. The government went even further and forwarded the names to several intelligence services outside of Canada. Later, in September, the Extra-Parliamentary Opposition appeared as a subject in a selection of slides shown to a group that included Trudeau as part of a presentation by the force on the present and the future of radicalism.[64]

Had such an organized menace that had emerged from the halls of academe really infiltrated the walls of government? As early as 1972 the Security Service itself began to have some doubts, and it moved to distance itself from its own dire warnings about both Praxis and the Extra-Parliamentary Opposition. A senior officer admitted that no evidence of a 'formal "E.P.O." membership' in government existed and that the Security Service's analyses had been based on developments in the Canadian New Left in 1969 and 1970 and thus were now 'dated.' 'For example,' he wrote, 'I believe we would revise certain assumptions ... in light of developments in the New Left field and Government sector in 1971 and 1972. One of the major revisions would be the hypothesis that there is a vast conspiratorial plot on the part of the proponents of radical EPO, other elements of the New Left ... and persons employed by the Federal Government.' Unable to openly admit that a mistake had been made, he denied 'that this hypothesis was invalid or unworthy of monitoring and investigation in an operational sense at the time [but] ... with the advantage of hindsight that this hypothesis does not seem valid today ...' He concluded by expressing apprehension that other government departments might be using the 'exaggerated' analysis in dealing with their employees.[65]

By then, however, the damage had been done. When the story of the 'blacklist' emerged in 1977, an uproar ensued in the House of Commons. Privately, Robin Bourne, now the assistant deputy minister (police and security) in the Solicitor General's Department, blamed the entire matter on the 'pervading atmosphere' at the time. As late as 1979, in its brief to the McDonald Commission, 'D' Ops continued to push the fiction of an organized EPO faction functioning within government. It was left to the McDonald Commission in its final report to finally dispel the notion. 'There never was, in Canada or elsewhere, any group or organization that styled itself as the Extra Parliamentary Opposition,' it concluded, adding that the 1971 Security Service report suffered from poor analysis, exaggerated rhetoric, and faulty logic.[66]

That reprimand arrived too late for the victims. Checkmate officially ended in December 1974 and the RCMP proceeded to destroy the

operational records to avoid, in the words of Ron Yaworski who had witnessed the problems for the FBI after some of its COINTELPRO files were
stolen and made public, 'the likelihood of adverse publicity.' The following year the government gave official licence to operations for
countersubversion, when for the first time ever it provided the Security
Service with a mandate that included the power to 'counter' and 'deter'
threats to the state. The extent to which it used countermeasures after
1975 is not known, but evidence is available to indicate that such operations were being considered in at least one instance: a 1976 Security
Service report about Maoists at the University of Guelph included a
category entitled 'Counter Measures,' under which it was noted that
none were necessary since the targeted group had a 'built-in self destruct
mechanism.'[67]

With the destruction of Special Operations Group records, only those
involved in it know for certain what the RCMP did during this period.
Even the leaders of the Mounted Police and the politicians could not be
sure, as in the example of a publisher and one of its authors, Stan
Hanson, who obtained a master's degree in history after completing a
thesis about the 1931 Estevan strike and riot. Soon after getting a job at
the University of Saskatchewan in 1971 he found an unfamiliar visitor in
his office one morning. The individual displayed identification confirm-
ing that he was a member of the Security Service and proceeded to
question Hanson about his relationship with James Lewis & Samuel,
Publishers, later James Lorimer and Company, which had approached
Hanson about publishing his thesis. It was this that the Mountie focused
on, asking the increasingly perplexed history graduate whether he intended to publish his work. Hanson's curiosity was piqued by the fact
that he had only discussed the matter with two people, his wife and the
representative from the publisher. When he asked the policeman about
the source of his information, the officer replied: 'we tend to keep track
of people involved with or involved in the study of radical political or
labour groups.'[68]

How had the RCMP learned about the publisher's interest in the
thesis? One possible answer is related to the 'dirty tricks' carried out in
the 1970s. In 1971 someone had broken into the office of James Lewis
and Samuel. Had it been a member of the Security Service? This was a
question asked within the RCMP in 1977 in the wake of the revelations
related to Praxis. The answer given to heads of the RCMP after file
searches and interviews with those who had worked in the Service's
Toronto office in 1971, was no. Instead, someone from within the pub-

lisher had supplied copies of correspondence and manuscripts to the Security Service in April 1971.[69]

After many reports from universities and the experience surrounding the phantom Extra-Parliamentary Opposition, even the RCMP had to realize that a new atmosphere existed on campuses in Canada. Resistance to change remained, however. The last gasp of the old order occurred in 1977 and involved the annual Learned Societies meeting, which was meeting in Fredericton, New Brunswick. One of those in attendance, a student in a humanities discipline, was also a police informant. After the conference he or she wrote a remarkable assessment of it:

> For a young academic on the make, the chance to present a research paper at the Learneds is a golden opportunity to impress his elders and get a job ... [G]iven the current tight academic job market, there is a great competition to present papers ...
>
> To an outsider, many of the activities are boring. A typical session consists of lots of free coffee, the reading of one or two research papers, some discussion, some questions from the floor, and then more free coffee. The action goes on at the pubs ... An important factor is that government grants usually pay for the travelling costs of all participants so that for an academic the Learneds are either a subsidized job hunt or a subsidized vacation.[70]

Marxists at Fredericton became the focus of the report. Remarking on the attendance at the business meetings of the Labour History Group and the Political Economy Network, the informant observed that the two groups displayed 'a semi-religious fervour in the manner in which most members see almost a moral duty to use their intelligence and teaching positions to spread the cause of marxism.' The prescient source went so far as to warn that Marxist scholars intended to try to gain access to secret RCMP Security Service records like the one that he or she was in the process of writing and that the RCMP had been accumulating about the Learneds over the previous seventeen years. 'They will claim that it is vital to their research but their goal, as stated several times in the company of other marxists, is to prove that the RCMP is in their terms, "an agent of state repression" and thus to try to discredit the RCMP.' At this point there is a cryptic handwritten comment, 'They've missed the boat,' referring either to the McDonald Commission, which was about to begin, or the destruction of sensitive documents that had already occurred.[71]

Even more remarkable than this report was the internal debate that it triggered in the Security Service. The information sent from Fredericton clearly represented an escalation of coverage in the area of higher education, just as other Security Service operations were coming under increasing scrutiny by politicians, the courts, the media, and the general public. The initial response from the author's superiors was positive. One policeman noted that the report provided an excellent opportunity to follow the activities of Marxists. His own superior, Superintendent M.J. Spooner, who as a student at Queen's University in 1962 had spied on a campus meeting, also praised the document.[72]

It was at this point, however, that some dissension about the report began to appear. Spooner's superior disagreed that the document demonstrated the utility of reporting every year on the Learned Societies conferences, agreeing only that it remained important to maintain 'permanent sources in academe.'[73] The most sustained critique, however, appeared in May 1978, when Inspector J.H. Brookmyre argued that the attendance of Marxists at the Learneds was something that had to be tolerated in a democratic society. He went so far as to suggest that such detailed coverage was outside the mandate of the Security Service and that the threat posed by those attending the Learneds was weak: 'There is *nothing* to indicate these academics (intelligentsia) intend to use or encourage the use of force, violence or criminal means – or create or exploit civil disobedience.' Equivalent intelligence, added Brookmyre, could be obtained more simply by a close reading of newspapers.[74]

Although Brookmyre had not ruled out continued coverage, clearly he and others realized that what was gathered did not justify either the methods or the risks, especially with the force coming under increasing scrutiny from a wide range of sources. The first instance of political scrutiny came from the Keable Commission, appointed on 15 June 1977 by the recently elected Parti Québécois government to investigate RCMP wrongdoing. A month later Solicitor General Francis Fox rose in the House of Commons to announce the creation of the Royal Commission to Investigate Certain Activities of the Royal Canadian Mounted Police, or the McDonald Commission, presided by D.C. McDonald. The Security Service's world was reeling.

Other factors were at work as well in changing the world of the Security Service. Throughout the decade it had continued to transform itself internally into a more sophisticated entity. The Operational Priorities Review Committee it created in 1977 represented a major development. It was an attempt to modernize operations by bringing in rigid criteria in the choice of groups and individuals for intrusive forms of surveillance. Technical resources had evolved as well. Early in the decade, computers arrived, and demonstrations, meetings, and individuals could now be, and on occasion were, videotaped or filmed. Around-the-clock monitoring of radio and television stations was carried out on a permanent basis at headquarters. Most significant for the RCMP, it finally became an employer of women as regular members and officially bilingual in the 1970s. As late as 1969 'C' Division in Montreal was cautioned against submitting reports in French because headquarters lacked the ability to deal with them. This changed dramatically over the following ten years, as important documents began to appear in both official languages and large numbers of reports, although almost exclusively from Quebec and New Brunswick, began to be submitted in French.[75]

Change was occurring all around. In the new atmosphere of the McDonald Commission era, the Security Service sought to jettison anything that created the potential for negative publicity. The RCMP planned to take a low-key approach to the new separatist government in Quebec, fearing that anything aggressive would be 'counter-productive.' The Security Service already had a source, Claude Morin, in the highest levels of the Lévesque administration. It was also concerned about the French-language abilities of its Quebec members and about whether those who were Francophone could be trusted to spy on the PQ government. Because of this limitation, Chief Superintendent Donald Cobb recommended 'expanded access to communications interceptions' as the best means for increased investigation of the government of Quebec.[76]

What Cobb recognized was that far from seeking to restrain the Security Service, the government of Prime Minister Pierre Trudeau wanted it to actively investigate the new separatist government. Trudeau expressed his wishes in a draft letter that encouraged (but did not explicitly state or order) the RCMP to avoid interpreting the 1975 mandate as restricting investigations of subversive activity even if the use of violence was not being advocated.[77]

With Trudeau's wishes becoming known, the Security Service, apparently to protect itself, spelled out explicitly that the government's policy directive would entail recruiting 'sources and agents within the Parti québécois,' monitoring the educational sector for separatist activities, and 'physical surveillance, electronic surveillance (when authorized), and surreptitious photography.' These were all methods that had previously been used against separatists but which would now be employed against a democratically elected provincial government.[78]

The Security Service was not alone in being concerned about the aims of Canada's prime minister. The commissioner of the RCMP and the head of the Security Service met repeatedly with Solicitor General Francis Fox and two senior bureaucrats from his department, Roger Tassé and Robin Bourne, to discuss Trudeau's wishes. In a letter drafted by Tassé and sent to the Privy Council Office, the officials did not equivocate: 'We have concluded that if it is the wish of the Government that the Security Service investigate activities aimed at the separation of a province from the Canadian federation, then the matter must be faced squarely. The draft letter from the Prime Minister to the Solicitor General is, in our opinion, not specific enough. In fact, Mr. Fox has made it clear that he would not feel comfortable with any change in current Security Service activities in Quebec on receipt of that letter alone.' Should Trudeau offer more explicit instructions, Tassé warned of potential consequences:

> Is it in fact a proper function of one element of a national police force to collect information about a provincial government? If the information collected is to be of any value, it must mean that the members of the provincial cabinet could become targets of covert surveillance. For how long would it be possible to keep this activity from public knowledge? In other words, is the value of the information collected going to be worth the political damage done to the Federal Government and the long term damage which will probably be done to the R.C.M.P. by public disclosure of this activity. The R.C.M.P. cannot afford to become suspected of 'political spying.'[79]

The RCMP continued to maintain an interest in issues of national unity but apparently not as directly as Trudeau had sought. This activity was extremely sensitive, so much so that when the subject came before the McDonald Commission it was decided that some of the RCMP documents would be viewed by Mr Justice McDonald and his two fellow commissioners but not be made public.[80]

It was not just in the field of national unity that the Security Service had become skittish. Key Sectors, a program that had once seemed on the cutting edge, was officially shut down in 1977, although in spirit it lingered on into the early years of CSIS. The force's 'VIP program,' a collection of files on 668 politicians and bureaucrats at all three levels of government, was stopped except for files on a handful of individuals who continued to be targeted. Security Service offices that had been established decades earlier in small communities to monitor the activities of East European Communists, closed their doors.[81]

In this new era, 'passive collation' became the operative phrase as the force moved away from actively seeking information on what had been hot topics. In June 1980 the order went out that all 'educational' files involving universities, community colleges, and such academic organizations as the Canadian Association of University Teachers were to be shifted to the 'passive mode,' although it was quickly added that the presence of 'subversive elements' in these agencies would continue to be investigated using more active methods.[82]

Nearing its end in the late 1970s, the countersubversion branch of the Security Service increasingly resembled its form in the era before the rise of the New Left in the previous decade. In truth, traditional targets, such as the Communists, Maoists, and Trotskyists, had never been abandoned; they just did not seem as significant as did movements connected with the New Left or Quebec separatism. Now, at the end of the 'me decade,' they again became the *raison d'être* for the countersubversion branch. But that renewed emphasis did not come without a degree of hesitation, especially after the shockwaves produced by the McDonald Commission report. In its wake, the Security Service received explicit permission from Solicitor General Robert Kaplan to continue its surveillance of the Communist Party of Canada.[83]

The traditional focus still involved trips onto campuses. At the Université Laval, Mounties spied on activities of the Ligue d'Ouvriers Révolutionnaire, which had established a table in the foyer of a campus building, in 1977. Another report from Laval described attempts by Trotskyist elements within the Department of Sociology to encourage the 'mobilization of first-year students.'[84] At McMaster University in October 1977 a Mountie secretly covered a conference about Poland and Ukraine. He or she noted the 'objective' tone of the event except for a paper by Professor Adam Bromke, then the head of the Political Science Department, who challenged the prevailing consensus about the Soviet Bloc.[85]

At times even the rationale for monitoring the usual countersubversion targets seemed weak. After commenting on the printing and book facilities of the Communist Party of Canada (Marxist-Leninist) and of one of its front groups, the Guelph Student Movement, the author of a report admitted that with only thirteen members the party in the Kitchener-Waterloo-Guelph area was 'spread pretty thin.' Did that mean an end to coverage and the transfer of resources elsewhere? No; continued investigation was recommended although less attention could be paid to front groups.[86]

The decline in the interest the Security Service paid to university campuses in the late 1970s continued into the 1980s. In a climate of heightened media and political scrutiny, the only safe targets were groups or activities that had been targeted for most of the cold war period. A source accompanied five busloads of protesters who journeyed from Quebec to Ottawa in March 1981 to protest recently elected U.S. president Ronald Reagan's first official visit to Canada as part of the effort to keep track of the growing peace movement and of attempts to infiltrate disarmament groups like Operation Dismantle.[87]

For the Security Service's countersubversion wing it was business as usual with its established targets, namely Maoists, Trotskyists, and Communists, across the country. The transfer of security activities to a new civilian agency loomed near, and in its final days in the early 1980s the Security Service returned to its countersubversion roots.

9

Conclusion: From CSIS to APEC

For us, this is old history.
> RCMP spokesperson Sergent Mike Gaudet on revelations about
> RCMP spying on universities and high schools
> during the cold war, 1998

RCMP Infiltrated Student Groups: Used Intelligence to Arrest Activists at
APEC Summit
> *Toronto Star*, 1998

These are matters CAUT has discussed with your predecessors as far back as
1963 and appear to be relevant matters for further discussion now.
> Thomas Booth, CAUT president, and James L. Turk, CAUT
> executive director, to RCMP commissioner Guiliano Zaccardelli, 2001

In Canada, old security services do not fade away, they just get absorbed
by other ones. In 1919 the Dominion Police discovered that merging
with the Royal North-West Mounted Police actually meant eradication.
In an event that went uncelebrated, the Royal Canadian Mounted Police
entered the Canadian scene in 1920, and it would later spawn a Security
Service. Sixty-four years after the RCMP was established, a major part of
its soul was severed by official edict when the Canadian Security Intelligence Service was born on 16 July 1984. It represented the biggest
offspring of the McDonald Commission. The agency came with a specific
mandate that specified its targets and with outside review bodies, in the
form of an inspector general and the Security Intelligence Review Committee (SIRC).

Despite the appearance of a new beginning, CSIS was, in fact, more of the same. Security Service members interested in remaining in the spy business joined the new agency. Many even kept their desks. All told, the original population of the new spy agency consisted of a majority of the old.[1] Up until the late 1980s, CSIS was little different from the Security Service of a decade earlier. The instructional books were the same, and the RCMP's Operational Priorities Review Committee became the Target and Approval Review Committee. Even the movement away from investigations into countersubversion to counterterrorism and counter-intelligence work actually started under the old Security Service, speeded along by several terrorist acts, including the bombing of Litton Systems in Toronto and the murder of a Turkish government official in Ottawa in the early 1980s.[2] The changes underway were already quite marked in the Security Service before it's demise in 1984 (see Table 9.1). A similar trend was apparent in the Security Service's use of technical sources in the same period (see Table 9.2).

In the countersubversion operations that remained after the transition to CSIS, old problems re-emerged. Many of the difficulties involved the troublesome role of dealing with the nebulous concept of subversion, which the new agency recognized. '[Countersubversion] targets are perhaps the most difficult of the CSIS targets to identify,' noted the proposed revision of the operational manual, 'because they often are Canadians who hold dissenting views but who are not otherwise distinctive.'[3] But countersubversion work against traditional targets continued in the early years of CSIS. From the Kitchener office, for example, appeared a November 1984 report on local Maoist activity, primarily in the form of front groups at the University of Guelph and the University of Waterloo.[4]

That trend would not last. The arrival of the government of Brian Mulroney neatly coincided with the introduction of CSIS. While in opposition, the Conservatives had been strong critics of both RCMP excesses and the complicity and perfidy of Pierre Trudeau's Liberals. Now in government, they had the opportunity to bring about change. In July 1987 the Conservatives appointed the Independent Advisory Team under Gordon Osbaldeston, a former clerk of the Privy Council, to investigate problems associated with CSIS. The Osbaldeston Report, with its clear focus on the countersubversion branch, arrived on the government's desks in the fall of that year. The choice for the government, argues journalist Richard Cleroux, was not difficult. Countersubversion 'amounted to no more than ten percent of the personnel or about five

TABLE 9.1
The use of operational personnel by the RCMP's Security Service, 1981–4

	1981–2		1982–3		1983–4	
Category	Percentage	Change from previous year	Percentage	Change from previous year	Percentage	Change from previous year
Counter-intelligence	55	not available	55.3	+.3	62.54[a]	+1.74
Foreign interference	8	not available	5.5	-2.5	not available	not available
Counterterrorism	8	not available	14.8	+6.8	16.04	+1.24
Countersubversion	21	not available	17.0	-4.0	13.83	-4.41
Security screening	8	not available	7.4	-.6	7.59	+.19

Source: CSIS, Access request 117-2000-22, 'The Role, Tasks, and Methods of the RCMP Security Service,' Annual reports of the RCMP Security Service, 1982–3, 1983–4.
[a]Foreign interference appears to have been added into counter-intelligence.

TABLE 9.2

Warrants for technical sources (telephone intercepts, etc.) issued by the solicitor general to the RCMP Security Service in the 1980s

Category	On 1 April 1981	New	Total, 1981–2	on 1 April 1982	New	Total 1982–3	on 1 April 1983	New	Total, 1983–4
Counter-intelligence	181	85	266	164	119	283	194	103	297
Counterterrorism	34	12	46	22	125	147	124	75	199
Countersubversion	57	34	91	50	21	71	39	34	73
Total	272	131	403	236	265	501	357	212	569

Source: CSIS, Access request 117-2000-22, 'The Role, Tasks, and Methods of the RCMP Security Service,' Annual reports of the RCMP Security Service, 1982–3, 1983–4.

percent of the budget ... and drew about fifty percent of the criticism directed at CSIS by civil libertarians.'[5]

The countersubversion branch was slowly closed down. Of the approximately 57,000 files on individuals that CSIS had maintained in the countersubversion branch, around 54,000 were considered worthless and slightly more than 3,800 worthy of further monitoring through open sources; only one hundred individuals continued to have their lives examined using the most intrusive measures possible. As for organizations, eighteen targets, all rather traditional, accounted for many of the 3,800 people, some of whom were on university campuses, and they became the responsibility of the Analysis and Production Branch, which continued to monitor them using open sources. The CSIS countersubversion targets in 1988 were the Alliance for Socialist Action (Trotskyist), Canada-USSR Association, Canadian Party of Labour, Canadian Peace Congress, Collectif des Révoltés (Trotskyist), Communist Party of Canada (Quebec), Congress of Canadian Women, Gauche Socialiste (Trotskyist), Groupe Marxiste-Léniniste Libre, Groupe Socialiste de Travailleurs (Trotskyist), International Socialists (Trotskyist), Ligue des Travailleurs (Trotskyist), Quebec Peace Council, Quebec Women's League, Revolutionary Workers League (Trotskyist), Société Culturelle Québec-URSS, Trotskyist League of Canada, and Young Communist League of Canada-Quebec.[6]

One of the pertinent questions as the countersubversion branch neared its death was what to do with thousands of pages of now-irrelevant documents, including records related to universities, that had been collected by the RCMP over six decades. The Security Service, with the federal government's permission had already destroyed 208,481 of its files between July 1983 and May 1984. With the appearance of the new spy agency, a decision was made to transfer some of the records to the National Archives of Canada. In 1987 CSIS created the National Archives Requirements Unit to review the documents in consultation with archivists. Out of nearly 500,000 records, 440,000 were destroyed. Twenty-nine thousand made the trip to the archives and 28,000 were retained at CSIS because of continuing value. The embarrassment factor was considered in at least one case when the records were being reviewed. After assessing a single volume in the collection relating to McGill University, an employee of CSIS was sure that the file deserved to be destroyed, since Canada's new spy service had 'no need for a file to be specifically opened on a university. [deleted] Keeping such a file can only bring us problems.'[7]

More than just RCMP records posed a difficulty for CSIS – an agency even more concerned than its predecessor with keeping a low profile – when it came to its dealings with universities. In the waning days of the government of Pierre Trudeau in the early 1980s, Robert Kaplan, the solicitor general of the day, changed the ministerial directive governing security investigations on campuses. The previous one had been in place since September 1971, when Jean-Pierre Goyer, to the anger of some in the Mounted Police, required each use of technical and paid human sources on campus to be approved in advance by the solicitor general. A loophole in Goyer's revision was the separation of paid informants from unpaid. Kaplan's instruction lumped together all informants; every use of them required the permission of the solicitor general before they could be used on campuses. Kaplan had been concerned about the issue after the McDonald Commission had made reference to it, and he finally found an opportunity, with the birth of the new agency, 'to protect a cornerstone of free thought in our society.'[8]

CSIS did not share his noble sentiments, perceiving the policy shift as a nuisance. An opportunity to seek its amendment arrived with the Conservative government of Brian Mulroney. The agency soon began asking the new solicitor general, Perrin Beatty, for revisions, portraying the issue not as one of protecting intellectual freedom but as one of ensuring proper on-campus intelligence gathering. Even the old Security Service cliché of the university as a sanctuary for terrorists and other nefarious figures was deployed. What CSIS sought to end was the constant need to seek permission from the solicitor general every time it wanted to use human sources on university campuses. If permission was granted, CSIS received the following generic reply from the solicitor general:

Dear Mr. [Ted] Finn [CSIS Director]:

I am writing in reply to your letter ... concerning your request to use a human source on campus to monitor [deleted: name of targeted organization].

I have carefully considered this case in the light of the current policy and the mandate of the Service as established by the CSIS Act. The recruitment activities and program of [deleted: name of targeted organization] on university campuses clearly indicates that 'something specific is happening beyond the general free flow of ideas.' I, therefore, approve your request to use the human source on the campuses [deleted: names of universities] subject to the observance of the operational guidelines set out in your letter.

Please keep me informed of any significant developments in this case.[9]

CSIS was mistaken, however, if it thought Beatty might be sympathetic to its case. He expressed concern instead about 'source activity on campus,' arguing that it was better to continue with the existing policy than to stir up the old problems with CAUT. The recently formed SIRC, CSIS's watchdog, investigated the issue of informants at universities for its 1986–7 annual report and reported that the intelligence organization was complying with existing policy.[10]

Nonetheless, CSIS continued to lobby for change. By 1987 Beatty had moved on to a different cabinet post and James Kelleher had become the new political master. His deputy minister described to him CSIS's unhappiness and suggested one of two courses of action: the status quo, or a change that would give it more leeway to use campus informants, while still facing scrutiny from SIRC and the inspector general. Kelleher opted in February for the status quo.[11]

Again, however, Canada's chief spy agency did not give up on the issue. It reappeared in 1993, during the short-lived administration of Prime Minister Kim Campbell, when Doug Lewis was her minister of public safety. A deal appeared attainable, to the point that a new ministerial direction was prepared by the National Security Directorate for Lewis to sign. The catastrophic election campaign for the Conservatives intervened in October, however, and the Liberals, the party that had put restraints in place in 1963, 1971, and 1984, returned to office. The lobbying by CSIS continued, nevertheless. In October 1994 the director of CSIS, Ward Elcock, wrote to the solicitor general in Jean Chrétien's government, Herb Gray, with a draft of a new ministerial direction. In support of his case, Elcock pointed out that most of the requests for the use of sources that Gray approved involved universities as 'venues of convenience' and not as academic institutions. He also offered a history lesson surrounding the issue and underlined that even SIRC, in its 1991 annual report, had argued the language of the 1984 ministerial direction 'was out of date' (the watchdog had launched an examination of the use of sources at universities after a rise in their number in both 1988 and 1989).[12] Everyone agreed on the necessity of using them and thus it was felt that the best route would be to rewrite the rules.[13]

The federal government was, however, still unconvinced. In January 1995 it asked for a review of CSIS's draft of the ministerial directive as it compared with the one that was put forward by the National Security Directorate in 1993. 'Whether by design or by oversight,' the author of the review warned the government, 'the CSIS MD ... goes beyond the modernisation of 1984 by stretching its governing principles. Thanks to some key omissions and the use of open-ended language, the CSIS MD would probably have the effect of opening up the policy horizon [resulting in] an expanded latitude with respect to the rationale for and the types of investigations it could pursue at post-secondary educational institutions.'[14]

Discussions continued through 1995. By November a compromise ministerial directive had been prepared and it was sent to the office of the solicitor general. Under the new directive, the minister's approval would continue to be required for the use of human sources against individuals 'whose activities are connected with the roles and functions of the educational institution' defined 'as teaching, study and research.' Now, however, the director of CSIS would be able to approve the use of informants against targets whose contact with universities was deemed 'incidental.' For the top bureaucrats in the solicitor general's department, however, the new draft and its expanded powers for the CSIS director remained problematic. In particular, the meaning of 'incidental' represented a major concern. After more discussions throughout 1996, a new directive acceptable to both CSIS and the bureaucrats was drafted; the approval of the solicitor general remained the final obstacle.

In February 1997 Gray's deputy minister advised him as to how the new document differed from the old. It allowed the director of CSIS to approve the use of a source when a university was used by a targeted organization (an example might be a White supremacist group) as a 'venue of convenience.' In order to do so, Canada's spy agency was required to 'possess information that the activity or meeting is to be closed or private, with participation by the general public, the academic community or students neither sought or encouraged. The activity is unrelated to academic life and is not intended to have an impact on the institution or its people.' It also included an 'urgent situations' clause allowing the director of CSIS to authorize, under certain circumstances, the use of an informant when the solicitor general was unable to do so. In these cases, CSIS was to be responsible for the decision and was to report promptly to the minister.

After asking for a minor clarification, Herb Gray authorized the new directive, which had been twelve years in the making, on 26 February 1997. As soon as it was implemented, however, problems arose. Eight months passed before the solicitor general was notified of a decision that had been taken on 18 August 1998 to authorize activities by a source on a campus. CSIS also chose to interpret the directive as allowing 'blanket authorizations' for the use of informants. In fact, the first authorization by the director under the 'venue of convenience' clause involved a broader activity than the government had originally envisioned possible under the new policy.[15]

Why was this matter of such concern to CSIS that it spent over a decade lobbying for reform? Because, very simply, the agency continued – and continues – to be interested in what occurs at universities. Both on and off campuses, however, targeting now has far more to do with combating violence, terrorism, and espionage than the traditional subversive elements of the Security Service era. Targets connected to subversion, as defined in Section 2(d) of the act creating CSIS, now require the specific authorization of the solicitor general. There was not a single such investigation in the period covered by the 1998–9 report of SIRC.[16]

Instead, CSIS concentrates on counter-intelligence and, especially since the end of the cold war, counterterrorism and transnational crime. Who can argue against a state agency fighting terrorism and violence on Canadian soil?[17] The application of the label of 'terrorist,' however, involves a little-recognized shade of grey. The attacks of 11 September 2001 were terrorism incarnate. But is a group that uses violence to combat a repressive regime, for example, really a terrorist organization? Should the labelling by dictatorships of their opponents as 'terrorists' be accepted? Was the African National Congress, which was monitored by the Security Service and no doubt CSIS in its early days, a terrorist organization? Are peaceful activities conducted on behalf of such groups in Canada worthy of state scrutiny? Is it accurate to label those who vandalize property as terrorists, as the United Kingdom has done? What about justifying the investigation of peaceful opponents of government foreign policy, as the FBI did in the early 1980s, when it went after groups opposed to the Reagan administration's policy towards El Salvador on the grounds that they posed a terrorist threat? What is the most effective method for dealing with terrorism? Are current institutions, developed during the cold war, capable of responding to new threats? Finally, is it ever in the interest of an intelligence agency to downplay a potential threat? These questions and more need to be asked,[18] but after 11 September and the rush to pass legislation and to follow the lead of the United States, they most likely will not be.

In this new era and the rapid passage of anti-terrorism legislation, the likelihood that those who engage in peaceful dissent will be investigated is great. Even CSIS's official and often-repeated mantra that it does not spy on legal activities is not as unequivocal as it sounds. After all, how does the agency determine whether an activity is legal without investigat-

ing it, although admittedly the methods employed might involve freely
available information. The same point applies to the notion of a 'threat,'
a term that has replaced the security labels of the past, like enemy alien,
Communist, and subversive. According to the Canadian Armed Forces,
'in the absence of a security threat [the National Counter-Intelligence
Unit] does not collect information on individuals, legal assemblies or
organizations.'[19] But, of course, it is the state that determines in the first
place who or what represents a 'threat.'

In writing this book I repeatedly faced questions regarding CSIS's
current activities on university campuses. Generally, there is little continuity with what came before, at least in terms of countersubversion. The
activities of CSIS are circumscribed by its governing legislation, by the
Security Intelligence Review Committee, and by fear of political and
public opinion. Nevertheless, CSIS does still perform campus-related
work. That it spent twelve years seeking the reform of the ministerial
directive governing the use of human sources on campuses is ample
evidence of this. So what does CSIS do on campuses? First, there is the
work that is incidental to the nature of universities. This is what the
reform of the ministerial directive was primarily aimed at. It could
involve, for example, investigating a White supremacist organization or
some other targeted group using university facilities to stage meetings.

The other justifications for campus work more closely resemble those
of the Security Service era. Counter-intelligence and counterterrorism
are the primary examples. In the case of the former, students and faculty
studying or working in Canada, especially in research connected to
technology, who are from countries such as Russia, Iran, Iraq, North Korea,
Libya, Sudan, or China are of interest to CSIS for two reasons. First, they
represent potential gatherers of highly valuable information on behalf of
the intelligence services of their native countries, not only in terms of
technological data but also about other students and faculty from their
home country. Secondly, they may be seeking to monitor the actions of
others from their countries who are in Canada or even to pressure their
fellow citizens into supplying sensitive information. In turn, CSIS would
have an interest in recruiting informants among members of these same
nationalities or in turning an intelligence agent from abroad using the
cover of academe into a double agent who would work on behalf of
Canada. Even Canadian academics having contact with individuals
from these countries can come under suspicion, as two geology professors
at the University of Toronto discovered in 1990 when their departmental secretary revealed to them that she had worked as an infor-

mant for CSIS since 1986; CSIS was concerned that the men, who had close academic ties to the Soviet Union, were working on behalf of Soviet intelligence.

Since 11 September 2001, counterterrorism has outpaced counter-intelligence as a justification for investigations on campuses. In Canada's southern neighbour, students from Muslim nations were targeted for questioning by law enforcement officials after it was revealed that one of the nineteen hijackers had entered the United States on a student visa. In Canada suspicions of Muslim students predated 11 September. The Canadian military's National Counter-Intelligence Unit investigated the purchase in 1998 of a building in Moncton by Muslim students at the University of New Brunswick, who were seeking to convert it into a mosque. In another example, an international student at a Canadian university who attended a dinner in 2000 with a diplomat from his native country, a country on the United States' list of nations that support terrorism, had a visit the next day from two members of CSIS. They had acquired his address either through surveillance of the gathering or from someone in attendance at it, and questioned him about what had transpired at the dinner.[20]

Then there is the concept that developed during the 1960s, namely the threat of domestic violence. First Nations are currently the focus, as both the RCMP and CSIS, in a vestige of colonialism that is almost unnoticed by the mainstream media, continue regularly to investigate Aboriginal communities under the pretext of the 'potential for violence.' This reflects a centuries-long stereotype of the 'savage,' and it also demonstrates that under the category of 'violence' almost any sort of monitoring can be justified. This was something that the RCMP Security Service recognized when it expanded its coverage in Quebec after the 1980 referendum on the grounds of the threat of violence.[21] It was also a reality that Tony Hall, a member of the Native Studies Department at the University of Lethbridge, experienced on two separate occasions. The first occurred in 1990, when members of CSIS visited the president of his university to discuss Hall's efforts on behalf of the Lonefighter Society, a group that was determined to halt the construction of the Oldman River dam in Alberta. The second occurred just before the 2001 Summit of the Americas in Quebec City, when he received a visit in his university office from Sergeant G.C. Cramer, a member of the RCMP's National Security Investigations Section (NSIS). Cramer wanted to question Hall about some of his writings that had appeared on the Internet and about his involvement in the Alternative Peoples' Summit scheduled to take place just before the politicians gathered in Quebec City. Cramer's appearance on campus prompted CAUT to complain to the commissioner of the RCMP, Guiliano Zaccardelli, and to request a meeting about the work carried out on campus, as it had done in the early 1960s. The battle was underway once again.[22]

CSIS's involvement in security matters hardly seems surprising, but why would the RCMP be involved in such investigations? That the RCMP still plays an important role in Canadian security intelligence work was little recognized until the infamous 'pepper spray' incident at the University of British Columbia during the Asia-Pacific Economic Cooperation conference.[23] As part of its National Security Investigations Directorate, which in 1989 had a budget of $7.7 million and a staff of 144, the RCMP, through its National Security Investigations Section, carries out intelligence work under the little known Security Offences Act, passed in 1984 at the same time as the CSIS act.[24] In part, there was a need for the section, given that CSIS lacks the power to make arrests. Under this new legislation, the Mounted Police have the responsibility for protecting visiting dignitaries, hence its appearance on the campus of UBC in 1997. It also continues to dabble in broader security investigations and 'investigates criminal offences related to national security.' Its 'duties include: responsibilities assigned to the RCMP under Section 6(1) Security Offences Act; ideologically motivated criminal activity such as environmental/animal rights extremism, white supremacism/neo-Nazi-ism; aboriginal extremism; and other criminal extremism.'[25]

Freed from its tainted history with the death of the Security Service, and outside the purview of SIRC, the RCMP has rebuilt its intelligence role. In the official and unofficial discourse this has been portrayed as problematic, since it has led to a rivalry with CSIS, one that became evident during the investigation of the Air India bombing and in the controversy of the joint CSIS-RCMP investigation, codenamed 'Project Sidewinder,'[26] of the collaboration between Chinese triads and Chinese intelligence. Conversely, cooperation between CSIS, the RCMP, and other state institutions that operate domestic intelligence agencies, in particular the Department of National Defence and its National Counter-Intelligence Unit, which all came together during the APEC conference, raises potential dangers for civil liberties through the evasion of both government-mandated restrictions and review, something that concerned the McDonald Commission. SIRC recognized this in its 1999 report, when it remarked on the contradiction that CSIS faced scrutiny and regulations while at the same time other governmental agencies employed intelligence-gathering capabilities without the fear of outside review. If this situation continues, cautioned SIRC, a loss of public faith would be the result.[27]

These dangers were evident at the University of British Columbia in 1997. Unfortunately, media coverage has focused on the arrests and clashes and, of course, the image of a mounted policeman pepper-spraying peaceful demonstrators. Largely ignored was what the RCMP did in the days, weeks, and months before the conference. NSIS actively investigated the activities of a variety of peaceful anti-APEC groups under the mantle of protecting visiting dignitaries from 'threat of harm or embarrassment.' Beginning in January 1997, ten months before the conference, NSIS commenced investigatory and surveillance activities, including reading e-mail and performing criminal and security checks on protesters, all of which were negative. Despite the knowledge that the groups being investigated were clearly peaceful, the police continued their spying over subsequent months. With the exception of the monitoring of e-mail distribution lists – and in spirit this is no different than campus bulletin boards or information telephone lines of eras gone by – the Mounted Police employed tactics that were exactly the same as those of the old Security Service. Indeed, one of the senior Mounties involved at APEC, Superintendent T.W. Thompsett, had spied on Trotskyists when he was a member of the Security Service in 1969. One element that was missing with the new RCMP, however, was the verbal flair of its predecessor. The NSIS emphasis was on brevity, although it still found room to address ideology: 'General discussion (left-wing) concerning women's rights, indigenous people and APEC (poverty and low income issues). Information was presented.'[28]

The secret coverage extended from off-campus to on-campus, with no distinction being made between the two. At the University of British Columbia, a seventeen-year veteran Mountie was in disguise, both figuratively and literally, when he attempted to infiltrate a group of ten students dressed up in Hallowe'en costumes as part of a march across the campus that included a stop to add washable graffiti to the exterior of the residence of the university president. Constable Mitch Rasche, his face obscured with a Star Trek mask, was careful to report that he did not participate in the minor vandalism and that the entire event had 'a happy go lucky attitude.'[29]

Those words also apply to the RCMP's carefree attitude to its troublesome past. In its anniversary celebrations of 1998 and 1999 the force emphasized its nineteenth-century history while completely ignoring the more pertinent twentieth-century record. Of course, that track record is more difficult to gloss over from a public relations point of view. Instead, the RCMP pretends that this past either did not happen or, if it did, that it has no relevance to the post–Security Service era.[30] But it does. When in the fall of 1998 the Mounted Police blew up an oil shed in Alberta in an effort to prevent a farmer named Wiebo Ludwig from blowing it up himself, there seemed to be little understanding within the RCMP of the significance of the act in the context of the infamous barn burning of the 'dirty tricks' era.[31] State institutions ignore the past at their and society's peril.

Then there is the part of the RCMP's history that involves higher education. For police and intelligence services, universities remain under the official dogma that they are no different than other targets in Canadian society. However, to the politicians, the media, and the public they are. This was recognized at the beginning of the RCMP's intelligence role at the end of the First World War and it has remained true for the remainder of the twentieth century. The inherent and interconnected duality of both challenging the status quo while at the same time upholding and perpetuating it remains a constant for universities. It also means that what attracted both the RCMP and its opponents to universities will continue to catch the attention of their successors. Which is not to say that universities are somehow threatened by such forces. Public scrutiny, that long-time obstacle to the operations of security forces, continues to take place. The crucial role of academe as critical interrogators of the status quo, which is today in the form of neo-liberalism, is far more endangered by the penny-pinching and short-sighted policies of right-wing governments than from agencies of the Canadian state. In addition, campuses have remained relatively quiet over the last twenty-five years, to a large extent, as the Security Service itself has recognized, because of the insecurity fuelled by economic recession and uncertainty. This conservative era has led some, writing before 11 September, to see a permanent end to widespread state surveillance within democratic societies.[32]

Times can change quickly, however. In the 1950s, when Daniel Bell proclaimed the 'end of ideology,' the notion of widespread campus unrest and of open flouting of all sorts of societal conventions would have been scoffed at.[33] Yet change arrived quickly and in Canada the RCMP Security Service, with the encouragement of the federal government, expanded its operations at universities. 11 September 2001 may well mark the beginning of a new age, as did the 1960s. Already, democratic countries have passed laws giving far greater power to intelligence and law enforcement agencies than they had even during the cold war. In turn, there is little tolerance, especially in the United States but also in Canada, for the traditional dissent that universities offer. That intolerance is aimed not just at those who question the direction of the 'war on terrorism' but also at those who, in a more fundamental way, question the direction of American foreign policy, particularly in terms of globalization and the proposed National Missile Defense Program. Those who protest these global policy shifts, and campuses are one centre for those who do, will discover at first hand the true flexibility of the new anti-terrorism powers of big brother and sister. Already in May 2001 the RCMP had created a new unit, the Public Order Program, with the aim of being a 'centre of excellence' for dealing with anti-globalization protests.[34] Born out of the struggle between communism and capitalism and then labelled as ready for retirement at the end of the cold war, domestic intelligence agencies will have plenty of work for a long time to come.

Notes

1: Introduction

1 S.T. Wood, 'Tools for Treachery,' *R.C.M.P. Quarterly* 8 (April 1941), 394–7.
2 Reg Whitaker, *The End of Privacy: How Total Surveillance Is Becoming a Reality* (New York 1999), 5–37; Wesley K. Wark, 'Security Intelligence in Canada, 1864–1945: The History of a National Insecurity State,' in Keith Nelson and B.J.C. McKercher, eds., *Go Spy the Land: Military Intelligence in History* (Westport, CT, 1992), 157.
3 Regardless of its content, a file is by its very nature neither a neutral document nor isolated from other elements of intelligence operations, a point well made by Frank J. Donner in his description of the characteristics of American domestic security in *Protectors of Privilege: Red Squads and Police Repression in Urban America* (Berkeley 1990), 3: '(1) physical surveillance of a "subject," usually conducted in secret and frequently termed "information gathering" or "data collection," benign usages characteristic of a system of repression; (2) a body of techniques that, in addition to informer infiltration, ranged from observation and mail opening to wiretapping and photography; (3) the compilation and dissemination of files and dossiers about individuals and organizational "subjects"; (4) the assessment of file data; and (5) the aggressive use of such data to do injury to the subject.'
4 Royal Commission of Inquiry concerning Certain Activities of the Royal Canadian Mounted Police (hereafter McDonald Commission), *Second Report: Freedom and Security under the Law* (Ottawa 1981), 1: 518; CSIS, Access request 117-1998-71, 'Contacts–Police–Canada,' vol. 5, Inspector J.G. Long to William Kelly, 28 July 1967; CSIS, Access request 117-2000-22, 'The Role, Tasks, and Methods of the RCMP Security Service'; Annual reports of the RCMP Security Service, 1982–83, 1983–4.

5 Gregory S. Kealey, 'The Early Years of State Surveillance of Labour and the Left in Canada: The Institutional Framework of the Royal Canadian Mounted Police Security and Intelligence Apparatus, 1918–26,' *Intelligence and National Security* 8 (1993): 129–48; Kealey, 'The Surveillance State: The Origins of Domestic Intelligence and Counter-Subversion in Canada, 1914–21,' *Intelligence and National Security* 7 (1992): 179–210; Reg Whitaker and Gary Marcuse, *Cold War Canada: The Making of a National Insecurity State, 1945–1957* (Toronto 1994); Reg Whitaker, 'The Politics of Security Intelligence Policy-Making in Canada: 1, 1970–84,' *Intelligence and National Security* 6, no. 4 (1991): 649–68.

6 John Sawatsky, *Men in the Shadows: The RCMP Security Service* (Toronto 1980); Sawatsky, *For Services Rendered: Leslie James Bennett and the RCMP* (Toronto 1982).

7 Sawatsky, *Men in the Shadows*; Michael McLoughlin, *Last Stop Paris: The Assassination of Mario Bachand and the Death of the FLQ* (Toronto 1998); Jeff Sallot, *Nobody Said No: The Real Story about How the Mounties Always Get Their Man* (Toronto 1979); Robert Dion, *Crimes of the Secret Police* (Montreal 1982).

8 Frank J. Donner, *The Age of Surveillance: The Aims and Methods of America's Political Intelligence System* (New York 1980); Donner, *Protectors of Privilege*; Ward Churchill and Jim Vander Wall, eds., *The COINTELPRO Papers: Documents from the FBI's Secret Wars against Dissent in the United States* (Boston 1990); Ellen W. Schrecker, *No Ivory Tower: McCarthyism and the Universities* (New York 1986); Athan G. Theoharis, *Spying on Americans: Political Surveillance from Hoover to the Huston Plan* (Philadelphia 1978); and Theoharis and John Stuart Cox, *The Boss: J. Edgar Hoover and the Great American Inquisition* (Philadelphia 1988).

9 'RCMP Infiltrated Student Groups: Used Intelligence to Arrest Activists at APEC Summit,' *Toronto Star*, 23 September 1998.

10 Paul Axelrod, *Making a Middle Class: Student Life in English Canada during the Thirties* (Montreal and Kingston 1990), 10–15, 23; A.B. McKillop, *Matters of Mind: The University in Ontario, 1791–1951* (Toronto 1994), 204–12.

11 Ralph Miliband, *The State in Capitalist Society: The Analysis of the Western System of Power* (London 1969), 221, 231.

12 For the American situation, see Schrecker, *No Ivory Tower*; Sigmund Diamond, *Compromised Campus: The Collaboration of Universities with the Intelligence Community, 1945–1955* (New York 1992); for Canada, see Michiel Horn, *Academic Freedom in Canada* (Toronto 1999); and for a discussion of academic freedom in the United Kingdom, see Conrad Russell, *Academic Freedom* (London 1993).

13 CSIS, Access request 117-1999-14, Instructions re: 'Subversive Investigation and Correspondence,' Superintendent Vernon Kemp to O.C. Montreal, 31 March 1944; Interview with 'A,' a former Security Service member, 20 April 1998. Pseudonyms are used for former Security Service members who wished to remain anonymous.

14 Keith Walden, 'Respectable Hooligans: Male Toronto College Students Celebrate Hallowe'en, 1884–1910,' *Canadian Historical Review* 68, no. 1 (1987), 1–34.

15 For more on the construction of enemies in the era of national security, see Gary Kinsman, with Dieter K. Buse and Mercedes Steedman, 'How the Centre Holds – National Security as an Ideological Practice,' in Gary Kinsman, Dieter K. Buse, and Mercedes Steedman, eds., *Whose National Security? Canadian State Surveillance and the Creation of Enemies* (Toronto 2000), 278–85.

16 Craig Heron and Myer Siemiatycki, 'The Great War, the State, and Working Class Canada,' in Craig Heron, ed., *The Workers' Revolt in Canada, 1917–1925* (Toronto 1998); Ivan Avakumovic, *The Communist Party in Canada: A History* (Toronto 1975), 35, 119–20.

17 Robert Louis Benson and Michael Warner, eds., *Venona: Soviet Espionage and the American Response, 1939–1957* (Laguna Hills, CA, 1996).

18 Harvey Klehr, John Earl Haynes, and Kyrill M. Anderson, *The Soviet World of American Communism* (New Haven, CT, 1998), 112, 132.

19 Christopher Andrew and Vasili Mitrokhin, *The Mitrokhin Archive: The KGB in Europe and the West* (London 1999), 373.

20 Klehr, Haynes, and Anderson, *The Soviet World of American Communism*, 151.

21 Jacob Weisberg, 'Cold War without End,' *New York Times Magazine* 28 (November 1999), 116–23, 155–8; Ronald Radosh, *Commies: A Journey through the Old Left, the New Left and the Leftover Left* (New York 2001).

22 Harvey Klehr, John Earl Haynes, and Fridrikh Igorevich Firsov, *The Secret World of American Communism* (New Haven, CT, 1995), 71; Andrew and Mitrokhin, *The Mitrokhin Archive.*

23 Klehr, Haynes, and Anderson, *The Soviet World of American Communism*, 73–4.

24 The quote is from a 24 March 1936 telegram from Moscow to New York, as reproduced in Benson and Warner, *Venona*, 199.

25 Allen Weinstein and Alexander Vassiliev, *The Haunted Wood: Soviet Espionage in America – The Stalin Years* (New York 1999), 300–4; National Archives of Canada, RG 146, Records of the Canadian Security Intelligence Service, vol. 3331, file AH-2000-00111, Commissioner J.H. MacBrien to O.D. Skelton, undersecretary of state for external affairs, 15 December 1933; John Earl Haynes and Harvey Klehr, *Venona: Decoding Soviet Espionage in America*

(London 1999), 28, 79–82, 183–4; Peter Shipley, *Hostile Action: The KGB and Secret Soviet Operations in Britain* (London 1989), 28, 155.

26 Telephone conversation with 'F,' a former Security Service member, 3 March 1998.

27 Letter from Derek Gee, a former Security Service member, to the *Ottawa Citizen*, 11 June 1998.

28 Klehr, Haynes, and Firsov, *The Secret World of American Communism*, 326.

29 Ellen Schrecker, *Many Are the Crimes: McCarthyism in America,* (New York 1998), xiii, 4–5; John Manley, 'Introduction,' in Gregory S. Kealey and Reg Whitaker, eds., *R.C.M.P. Security Bulletins: The Depression Years, Part V, 1938–1939* (St John's 1997), 24–6; Bryan Palmer, 'Introduction,' in *A Communist Life: Jack Scott and the Canadian Workers' Movement, 1929–1985* (St John's 1988), 6–7, as cited in Manley, 'Introduction'; Gordon Lunan, *The Making of a Spy: A Political Odyssey* (Toronto 1995).

30 Victor Navasky, 'Cold War Ghosts: The Case of the Missing Red Menace,' *Nation*, 16 July 2001, 40.

31 Schrecker, *Many Are the Crimes*, 4.

32 The three spy scandals were the Igor Gouzenko defection, the trial of Julius and Ethel Rosenberg, and the defection of Vladimir Petrov.

33 Oleg Kalugin and Fen Montaigne, *Spymaster: My Thirty-Two Years in Intelligence and Espionage against the West* (London 1994), 55–6.

34 Markus Wolf, *Man without a Face: The Autobiography of Communism's Greatest Spymaster* (New York 1997), 284–5.

35 Walter Schneir and Miriam Schneir, 'Cables Coming in from the Cold,' *Nation*, 5 July 1999. 38.

36 John Barron, *KGB Today: The Hidden Hand* (New York 1985), 315–54; Leo Heaps, *Hugh Hambleton, Spy: Thirty Years with the KGB* (Toronto 1983), 101–63.

37 Andrew and Mitrokhin, *The Mitrokhin Archive*, 272; CSIS, 'Briefing Notes from Assistant Director of Operations to Director, Counter Intelligence,' 13 September 1999; CSIS, 'Briefing Note for the Solicitor General of Canada,' 16 September 1999.

38 Peter Worthington, 'Traitors in Our Midst,' *Ottawa Sun*, 30 September 1999; Stewart Bell, 'KGB Plans to Sabotage Canada Revealed,' *National Post*, 14 September 1999; 'Mystery KGB Agent in the Civil Service "Is Still Alive,"' *Times*, 30 September 1999.

39 For more on the post-1945 hunt for subversives in the West, see Reg Whitaker, 'Cold War Alchemy: How America, Britain and Canada Transformed Espionage into Subversion,' *Intelligence and National Security* 15, no. 2 (2000), 177–210.

40 Elizabeth Grace and Colin Leys, 'The Concept of Subversion and Its Implications,' in C.E.S. Franks, ed., *Dissent and the State* (Toronto 1989), 62.
41 *Canadian Oxford Dictionary* (Toronto 1998), 1448.
42 Fulton as quoted in Carl Betke and S.W. Horrall, *Canada's Security Service:
A History* (Ottawa 1978), 2: 756.
43 CSIS, Access request 117-2000-22, 'Memorandum to the Cabinet,' 7 March
1975.
44 Donner, *Protectors of Privilege*, 76.
45 McDonald Commission, Testimony of Warren Allmand, vol. 115, 17764–7.
46 NA, RG 146, vol. 2910, file 97A-00062, 'Learned Societies,' pt 2, Report
of [deleted: name of informant], and handwritten comment by unknown,
4 July 1977.
47 Interview with Peter Marwitz, a former Security Service member, 21 August
1997.
48 Fiona Capp, *Writers Defiled* (South Yarra, Australia, 1993), 90.
49 NA, RG 146, vol. 2777, Report re: 'Combined Universities Campaign for
Nuclear Disarmament,' 29 October 1963; ibid., vol. 78, file 98-A-00026,
'Dalhousie University,' pt 1, Report re: 'Combined Universities Campaign
for Nuclear Disarmament,' 16 March 1962.
50 Ibid., vol. 65, file 1027-97-A-00044, 'Frank Underhill,' pt 1, Superintendent
Vernon Kemp to the commissioner, 29 January 1940.
51 Ibid., vol. 2760, file 96-A-00057, Report of Constable Ritchie, 29 November
1948.
52 Ibid., vol. 5008, file 97-A-00076, 'RCMP Investigations on Campus-Work,'
pt 7, 'Academe and Subversion,' June 1970.
53 J. Edgar Hoover, *Communist Target – Youth* (Washington 1960), 1.
54 Axelrod, *Making a Middle Class*, 133, 137–8.
55 Doug Owram, *Born at the Right Time: A History of the Baby-Boom Generation*
(Toronto 1996), 178.
56 'Intelligence Bulletin, Weekly Summary February 12, 1940,' in Gregory S.
Kealey and Reg Whitaker, eds., *R.C.M.P. Security Bulletins: The War Series,
1939–1941* (St John's 1989), 140–1.
57 NA, RG 146, volume 25, file 93-A-00077, Report of Corporal J.W. Townsend, 'York Composite Report,' April 1973–April 1974.
58 William C. Sullivan and Bill Brown, *The Bureau: My Thirty Years in Hoover's
FBI* (New York 1979).
59 Confidential interview; from the Access to Information Act: '13 (1) Subject
to subsection (2), the head of a government institution shall refuse to
disclose any record requested under this Act that contains information that
was obtained in confidence from (*a*) the government of a foreign state or

an institution thereof; (*b*) an international organization of states or an institution thereof; (*c*) the government of a province or an institution thereof; or (*d*) a municipal or regional government established by or pursuant to an Act of the legislature of a province or an institution of such a government ... 15 (1) The head of a government institution may refuse to disclose any record requested under this Act that contains information the disclosure of which could reasonably be expected to be injurious to the conduct of international affairs, the defence of Canada or any state allied or associated with Canada or the detection, prevention or suppression of subversive or hostile activities, including, without restricting the generality of the foregoing, any such information ... 19 (1) Subject to subsection (2), the head of a government institution shall refuse to disclose any record requested under this Act that contains personal information as defined in section 3 of the *Privacy Act*.'

60 McDonald Commission, Testimony of Warren Allmand, vol. 117, 18278.
61 Wark, 'Security Intelligence in Canada, 1864–1945,' 157.
62 In 1998 it was revealed that MI5 held files on its political boss, Home Secretary Jack Straw, and another cabinet minister, Peter Mandelson, from the time they were student politicians in the late 1960s and early 1970s. Richard Norton Taylor, Owen Bowcott, and Michael White, 'MPs To Question MI5 over Secret Files,' *Guardian Weekly*, 31 August 1997; Philip Johnston, 'Straw To Shed Light on MI5 "subversives" files,' *Daily Telegraph*, 20 July 1998.

2: Spying, RCMP-Style: History, Organization, and Tactics

1 RCMP Archives, Personnel record of S.L. Warrior.
2 The best studies of the Mounted Police in this era are Gregory S. Kealey, 'The Early Years of State Surveillance of Labour and the Left in Canada: The Institutional Framework of the Royal Canadian Mounted Police Security and Intelligence Apparatus, 1918–26,' *Intelligence and National Security* 8, no. 3 (fall 1993), 129–48; Kealey, 'The Surveillance State: The Origins of Domestic Intelligence and Counter-Subversion in Canada, 1914–21,' *Intelligence and National Security* 7, no. 3 (1992), 179–210; Kealey, 'State Repression of Labour and the Left in Canada, 1914–20: The Impact of the First World War,' *Canadian Historical Review* 73, no. 3 (1992), 281–314; S.W. Horrall, 'The Royal North-West Mounted Police and Labour Unrest in Western Canada, 1919,' *Canadian Historical Review* 61, no. 2 (1980), 169–90; Carl Betke and S.W. Horrall, *Canada's Security Service: An Historical Outline, 1864–1966* (Ottawa 1978), vol. 1.
3 Betke and Horrall, *Canada's Security Service*, 78–93, 122–30, 160–75, 225.

More insight into this period will soon be arriving through the work of Kealey, for a preview, see his 'The Empire Strikes Back: The Nineteenth-Century Origins of the Canadian Secret Service,' *Journal of the Canadian Historical Association* 10 (1999), 1–12.

4 For more on this transformation, see Robert Craig Brown and Ramsay Cook, *Canada, 1896–1921: A Nation Transformed* (Toronto 1974).

5 Canada, House of Commons, *Debates*, 12 February 1914: 710; Bill Waiser, *Park Prisoners: The Untold Story of Western Canada's National Parks* (Saskatoon 1995), 6; NA, RG 18, Records of the Royal Canadian Mounted Police, vol. 469, file 456, Perry to comptroller, 24 August 1914; ibid., file 511, Perry to comptroller, 13 October 1914.

6 Bernard Porter, *Plots and Paranoia: A History of Political Espionage in Britain, 1790–1988* (London 1992), 108–9; Clive Emsley, *Policing and Its Context, 1750–1870* (London 1983), 86.

7 Douglas Haig, as quoted in Christopher Andrew, *Her Majesty's Secret Service: The Making of the British Intelligence Community* (New York 1986), 238.

8 *Regina Leader-Post*, 22 September 1933; Editorial: 'Are We Really Recruiting Youngsters to Spy on Each Other?' *Maclean's*, 15 July 1961.

9 Superintendent Christian Junget, as quoted in Horrall, 'The Royal North-West Mounted Police and Labour Unrest in Western Canada, 1919,' 175; NA, RG 18, vol. 537, file 432, Report of Secret Agent 25, 11 August 1917; ibid., Perry to comptroller, 28 August 1917; ibid., comptroller to Colonel Hugh Clark, 1 September 1917.

10 NA, RG 18, vol. 19, file 11, pt 1, Report of Detective Sergeant S.L. Warrior, 19 October 1917.

11 Richard Pipes, ed., *The Unknown Lenin: From the Secret Archive* (New Haven, CT, 1996), 8.

12 Cahan to Borden, 14 September 1918 and 21 October 1918, as quoted in Donald Avery, *'Dangerous Foreigners': European Immigrant Workers and Labour Radicalism in Canada, 1896–1932* (Toronto 1979), 75.

13 NA, RG 18, vol. 599, file 1309-1335, Circular memo no. 807, Re: 'Bolshevism,' 6 January 1919.

14 Ibid., 'Circular Memo no. 807A,' re: Detectives and Bolshevism, 6 January 1919.

15 Ibid., 'Circular Memo no. 807B,' 5 February 1919.

16 Andrew, *Her Majesty's Secret Service*. For the United Kingdom, see also Richard Thurlow, *The Secret State: British Internal Security in the Twentieth Century* (Oxford 1994); Porter, *Plots and Paranoia*; Bernard Porter, *The Origins of the Vigilant State: The London Metropolitan Police Special Branch before the First World War* (London 1987).

17 Richard Gid Powers, *Secrecy and Power: The Life of J. Edgar Hoover* (New York 1987), 36–129.
18 Horrall, 'The Royal North-West Mounted Police and Labour Unrest in Western Canada,' 169–70.
19 Betke and Horrall, *Canada's Security Service*, 1: 349–51.
20 C.W. Harvison, *The Horsemen* (Toronto 1967), 58–96.
21 McDonald Commission, *Freedom and Security under the Law* (Ottawa 1981), 1: 58–9.
22 Betke and Horrall, *Canada's Security Service*, 2: 607.
23 Copy of a recruiting poster in author's posession.
24 Raymond Rodgers, 'Wanted: Intelligence in the RCMP,' *Saturday Night*, 24 June 1961; Harvison as quoted in *Toronto Telegram*, 14 June 1963, as cited in Edward Mann and John Alan Lee, *The RCMP vs. the People: Inside Canada's Security Service* (Don Mills, ON 1979), 123.
25 Interview with 'A,' a former Security Service member, 18 April 1998; Recollections of 'D,' a former Security Service member, 2 August 1999.
26 Interview with 'B,' a former Security Service member, 20 May 1998; Interview with Peter Marwitz, a former Security Service member, 20 February 1998; Recollections of 'C,' a former Security Service member, 20 February 1999; Recollections of 'D.'
27 Betke and Horrall, *Canada's Security Service*, 2: 696; CSIS, Access request 89-A-63, 'Annual Report "D"' Branch, 1958–1959, 5; K.G. Stroud, a former Security Service member, to author, 1 April 1998; NA, RG 25, Records of the Department of External Affairs, vol. 8562, file 50364-40, pts 1–2, Superintendent Kenneth Hall to G.G. Crean, 5 March 1955, 26 July 1955, 31 January 1957; Interview with Marwitz, 21 August 1997; McDonald Commission, vol. 28, 4649–52; R.N. Carew Hunt, *The Theory and Practice of Communism: An Introduction* (London 1957).
28 Recollections of 'C,' 20 February 1999.
29 Ibid.
30 Interview with Donald J. Inch, a former Security Service member, 1 March 1998; Interview with Marwitz, 21 August 1997; CSIS, Access request 117-1999-6, '"I" Directorate Manual of Filing'; Recollections of 'C.'
31 Interview with Inch; Interview with 'A.'
32 CSIS, Access request 89-A-63, 'Counter-Espionage Section–Headquarters Special Branch, April 1st, 1949–March 31st, 1950,' 20–1. John Starnes, director-general of the Security Service from 1969 to 1973, testified at the McDonald Commission that he informed Solicitor General George McIlraith at a meeting on 24 November 1970 that 'the RCMP, had, in fact,

been carrying out illegal activities for two decades,' but McIlraith denied having received this information. McDonald Commission, Testimony of George McIlraith, vol. 118, 18430–1.

33 McDonald Commission, Testimony of John Starnes, vol. 103, 16325–6; Anonymous to author, 22 March 1999.

34 M. Wesley Swearingen, *FBI Secrets: An Agent's Exposé* (Boston 1995), 23–4; Ward Churchill and Jim Vander Wall, eds., *The COINTELPRO Papers: Documents from the FBI's Secret Wars against Dissent in the United States* (Boston 1990), 33–9. The author of the project aimed at the CPUSA was William Sullivan, a senior member of the FBI, who later broke with Hoover and whose autobiography was published posthumously; see William C. Sullivan, with Bill Brown, *The Bureau: My Thirty Years in Hoover's FBI* (New York 1979). For more information on those who infiltrated the CPC on behalf of the FBI, see Schrecker, *Many Are the Crimes*, 196–8. An illegal entry by MI5 in the United Kingdom in 1955 is described in Peter Wright's autobiography: Peter Wright, with Paul Greengrass, *Spy Catcher: The Candid Autobiography of a Senior Intelligence Officer* (New York 1987), 70–2.

35 McDonald Commission, *Freedom and Security Under the Law*, 1:267–8. The text of the letter is available at NA, RG 33/128, Records of the McDonald Commission, Access request AH-1998-00059, Accession 1992–93/251, box 130, file 'Covert Measures–Check Mate–"D" Operations,' 21 March 1956. For the problems Khrushchev's speech and the Soviet invasion of Hungary caused the Labour Progressive Party, see Merrily Weisbord, *The Strangest Dream: Canadian Communists, the Spy Trials, and the Cold War* (Toronto 1983), 214–23, and Norman Penner, *Canadian Communism: The Stalin Years and Beyond* (Toronto 1998), 237–49.

36 McDonald Commission, *Freedom and Security under the Law*, 1: 149–60, 204, Interview with Warren Allmand, 25 February 1999.

37 Marwitz to author, 3 March 1998.

38 Interview with Martin Loney, a former Simon Fraser University Student Council president, 16 February 1998; Andrew Wernick, a former University of Toronto student, to author, 31 October 1998; Phillip Resnick, a former University of Toronto student, to author, 28 April 1998; Peter Warrian, a former University of Waterloo student, to author, 16 October 1998; Interview with Marwitz, 17 February 1998.

39 Jeff Sallot, *Nobody Said No: The Real Story about How the RCMP Always Get Their Man* (Toronto 1979), 147.

40 Frank J. Donner, *The Age of Surveillance: The Aims and Methods of America's Political Intelligence System* (New York 1980), 464.

41 In the United Kingdom, for example, in 1998 approximately 50,000 inform-
    ants were in the employ of police forces. Duncan Campbell, 'Police Fear for
    Informers,' *Guardian Weekly*, 18 October 1998.

42 Stanislav Levchenko, *On the Wrong Side: My Life in the KGB* (Washington
    1988), 106. For a variation on the M.I.C.E. concept, see Stan A. Taylor and
    Daniel Snow, 'Cold War Spies: Why They Spied and How They Got
    Caught,' *Intelligence and National Security* 12, no. 2 (1997), 101–25; Malin
    Åkerström, *Betrayal and Betrayals: The Sociology of Treachery* (New York 1991),
    21–2, 122.

43 Interview with 'A'; Recollections of 'C'; Marwitz to author, 12 June 1998.

44 Gordon Thomas, *Gideon's Spies: The Secret History of the Mossad* (New York
    1999), 5; Interview with 'A'; James T. Stark, *Cold War Blues: The Operation
    Dismantle Story* (Hull, QC, 1991), 320–62. John Marks, *The Search for the
    'Manchurian Canadidate': The CIA and Mind Control* (New York 1979), 44–9.

45 NA, RG 146, vol. 2774, file 94-A-00057, University of Saskatchewan, pt 3,
    Report of Corporal R.L. Firby, 2 February 1964. The would-be informant
    maintained his previous political ties, appearing in a Liberal Party television
    commercial during the 1999 Saskatchewan provincial election and running
    for the party in the 2000 federal election.

46 Marwitz to author, 12 June 1998; *Dalhousie Gazette*, 26 November 1981; 'A'
    to author, 19 December 1998. Also lending credibility to the Dalhousie
    University student's account are the memoirs of two FBI sources, one of
    whom, Larry Grathwohl, supplied information on connections between the
    Weather Underground and the Front de Libération du Québec. William
    Tulio Divale, with James Joseph, *I Lived inside the Campus Revolution* (New
    York 1970); Larry Grathwohl, *Bringing Down America: An FBI Informer with the
    Weathermen* (New Rochelle, NY 1976). It is suggested in Ward Churchill and
    Jim Vander Wall, *Agents of Repression: The FBI's Secret Wars against the Black
    Panther Party and the American Indian Movement* (Boston 1990), 47, that these
    two books represent a campaign of disinformation by the FBI to discredit
    the New Left; while this may be true of the Grathwohl book, which reveals
    little about the FBI, the other work is openly critical of the FBI and gives
    details of the handling of sources. Louis Fournier, *F.L.Q.: The Anatomy of an
    Underground Movement* (Toronto 1984), 194.

47 NA, RG 146, vol. 57, file 96-A-00048, pt 7, RCMP transit slip, 8 February
    1971. The coded designation remained in use as late as 1998, when the
    Mounted Police's 'K' Division in Alberta blew up an oil shed to establish
    the credibility of an informant code-named K4029. Eoin Kenny, 'Crown's
    Key Witness Loses Temper,' *Canadian Press*, 14 March 2000; Interview with
    'B,' 20 May 1998.

48 Interview with Richard Bickley, 18 August 1996.
49 NA, RG 146, vol. 2768, file 96-A-00045, 'Carleton University,' pt 7, Director
   of security for chief of the defence staff to M.D. Sexsmith, 20 January 1976.
50 Interview with Marwitz, 21 August 1997; CSIS, Access request 89-A-63,
   'Annual Report on "D" Section,' 1954–1955, 1(b).
51 'F,' a former Security Service member, to author, 24 March 1999. For a
   study of the previous system, see Gregory S. Kealey, 'Filing and Defiling:
   The Organization of the State Security Archives in the Interwar Years,' in
   Franca Iacovetta and Wendy Mitchinson, eds., *On the Case: Explorations in
   Social History* (Toronto 1998), 88–105.
52 NA, RG 146, vol. 4267, file 98-A-00047, Leopold Infeld, pt 1, Memorandum,
   29 October 1952; ibid., vol. 2787, file 96-A-00045, 'University of British
   Columbia,' pt 21A, 'Education–British Columbia,' 7 August 1969; Michael
   McLoughlin, *Last Stop Paris: The Assassination of Mario Bachand and the Death
   of the FLQ* (Toronto 1998), 201.
53 CSIS, Access request 89-A-63, 'Annual Report on "D" Section,' 1955–1956,
   3; Wright, *Spy Catcher*, 52.
54 CSIS, Access request 89-A-63, 'Annual Report on "D" Section,' 1954–1955,
   1(a); Interview with 'A'; Horrall and Betke, *Canada's Security Service*, 2: 664–
   6; CSIS, Access request 117-99-14, Report from Sault Ste Marie SIS, 19
   September 1961.
55 CSIS, Access request 117-1999-14, Report from Sault Ste Marie SIS, 19
   September 1961; Interview with 'A'; Len Scher, *The Un-Canadians: True
   Stories of the Blacklist Era* (Toronto 1992), 125–7; Horrall and Betke, *Canada's Security Service*, 2: 684; NA, RG 146, vol. 5008, file 97-A-00076, pt 2, 'The
   Communist Program for Control of Youth and Intellectuals,' August 1961.

3: In the Beginning, 1920–1945

1 Reg Whitaker has addressed the 'curious complicity between the Canadian
  state and the Communists' in 'Left-Wing Dissent and the State: Canada in
  the Cold War Era,' in C.E.S. Franks, ed., *Dissent and the State* (Toronto
  1989), 194.
2 Gary Kinsman, with Dieter K. Buse and Mercedes Steedman, 'How the
  Centre Holds – National Security as an Ideological Practice,' in Gary
  Kinsman, Dieter K. Buse, and Mercedes Steedman, eds., *Whose National
  Security? Canadian State Surveillance and the Creation of Enemies* (Toronto
  2000), 278–85. Richard J. Aldrich, *Intelligence and the War against Japan:
  Britain, America and the Politics of Secret Service* (New York 2000), 64, provides
  a practical example of the impact on intelligence of the social construction

of threats: before December 1941, people, especially those in positions of power, constantly played down the Japanese military threat in the Pacific because their racism could not perceive how 'the wogs of the East,' as Winston Churchill called them, could pose a threat.

3 For more on the nature of subversion in the post-1945 period, see Reg Whitaker, 'Cold War Alchemy: How America, Britain, and Canada Transformed Espionage into Subversion,' *Intelligence and National Security* 15, no. 2 (2000), 177–210.

4 Paul Axelrod, *Making a Middle Class: Student Life in English Canada during the Thirties* (Montreal and Kingston 1990), 22–3. A survey in 1965 by the Canadian Union of Students found that 35 per cent of undergraduates were drawn from the working class. See Myrna Kostash, *Long Way from Home: The Story of the Sixties Generation in Canada* (Toronto 1980), 77.

5 Greg Marquis, 'Working Men in Uniform: The Early Twentieth-Century Toronto Police,' *Histoire sociale/Social History* 20, no. 40 (1987), 259–77.

6 Axelrod, *Making a Middle Class*, 27. The yearly wage for a Mountie is based on the daily wage, which was raised to $1.25 a day in 1935. S.W. Horrall, *The Pictorial History of the Royal Canadian Mounted Police* (Toronto 1973), 34. The yearly cost for a student remained consistent throughout the interwar period. The *Varsity*, the University of Toronto student newspaper, estimated in 1922 that the annual cost for a male arts student was $595. A.B. McKillop, *Matters of the Mind: The University in Ontario, 1791–1951* (Toronto 1994), 416.

7 CSIS, Access request 88-A-60, RCMP records relating to J.S. Woodsworth, O.C. 'G' Division to Perry, 24 March 1920. There is no record on whether any action was taken. For more on the dismissals at the University of Saskatchewan, see Michael Hayden, *Seeking a Balance: The University of Saskatchewan, 1907–1982* (Vancouver 1983), 85–115.

8 'J.S. Woodsworth in Address Tells the "Inside" of Strike,' *Saskatoon Daily Star*, 23 March 1920.

9 RCMP, Personnel records of Cecil Thoroton Hildyard, Report of C.T. Hildyard, 24 March 1920.

10 Ibid.; 'Liberty of Speech,' *Saskatoon Daily Star*, 27 March 1920: 4.

11 NA, RG 146, vol. 2782, file 96-A-00045, 'University of British Columbia,' pt 1, re: 'Federated Labor Party of Canada,' 6 January 1921; ibid., Report of Mundy, 15 January 1921; ibid., Report of Inspector Shoebotham, 11 March 1921. For more about Clearihue, see Sydney W. Jackman and Ronald R. Jeffels, eds., *Joseph Badenoch Clearihue* (Victoria 1967).

12 NA, RG 146, vol. 2782, file 96-A-00045, 'University of British Columbia,' pt 1, re: 'University of British Columbia,' 27 March 1923.

13 *Vancouver Daily World,* March 28, 1923.

14 NA, RG 146, vol. 2782, Report of Mundy, 16 April 1923; ibid., Report of RCMP source, 19 April 1923.

15 Ibid., Report of RCMP source, 22 April 1923.

16 Ibid., Report of RCMP source, 29 April 1923; ibid., Inspector Shoebotham to Starnes, 11 May 1923.

17 Ibid., Memorandum from Starnes, 14 May 1923.

18 Ibid., vol. 2787, Starnes to O.C. 'E' Division, 21 May 1923.

19 Frank J. Donner, *The Age of Surveillance: The Aims and Methods of America's Political Intelligence System* (New York 1980), 464.

20 NA, RG 18, vol. 1933, file G-57-9-1, '"K" Division Confidential Monthly Report,' November 1919.

21 CSIS, Access request 88-A-60, RCMP records relating to J.S. Woodsworth, Starnes to Duffus, 27 November 1925. Starnes's message did not reach all of his employees. A report on a speech by Woodsworth to McGill University's Labour Research Club was made in December 1926. See NA, RG 146, vol. 3042, file 98-A-00082, pt 1, Report by Constable I. Delvallet, 8 December 1926.

22 CSIS, Access request 117-1989-27, RCMP records related to William Irvine, Assistant Commissioner J.A. McGibbon to the comptroller, 17 June 1919; Pennefather to commissioner, 20 November 1919; Jas Ritchie to Starnes, 5 April 1926. University of Alberta Professor Anthony Mardiros, on whom the RCMP started a file in the 1950s, would profile Irvine's life in *William Irvine: The Life of a Prairie Radical* (Toronto 1979).

23 William Rodney, *Soldiers of the International: A History of the Communist Party of Canada* (Toronto 1968), 57, 152.

24 Gregory S. Kealey and Reg Whitaker, eds., *R.C.M.P. Security Bulletins: The Early Years, 1919–1929* (St John's 1994); CSIS, Access request 88-A-25, Maurice Spector, Superintendent A.W. Duffus to commissioner, 22 September 1922.

25 Richard Cornell, *Youth and Communism: An Historical Analysis of International Communist Youth Movements* (New York 1965), 54–5.

26 British intelligence suspected Soviet trade offices of being fronts for espionage operations. In May 1927 British authorities raided the offices of the All-Russian Cooperative Society (Arcos). Despite an extensive search through the material they seized, no evidence of espionage could be found. Christopher Andrew, *Her Majesty's Secret Service: The Making of the British Intelligence Community* (New York 1986), 332.

27 NA, RG 146, vol. 3042, file 98-A-00084, McGill Labour Club, pt 1, Report of no. 30, 26 October 1926.

28 Ibid., Report of Corporal F.R. Hassey, 22 November 1926; ibid., Report of Corporal F.R. Hassey, 14 April 1927.

29 NA, RG 146, vol. 3042, file 98-A-00084, 'McGill Labour Club,' pt 1, Inspector T. Dann to Commissioner Starnes, 27 October 1926.

30 Ibid., Report of Constable I. Delvallet, 7 November 1927; ibid., Starnes to Superintendent H.M. Newson, 15 November 1927; ibid., Starnes to Senator Andrew Haydon, 15 November 1927.

31 Andrew, *Her Majesty's Secret Service*, 322–3.

32 John Herd Thompson, with Allen Seager, *Canada: 1922–1939: Decades of Discord* (Toronto 1990), 226.

33 Whitaker, 'Left-wing Dissent and the State,' 191–210.

34 Lita-Rose Betcherman, *The Little Band* (Ottawa 1982).

35 Inspector J.W. Phillips to Commissioner MacBrien, as quoted in Paul Axelrod, 'Spying on the Young in Depression and War: Students, Youth Groups, and the RCMP,' *Labour/Le Travail* 35 (spring 1995), 46.

36 David Lewis discussed the club in his autobiography, *The Good Fight: Political Memoirs, 1909–1958* (Toronto 1981), 27–8. See also Eugene Forsey, *A Life on the Fringe: The Memoirs of Eugene Forsey* (Toronto 1990), 20–9. The RCMP also began a large file on Lewis while he was at McGill University in this period and continued it more than fifty years; see Jim Bronskill, 'RCMP Spied on ex-NDP Leader,' *Ottawa Citizen*, 23 November 2001.

37 Axelrod, 'Spying on the Young,' 46.

38 Axelrod, *Making a Middle Class*, 135–6; Superintendent H.A.R. Gagnon, as quoted in Paul Axelrod, 'The Student Movement of the 1930s,' in Paul Axelrod and John G. Reid, eds., *Youth, University, and Canadian Society: Essays in the Social History of Higher Education* (Montreal and Kingston 1989), 217; Dashan Singh, as quoted in Axelrod, *Making a Middle Class*, 135.

39 Robert Cohen, *When the Old Left Was Young: Student Radicals and America's First Mass Student Movement, 1929–1941* (New York 1993), xvi, 44–53, 328–9. Cohen includes a list of forty-three universities at which sources supplied the FBI with information about students or student activities (ibid., 325–36).

40 The investigation of the SCM is documented but the organization would not be the subject of its very own file until the late 1950s; between 1958 and 1973, over 40,000 pages would be gathered in the RCMP's file. Isabelle Tessier, NA, to author, 13 October 1998. For more on the SCM in this period, see Catherine Gidney, 'Poisoning the Student Mind?: The Student Christian Movement at the University of Toronto, 1920–1965,' *Journal of the Canadian Historical Association* 8 (1997), 147–63.

41 Cornell, *Youth and Communism*, 58–9.

42 NA, RG 146, vol. 4946, Special Constable James S. Cross, 'History of Communism among the Youth in Canada, 1923–1947,' September 1947.

43 NA, RG 146, vol. 24, file 93-A-00019, University of Toronto, pt 4, Report of
    Detective Corporal [illegible], 17 December 1935. For an examination of
    this era at the University of Toronto, see Ian Montagnes, *An Uncommon
    Fellowship: The Story of Hart House* (Toronto 1969); Escott Reid, *Radical
    Mandarin: The Memoirs of Escott Reid* (Toronto 1989), 27–92.

44 Gary Kinsman, '"Character Weaknesses" and "Fruit Machines": Towards an
    Analysis of the Anti-Homosexual Security Campaign in the Canadian Civil
    Service,' *Labour/Le Travail* 35 (1995), 133–61; Christabelle Sethna, 'The
    Cold War and the Sexual Chill: Freezing Girls out of Sex Education,' *Cana-
    dian Woman Studies/Les Cahiers de la Femme* 17, no. 4 (1998), 57–61; Whita-
    ker, 'Cold War Alchemy,' 193–205; Gary Kinsman, 'Constructing Gay Men
    and Lesbians as National Security Risks, 1950–1970,' in Gary Kinsman,
    Dieter K. Buse, and Mercedes Steedman, eds., *Whose National Security?
    Canadian State Surveillance and the Creation of Enemies* (Toronto 2000), 143–
    53; J. Edgar Hoover, *Masters of Deceit: The Story of Communism in America and
    How to Fight It* (New York 1958), 107; Elaine Tyler May, *Homeward Bound:
    American Families in the Cold War Era* (New York 1988), 94.

45 NA, RG 146, vol. 24, file 93-A-00019, University of Toronto, pt 4, Report of
    Constable R.R. Warner, 23 March 1936; ibid., Report of Constable R.W.
    Irvine, 17 April 1936.

46 The RCMP sponsored the university attendance of Lindsay and six others,
    and they all studied law (six of the seven already had university degrees).
    William and Nora Kelly, *The Royal Canadian Mounted Police: A Century of
    History, 1873–1973* (Edmonton 1973), 175.

47 NA, RG 146, vol. 2774, file 94-A-00057, University of Saskatchewan, pt 1,
    Report of Sergeant H.W.H. Williams, 19 March 1936.

48 'Thanksgiving Day,' *Sheaf*, 25 October 1935.

49 NA, RG 146, vol. 2774, file 94-A-00057, pt 1, Report of Constable M.F.A.
    Lindsay, 6 November 1935; ibid., Assistant Commissioner S.T. Wood to the
    attorney general of Saskatchewan, 9 Nov. 1935; Wood to Commissioner J.H.
    MacBrien, 30 March 1936.

50 NA, RG 146, Access request 98-A-00133, 'Memorandum: Communism in
    Canadian Colleges and Universities,' 12 July 1940; ibid., 'Subversive Condi-
    tions–Canadian Universities,' 8 July 1940. For more on the Brussels confer-
    ence, see Cornell, *Youth and Communism*, 62.

51 Axelrod, 'The Student Movement of the 1930s,' 219.

52 NA, RG 146, vol. 4946, James S. Cross, 'History of Communism among the
    Youth in Canada, 1923–1947,' September 1947; Axelrod, 'Spying on the
    Young in Depression and War,' 56; James Cross to author, 5 January 2001.

53 Interview with 'A,' a former RCMP Security Service member, 18 April 1998.

54 Martin Robin, *Shades of Right: Nativist and Fascist Politics in Canada, 1920–*

1940 (Toronto 1992), 265–80; Michael D. Behiels, *Prelude to Quebec's Quiet Revolution: Liberalism versus Neo-nationalism, 1945–1960* (Montreal and Kingston 1985), 26–30. For a detailed examination of the RCMP's response to the far right, see Michelle Lea McBride, 'From Indifference to Internment: An Examination of RCMP Responses to Nazism and Fascism in Canada from 1934 to 1941,' unpublished MA thesis, Memorial University of Newfoundland, 1997.

55 Ibid., 47–50; Cohen, *When the Old Left Was Young*, 79–80; McKillop, *Matters of the Mind*, 449.

56 NA, RG 146, vol. 65, file 97-A-00044, 'Frank Underhill,' pt 1, Memorandum Kemp, 26 January 1940.

57 CSIS, Access request 85-A-88, Report of Constable H.W. Kirkpatrick, 2 March 1939.

58 Ibid., Report of Constable C.W. Goldsmith, 19 February 1940; ibid., Kemp to Commissioner, 4 March 1940.

59 Ibid., Report of Superintendent Gagnon, 30 January 1940; ibid., Kemp to commissioner, 2 February 1940.

60 For more on the RCMP's male identity, see Steve Hewitt, 'The Masculine Mountie: The Mounted Police as a Male Institution,' *Journal of the Canadian Historical Association* 6 (1996), 153–74.

61 Fiona Capp, *Writers Defiled* (South Yarra, Australia 1993), 50–3.

62 NA, RG 146, vol. 2757, file 96-A-00045, Queen's University, pt 2, Report of Constable M.G. Johnston, 5 February 1963.

63 Allen Weinstein and Alexander Vassiliev, *The Haunted Wood: Soviet Espionage in America – The Stalin Years* (New York 1999), 54, 62–5; Veronica A. Wilson, 'Elizabeth Bentley and Cold War Representation: Some Masks Not Dropped,' *Intelligence and National Security* 14, no. 2 (summer 1999), 49–69.

64 NA, RG 146, vol. 65, file 97-A-00044, Frank Underhill, pt 1, Report of Kemp, February 1940; CSIS, Access request 85-A-88, Assistant Commissioner R.R. Tait to Commissioner Wood, 29 January 1940; NA, RG 146, vol. 65, file 97-A-00044, pt 1, Kemp to Wood, 29 January 1940.

65 NA, RG 146, vol. 65, file 97-A-00044, pt 1, Memorandum of Kemp, 26 January 1940. Kemp, in invoking the concept of citizenship, provides further evidence to support the contention of some historians that the concept, as defined in the interwar period, is far from neutral. See Tom Mitchell and James Naylor, 'The Prairies: In the Eye of the Storm,' in Craig Heron, ed., *The Workers' Revolt in Canada, 1917–1925* (Toronto 1998), 211–15.

66 CSIS, Access request 85-A-88, Kemp to commissioner, 26 January 1940; ibid., Report of Kemp and informant, 8 March 1940.

67 NA, RG 146, vol. 65, file 97-A-00044, pt 1, Report of C.J. Zryd, 26 March 1935.

68 CSIS, Access request 85-A-88, Kemp to commissioner, 26 January 1940. Emphasis in original.

69 NA, RG 146, vol. 65, file 97-A-00044, pt 1, Report of Special Consta- ble Mervyn Black, 20 February 1940. For more on Mervyn Black's rather interesting career in the RCMP, see Gregory S. Kealey, 'Introduction,' in Gregory S. Kealey and Reg Whitaker, eds., *R.C.M.P. Security Bulletins: The Depression Years, Part I, 1933–1934* (St John's 1993), 12–15.

70 H.S. Ferns, *Reading from Left to Right: One Man's Political History* (Toronto 1983), 119, 181; Michiel Horn, *Academic Freedom in Canada: A History* (Toronto 1999), 148–9.

71 NA, RG 146, vol. 24, file 93-A-00019, University of Toronto, pt 4, Kemp to commissioner, 20 February 1940.

72 *Toronto Telegram,* 18 March 1940.

73 NA, RG 146, vol. 65, file 97-A-00044, pt 1, Report of Constable S.O.F. Evans, 4 March 1940; ibid., Memorandum of Kemp, 4 March 1940; ibid., pt 2, Report of Constable Jenkins, 22 December 1941.

74 Ibid., Report of Constable N.O. Jones, 13 May 1940. For more on the nature of RCMP security files in the interwar period, see Gregory S. Kealey, 'Filing and Defiling: The Organization of the State Security Archives in the Interwar Years,' in Franca Iacovetta and Wendy Mitchinson, eds., *On the Case: Explorations in Social History* (Toronto 1998), 88–105.

75 NA, RG 146, vol. 65, file 1027-97-A-00044, pt 1, Personal History File of Frank Underhill, 13 August 1940.

76 NA, RG 146, vol. 24, file 93-A-00019, pt 4, Tait to the commissioner, 27 December 1939; NA, RG 146, vol. 65, file 97-A-00044, pt.1, Report of Kemp, re: 'Subversive Activities–"O" Division,' 20 December 1939; ibid., Kemp to the commissioner, 29 January 1940.

77 R. Douglas Francis, *Frank Underhill: Intellectual Provocateur* (Montreal and Kingston 1986), 115–16.

78 NA, RG 146, vol. 65, file 97-A-00044, pt 1, Meeting re: 'Underhill,' 17 Sep- tember 1940. To correct the problem of a lack of evidence, a policeman noted that should Underhill speak at Couchiching again his remarks would be recorded; see ibid., pt 2, Report of Constable Jenkins, 3 June 1942. Ibid., Report re: 'Underhill Frank (Prof),' 21 December 1940; Francis, *Frank Underhill,* 95–6, 120–7.

79 Ibid., pt 2, Report of Assistant Corporal H.R. Jenkins, 3 May 1943.

80 Ibid., Memorandum by [deleted], 10 December 1947; ibid., Memorandum

to Inspector Leopold, 10 December 1947. Don Wall, who served as a civilian member with the RCMP in the 1950s, suggests Inspector Bob McNeil, father of newscaster and author Robert (Robin) McNeil, as a possible author of this passage. Interview with Don Wall, 7 May 1998.
81 Ibid., 'Report regarding Frank Underhill,' 14 December 1964; ibid., Report of Inspector J.L. Forest, 14 December 1964.
82 Escott Reid, *Radical Mandarin: The Life of Escott Reid* (Toronto 1989), 143–4.
83 This point is also made in Reg Whitaker and Gary Marcuse, *Cold War Canada: The Making of a National Insecurity State, 1945–1957* (Toronto 1993), 220.
84 The impact of this legislation on the CPC is described in several places. See, for example, Peter Hunter, *Which Side Are You On, Boys: Canadian Life on the Left* (Toronto 1988); William Repak and Kathleen M. Repak, *Dangerous Patriots: Canada's Unknown Prisoners of War* (Vancouver 1982).
85 NA, RG 146, vol. 2760, file 96-A-00057, Report of Constable A.F. Wilcox, 20 April 1941; ibid., vol. 24, file 93-A-00019, pt 4, Report of Constable H.R. Jenkins, 23 October 1941; ibid., vol. 2777, file 96-A-00045, 'University of Alberta,' pt 1, re: 'Tim Buck–Communist,' 25 October 1943; ibid., vol. 79, file 98-A-00004, re: 'Communism in Canada–Survey of,' 17 May 1944; ibid., vol. 2782, file 96-A-00045, 'UBC,' pt 1, Report of [deleted], re: 'Young Communist League,' 5 March 1942; ibid., vol. 2790, file 98-A-00133, 'Education–Canada–General,' pt 1, Report of secret agent, 26 October 1943; ibid., Report of Corporal C.W. Bishop, 10 December 1943; ibid., vol. 24, file 93-A-00019, 'University of Toronto,' pt 4, Superintendent F.W. Schutz, to commissioner, 17 September 1943.

4: Scarlet and Reds on Campus, 1946–1960

1 RCMP, *Law and Order in Canadian Democracy: A Series of 20 Lectures Prepared by the Royal Canadian Mounted Police on Crime and Police Work in Canada* (Ottawa 1949), 137.
2 Reg Whitaker and Gary Marcuse, *Cold War Canada: The Making of a National Insecurity State, 1945–1957* (Toronto 1994), 99–100.
3 Herbert Romerstein and Eric Breindel, *The Venona Secrets: Exposing Soviet Espionage and America's Traitors* (Washington 2000); Nigel West, *Venona: The Greatest Secret of the Cold War* (Toronto 1999); John Earl Haynes and Harvey Klehr, *Venona: Soviet Espionage in America in the Stalin Era* (New Haven, CT, 1999). For a critique of the accuracy of Venona, see Walter Schneir and Miriam Schneir, 'Cables Coming in from the Cold,' *Nation*, 5 July 1999, 38.

4 Allen Weinstein and Alexander Vassiliev identify a total of fifty-eight agents
   operating on behalf of the NKVD, the ancestor of the KGB, in the United
   States between 1933 and 1945. In their examination of the Venona documents, which included messages by agents run by both the NKVD and the
   GRU, the Soviet military intelligence, John Earl Haynes and Harvey Klehr
   suggest 349 citizens and residents in the United States had 'a covert relationship with Soviet intelligence' in the period covered by the documents.
   They admit that this figure may be exaggerated because of the possibility of
   multiple code names for the same persons. On the other hand, they note
   that the names discovered through Venona represent only a partial look at
   Soviet espionage during the cold war. Allen Weinstein and Alexander Vassiliev, *The Haunted Wood: Soviet Espionage in America – The Stalin Era* (New
   York 1999), xxi–iv; Haynes and Klehr, *Venona*, 339; Daniel Patrick
   Moynihan, *Secrecy: The American Experience* (New Haven, CT, 1998), 144–6,
   202–27.
5 Ronald Radosh and Joyce Milton, *The Rosenberg File* (New Haven, CT, 1997);
   Ellen Schrecker, *Many Are the Crimes: McCarthyism in America* (New York
   1998), 154.
6 Ellen Schrecker, *No Ivory Tower: McCarthyism and the Universities* (New York
   1986), 258, 291–3.
7 John Kenneth White, *Still Seeing Red: How the Cold War Shapes the New American Politics* (Boulder, CO, 1997), 69.
8 J.L. Granatstein, *Yankee Go Home: Canadians and Anti-Americanism* (Toronto
   1996), 110.
9 Watson Kirkconnell, 'Communists on the Canadian Campus Are Now
   Briefed for Their Missions,' *Saturday Night*, 18 January 1949, 6–9. For more
   on Watson Kirkconnell, see J.R.C. Perkin and James B. Snelson, *Morning in
   His Heart: The Life and Writings of Watson Kirkconnell* (Halifax 1986).
10 'University Students Charge Reds Trying to Exploit the Veterans,' *Ottawa
   Evening Journal*, 13 December 1946.
11 *Quebec Chronicle-Telegraph*, 18 March 1946, as quoted in Paul Dufour, '"Eggheads" and Espionage: The Gouzenko Affair in Canada,' *Journal of Canadian Studies* 16, nos. 3–4 (fall–winter 1981), 188–98. For more on the
   commission, including partial transcripts, see J.L. Granatstein and Robert
   Bothwell, *The Gouzenko Transcripts: The Evidence Presented to the Kellock-
   Taschereau Royal Commission of 1946* (Ottawa 1982).
12 'Speaker Raps Colleges,' *Vancouver Daily Province*, 19 April 1947; Canada.
   House of Commons, *Debates*, 19 March 1946: 66.
13 NA, RG 146, vol. 5008, file 97-A-00076, pt 4, '*Canadian Tribune*,' 1949; NA,
   MG 28, IV 4, Communist Party of Canada Papers, vol. 84, file 142, 'Draft:

Main Propositions for the National Committee Meeting, November 15–18, 1963'; ibid., vol. 15, file 14, 'Fight Fee Hike'; ibid., vol. 57, file 12, *Communist Viewpoint*, 15 January 1959; ibid., vol. 55, file 2, 1972; RG 146, vol. 69, file 96-A-00045, 'University of Toronto,' pt 23, 'University of Toronto Composite Report April '74–April '75.'

14 NA, RG 146, vol. 2760, file 96-A-00057, Report of Ritchie, 12 February 1946.

15 The extent of the RCMP's investigation of Hitschmanova is unknown. She died at the beginning of August 1990, meaning that under the provisions of the Access of Information Act her file can be applied for in August 2010. NA, RG 146, vol. 2777, file 96-A-00045, 'University of Alberta,' pt 1, Report of Inspector C. Batch, 21 January 1947; ibid., vol. 75, file 96-A-00045, 'McGill University,' pt 70, Unitarian Men's Club, 14 December 1960; Recollections of 'C,' a former Security Service member, 20 February 1999.

16 CSIS, Access request 89-A-63, 'Annual Report–Anti-Communist Section Special Branch,' 5; NA, RG 146, vol. 24, file 93-A-00019, pt 4, Canadian embassy to L.B. Pearson, 25 October 1948. The visits of Canadian students to the Eastern bloc continued into the 1950s; see Nicole Neatby, 'Student Leaders at the University of Montreal from 1950–1958: Beyond the "Carabin Persona,"' *Journal of Canadian Studies* 29, no. 3 (fall 1994), 32.

17 NA, RG 146, vol. 23, file 93-A-00088, 'McGill University, 1946–50 (Eastern Section)–Subversive Activities in,' 15 September 1948.

18 Ibid., Report re: 'McGill Student Veterans Society,' 19 May 1947; ibid., Inspector W.M. Brady to the commissioner, re: 'Student Christian Movement,' 13 January 1948; ibid., 3402, file 98-A-00082, pt 2, RCMP transit slip, 20 December 1967. In 1948, for a brief time, the club was taken over by a group of Progressive Conservatives in a right-wing coup. Among the newcomers was a young Zbigniew Brezinski, future national security advisor for the presidential administration of Jimmy Carter: see 'McGill Club Bans Dubious Politics,' *Montreal Gazette*, 28 October 1948.

19 CSIS, Access request 88-A-36, 'Security Service "D" Operations Presentation to the McDonald Commission,' October 1979.

20 Yuri Modin, *My Five Cambridge Friends: Philby, Burgess, MacLean, Blunt, and Cairncross* trans. Anthony Roberts (New York 1994).

21 CSIS, Access request 120-2-14, 'Operation Feather Bed, Aide Memoire,' 19 November 1979; ibid., Memorandum from Inspector [deleted: *Terry Guernsey*], 7 December 1962. It is even rumoured that Pierre Trudeau had his own Feather Bed file; see John Sawatsky, *For Services Rendered: Leslie James Bennett and the RCMP Security Service* (Toronto 1982), 253–9.

22 NA, RG 146, vol. 24, file 93-A-00019, pt 4, Report from 'C' Division, Montreal, 11 March 1949.

23 RCMP, *Law and Order in Canadian Democracy*, 137.

24 *Canadian Tribune*, 4 April 1949; NA, RG 146, vol. 23, file 93-A-00088, Report of Constable C.J. Young, 8 March 1949; 'University Campus Free of "Communist Trouble,"' *Ottawa Citizen*, 5 March 1949.

25 'More on Carleton and Tim Buck,' *Ottawa Journal*, 21 March 1949.

26 NA, RG 146, vol. 2768, file 96-A-00045, 'Carleton University,' pt 1, 'Labour Progressive Party,' 4 April 1956.

27 Lionel S. Lewis, *Cold War on Campus: A Study of the Politics of Organizational Control* (London, 1997), 23.

28 NA, RG 146, vol. 2772, file 96-A-00045, 'University of Manitoba,' pt 1, 'Subversive Activities in the University of Manitoba,' 26 January 1951; ibid., vol. 2790, file 98-A-00133, pt 1, 16 March 1949; 'More on Carleton and Tim Buck,' *Ottawa Journal*, 21 March 1949; 'Peace Council Banned at UBC,' *Vancouver Daily Province*, 22 February 1949; 'MacDonald Issues Call For Red Probe at UBC,' *Vancouver News Herald*, 19 February 1949; 'Some Necessary House Cleaning,' *Financial Post*, 12 March 1949; 'Should Communists Be Teachers?' *Ottawa Journal*, 12 March 1949; 'Young Canada Red Target,' *Vancouver Daily Province*, 3 February 1949.

29 Whitaker and Marcuse, *Cold War Canada*, 163–4.

30 NA, RG 146, vol. 2777, file 96-A-00045, 'University of Alberta,' pt 1, Memorandum to Inspector Leopold, 12 February 1949; ibid., vol. 2793, file 98-A-00129, pt 2, 'Communist Threat to Universities,' 29 April 1968; ibid., vol. 2790, file 98-A-00133, 'Education–Canada, General,' pt 1, [deleted: *Supt. George McClellan*] to division commanders, 22 January 1949; ibid., [deleted: name of an RCMP officer] commanding 'J' Division to the commissioner, 4 April 1949.

31 Radosh and Milton, *The Rosenberg File*, 56–7; Oleg Kalugin and Fen Montaigne, *Spymaster: My 32 Years in Intelligence and Espionage against the West* (London 1994), 55–6; CSIS, Access request 89-A-63, 'Annual Report 1951/52, Report of Counter-Espionage Section,' 5. One example of a person who broke off with the party was a KGB agent code-named Gideon, whose career is profiled in Sawatsky, *For Services Rendered*, 33–63.

32 NA, RG 146, vol. 2793, file 98-A-00129, Memorandum for Mr McClung, 9 March 1959.

33 Ibid., Transit slip, 9 March 1959; Whitaker and Marcuse, *Cold War Canada*, 359.

34 NA, RG 146, vol. 2793, file 98-A-00129, Transit slip, 9 March 1959.

35 NA, R-09107 (2), Accession: 1987-0259, ISN: 61911, Gary Marcuse, Interviews with Mark McClung, 15 January 1983, 15 December 1983.

36 Michiel Horn, *Academic Freedom in Canada: A History* (Toronto 1999), 203–

11; NA, RG 146, vol. 4276, file 98-A-00047, Leopold Infeld, pt 1, Report of [deleted: name], 21 August 1946; Leopold Infeld, *Why I Left Canada: Reflections on Science and Politics*, trans. by Helen Infeld (Montreal and London 1978), 28–9.

37 NA, RG 146, vol. 4296, file 98-A-00047, Report of [deleted: name], re: 'Dr. Leopold Infeld,' 17 April 1948.

38 Ibid., Inspector J. Leopold for officer in charge of Special Branch, 4 July 1949; Whitaker and Marcuse, *Cold War Canada*, 107; Horn, *Academic Freedom in Canada*, 205–11; Infeld, *Why I Left Canada*, 26.

39 NA, RG 146, vol. 4276, file 98-A-00047, Leopold Infeld, pt 1, 'Joint Intelligence Bureau, Appendix B to Special Report,' 18 January 1956; James Eayrs, *In Defence of Canada: Indochina, Roots of Complicity*, vol. 5 (Toronto 1983), 247.

40 Ibid., 4762, file 98-A-00047, pt 5, J.K. Starnes to commissioner, 30 November 1960.

41 Leopold Infeld, 'The Katyn Provocation,' *Pacific Tribune*, 21 March 1952.

42 NA, RG 146, vol. 79, file 98-A-00004, pt 1, Report of [deleted], 14 March 1939; ibid., Report of Constable Archbold, 9 April 1940; ibid., Superintendent R.E. Mercer to the commissioner, 15 May 1940; ibid., Superintendent J. Kelly to O.C. 'K' Division, 17 May 1940; Horn, *Academic Freedom in Canada*, 150–1.

43 NA, RG 146, vol. 79, file 98-A-00004, RCMP files relating to George Hunter, pt 1, 'Report on George Hunter,' 22 April 1949; ibid., pt 1, Re: 'Subversive Activity within the University of Alberta–Edmonton,' 2 June 1949; ibid., ibid., Report of Edmonton Special Branch, 15 July 1949; CSIS, Access request 89-A-63, 'RCMP Special Branch, Annual Report, 1946/47,' 2; Horn, *Academic Freedom in Canada*, 195–7; Dufour, '"Eggheads" and Espionage,' 188–98.

44 H.S. Ferns, *Reading from Left to Right: One Man's Political History* (Toronto 1983), 288–95. In 1946, Ferns had been tied to the Gouzenko spy scandals by an inaccurate translation of a Soviet document. Whitaker and Marcuse, *Cold War Canada*, 107–10.

45 NA, RG 146, vol. 3402, file 98-A-00082, pt 2, Report of [deleted: RCMP officer's name], 8 March 1949; ibid., vol. 2760, file 96-A-00057, 21 February 1949. Another report of a campus appearance by Ryerson, twenty-seven years after the University of Western Ontario talk, appears in ibid., vol. 2724, file 96-A-00057, 'Mount Allison University,' 25 November 1976.

46 Ibid., vol. 59, file 96-A-00169, pt 1, 'Communist Activity among Youth,' 8 November 1963; Len Scher, *The UnCanadians: True Stories of the Blacklist Era* (Toronto 1992), 213–18.

47 Interview with Daniel Goldstick, former student politician, 7 August 1999.

48 NA, RG 146, vol. 2777, file 96-A-00045, pt 1, to Inspector Parsons, no date; ibid., Inspector C. Batch, to O.C., Edmonton, 30 January 1947.

49 Ibid., 'Subversive Activities within the University of Alberta,' 1 February 1956; ibid., Inspector N.O. Jones to O.C., 'K' Division, 22 February 1956.

50 Ibid., 2772, file 96-A-00045, pt 1, Report of Corporal C.S. Hogg, 5 December 1949; ibid., vol. 2761, file 96-A-00045, pt 5, 'U. of T., Subversive Activities within,' 28 February 1961.

51 Ibid., vol. 3402, file 98-A-00082, pt 2, Report of J/D, 8 March 1949.

52 Ibid., vol. 24, file 93-A-00019, pt 4, Report of Inspector A.W. Parsons, 7 January 1949; ibid., vol. 2777, file 96-A-00045, pt 1, re: 'Dr. Mayo,' 16 December 1948; ibid., vol. 2782, file 96-A-00045, pt 2, re: 'S.S. Islandside,' 19 November 1948; ibid., vol. 2761, file 96-A-00045, pt 4, 'Subversive Activities within the U. of T.,' 18 December 1953; Steve Hewitt, 'Spying 101: The RCMP's Secret Activities at the University of Saskatchewan,' *Saskatchewan History* 47, no. 2 (fall 1995), 20–31.

53 NA, RG 146, vol. 2761, file 94-A-00057, pt 1, Inspector H.C. Forbes to the O.C. 'F' Division, 9 May 1952.

54 Ibid., vol. 2768, file 96-A-00045, 'Carleton University,' pt 1, Inspector Jones to O.C. 'A' Division, 31 January 1957; ibid., Report of Constable G.E. Land, 2 February 1957.

55 Ibid., vol. 2777, file 96-A-00045, University of Alberta, pt 2, Report of Constable R.C. Francis, 18 February 1952.

56 Ibid., pt 3, Inspector L.R. Parent to 'K' Division, re: 'Edmonton Philosophical Society,' 9, 31 October 1958; ibid., 'Subversive Activities within the University of Alberta,' 19 January 1959; Mel Hurtig, *At Twilight in the Country: Memoirs of a Canadian Nationalist* (Don Mills, ON, 1996), 36–7. As for the allegation that another of his acquaintances, Harry Gunning, was considered to be sympathetic to the subversive cause, Hurtig gave a simple response: 'If Harry Gunning was a subversive then Ralph Klein is a Trotskyist.' Interview with Mel Hurtig, 16 September 1998.

57 CSIS, Access request 89-A-63, 'Annual Report, 1949/50'; NA, RG 146, vol. 2782, file 96-A-00045, pt 3, 'Communist Activity at the University of British Columbia,' 24 October 1950.

58 '"Feeble Red Cell" Seen at McMaster,' *Toronto Telegram,* 19 May 1953; NA, RG 146, vol. 74, file 96-A-00045, pt 59, Report of [deleted: name of Mountie], re: 'Communist Activities–McMaster University,' 30 May 1953; ibid., Report of [deleted: name of Mountie], re: 'Communist Activities–McMaster University,' 29 November 1952.

59 Ibid., vol. 2760, file 96-A-00057, 'Subversive Activities,' 22 December 1952;

ibid., 'Subversive Activities at the University of Western Ontario,' 16 May 1958; ibid., Report of Constable Ritchie, 25 June 1951; ibid., Report of Ritchie, 11 June 1953; ibid., vol. 75, file 96-A-00045, pt 70, 'National Federation of Canadian University Students,' 21 January 1952.

60 Ibid., vol. 2761, file 96-A-00045, pt 4, 'Subversive Activities within the U. of T.,' 18 December 1952; ibid., 'Literature–Communist (Nature and Extent of: Production & Distribution), Canada Generally,' 7 June 1952; ibid., 'Literature–Communist (Nature & Extent of: Production & Distribution), Canada Generally,' 11 March 1954.

61 Ibid., *Varsity*, 9 January 1953.

62 Whitaker and Marcuse, *Cold War Canada*, 364–7; Carl Betke and S.W. Horrall, *Canada's Security Service: A History* (Ottawa 1978), 2: 657–8; Norman Penner, *Canadian Communism: The Stalin Years and Beyond* (Toronto 1988), 226; Lawrence S. Wittner, *One World or None: A History of the World Nuclear Disarmament Through 1953* (Stanford, Calif. 1993), 211–14.

63 Betke and Horrall, *Canada's Security Service*, 2: 591.

64 NA, RG 146, vol. 2772, file 96-A-00045, University of Manitoba, pt 1, Inspector W.J. Monaghan to O.C., 'D' Division, 20 December 1950.

65 Ibid., vol. 2761, file 96-A-00045, pt 5, 'University of Toronto Subversive Activities in,' 24 February 1958.

66 Douglas Owram, *Born at the Right Time: A History of the Baby-Boom Generation* (Toronto 1996), 165, 218–19; *Ottawa Citizen*, 19 December 1960. Nicole Neatby has written extensively about activism among francophone students during the 1950s; see her *Carabins ou activistes?: L'idéalisme et la radicalisation de la pensée étudiante à l'Université de Montréal au temps du Duplessisme* (Montreal 1997); Neatby, 'Student Leaders at the University of Montreal from 1950 to 1958,' 26–44; Stephen Endicott, *James G. Endicott: Rebel Out of China* (Toronto 1980), 328–9.

67 J.L. Granatstein, *Canada, 1957–1967: The Years of Uncertainty and Innovation* (Toronto 1986), 106–9.

5: Controversy and Contravention

1 Headquarters in Ottawa was not pleased with the failed attempt at recruiting: 'we must avoid any further indiscretion which might prove disastrous and embarrassing.' NA, RG 146, vol. 78, file 98-A-00027, pt 2, Superintendent Milligan to officer commanding, RCMP–Quebec Sub/Division, 16 May 1961.

2 As quoted in 'Sequel to an article from *Le Çarabin*; If You Do Not Like the Atom Bomb, Beware the R.C.M.P.,' *La Presse*, 23 May 1961, in House of

Commons, *Debates*, 9 June 1961. (The English translation was done by the House of Commons translation bureau.)

3 In the 1920s and 1930s social democratic politicians J.S. Woodsworth and M.J. Coldwell had spoken out against RCMP security intelligence activities, but there was no significant effort to restrict them. In 1959 the Co-operative Commonwealth Federation member of Parliament Douglas Fisher asked in the House of Commons about RCMP spying on Finnish citizens in his northern Ontario riding but, perhaps because the matter pertained to members of an ethnic minority, it received little attention. See Carl Betke and S.W. Horrall, *Canada's Security Service: A History* (Ottawa 1978), 2: 756. That scrutiny continued with the McDonald Commission and the Security Intelligence Review Committee, both of which were flawed in their depiction of these events and of their significance. McDonald Commission, *Second Report: Freedom and Security under the Law* (Ottawa 1981), 1: 347, 490–1; Donald C. Savage, 'Academe and Subversion: McDonald Commission and the Universities,' *CAUT Bulletin* 28, no. 6 (1981), 9–11; Security Intelligence Review Committee, 'A Review of CSIS Intelligence Activities,' *SIRC Annual Report, 1998–99* (Ottawa 1999), 16–20.

4 McGeorge Bundy, *Danger and Survival: Choices about the Bomb in the First Fifty Years* (New York 1990), 334, 342; Lawrence S. Wittner, *Resisting the Bomb, 1954–1970: A History of the World Nuclear Disarmament Movement* (Stanford, CA, 1997), 2: 87.

5 Bryan D. Palmer, *E.P. Thompson: Objections and Oppositions* (London 1994), 72–3, 126–8; Stephen Endicott, *James G. Endicott: Rebel Out of China* (Toronto 1980), 328–9; Wittner, *Resisting the Bomb*, 44–51; NA, RG 146, Access request 97-A-00172, 'New Left Committee–Canada,' Commissioner C.W. Harvison to Minister of Justice E.D. Fulton, 24 February 1961.

6 Wittner, *Resisting the Bomb*, 197, 203. For more on the Voice of Women, see Kay Macpherson, *When in Doubt, Do Both: The Times of My Life* (Toronto 1994), 89–117.

7 NA, RG 146, vol. 5008, file 97-A-00076, pt 2, Harvison to Fulton, 4 July 1961; 'Fulton Cites Red Threat in Canada,' *Ottawa Journal*, 1 June 1961.

8 NA, RG 33/128, Access request 98-A-00034, box 105, file 6000-6-60.4, Superintendent W.H. Kelly to officers commanding divisions, 21 June 1961.

9 The appearance of Soviet students concerned both the RCMP and the Department of External Affairs. Those who visited were not ordinary students: they tended to be in their thirties, or even in their forties, and appeared to be selected as ambassadors for communism or as intelligence gatherers. Internal discussions took place about whether to restrict the age

of those who could visit Canada. Peter Marwitz, former Security Service member, to author, 11 November 1999.

10 John Ranelagh, *The Agency: The Rise and Decline of the CIA* (New York 1986), 250–1; Angus Mackenzie, *Secrets: The CIA's War at Home* (Los Angeles 1997), 19–25. For more on the CIA's funding of a wide variety of cultural organizations during the cold war, see Frances Stonor Saunders, *Who Paid the Piper? The CIA and the Cultural Cold War* (London 1999).

11 NA, RG 146, vol. 78, file 98-A-00027, pt 2, 'National Federation of Canadian University Students,' 6 December 1961; ibid., vol. 2757, file 96-A-00045, pt 1, Report of Constable M.G. Johnston, 8 November 1962. Stewart Goodings, NFCUS president at the time remembers the excitement he and his fellow executive members felt at the presence of the two Soviets. Unlike the source, who was one of his colleagues, he was not impressed by the American; interview with Stewart Goodings, 18 February 1999. For other work on campuses at this time, see NA, RG 146, vol. 2770, file 95-A-00094, pt 1, Inspector D.F. Fitzgerald to NCO i/c Sudbury, 6 November 1961; ibid., vol. 2777, file 96-A-00045, pt 4, 'General Conditions and Subversive Activities within the University of Alberta,' 18 October 1962; ibid., vol. 2872, file 96-A-00045, pt 5, 'Communist Party of Canada–Students' Club–U.B.C.,' 22 October 1962; ibid., vol. 2760, file 96-A-00057, 'University of Western Ontario,' pt 1, RCMP transit slip, 20 November 1961; ibid., vol. 2262, file 94-A-00067, pt 5, Report of Constable J.A. Bezzola, 19 February 1963.

12 According to Don Wall, a civilian member of the Security Service, Ken Green, was most likely the author of the 1961 document. Interview with Don Wall, 7 May 1998; John Sawatsky, *Men in the Shadows: The RCMP Security Service* (Toronto 1980), 108–10; NA, RG 146, vol. 5008, file 97-A-00076, pt 2, 'The Communist Program for Control of Youth and Intellectuals,' 1, 3.

13 'The Communist Program for Control of Youth and Intellecuals,' 12. What the RCMP failed to mention was that David Shugar, Eric Adams, and Matthew Nightingale were acquitted. In addition, Raymond Boyer received a two-year sentence, while Harold Gerson was sentenced to five years. See Reg Whitaker and Gary Marcuse, *Cold War Canada: The Making of a National Insecurity State, 1945–1957* (Toronto 1994), 106–7, 432. Christopher Andrew and Oleg Gordievsky, *KGB: The Inside Story* (Toronto 1990), 144.

14 'The Communist Program for Control of Youth and Intellectuals,' 2–3; J. Edgar Hoover, *Communist Target – Youth: Communist Infiltration and Agitation Tactics* (Washington 1960).

15 NA, RG 146, vol. 5008, file 97-A-00076, pt 2, 'The Communist Program for Control of Youth and Intellectuals,' attachment.

16 Ibid., 14.

17 Ibid., pt 6, 'RCMP Inquiries on University Campuses,' 23 June 1970. This was one of two internal reports on the subject of RCMP investigations on campuses that the force had prepared in 1970.

18 'RCMP: How the RCMP Spies on Students,' *Viewpoint* 2, no. 5 (1962); 'RCMP Campus Capers Attacked,' *Ottawa Citizen*, 14 December 1962.

19 NA, MG 32, B39, Donald Fleming Papers, vol. 96, file 'R.C.M.P. University Students and Teachers, 1962,' Harvison to Fleming, 18 December 1962; C.W. Harvison, *The Horsemen* (Toronto 1967), 208, 244–67.

20 NA, RG 146, vol. 5008, file 97-A-00076, pt 3, reports from December 1962 and January 1963. The information received by headquarters became a one-page memo and was submitted to the minister of justice; see NA, MG 32, B39, vol. 96, file 'R.C.M.P. University Students and Teachers,' 1962, 'A Summary of RCMP Activity in Universities Generally during the Six Months Preceding December 1st, 1962.'

21 Ibid., Lowell Murray to Harvison, 15 May 1962; ibid., vol. 98, file R.C.M.P. University Students and Teachers, 1963, Fleming to J.H. Stewart Reid, 3 January 1963.

22 Donald Fleming, *So Very Near: The Political Memoirs of the Honourable Donald M. Fleming,* Vol. 2, *The Summit Years* (Toronto 1985), 543–4.

23 NA, MG 32, B39, vol. 96, file 'RCMP–Memos to the Minister from R.C.M.P. Commissioner,' pt 9, Fleming to Harvison, 22 November 1962; ibid., file 'R.C.M.P. University Students and Teachers,' 1962, Deputy Commissioner G.B. McClellan to Fleming, 30 November 1962; ibid., Fleming to Harvison, 17 January 1963.

24 Ibid., Harvison to Fleming, 21 January 1963; Canada, House of Commons *Debates*, 1962–3: 2920.

25 'Political Activities Checked by Police,' *Ubyssey*, 18 January 1963; 'RCMP Enlisting Informants Approach Carleton Student,' *Silhouette*, 1 February 1963; 'Are the RCMP Investigating Us?' *Dalhousie Gazette*, 21 February 1963.

26 NA, RG 146, vol. 2757, file 96-A-00045, pt 2, Report of Constable M.G. Johnston, 9 January 1963.

27 Ibid., vol. 2770, file 95-A-00094, Laurentian University, pt 1, S/Inspector J.L. Forest to the commissioner, 28 November 1962; ibid., vol. 5008, file 97-A-00076, pt 4, Report from Superintendent N.W. Jones, 4 February 1963; ibid., vol. 2924, file 97-A-00152, pt 1, re: 'National Federation of Canadian University Students,' 7 February 1963; ibid., vol. 59, file 96-A-00169, pt 2, Aide-mémoire, 1980 (an assessment of the RCMP's file on the CAUT prepared during the McDonald Commission's hearings); ibid., vol. 59, file 96-A-00169, pt 1, D.S.I. to all divisions, 14 June 1968; ibid., CAUT, pt 1, 27 April 1964; ibid., Memorandum of Inspector J.E.M. Barrette, re: 'CAUT

and Stewart Reid,' 28 June 1963; ibid., vol. 5008, file 97-A-00076, pt 5, 'Canadian Association of University Teachers–Canada,' 20 October 1965.

28 'RCMP Campus Activities Criticized by Professors: Commissioner Says Force Questioned Students,' *Kingston Whig-Standard*, 21 March 1963; 'Harvison Defends Investigations,' *Gateway*, 22 March 1963.

29 'RCMP Campus Activities Criticized by Professors: Commissioner Says Force Questioned Students,' *Kingston Whig-Standard*, 21 March 1963; NA, RG 146, vol. 5008, file 97-A-00076, pt 4, McClellan to Fleming, 26 March 1963.

30 Diefenbaker Canada Centre Archives, MG 01, XII, A/711, vol. 27, Harvison to Sidney Katz, 13 April 1963; Sidney Katz, 'RCMP: Inside Canada's Secret Police,' *Maclean's*, 20 April 1963: 13–15, 32–41.

31 NA, RG 146, vol. 2777, file 96-A-00045, 'University of Alberta,' pt 5, 'Combined Universities Campaign for Nuclear Disarmament, University of Alberta (Communist Activities Within)–Edmonton, Alberta,' 29 October 1963.

32 'RCMP Activities on Campus,' *CAUT Bulletin* 12 (October 1964), 56.

33 House of Commons, *Debates*, 14 December 1962: 2653; ibid., 18 December 1962: 2773; 'Redcoats Still Hunt Campus Reds,' *Ubyssey*, 31 January 1964.

34 Records of the Privy Council Office (PCO), Access request 135–2/98-A-00086, 'Minutes of the 74th Meeting of the Security Panel,' 31 October 1963.

35 RCMP memorandum dated 24 December 1963, as quoted in McDonald Commission, *Second Report*, 1: 342; 'RCMP Activity on Campus,' *CAUT Bulletin* 12 (October 1964): 56.

36 Interview with Don Wall, 7 May 1998. Wall was at the meeting as a representative of the Privy Council Office; McDonald Commission, *Second Report*, 1: 342.

37 'Redcoats Still Hunt Campus Reds,' *Ubyssey*, 31 January 1964; Peter Bower, 'I Spy with My Little Red Eye,' *Martlet*, 10 March 1964; NA, RG 146, vol. 5008, file 97-A-00076, pt 4, [deleted: *Robert Thompson, Social Credit, Member of Parliament (Red Deer)*], to Commissioner G.B. McClellan, 29 November 1963.

38 Ibid., pt 6, 'RCMP Inquiries on University Campuses,' 23 June 1970; McDonald Commission, *Second Report*, 1: 486–7 (this section of the McDonald Commission report confuses two separate issues: surveillance on university campuses and the recruitment of sources on university campuses); 'Mr Ward and the Mounties,' *Ottawa Journal*, 23 February 1967; 'RCMP "spies" on the campus,' *Ottawa Citizen*, 23 February 1967; 'RCMP

Must Interview Students, Pennell Says,' *Globe and Mail*, 23 February 1967; 'RCMP Spy Bids in 50s,' *Toronto Telegram*, 22 February 1967.

39 Interview with 'B,' a former Security Service member, 20 May 1998; Interview with Donald J. Inch, a former Security Service member, 1 March 1998; Recollections of 'C,' a former Security Service member, 20 February 1999.

40 NA, RG 146, Access request 98-A-00133, 'Education–Canada, General,' Notes from Assistant Commissioner Lemieux to Superintendent Bella, 22 January 1959.

41 Ibid., vol. 2757, file 96-A-00045, pt 1, Report of Constable M.G. Johnston, 8 November 1962; ibid., S/Inspector J.L. Forest to Kingston S.I.B., 20 November 1962.

42 Ibid., vol. 29, file 93-A-00039, York University, pt 1, Report of Constable T.L. Beckett, 8 November 1968.

43 Ibid., vol. 2774, file 94-A-00057, University of Saskatchewan, pt 3, Report of Constable J.C. Dudley, 17 February 1967.

44 Ibid., vol. 28, file 93-A-00038, pt 1, 'Assessment of Political Activities at Sir George Williams University (Sept. 1964 to June 1968),' Prepared by Constable J.J.L. Jodoin, December 1968; Interview with Terry Copp, a faculty member at Sir George Williams University in 1968, 8 September 1998.

45 NA, RG 146, vol. 28, file 93-A-00038, pt 1, 'Assessment of Political Activities at Sir George Williams University,' ibid., vol. 2771, file 96-A-00045, pt 1, 'Waterloo Lutheran University,' 19 May 1970.

46 Ibid., vol. 29, file 93-A-00039, York University, pt 1, Report of Corporal A. Cevraini, 25 September 1968; ibid., vol. 2731, file 96-A-00045, 'Université de Montréal,' pt 2, 6–21 May 1969; interview with 'A,' a former Security Service member, 18 April 1998; NA, RG 146, vol. 28, file 93-A-00038, pt 1, 'Assessment of Political Activities at Sir George Williams University.'

47 Ibid., vol. 5008, file 97-A-00076, pt 7, 'Academe and Subversion,' June 1970.

48 This is not to suggest that Mounted Police students were deliberately sent to universities to collect intelligence. If such had been the case, according to one former Security Service member, the RCMP would have sent younger members to blend in, not men in their thirties. 'D,' a former Security Service member, to author, 14 August 1999.

49 NA, RG 33/128, Access request 98-A-00034, box 105, file 6000-5-60.6, [deleted: name of Mountie] to officer i/c sources, 24 October 1968; ibid., Transit slip, 25 October 1968; ibid., assistant D.S.I. to D.S.I., 28 October 1968.

50 NA, RG 146, vol. 2991, file 98-A-00079, pt 1, Raid against "Rising up Angry,"' 30 December 1970; ibid., vol. 39, file 94-A-00130, pt 1, 'Vancouver Police,' 1 October 1970.

51 Ibid., vol. 2772, file 96-A-00045, pt 3, director of security for Canadian
    Military, to Assistant Commissioner W.L. Kelly, 31 April 1965; ibid., vol.
    2762, pt 14, R.L. McGibbon to the commissioner, 24 January 1968; ibid.,
    vol. 2760, file 96-A-00057, Memorandum to Sergeant Fred Schultz from
    Corporal Surgenor, 26 March 1970.
52 Ibid., vol. 2793, file 98-A-00129, Higgitt to Directorate of Security, Canadian
    Forces, 29 April 1968. Bennett had no recollection of what the matter with
    the Department of National Defence involved. Four years later, in 1972, he
    was let go because of false accusations that he was a Soviet mole. Leslie
    James Bennett to author, 8 September 1999.
53 NA, KG 146, vol. 2760, file 96-A-0005, Memorandum to Department of
    National Defence from RCMP, 8 April 1970.
54 Ibid., vol. 2750, file 96-A-00045, 'Protests and Demonstrations Quebec
    Province,' 5 February 1970.
55 Ibid., vol. 2774, file 97-A-00139, Higgitt to under-secretary of state for
    external affairs, 27 May 1969; ibid., vol. 75, file 96-A-00045, pt 71,
    J.J. McCardle, to the commissioner, 30 April 1968; ibid., vol. 2793,
    file 98-A-00129, J.J. McCardle, to Deputy Commissioner W.H. Kelly,
    and responding comments, 9 November 1967.
56 Ibid., vol. 2786, file 96-A-00045, pt 12, Art Butroid to Assistant Commis-
    sioner W.L. Higgitt, 16 September 1968; CSIS, Access request 117-1999-14,
    Instructions, re: 'Subversive Investigation and Correspondence,' McClellan
    to officers commanding, 12 September 1951.
57 NA, RG 146, vol. 2762, file 96-A-00045, pt 14, R.L. McGibbon to commis-
    sioner, 24 January 1968; Jeffrey T. Richelson and Desmond Ball, *The Ties
    That Bind: Intelligence Cooperation between the UKUSA Countries – the United
    Kingdom, the United States of America, Canada, Australia and New Zealand*
    (London 1990), 90.
58 NA, RG 33, Access request 98-A-00034, box 105, file 6000-5-60.6, [deleted:
    name] to officer i/c sources, 24 October 1968.
59 Memorandum of Assistant Commissioner Leonard Higgitt, 29 November
    1967, as quoted in McDonald Commission, *Second Report*, 1: 343–6. For
    more specific details on this operation, see NA, RG 33, Access request
    98-A-00034, box 105, file 6000-5-60.6, D.S.I. to divisions, 31 January 1968.
60 McDonald Commission, *Third Report: Certain R.C.M.P. Activities and the
    Question of Governmental Knowledge* (Ottawa 1981), 182.
61 NA, RG 33, Access request 98-A-00034, box 105, file 6000-6-60.6, re:
    'Contacts–Key Sectors–Canada,' 11 March 1968.
62 NA, RG 146, vol. 2792, file AH-1999-00101, 'Education Canada,' pt 27,
    [deleted: name] to Inspector Chisholm, 7 October 1969; McDonald Com-

mission, *Freedom and Security Under the Law*, 1: 347. There is no reference to any liaison with the Security Service in Claude Bissell's memoirs of his tenure as president of the University of Toronto. He did, however, express his concern 'about the possible use of force to gain student political goals' after the disruption of a speech in Toronto in February 1969 by former University of California–Berkeley president Clark Kerr. Claude Bissell, *Halfway Up Parnassus: A Personal Account of the University of Toronto, 1932–1971* (Toronto 1974), 139.

63 Kenneth Strand to author, 3 February 1999; NA, RG 146, vol. 2262, file 94-A-00057, pt 3, Report of Sergeant R.L. Firby, 10 June 1965; Department of Foreign Affairs and International Trade, Access request A-1998-0356/mh, file 29-16-2-1, 'New Left,' Memorandum of E.R. Rettie, 4 June 1969.

64 NA, RG 146, vol. 2778, file 96-A-00045, pt 12, Constable Moodie to O.C. 'K' Division, S and I Branch, 13 August 1969; ibid., vol. 5008, file 97-A-00076, pt 6, J.E.M. Barrette to O.C.s, 5 March 1970.

65 Ibid., vol. 5008, file 97-A-00076, pt 6, 'RCMP Inquiry on University Campuses–Appendices,' 23 June 1970.

66 Ibid., vol. 2757, file 96-A-00045, pt 2, Higgitt to Solicitor General George J. McIlraith, 9 January 1970. 'Explain RCMP Policy in Campus Probes: Queen's Principal,' *Globe and Mail*, 30 May 1970; ibid., Inspector R.M. Shorey to director, Security and Intelligence, 9 January 1970.

67 Ibid., pt 3, Assistant Commissioner C.J. Sweeny to Barrette, 5 June 1970; ibid., Watts to Higgitt, 19 June 1970; ibid., Drafts, Higgitt to Watts, 22 July 1970; ibid., Drafts, Higgitt to Watts, 20, 21 July 1970; ibid., Report of Sergeant B.L. Campbell, 3 June 1970; ibid., vol. 2756, file 96-A-00045, pt 3, Transit slip, 10 July 1970.

68 Ibid., vol. 5008, file 97-A-00076, pt 8, Beavis to commissioner, 5 April 1971; ibid., pt 9, John Starnes to Don Wall, 7 June 1971; 'Queen's Senate Endorses Earlier Stand on "Snooping,"' *Kingston Whig-Standard*, 26 November 1971.

69 Interview with 'B,' 20 May 1998; NA, RG 33, Access request, 98-A-00034, box 105, file 6000-5-60.6, Memorandum from officer in charge of sources, 'RCMP Enquiries on University Campuses,' 29 April 1970.

70 Peter Worthington, '"Academic Freedom" Keeps RCMP Off the Campus,' *Toronto Telegram*, 14 October 1970; interview with Peter Marwitz, 17 February 1998; McDonald Commission, vol. 170, 23312; NA, RG 146, vol. 5008, file 97-A-00076, pt 6, 'O' Division to assistant D.S.I., 14 October 1970; *Report of the Royal Commission on Security* (abridged version) (Ottawa 1969), 37.

71 NA, RG 146, vol. 30, file 93-A-00069, pt 1, Higgitt to E.T. Galpin, 30 April 1968; Department of Foreign Affairs and International Trade, Access

request A-1998-0356/mh, file 29-16-2-1, New Left, Higgitt to E.T. Galpin, 30 April 1969. Three different versions of this document have been cleared under the Access to Information Act and all three contain different excisions, including the removal of the name of Trent University in one of them. Ibid., access request A-1999-0149, file 29-16-1-1, New Left, E.R. Rettie to Mr Williamson, 6 May 1969.

72 NA, RG 146, vol. 22, file 93-A-00058, Aide-Mémoire of Assistant Commissioner J.E.M. Barrette, 5 November 1969. Wall admits that the Trudeau government's approach represented a violation of the earlier agreement with the CAUT; interview with Don Wall, 7 May 1998. Lalonde had no 'recollection' of the matter; Marc Lalonde to author, 4 January 1999

73 McDonald Commission, *Second Report*, 1: 492.

74 NA, RG 146, vol. 5008, file 97-A-00076, pt 7, 'Academe and Subversion,' June, December 1970.

75 Ibid., June 1970. The deleted passages appear in Privy Council Office, Access request 135-2/98-A-00024, 'Academe and Subversion,' June 1970.

76 NA, RG 146, vol. 5008, file 97-A-00076, pt 7, 'Transcript of Prime Minister's Remarks on the CBS Program "Sixty Minutes,"' 8 December 1997; Privy Council Office, Access request 135–2/98-A-00024, 'Minutes of Cabinet Meeting of 23 December 1970.'

77 John Starnes to author, 8 May 1998.

78 NA, RG 33/128, Access request 98-A-00032, exhibit M27, Memorandum of John Starnes, 21 December 1970. At this meeting the cabinet committee agreed in principle to lift the alleged restrictions. The entire cabinet confirmed the decision two days later.

79 NA, RG 146, vol. 5008, file 97-A-0076, [deleted: name] to Inspector Spooner, 20 January 1971; ibid., pt 8, Message from Sudbury S.I.S., 17 March 1971; ibid., pt 8, Action request, D.S.I. to Superintendent Chisholm, February or March 1971.

80 Privy Council Office, Access request 135-2/98-A-00024, 'Cabinet Minutes of September 30, 1971'; ibid., 'Memorandum to Cabinet from Jean-Pierre Goyer,' 17 September 1971

81 McDonald Commission, *Second Report*, 1: 489. The use of technical sources (wiretaps of telephones and listening devices) was not discussed at the November 1963 meetings; NA, RG 146, vol. 5008, file 97-A-00076, pt 8, Goyer to [deleted: name of academic], 24 November 1971; Jean-Pierre Goyer to author, 16 June 1998.

82 NA, RG 33/128, Access request 98-A-00032, O.M. Davey to John Starnes, 29 February 1972; John Starnes to author, 26 January 2000.

83 John Starnes, as quoted in McDonald Commission, *Second Report*, 1: 490. Starnes's emphasis. His autobiography . *Closely Guarded: A Life in Canadian Security and Intelligence* (Toronto 1998), does not mention the university controversy.

84 Interview with former Solicitor General Warren Allmand, 25 February 1999.

6: From the Old Left to the New Left

1 NA, RG 146, vol. 78, file 98-A-00027, pt 2, Superintendent W. Milligan to commissioner, 16 October 1961; ibid., vol. 78, file 98-A-00027, pt 2, 'Combined Universities Campaign for Nuclear Disarmament,' 3 November 1961; ibid., Reports re: 'Combined Universities Campaign for Nuclear Disarmament, Laval,' 4, 16 October 1961.

2 Lawrence Wittner, *Resisting the Bomb: A History of the World Nuclear Disarmament Movement, 1954–1970* (Stanford, CA, 1997), 443.

3 Trotskyists had been targeted for decades because of their radicalism and because of a belief among security services that their Communist enemies had infiltrated their organizations. See John Earl Haynes and Harvey Klehr, *Venona: Decoding Soviet Espionage in America* (New Haven, CT, 1999), 251–2.

4 Higgitt memorandum re: 'Mounties on Campus,' as quoted in McDonald Commission, *Freedom and Security under the Law, Second Report*, 1: 343–7.

5 'Robarts against UWO Communists,' *Gazette*, 8 January 1963; NA, RG 146, vol. 2761, file 96-A-00045, 'University of Toronto,' pt 7, University of Toronto, Communist Activities within,' 1964; ibid., vol. 2777, file 96-A-00045, 'University of Alberta,' pt 4, 'General Conditions and Subversive Activities Within,' 18 October 1962.

6 Ibid., vol. 4230, file 98-A-00028, 'Communist Party of Canada–Professional Section,' 29 May 1964; ibid., vol. 2783, file 96-A-00028, 'Communist Infiltration of Educational Process,' 6 October 1964.

7 Ibid., 'Communist Infiltration of Educational Process,' 13 July 1964; ibid., vol. 2779, Education–British Columbia, pt 3, 'B.C. Parent-Teacher Association–Subversive Activities in,' 26 October 1961.

8 Ibid., vol. 2783, file 96-A-00045, pt 7, 'Fair Play for Cuba Committee–Communist Activities Within,' 16 July 1963.

9 Ibid., vol. 65, file 97-A-00044, 'Frank Underhill,' pt 2, 'Canadian Broadcasting Corporation, Communist Activities within,' 27 November 1963; ibid., vol. 75, file 96-A-00045, 'McGill University,' pt 72, 'Students for a Democratic Society,' 10 February 1969. The last report has been excised under Access provisions but RCMP officer Gus Begalki has written below it:

'Another case where C.B.C. interviews serve to finance Radical trend, etc.'

10 Ibid., vol. 2760, file 96-A-00057, 'Communist activities within UWO,' 19 June 1962; ibid., vol. 2782, file 96-A-00045, pt 5, 'In a Letter from B.C.,' 27 April 1962; ibid., vol. 2783, file 96-A-00045, pt 20, 'UBC,' 28 October 1969.

11 Ibid., vol. 59, file 96-A-00169, pt 1, 'U. of T. *Staff Bulletin*,' 15 November 1965; ibid., vol. 5008, file 97-A-00076, pt 6, 'RCMP Inquiries on Campus-Appendix 3,' 23 June 1970.

12 Ibid., vol. 2760, file 96-A-00057, 'University of Western Ontario,' 10 June 1970; ibid., vol. 2728, 'SGWU,' pt 1, 'Subversive Activities in Canadian Universities,' 9 December 1965; ibid., vol. 2759, file 98-A-00066, 'Brock University,' pt 2, 'Report of Niagara Falls,' 31 October 1969; ibid., vol. 2910, file 97-A-00062, 'Learned Societies,' pt 1, 'Canadian Association of Slavists–Canada,' 19 September 1969.

13 NA, RCMP Records relating to Daniel Goldstick, Report of [deleted: name of Mountie], 21 December 1964; ibid., Report of [deleted: name of Mountie], 16 December 1965; ibid., Report of [deleted: name of Mountie], 22 February 1966; ibid., Report of [deleted: name of Mountie], 1 June 1966; ibid., Report of [deleted: name of Mountie], 9 January 1975.

14 NA, RG 146, vol. 59, file 96-A-00169, Laurentian University, pt 1, 'Laurentian University, Sudbury, Ont., Communist Activities within,' 6 November 1961.

15 Ibid., vol. 2756, file 93-A-00051, pt 7, 'York Misc.,' 18 December 1961; ibid., vol. 2761, file 96-A-00045, pt 7, Report of Constable W.G. Elkeer, 18 December 1964; ibid., 'U. of T.,' 20 February 1964; ibid., vol. 59, file 96-A-00169, pt 1, 'U. of T. *Staff Bulletin*,' 15 November 1965.

16 NA, MG 28, IV 4, vol. 84, file 142, Reel H-1583, 5–6; Reel H-1587, 'Draft: Main Propositions for the National Committee Meeting, November 15–18, 1963,' 5 November 1963; NA, RG 146, vol. 5008, file 97-A-00076, pt 4, 'YCL–16th National Convention,' December 1962; ibid., vol. 2762, file 96-A-00045, pt 14, Superintendent C.S. Hogg to Commissioner, 24 January 1968.

17 Ibid., vol. 743, file 97-A-00172, New Left Committee, pt 1, George McClellan to E.D. Fulton, 30 March 1961; ibid., vol. 2779, file 98-A-00170, Education–British Columbia, pt 1, 'Communist Party of Canada–Greater Vancouver Area Convention–1962,' 19 March 1962; ibid., vol. 2777, file 96-A-00045, 'University of Calgary,' pt 3, 19 January 1970. The last provides an example of a collection of internal party documents and includes a letter that was most likely addressed to William Kashtan, leader of the party in the 1970s:

Dear Bill,

An interesting development over the weekend that You will like to hear. Yesterday we had a small meeting with a group from the University. The three who came to the meeting belong to a group on the Campus, which call themselves 'The Collective.' There are about 24 young people in this group, and the 3 who met with us represent the leadership.

They have told us that they are dissatisfied with the New Left as represented by the people on the Campus, and feel that words must be accompanied by action. All 3 have told us, that they are Communists although they do not belong to our Party ... You will meet these people when You are here Saturday and You will form Your own opinions of them. I think that perhaps we should give some thought, at this stage, to invite our YCL organizer from the east for a meeting with them, as the action plan of the YCL is probably exactly what would keep this group from falling apart.

At the same time it may perhaps be wise if you could get in touch with our Party in Victoria and get some background on Colin Constant. He claims to have been fired from CYC there for being a Communist ... Sincerely, [deleted: name]

18 NA, RG 146, vol. 2763, file 96-A-00045, pt 23, 'League for Socialist Action,' 3 February 1970; ibid., vol. 56, file 96-A-00048, pt 5, 'Report of Corporal D.M. Crimp,' 18 March 1969; ibid., vol. 2769, file 97-A-00139, pt 1, 'Young Socialists, Guelph-Waterloo, Ontario,' 18 December 1969; ibid., vol. 2762, file 96-A-00045, pt 21, 'League for Socialist Action,' 20 May 1969. For background on the League for Socialist Action and the Young Socialist Alliance, see Roger O'Toole, *The Precipitous Path: Studies in Political Sects* (Toronto 1977), 12–32.

19 NA, RG 146, vol. 2159, file 98-A-00030, 'Organizational Assessment Form–Internationalists,' 4 August 1969; ibid., vol. 2950, file 98-A-00078, pt 1, re: 'Organizational Assessment Form–Canadian Communist Movement,' 14 November 1969; ibid., vol. 2787, file 96-A-00045, pt 25, 'The Canadian Communist Movement (Marxist-Leninist),' no date; ibid., vol. 3718, file 98-A-00082, pt 3, 'Quebec Student Movement,' 5 August 1970; ibid., vol. 2778, file 96-A-00045, Simon Fraser University, pt 25, 'The Canadian Communist Movement,' [1969].

20 Ibid., vol. 2762, file 96-A-00045, 'University of Toronto,' pt 22, 'Canadian Student Movement,' 30 September 1969.

21 Alvin Finkel, *Our Lives: Canada after 1945* (Toronto 1997), 54–5, 127–8; Robert Wright, 'History Underdosing: Pop Demography and the Crisis in Canadian History,' *Canadian Historical Review* 81, no. 4 (December 2000), 663–5.

22 Doug Owram, *Born at the Right Time: A History of the Baby-Boom Generation* (Toronto 1996); Cyril Levitt, *Children of Privilege: Student Revolt in the Sixties:*

A Study of Student Movements in Canada, the United States, and West Germany (Toronto 1984), 50; 'Universities Face Record Enrolments,' *Vancouver Sun*, 31 August 1968; Peter Warrian, 'Education: Democratization and Decolonization,' in Tim and Julyan Reid, eds., *Student Power and the Canadian Campus* (Toronto 1969), 24–5; Nigel Roy Moses, 'All That Was Left: Student Struggle for Mass Student Aid and the Abolition of Tuition Fees in Ontario, 1946–1975' (PhD dissertation, University of Toronto, 1995), 79–81; Myrna Kostash, *Long Way from Home: The Story of the Sixties Generation in Canada* (Toronto 1980), 71–3, 77–8, 96.

23 Mary Louise Adams, *The Trouble with Normal: Postwar Youth and the Making of Heterosexuality* (Toronto 1997), 137; J. Edgar Hoover, *Masters of Deceit: The Story of Communism in America and How to Fight It* (New York 1958), 107; Elaine Tyler May, *Homeward Bound: American Families in the Cold War Era* (New York 1988), 94; Philip G. Altbach, *Student Politics in America: A Historical Analysis* (New York 1974), 203.

24 Maurice Isserman and Michael Kazin, *America Divided: The Civil War of the 1960s* (New York 2000), 171; Maurice Isserman, *If I Had a Hammer: The Death of the Old Left and the Birth of the New Left* (New York 1987), xiii, 3, 115; Bryan D. Palmer, *E.P. Thompson: Objections and Oppositions* (London 1994), 70–80.

25 Tom Hayden, *Reunion: A Memoir* (New York 1988), 78–81, 201; Moses, 'All That Was Left,' 36; C. Wright Mills, *The Power Elite* (New York 1956); Herbert Marcuse, *One-Dimensional Man* (Boston 1964)

26 Seymour Martin Lipset, *Rebellion in the University* (Boston 1971), 46, 60; 'A Conversation with Todd Gitlin,' *CBC Ideas* transcript, 1997; David MacGregor, a 1960s Canadian student activist, to author, 12 July 2001; Moses, 'All That Was Left,' 179–80.

27 George Grant, *Lament for a Nation: The Death of Canadian Nationalism* (Toronto 1965); Kostash, *Long Way From Home*, xxxiii, 191–207.

28 John A. Andrew, III, *The Other Side of the Sixties: Young Americans for Freedom and the Rise of Conservative Politics* (New Brunswick, NJ, 1997), 29–30; Tom Hayden, 'Port Huron Statement of the Students for a Democratic Society,' 1962, http://ppl.nhmccd.edu/~craigl/primary_folder/29.c.01.Port_Huron.html; Jerry Farber, *The Student as Nigger: Essays and Stories* (New York 1969); Isserman, *If I Had a Hammer*, 202; Ron Jacobs, *The Way the Wind Blew: A History of the Weather Underground* (London 1997).

29 Moses, 'All That Was Left,' 72–4, 189–95; NA, RG 146, vol. 363, file 98-A-00102, S/Inspector, assistant SIB officer, to commissioner, 30 August 1968.

30 Ibid., vol. 2768, file 96-A-00045, pt 2, Report of Constable D.G. McIntyre,

20 October 1965; ibid., Witherden to commissioner, 29 October 1965; ibid., vol. 2783, file 96-A-00045, 'UBC,' pt 9, 'Seminar on American Foreign Policy,' 7 December 1965; ibid., 'UBC, Communist Activities within,' 10 August 1965; ibid., vol. 2761, file 96-A-00045, 'University of Toronto,' pt 8, 'U. of T., Communist Activities within,' 23 February 1965.

31 NA, RG 146, vol. 738, file 98-A-00026, 'Student Union for Peace Action,' pt 1, 'SUPA,' 27 June 1966.

32 NA, RG 146, vol. 2783, file 96-A-00045, pt 11, 'UBC,' 3 March 1967; George Woodcock, 'A Radical Dilemma,' in Tim and Julyan Reid, eds., *Student Power and the Canadian Campus* (Toronto 1969), 58–64.

33 NA, RG 146, vol. 2793, file 98-A-00129, Education–Briefs and Surveys–Canada, pt 2, 'Communist Threat to Universities,' 29 April 1968.

34 Ibid., vol. 59, file 96-A-00169, pt 1, 'Communist Activity among Youth Particularly in the Educational Field,' no date. For more on the RCMP's monitoring of high school students and groups, see Christabelle Sethna, 'High School Confidential: RCMP Surveillance of Secondary School Activists,' in Dieter Buse, Gary Kinsman, and Mercedes Steedman, eds., *Whose National Security? Canadian State Surveillance and the Creation of Enemies* (Toronto 2000), 121–8.

35 The FBI solicited advice on how to deal with the New Left from its regional branches. The Newark office remarked on the 'unique task' of curtailing the New Left. Holding the movement up to ridicule was out because of the fondness of radicals for 'nonconformism in dress and speech, neglect of personal cleanliness, used of obscenities (printed and uttered), publicized sexual promiscuity, experimenting with and the use of drugs, filthy clothes, shaggy hair, wearing of sandals, beads, and unusual jewelry.' Eventually the office recommended the promotion of factionalism within the movement, the very factor that led to the disintegration of the New Left later in the 1960s. FBI memorandum dated 27 May 1968; reprinted in Churchill and Vander Wall, *The COINTELPRO Papers*, 181–2; Nelson Blackstock, *COINTELPRO: The FBI's Secret War on Political Freedom* (New York 1976), 124; William C. Sullivan, *The Bureau: My Thirty Years in Hoover's FBI* (New York 1979).

36 Central Intelligence Agency, Freedom of information request F-1998-01934, 'Restless Youth,' September 1968, v–viii, 1–3, 16–17.

37 Ibid., i, 21.

38 Richard Gid Powers, *Secrecy and Power: The Life of J. Edgar Hoover* (New York 1987), 464–7; Athan G. Theoharis, *Spying on Americans: Political Surveillance from Hoover to the Huston Plan* (Philadelphia 1978), 147–8; Frank J. Donner, *The Age of Surveillance: The Aims and Methods of America's Political Intelligence System* (New York 1980), 270–1; *Report to the President by the Commission on*

CIA Activities within the United States (New York 1975), 130–50; Harry Rositzke, *The CIA's Secret Operations: Espionage, Counterespionage, and Covert Action* (New York 1977), 217.

39 NA, RG 33/128, Access request AH-1998-00059, accession 1992–93/251, box 130, file 'Covert Measures–Check Mate–"D" Operations,' John Starnes to D.S. Maxwell, 23 July 1970. This record is one more example of the vagaries of the Access to Information system. A heavily censored version of Starnes's letter, minus the comments of British intelligence, appears in CSIS, Access request 117-90-123, Starnes to Maxwell, 23 July 1970.

40 ASIO, 'Peaceful Co-existence and the Role of the "New Left,"' 1970. For more on the history of security intelligence in Australia, see David McKnight, *Australia's Spies and Their Secrets* (St Leonards, Australia 1994); Fiona Capp, *Writers Defiled* (South Yarra, Australia 1993); Frank Cain, *The Australian Security Intelligence Organization: An Unofficial History* (London 1994).

41 NA, RG 146, vol. 25, file 93-A-00019, pt 6, Report of Constable T.L. Beckett, 'Student Activism–Metropolitan Toronto,' October 1968. Some of the deleted material in this version can be found in a copy in ibid., vol. 2762, file 96-A-00045, 'University of Toronto,' pt 18. Other American studies generally reached similar conclusions about the background of student activists; see Lipset, *Rebellion in the University*, 80–1.

42 Ibid., vol. 2762, file 96-A-00045, University of Toronto, pt 18, Report of Constable T.L. Beckett, October 1968.

43 Ibid., vol. 2760, file 96-A-00057, Report of Inspector R. Whittaker, 4 April 1966.

44 Interview with former Simon Fraser University student president, Martin Loney, 16 February 1998.

45 NA, RG 146, vol. 2778, file 96-A-00045, pt 12, Report of Constable J.D. Moodie, 15 December 1969; ibid., vol. 2922, file 98-A-00196, Superintendent H.C. Draper to C/M i/c research, 29 May 1969; Jack Granatstein, *Yankee Go Home? Canadians and Anti-Americanism* (Toronto 1996), 192–216; 'The De-Canadianization of our Universities,' *Canadian Tribune*, 2 April 1969; Sheldon Alberts, 'Trudeau Considered Pulling Out of NATO,' *National Post*, 10 February 2000.

46 NA, RG 146, vol. 2774, file 94-A-00057, pt 7, Report of W.P. Lozinski, 27 November 1968; ibid., vol. 74, file 96-A-00045, pt 60, 'McMaster University,' 26 November 1970.

47 Ibid., vol. 56, file 96-A-00048, pt 6, Report of [deleted: name of Mountie], 10 April 1970.

48 Ibid., vol. 2760, file 93-A-00057, 'University of Western Ontario,' 25 October 1967.

49 Ibid., vol. 2776, file 96-A-00045, pt 2, 'The University of Calgary,' 20 November 1968; ibid., vol. 74, pt 62, 'Marxist Conference Waterloo, Ontario, 8–11 Oct 70,' 13 October 1970; ibid., vol. 2757, file 96-A-00045, Queen's University, pt 2, 29 March 1968; ibid., Report of Corporal D.J. Mulvenna, 8 March 1968; Hamar Foster, co-editor of *Heresy*, to author, 20 January 1998.

50 NA, RG 146, vol. 24, file 93-A-00047, re: 'Education–PEI,' 11 July 1969; ibid., RCMP transit slip re: 'Dalhousie University,' 23 July 1969.

51 Ibid., vol. 2758, file 96-A-00045, pt 2, 'University of Windsor,' 5 February 1968; ibid., vol. 2774, file 94-A-00057, pt 7, 'RCMP Report,' 3 December 1968; ibid., vol. 24, file 93-A-00047, re: 'University of Prince Edward Island Student Protest Demonstration,' 27 January 1970; ibid., Report of Corporal E.F. McCue, 27 January 1970; ibid., Report of Corporal H.V. Cameron, 25 March 1970.

52 A reference to the University of New Brunswick in this report was undoubtedly to the case of Norman Strax, an American physicist who was suspended over a protest against the introduction of identification cards at the university. The Strax case bewildered local Mounties who did not know how to interpret his actions. 'Professor Strax is what might be called an activist politically,' wrote Constable Charlie Cattle. 'For reasons I don't pretend to understand he objects to the compulsory use of identity cards in the library at U.N.B.' NA, RG 146, vol. 28, file 93-A-00038, pt 1, Report of Constable C.A. Cattle, 28 October 1968. For more on the Strax incident, see John Braddock, 'Strife on Campus,' in Tim and Julyan Reid, eds., *Student Power and the Canadian Campus* (Toronto 1969), 115–24.

53 NA, RG 146, vol. 25, file 93-A-00019, pt 5, re: 'Simon Fraser University,' fall 1968. For more on the career of Halperin, see Don S. Kirschner, *Cold War Exile: The Unclosed Case of Maurice Halperin* (London 1995). In his examination of Halperin's story, Kirschner concludes that the academic was a Soviet agent during World War Two. Venona decryptions confirm that Halperin did spy on behalf of the Soviet Union while working for the U.S. government during the Second World War, but there is no evidence that he was still an active agent when he surfaced at Simon Fraser University. See John Earl Haynes and Harvey Klehr, *Venona: Decoding Soviet Espionage in America* (London, 1999), 100–4.

54 NA, RG 146, vol. 2786, file 96-A-00045, pt 17, Higgitt to C.O.s, 21 January 1969.

55 Ibid., Higgitt to CO.s, 21 January 1969; ibid., vol. 2262, file 94-A-00057, pt 7, Report of Corporal J.W. Dafoe, 9 October 1968.

56 Ibid., vol. 2787, file 96-A-00045, pt 20, 'General Conditions and Subversive Activities, British Columbia,' 6 June 1969.

57 Carl Betke and S.W. Horrall, *Canada's Security Service: A History* (Ottawa 1978), 2: 665.

58 CSIS, Access request 88-A-18, Instructions re: 'Subversive Investigations and Correspondence,' 1 November 1967; NA, RG 146, vol. 2755, file 98-A-00130, pt 1, [deleted: name of Mountie] for DSI to officer i/c SIB 'O' Division, Toronto, 17 February 1967; ibid., vol. 2755, file 98-A-00130, pt 1, RCMP transit slip, 16 February 1967.

59 CSIS, Access request 88-A-18, Memorandum of Superintendent Draper for D.S.I., 7 November 1967; NA, RG 146, vol. 2772, file 98-A-00130, pt 1, [deleted: name of Mountie] for director, Security and Intelligence, to divisional C.O.s and officers i/c S.I.B. 'C,' 'E,' and 'O,' re: 'Instructions re: Subversive Investigations and Correspondence,' 15 September 1970.

60 Interview with 'A,' a former Security Service member, 18 April 1998.

61 CSIS, Access request 117-98-71, 'Contacts–Key Sectors–Canada, Memorandum of Directing N.C.O., Key Sectors,' 15 December 1971.

62 NA, RG 146, vol. 2772, file 98-A-00130, 'Education–List of Persons Employed, Manitoba and Ontario,' pt 1, [deleted: name of Mountie] for D.S.I. to officer i/c S.I.B. 'O' Division, Toronto, 1 February 1968.

63 Ibid., vol. 2755, file 98-A-00130, [deleted: name of Mountie] for D.S.I. to C.O. 'A'–Ottawa, 30 November 1967; ibid., [deleted: name of Mountie] for DSI to 'O' Division officer i/c SIB, 30 November 1967.

64 Ibid., vol. 2772, file 98-A-00130, pt 1, Memorandum to divisions and officers, 17 March 1969.

65 Anonymous to author, 16 February 1999. Not only has CSIS excised the names of individuals in documents provided under the Access to Information Act but it has also removed the names of academic departments. A complaint to the federal information commissioner that the total number of names deleted should be listed was ruled invalid; that number too is apparently a secret. John Reid, information commissioner of Canada, to author, 10 May 1999.

66 NA, RG 146, vol. 2755, file 96-A-00130, pt 1, Report of London SIS, 1 March 1969.

67 Ibid., 'University of Toronto,' 16 January 1969.

68 CSIS, Access request 88-A-18, 'Key Sectors–Canada,' 7 November 1967.

69 NA, RG 33/128, Access request 98-A-00034, box 105, file 6000-5-60.6, Memorandum from Sub Inspector D.G. Cobb, 26 March 1968; John Sawatsky, *Men in the Shadows: The RCMP Security Service* (Toronto 1983), 249.

70 NA, RG 146, vol. 2991, file 98-A-00079, New Left Caucus, pt 1, '*Here and Now,*' 7 April 1970.

71 Ibid., vol. 2774, file 94-A-00057, Superintendent R.J. Ross, to the commissioner, 18 August 1969; ibid., Assistant Commissioner Higgitt, to DOP (SPO), 14 March 1969; ibid., vol. 2778, file 96-A-00045, pt 11, Inspector Witherden to commissioner, 12 December 1968.

72 Ibid., vol. 2760, file 96-A-00057, 'Activists at UWO,' 16 July 1969.

73 Ibid., vol. 2774, file 94-A-00057, University of Saskatchewan, pt 7, Superintendent R.J. Ross to the commissioner, 18 August 1969.

74 Ibid., vol. 22, file 93-A-00058, re: 'Education–Nova Scotia,' 18 August 1969; ibid., Report of Constable A.B. Brown, re: 'Education in Nova Scotia,' 11 August 1969; ibid., vol. 30, file 93-A-00069, pt 2, re: 'Education–Ontario,' 13 August 1969; ibid., vol. 2787, file 96-A-00045, pt 21, 'Education–British Columbia,' 7 August 1969; ibid., vol. 74, file 96-A-00045, pt 59, 'Education–Ontario,' 13 August 1969; ibid., vol. 2787, file 96-A-00045, pt 21, 7 August 1969; ibid., vol. 2762, file 96-A-00045, 'U. of T.,' pt 21, re: 'Education–Ontario,' 12 August 1960. For more on Yorkville and Rochdale, see Owram, *Born at the Right Time*, 185–6, 210–15.

75 For more on personalities and problems of the University of Toronto in this era, see Bob Rae, *From Protest to Power* (Toronto 1997), 37–40; Claude Bissell, *Halfway up Parnassus: A Personal Account of the University of Toronto, 1932–1971* (Toronto 1974); and Robin Ross, *The Short Road Down: A University Changes* (Toronto 1984). Bob Rae, like his fellow student politicians at the time, including Steven Langdon, had his own RCMP file. See Dean Beeby, 'RCMP Spied on Bob Rae,' *Canadian Press*, 19 September 1993.

76 NA, RG 146, vol. 22, file 93-A-00016, Superintendent M. Chisholm to officer i/c 'D' Branch, 6 October 1970; ibid., Report of Sergeant D.R. Roller, 10 November 1970; ibid., Ken Green to Roller, 10 November 1970. D.R. Roller to author, 5 April 1998.

77 Ibid., vol. 22, file 93-A-00016, Report of Sergeant D.R. Roller, December 1970; ibid., vol. 4127, file 95-A-00133, pt 1, Report of Sergeant E.E. Chetner, 10 February 1970.

78 Ibid., Report of Sergeant D.R. Roller, December 1970; ibid., vol. 2787, file 96-A-00045, pt 21A, 'Education–B.C.,' 7 August 1969.

79 Ibid., vol. 2763, file 96-A-00045, pt 27, 'University of Toronto,' 1 October 1970.

80 NA, RG 33/128, Access request, AH-1998-00059, Accession 1992–93/251, box 130, file 'Covert Measures–Check Mate–"D"' Operations, Memorandum for File from John Starnes, 8 October 1970.

81 CSIS, Access request 117-90-123, John Starnes to D.S. Maxwell, 23 July 1970.

7: The Crisis Years, 1968–1970

1 NA, RG 146, vol. 2732, file 96-A-00045, 'Université de Montreal,' pt 9, Report re: 'University of Montreal,' 29 December 1970.

2 Ward Churchill and Jim Vander Wall, eds., *The COINTELPRO Papers: Documents from the FBI's Secret Wars Against Dissent in the United States* (Boston 1990), 177; Todd Gitlin, *The Sixties: Years of Hope, Days of Rage*, 3rd ed. (Toronto 1993), 306–9.

3 NA, RG 146, vol. 2785, file 96-A-00045, pt 4, Superintendent H.P. Tadeson, 27 October 1967; ibid., vol. 39, file 94-A-00130, pt 2, Superintendent H.P. Tadeson to Commissioner, 7 June 1968.

4 Ibid., vol. 2785, file 96-A-00045, SFU, pt 1, 'Simon Fraser University,' 20 February 1967; ibid., pt 4, Report of [deleted: name], 24 October 1967; ibid., vol. 24, file 93-A-00019, pt 3, RCMP briefing paper, 'Unrest at SFU,' 1968.

5 Ibid., vol. 2785, file 96-A-00045, pt 7, 'Simon Fraser University,' 6 June 1968; ibid., vol. 2786, file 96-A-00045, pt 12, re: 'Simon Fraser University, Vancouver,' 11 September 1968; ibid., vol. 2785, file 96-A-00045, pt 13, 'E' Division to commissioner, 26 September 1968.

6 Ibid., vol. 2786, file 96-A-00045, pt 10, A. Butroid to Superintendent H.C. Draper, 12 August 1968; ibid., Butroid to Assistant Commissioner W.L. Higgitt, plus handwritten comments, 16 September 1968; Donald C. Savage, 'Keeping Professors Out: The Immigration Department and the Idea of Academic Freedom, 1945–90,' unpublished paper, 1990; Reg Whitaker, *Double Standard: The Secret History of Canadian Immigration* (Toronto 1987), 238–54; Alvin Finkel, 'Canadian Immigration Policy and the Cold War, 1945–80,' *Journal of Canadian Studies* 21 (1986), 53–70.

7 For an account of the occupation and of the era, see Tina Loo, 'Flower Children in Lotusland,' *Beaver* 68, no. 1 (1998), 36–41; Myrna Kostash, *Long Way from Home: The Story of the Sixties Generation in Canada* (Toronto 1980), 92–4.

8 NA, RG 146, vol. 2786, file 96-A-00045, pt 16, Inspector R.H. Simmonds, 'Simon Fraser University "Sit-in" November 20–23/68,' 2 December 1968.

9 Ibid., pt 15, 'E' Division to Commissioner, 22 November 1968.

10 As a citizen of the United Kingdom, Loney was well aware that being arrested could have had led to his deportation. Interview with Martin Loney, 16 February 1998; NA, RG 146, vol. 2786, file 96-A-00045, pt 16, Assistant Commissioner G.R. Engel to commissioner, re: 'Simon Fraser University "Sit-in," November 20/23, 1968,' 9 December 1968; ibid., Inspector R.H. Simmonds, 'Simon Fraser University "Sit-in" November 20–23/68,' 2 December 1968.

11 Interview with 'A,' a former Security Service member, April 1998; a former 'E' Division member, to author, 12 November 1996.

12 'D,' a former Security Service member to author, 8 September 1999; interview with 'B,' a former Security Service member, 20 May 1998; D.R. Roller to author, 5 April 1998.

13 NA, RG 146, vol. 2787, file 96-A-00045, pt 25, 'Simon Fraser University,' 9 January 1970.

14 Interview with Terry Copp, a former Sir George Williams University faculty member, 8 September 1998.

15 NA, RG 146, vol. 2762, file 96-A-00045, pt 19, 'Sir George Williams University,' 3 February 1969; ibid., Cobb to commissioner, 3 February 1969.

16 For more on the career of Warren Hart, see McDonald Commission, Testimony of Warren Hart, vol. 143.

17 NA, RG 146, vol. 3718, file 98-A-00082, pt 2, 'Sir George Williams University,' 3 March 1969.

18 'Deport Rioters Angry MPs Urge,' *Vancouver Sun*, 25 February 1969; Canada, House of Commons, *Debates*, 18 February 1969: 5640.

19 NA, RG 146, vol. 2783, file 96-A-00045, pt 17, 'Jerry Clyde Rubin,' 4 November 1968; ibid., vol. 2786, file 96-A-00045, pt 19, 'Agitation from Abroad,' 2 April 1969.

20 Ibid., vol. 5008, file 96-A-00045, pt 7, 'Simon Fraser University,' Appendix A, June 1970.

21 McDonald Commission, *Freedom and Security Under the Law* (Ottawa 1981), 1: 503; CSIS, Access request 117-99-14, Memorandum of Commissioner Higgitt, 12 June 1969.

22 NA, RG 146, vol. 2728, file 96-A-00045, pt 3, 'Sir George William's University–Subversive Activities,' 3 October 1968; 'Black Power at SGWU,' 25 October 1968; anonymous to author, 14 April 1998.

23 Ibid., vol. 2773, file 96-A-00045, pt 6, 'Paul Boutelle–Black Nationalist,' 10 December 1968. The Socialist Workers Party was a leading target of the FBI's COINTELPRO campaign. See Ward Churchill and Jim Vander Wall, *Agents of Repression: The FBI's Secret Wars against the Black Panther Party and the American Indian Movement* (Boston 1990), 395.

24 NA, RG 146, vol. 76, file 96-A-00045, 'McGill University,' pt 74, 'Operation McGill–an Analysis,' 26 November 1970.

25 Ibid., vol. 2728, file 96-A-00045, 'Sir George Williams University,' pt 4, 'General Conditions and Subversive Activities among Negroes,' 29 January 1969.

26 Ibid., vol. 2769, file 97-A-00139, 'University of Guelph, Black Power–Canada,' 12 March 1969.

27 Ibid., vol. 2758, file 96-A-00045, pt 4, 'University of Windsor,' 31 July 1969.

28 Ibid., vol. 2769, file 94-A-00057, pt 7, 'Telephone,' 2 December 1969; ibid., Superintendent E.R. Lysyk to commissioner, 2 December 1969; ibid., vol. 397, file 98-A-00107, pt 1, 'Black Panther Party–U.S.A.,' 1 December 1969; ibid., vol. 2778, file 96-A-00045, pt 12, 'Black Panther Party–U.S.A.,' 8 December 1969; Noam Chomsky, 'Introduction,' in Nelson Blackstock, *COINTELPRO: The FBI's Secret War on Political Freedom* (New York 1976), 12; Churchill and Vander Wall, *Agents of Repression*, 64–77.

29 Jeff Sallot, *Nobody Said No: The Real Story about How the Mounties Always Get Their Man* (Toronto 1979), 44–50.

30 'Mountie Links Visits of U.S. Agitators to Campus Troubles,' *Toronto Star*, 7 May 1969.

31 McDonald Commission, *Freedom and Security*, 1: 503–4.

32 NA, RG 146, vol. 94, file 94-A-00057, 'Red Power–Canada,' 26 February 1969.

33 Ibid., vol. 2769, file 96-A-00045, 'Lakehead University, Red Power–Canada,' 17 February 1969.

34 Ibid., vol. 94, file 94-A-00057, 'Metis Society of Saskatchewan,' 5 December 1969.

35 Ibid., Report of Constable J.S. Rae, 20 August 1969.

36 Michael McLoughlin, *Last Stop Paris: The Death of Mario Bachand and the FLQ* (Toronto 1998), 115; 'Bridge Is Destroyed in Bombing Outbreak on Waterloo Campus,' *Globe and Mail*, 2 November 1968; NA, RG 146, vol. 2784, file 96-A-00045, pt 21, 'UBC,' 11 February 1970; ibid., Telex to officer i/c S.I.B. 'E,' 2 February 1970.

37 Access request 117–1990–123, John Starnes to D.S. Maxwell, 23 July 1970; Starnes to author, 12 February 1999. The material removed under Access to Information Act provisions is available in NA, RG 33/128, Access request AH-1998-00059, Accession 1992–93/251, box 130, file 'Covert Measures– Check Mate–"D" Operations,' Starnes to Maxwell, 23 July 1970.

38 NA, RG 146, vol. 75, file 96-A-00045, pt 70, 'Universities Committee for Peace in Vietnam,' 30 May 1967; ibid., vol. 2759, file 96-A-00045, pt 6, 'Indo-China War Crimes Inquiry,' 19 February 1971.

39 Larry Hannant, *The Infernal Machine: Investigating the Loyalty of Canada's Citizens* (Toronto 1995), 78; Jeffrey T. Richelson and Desmond Ball, *The Ties That Bind: Intelligence Cooperation between the UKUSA Countries – the United Kingdom, the United States of America, Canada, Australia and New Zealand* (London 1990); S.W. Horrall and Carl Betke, *Canada's Security Service: A History* (Ottawa 1978), 2: 729–42; Len Scher, *The Un-Canadians: True Stories of the Blacklist Era* (Toronto 1992), 238–9.

40 NA, RG 146, vol. 755, file 94-A-00057, 'University of Saskatchewan,' pt 1,
    Inspector L.R. Parent to C.O. 'F' Division, 21 April 1965.
41 'A,' a former Security Service member, to author, 15 February 1999; NA,
    RG 146, vol. 2763, pt 26, 'Anti-Draft Movement in Toronto, 1970'; ibid., vol.
    2755, file 98-A-00130, pt 2, 'Report of "O" Division,' 18 September 1969;
    ibid., vol. 74, pt 61, 'Student Union for Peace Action,' 11 May 1967; ibid.,
    vol. 74, file 96-A-00045, pt 61, 'Transcript of "Ideas" "The Invisible Tile in
    the Mosaic: A Report on Americans Living in Canada," 26 August 1968.
    The Saint John, New Brunswick, office of the Security Service reported that
    war resisters in its area were employed at local high schools. 'They have
    been relatively inactive as far as is known,' added the report's author, 'but
    have maintained contact with the local negro element.' Ibid., vol. 2793, file
    98-A-00129, pt 2, 7 August 1969. For more on American war resisters in
    Canada, see James Dickerson, *North to Canada: Men and Women against the
    Vietnam War* (Westport, CT 1999), and Kostash, *Long Way from Home*, 41–68.
42 NA, RG 146, vol. 2783, file 96-A-00045, pt 11, 'UBC,' 20 February 1967;
    ibid., vol. 2759, file 96-A-00045, pt 5, 'William Spira,' 17 November 1969;
    ibid., vol. 2765, file 93-A-00039, pt 1, Report of T.L. Beckett, 21 October
    1968; ibid., vol. 2756, file 93-A-00051, Report of Corporal E.A.E. LaFontaine,
    11 April 1967; ibid., vol. 2763, file 96-A-00045, pt 28, 'Vietnam Mobilization
    Committee,' 4 December 1970; ibid., vol. 773, file 98-A-00029, 'Brock
    University, Protests and Demonstrations re: U.S. Action in Vietnam–
    Canada,' 5 November 1968; ibid., vol. 2762, file 96-A-00045, pt 19, 'Viet-
    namese Liberation Front Representatives on Tour in Canada–January–
    February,' 1969, 17 February 1969.
43 Ibid., vol. 2765, file 93-A-00051, 'York University,' Assistant Commissioner
    W.H. Kelly to R.C.M.P. liaison officer, Washington, 1 February 1967; ibid.,
    vol. 2664, file 98-A-00127, 'Protests and Demonstrations–Educational
    Institutions,' pt 2, Chisholm to officer i/c VIP Security Section, 7 October
    1971; ibid., Chisholm to officer i/c VIP Security Section, 1 November 1971.
44 Pierre Vallières, *White Niggers of America*, trans. by Joan Pinkham (New York
    1971). For background on the Quebec of this era, see Paul-André Linteau,
    et al., *Quebec since 1930*, trans. by Robert Chandos and Ellen Garmaise
    (Toronto 1991).
45 NA, RG 146, vol. 59, file 96-A-00169, 'Canadian Association of University
    Teachers,' pt 1, Communist Activity among Youth,' no date.
46 McLoughlin, *Last Stop Paris*, 19, 37, 127, 150–1; Louis Fournier, *F.L.Q.: The
    Anatomy of an Underground Movement*, trans. by Edward Baxter (Toronto
    1984), 41–2, 49–50, 192.
47 Carole de Vault and William Johnson, *The Informer: Confessions of an Ex-*

Terrorist (Toronto 1982), 90–2; McDonald Commission, Testimony of Jean-Pierre Goyer, vol. 122, 19,037; NA, RG 146, vol. 2772, file 98-A-00130, pt 1, [deleted: name of Mountie] to division C.O.s and Officers i/c S.I.B., 15 September 1970.

48 McDonald Commission, Testimony of John Starnes, vol. 101, 16,029, 16,031; McLoughlin, *Last Stop Paris*, 117.

49 NA, RG 146, vol. 2731, file 96-A-00045, pt 2, 'McGill University–Communist Activities within,' 5 January 1967; ibid., vol. 2758, file 96-A-00045, pt 3, University of Windsor, 4 February 1969; ibid., vol. 76, file 96-A-00045, pt 75, 'Jacques Parizeau,' 2 January 1972. Researchers will be able to request René Lévesque's RCMP file on 1 November 2007.

50 Ibid., vol. 75, file 96-A-00045, McGill University, pt 71, Parent to director of security intelligence, 30 July 1968.

51 J.F. Bosher, *The Gaullist Attack on Canada, 1967–1997* (Montreal and Kingston 1999).

52 One person at the Université de Moncton submitted information on campus events to the RCMP on university stationery. NA, RG 146, vol. 31, file 93-A-00089, 'Moncton University,' pt 1, [deleted: name] to O.C. R.C.M.P. Moncton, 3 March 1969; ibid., vol. 31, file 93-A-00089, pt 1, E.R. Rettie, under-secretary of state for external affairs, to the commissioner, 11 February 1969; ibid., Superintendent W.G. Hurlow to O.C. Moncton Sub-Division, 26 February 1969; ibid., Superintendent W.G. Hurlow to commissioner, 22 February 1969.

53 Ibid., vol. 30, file 93-A-00069, 'Sir George Williams University,' pt 1, Inspector Cobb to commissioner, 11 September 1969; ibid., vol. 31, file 93-A-00089, pt 1, Assistant Commissioner J.E.M. Barrette to under-secretary of state for external affairs, 12 September 1969.

54 Normand Lester, *Enquêtes sur les Services Secrets* (Montreal 1998), 332.

55 NA, RG 146, vol. 76, file 96-A-00045, 'McGill University,' pt 73, 18 March 1969; 'Two Arrested after Police Found "Spying" at Meeting,' *Montreal Star*, 24 March 1969; Reg Whitaker, 'Apprehended Insurrection? RCMP Intelligence and the October Crisis,' *Queen's Quarterly* 100 (1993), 390.

56 NA, RG 146, vol. 76, file 96-A-00045, pt 74, 'Operation McGill, an Analysis,' 26 November 1970; ibid., vol. 76, file 96-A-00045, pt 78, Memorandum of C/Superintendent J.E.M. Barrette, 28 March 1969; ibid., vol. 76, file 96-A-00045, pt 74, 'Operation McGill, an Analysis,' 26 November 1970. '8,000 Stopped in McGill Protest,' *Toronto Telegram*, 29 March 1969.

57 Ibid., vol. 2731, file 96-A-00045, pt 6, '*College of General and Professional Teaching*,' 6 June 1969.

58 Ibid., vol. 76, file 96-00045, pt 79, 'Collège d'Enseignement Général et Professionnel (CEGEP),' 12 May 1969.

59 Ibid., vol. 5008, file 97-A-00076, pt 7, 'Academe and Subversion,' June, December 1970. CSIS deleted the numbers in a request for access made to the National Archives of Canada. A request to the Privy Council Office, however, produced an intact document. PCO, Access request P.C. 135-2/ 98-A-00024, 'Academe and Subversion,' December 1970.

60 NA, RG 146, vol. 2731, file 96-A-00045, pt 6, 'University of Montreal,' 11 August 1969; ibid., pt 8, 'D' Section, re: 'University of Montreal,' 13 August 1970.

61 Whitaker, 'Apprehended Insurrection?,' 405; McLoughlin, *Last Stop Paris*, 150–1; Fournier, *The F.L.Q.*, 276–7; Robert Comeau to author, July 2001.

62 PCO, Acess request P.C. 135-2/98-A-00024, 'Academe and Subversion,' Appendix B, December 1970.

63 NA, RG 146, vol. 2771, file 96-A-00045, re: 'Communist Party of Canada– Marxist/Leninist Canada,' 19 October 1970; ibid., vol. 74, file 96-A-00045, pt 62, 'Subversive Separatist Activities–Canada,' 22 October 1970; interview with Professor Sidney Pobihushchy, 30 September 1997; 'Professors' Association Says It's Asking How Much Universities Helped the RCMP,' *University of Waterloo Gazette*, 30 November 1977.

64 Alexander's inclusion on the RCMP enemies list came as a complete surprise to him. He was on the board of Pestalozzi College, which, with the assistance of money from the Canadian government, was attempting to aid children on the street. Although separatists served on the same board, there were, to Alexander's knowledge, no FLQ members. Jon Alexander to author, 4 November 1998. The special enmity towards Frank and Parkins was probably based in part on a 6 November 1970 issue of the *Varsity*, which provided considerable humour at the expense of Canada's men in scarlet.

65 NA, RG 146, vol. 5008, file 97-A-00076, pt 7, 'Canadian University Press (CUP),' app. 2, July 1970; PCO, Access request P.C. 135-2/98-A-00024, 'Academe and Subversion,' Appendix B, December 1970.

8: Moving from Campus to Community, 1971–1984

1 Privy Council Office (PCO), Access request 173-A-003, 'Minutes of the 24 September 1971 Meeting of the Cabinet Committee on Security and Intelligence.' 28 October 1971. The assistant secretary in attendance was T.D. ('Ted') Finn, later the first director of the Canadian Security Intelligence Service. John Starnes predicted in 1970 that there was a high potential for violence in the coming decade; see McDonald Commission, vol. 170, 23374. CSIS, Access request 117-1991-102, 'The Threat to Security from Violence Prone Revolutionary Elements in Canada,' [24 September 1971].

2 Jeff Sallot, *Nobody Said No: The Real Story about How the RCMP Always Get Their Man* (Toronto 1979); Robert Dion, *Crimes of the Secret Police* (Montreal 1982); John Sawatsky, *Men in the Shadows: The RCMP Security Service* (Toronto 1980).

3 One potentially violent group targeted by the RCMP was the Partisan Party in Vancouver. Mounted Policeman Rick Bennett, operating under the pseudonym of Richard Benning, infiltrated the party. Bennett remained with the Security Service and then its successor, CSIS, where he was a deputy director as of February 2000. Sawatsky, *Men in the Shadows*, 267–77; 'CSIS To Reassign 30 Top Managers in March Shuffle,' *Globe and Mail*, 1 March 2000.

4 Richard E. Peterson, 'The Scope of Organized Student Protest,' in Julian Foster and Durward Long, eds., *Protest! Student Activism in America* (New York 1970), 78; Cyril Levitt, *Children of Privilege: Student Revolt in the Sixties* (Toronto 1984), 105.

5 NA, RG 146, vol. 5008, file 97-A-00076, pt 7, 'The University,' 24 March 1969. Somehow the RCMP acquired a copy of the text of Penfield's speech; see ibid., vol. 2664, file 98-A-00127, pt 1, Higgitt to [deleted: *FBI and/or CIA*], 29 July 1969. One example of Duart Farquharson's work is 'How Radicals Paralyzed a University,' *Ottawa Citizen*, 6 December 1968; McKenzie Porter, 'Tiny Crack-Pot Minority at U of T Are Agitators,' *Toronto Telegram*, 24 September 1969; Hartley Steward, 'The Quiet Campus: Student Militancy Is Muted – Maybe,' *Toronto Star*, 12 May 1973.

6 'Nursing Student Wins UBC Vote,' *Vancouver Sun*, October 1968; Myrna Kostash, *Long Way From Home: The Story of the Sixties Generation in Canada* (Toronto 1980), 97; Nigel Roy Moses, 'All That Was Left: Student Struggle for Mass Student Aid and the Abolition of Tuition Fees in Ontario, 1946–1975,' unpublished PhD dissertation, University of Toronto (1995), 81–2.

7 NA, RG 146, vol. 69, file 96-A-00045, pt 22, Toronto to Ottawa 'D' Ops, 25 March 1974.

8 Ibid., vol. 2950, file 98-A-00078, Report of [deleted: name of Mountie], 8 December 1971.

9 Ibid., vol. 2763, file 96-A-00045, pt 26, 'Education Ontario,' 31 July 1970.

10 Ibid., vol. 74, file 96-A-00045, pt 63, 'University of Waterloo,' 22 April 1974.

11 Ibid., vol. 69, file 96-A-00045, pt 23, 'University of Toronto,' 22 July 1974; ibid., vol. 373, file 98-A-00107, pt 1, University of Saskatchewan–Regina Campus,' 22 March 1971.

12 Ibid., vol. 60, file 96-A-00045, pt 22, Toronto to Key Sectors, Composite Report on the University of Toronto, 23 February 1973.

13 Ibid., vol. 25, file 93-A-00078, 'York University Composite Report, April 1974–April 1975.'

14 Ibid., vol. 2729, file 96-A-00045, pt 12, 'General Assessment at Sir George Campus,' 18 August 1975.

15 Ibid., vol. 57, file 96-A-00045, pt 12, 'University of Toronto Composite Report April 75–June 76,' June 1976.

16 CSIS, Access request 117-1998-71, 'Contacts–Key Sectors–Canada,' Memorandum of directing NCO, 15 December 1971.

17 Ibid., Report of Kamloops Security Service, 20 April 1972.

18 Ibid., 'Key Sectors: The Findings of the Key Sectors Program, 1971–73,' April 1974, Appendix B(3).

19 NA, RG 146, vol. 2773, file 96-A-00045, pt 9, Transit slip, 13 December 1972; ibid., 'University of Manitoba,' 2 January 1973.

20 Ibid., vol. 60, file 96-A-00045, pt 22, Toronto office to Key Sectors, 23 February 1973; ibid., vol. 2769, file 97-A-00139, pt 1, 'University of Guelph,' 14 August 1973; ibid., vol. 363, pt 2, 'McGill Daily,' 25 May 1972.

21 Ibid., vol. 60, file 96-A-00045, pt 22, RCMP transit slip, 22 June 1972.

22 Ibid., vol. 69, file 96-A-00045, pt 23, RCMP transit slip, 14 August 1974; ibid., re: 'Composite Report on the University of Toronto, 22 July 1974.' For more on the far right in Canada, see Warren Kinsella, *Web of Hate: Inside Canada's Far Right Network* (Toronto 1994).

23 NA, RG 146, vol. 2778, file 96-A-00045, pt 16, 'Education–Canada,' 31 August 1973; Memorandum of S/Sergent D.J. Frayn, 28 August 1973; 'University of Lethbridge,' 1973.

24 Ibid., vol. 2755, file 98-A-00130, Report of [deleted: name], 21 April 1972.

25 Ibid., vol. 22, file 93-A-00005, Parent to Bourne, 4 December 1972. The reference to the visit to Barrett's residence was removed under Access to Information provisions from one version of this document but was allowed to remain in another; see ibid., vol. 59, file 96-A-00169, pt 2, 'Vancouver Security Service Key Sectors Composite Report Period Feb. 1973 to Jan. 1974,' 25 February 1974; ibid., vol. 2784, file 96-A-00045, pt 26, 'Geography,' 19 December 1972; ibid., 'Vancouver Security Service Key Sectors Composite Report, June 1972 to February 1973'; ibid., vol. 2788, file 96-A-00045, pt 30, Simon Fraser University, 20 November 1972; ibid., vol. 39, file 94-A-00130, pt 1, Report of E. Downton, 6 October 1971.

26 Ibid., vol. 25, file 93-A-00078, Sergeant W.G. Rohr to officer i/c 'D' Operations, Toronto Security Service, 30 September 1975.

27 Ibid., vol. 42, file 95-A-00049, pt 5, re: 'University of Waterloo,' 24 January 1973.

28 Ibid., vol. 2771, file 96-A-00045, pt 1, 'Communist Party of Canada, (M/L) Kitchener–Waterloo, Guelph,' 5 February 1976.

29 SIS, Access request 117-1999-14, Instructions re: 'Subversive Investigation and Correspondence,' Starnes to Goyer, 8 August 1971.

30 NA, RG 146, vol. 76, file 96-A-00045, pt 75, 'Rabbi M. Kahane,' 10, 16 March
    1971; ibid., L.R. Parent to under-secretary of state for external affairs, 10
    March 1971; ibid., vol. 74, pt 60, 'McMaster Hillel,' 26 March 1970; ibid., pt
    76, 'Report on United Jewish People's Order–U of Manitoba, "D" Ops
    Jewish Sector,' 26 November 1974; ibid., 'McGill University, Composite
    Report, 1974–74, pt.2,' 18 July 1975; ibid., vol. 2787, file 96-A-00045, pt 28,
    'Free Jewish Community,' 5 November 1970; ibid., vol. 2773, file 96-A-00045,
    pt 8, 'Jews and Arabs,' 11 March 1970.

31 NA, RG 146, vol. 2729, file 96-A-00045, pt 11, 'Middle East Anti-Imperialist
    Coalition,' 4 February 1974; vol. 76, file 96-A-00045, pt 76, re: 'Association
    Humanitaire Québec-Palestine,' 18 April 1974; ibid., re: 'General Condi-
    tions and Subversive Activities amongst Arabs,' 13 February 1975.

32 Ibid., vol. 2778, file 96-A-00045, pt 17, Report of Constable A.B. Napier,
    7 July 1975.

33 Reg Whitaker, *Double Standard: The Secret History of Canadian Immigration*
    (Toronto 1987), 254–61.

34 NA, RG 146, vol. 2925, file 97-A-000152, pt 9, re: 'Latin American Working
    Group–Toronto,' 21 December 1973.

35 Ibid., vol. 76, file 96-A-00045, pt 75, 'McGill University–IRA,' 26 November
    1971; ibid., vol. 2769, file 98-A-00029, 'League for Socialist Action,'
    29 November 1971. For more on British intelligence and the IRA, see Tony
    Gerhagty, *The Irish War* (London 1998).

36 NA, RG 146, vol. 3189, file 98-A-00030, 'ANC,' 12 February 1982. Con-
    troversy erupted in June 2001 when a right-wing Canadian member of
    Parliament opposed honorary citizenship for former ANC leader Nelson
    Mandela on the grounds that he was a Communist and terrorist. It is likely
    that the Security Service would have agreed with that proposition. See
    'MP's Snub of Mandela "Stupid," "Appalling"; Mulroney Joins Attack,'
    National Post, 8 June 2001.

37 NA, RG 146, vol. 2910, file 97-A-00062, pt 1, 'Learned Societies–Canada,'
    20 April 1971; ibid., vol. 2782, file 96-A-00045, pt 8, 'University of Victoria,'
    11 April 1972.

38 Ibid., vol. 24, 93-A-00047, Pantry to the commissioner, 1 March 1972.

39 Ibid., vol. 69, file 96-A-00045, pt 23, University of Toronto Composite
    Report, June 76–June 77,' 1977; ibid., vol. 2733, file 96-A-00045, Syndicat
    des Professeurs de l'Université Laval,' 13 December 1976; ibid., 'University
    of Montreal,' 3 March 1976; ibid., vol. 25, file 93-A-00078, 'York University
    Composite Report,' 1975.

40 Ibid., vol. 69, file 96-A-00045, pt 22, re: 'Composite Report on the Univer-
    sity of Toronto,' 7 August 1973; ibid., vol. 2783, file 96-A-00045, pt 19,
    'Vancouver Women's Caucus,' 29 August 1969.

41 For background on many of the groups spied on by the Mounted Police, see Nancy Adamson, 'Feminists, Libbers, Lefties, and Radicals: The Emergence of the Women's Liberation Movement,' in Joy Parr, ed., *A Diversity of Women: Ontario, 1945–1980* (Toronto 1995), 252–80.

42 NA, RG 146, vol. 2763, file 96-A-00045, pt 26, 'Education Ontario,' 31 July 1970; Wendy Atkin, '"Babies of the World Unite": The Early Day-Care Movement and Family Formation in the 1970s,' in Lori Chambers and Edgar-André Montigny, eds., *Family Matters: Papers in Post-Confederation Canadian Family History* (Toronto 1998), 57–70.

43 NA, RG 146, vol. 2732, file 96-A-00045, pt 13, 'Ligue Socialiste Ouvrière,' 23 February 1973; ibid., vol. 2262, pt 1, 'Saskatoon National Conference of Women's Liberation Groups–Saskatoon,' 1 February 1971.

44 Ibid., vol. 2787, file 96-A-00045, pt 29, 'Youth International Party,' 3 March 1971; ibid., vol. 2159, file 98-A-00030, Kitchener to HQ, 15 March 1982; Ruth Rosen, *The World Split Open: How the Modern Women's Movement Changed America* (New York 2000), 239–60.

45 NA, RG 146, vol. 2760, file 96-A-00045, pt 6, 'Yearly Report on McMaster 1972–73,' 22 June 1973; ibid., vol. 2787, file 96-A-00045, pt 29, 'Gay Liberation Front,' 31 December 1970; ibid., vol. 2769, file 97-A-00139, re: 'University of Guelph, Ontario,' 15 May 1974; ibid., vol. 2774, file 95-A-00117, pt 8, 'Key-Sectors, Canada,' 3 August 1973.

46 Ibid., vol. 74, file 96-A-00045, pt 60, [deleted: name of the Mountie] to officer i/c 'O' Division, 12 September 1972; ibid., vol. 74, file 96-A-00045, pt 60, 'Canadian Radical Archives, Mills Memorial Library, McMaster University,' 20 January 1972.

47 Ibid., vol. 74, file 96-A-00045, pt 63, Major T.P. Haney to RCMP, 31 May 1977; 'University of Waterloo–Project Ploughshares,' 22 June, 28 July 1977; ibid., file 96-A-00045, pt 63, 'D' Ops Ottawa to Kitchener, 2 June 1977; J.H. Brookmyre to Major T.P. Haney, re: 'Project Ploughshares,' 18 August 1977.

48 Ibid., vol. 2727, file 96-A-00045, pt 4, Montreal Security Service to HQ, 15 November 1971; ibid., vol. 31, file 93-A-00089, pt 4, Report of J.J.G. Brodeur, 9 October 1975; Report of Corporal L.G. Leppington, 24 November 1972; Report of [deleted: name], 20 November 1972; ibid., vol. 2778, file 96-A-00045, pt 14, 'Front de Libération du Québec,' 24 February 1971; ibid., vol. 76, file 96-A-00045, pt 75 'McGill University–Robert Lemieux,' 23 September 1971; 'Lévesque and Kierans,' 8 October 1971; ibid., vol. 2773, file 96-A-00034, pt 9, 'Subversive Separatist Activities amongst French Canadians,' 14 January 1972.

49 McDonald Commission, Testimony of Murray Chisholm, vol. 169, 23254.

50 McDonald Commission, *Freedom and Security under the Law* (Ottawa 1981),

1: 268–9; McDonald Commission, Testimony of Murray Chisholm, vol. 169, 23236–40.

51 One of the most famous break-ins involved the Agence de Presse Libéra-tion du Québec, a separatist news agency. Thousands of pages of docu-ments were stuffed into hockey bags and taken away on the night of 5 October 1972. According to John Sawatsky, they were never used but this does not appear to be correct: in November an RCMP report on the *McGill Daily* noted it was a subscriber to the APLQ, information that was undoubt-edly obtained through the break-in. Sawatsky, *Men in the Shadows*, 247–51; NA, RG 146, vol. 363, file 98-A-00102, '*McGill Daily*,' 20 November 1972. Michael McLoughlin, *Last Stop Paris: The Assassination of Mario Bachard and the Death of the FLQ* (Toronto 1998). McLoughlin alleges that the RCMP, acting on the orders of the Trudeau government, murdered Bachard in Paris in 1971.

52 NA, RG 146, vol. 31, file 93-A-00089, pt 3, Report of [deleted: Mountie name], 25 September 1973; ibid., pt 3, Superintendent C.A.J. Philion to C.O. 'J' Division, 15 November 1972; ibid., vol. 2762, file 96-A-00045, pt 18, 'CP of C Toronto,' 25 November 1968.

53 McDonald Commission, Testimony of Murray Chisholm, vol. 169, 23212, 23216.

54 'A,' a former Security Service member, to author, 15 February 1999.

55 McDonald Commission, *Freedom and Security*, 1: 270.

56 Ibid., 272–3, 480; McDonald Commission, Testimony of Warren Allmand, vol. 117, 18270.

57 NA, RG 146, vol. 42, file 95-A-00049, pt 1, under-secretary of state for external affairs to Higgitt, 19 March 1969; ibid. Higgitt to the Department of External Affairs, 14 March 1969.

58 Ibid., Report of S/Sergeant Fred Schultz, 9 June 1970.

59 Ibid., pt 5, C/Superintendent S.V.M. Chisholm to A/Commissioner M.S. Sexsmith, 27 June 1977; ibid., 'Praxis Corp.,' 26 February 1971; ibid., pt 2, 'Praxis Corporation,' 15 April 1971; ibid., 'Praxis Corporation–Toronto,' Memorandum of Sergeant W. Ormshaw, 8 June 1971.

60 'RCMP Inquiry?' *Toronto Sun*, 29 May 1977.

61 Dimitrios J. Roussopoulos, 'Towards a Revolutionary Youth Movement and an Extra-Parliamentary Opposition in Canada,' in Dimitrios J. Roussopou-los, ed., *The New Left in Canada* (Montreal 1970), 149. Emphasis is in the original.

62 NA, RG 146, vol. 42, file 95-A-00049, pt 2, CSIS report on Gerry Hunnius, 22 January 1986; ibid., Praxis Corporation–Toronto, Memorandum Ormshaw, 8 June 1971; ibid., 'Revolutionary Extra-Parliamentary Opposi-

tion,' 11 April 1972; ibid., pt 4, 'Praxis Corporation,' 30 September 1971; ibid., pt 2, D.S.I. to C.O. 'D' Division, 16 February 1971.

63 Ibid., pt 5, 'Extra Parliamentary Opposition,' 7 June 1971; ibid., Goyer to Robert K. Andras, minister without portfolio, 15 June 1971.

64 Interview with M. Loney, 16 February 1998; *Globe and Mail*, 1 February 1977; *Globe and Mail*, 3 Feburary 1977; *Ottawa Citizen*, 4 February 1977; Canada, House of Commons, *Debates*, 2 February 1977: 2633–5.

65 NA, RG 146, vol. 42, file 95-A-00049, pt 5, 'Critique of SPARG Paper,' 21 November 1972; ibid., Parent to Robin Bourne, 12 October 1972.

66 Ibid., Bourne to Roger Tassé, 31 January 1977; CSIS, Access request 88-A-36, 'Security Service' "D" Ops Presentation to McDonald Commission,' October 1979; McDonald Commission, *Freedom and Security*, 1: 507–9.

67 McDonald Commission, Testimony of Ron Yaworski, vol. 303: 300, 367; NA, RG 146, vol. 2771, file 96-A-00045, 'Communist Party of Canada, Part B–Guelph,' 5 February 1976; McDonald Commission, *Freedom and Security*, 1: 75.

68 Interview with Stan Hanson, 19 February 1997.

69 NA, RG 146, vol. 42, file 95-A-00049, pt 5, D.D.G. (Ops.) to Inspector G. Powell, 8 June 1977; ibid., re: 'Enquiry re: B.E. [Break and Entry] & Theft from James, Lewis, & Samuel Publishing Co., Toronto (1971),' 9 September 1977; ibid., Superintendent J.A. Venner to D.D.G. Ops, 8 June 1977.

70 Ibid., vol. 2910, file 97-A-00062, pt 2, re: 'Learned Societies–Canada,' 4 July 1977.

71 Ibid.

72 Ibid., Inspector C. Scowen to area commander, southwestern Ontario Security Service, 8 July 1977; ibid., C/Superintendent M.J. Spooner, to D.D.G. Ops, 13 July 1977.

73 Ibid., handwritten comment appearing on Spooner letter, dated 28 July 1977.

74 Ibid., Inspector J.H. Brookmyre to i/c 'L' Ops, 11 May 1978. Although it marked a turning point, the report on the Fredericton Learneds was still being cited two years later, when the camaraderie between young Marxists in the Sociology Department at Ryerson College in Toronto was noted; see ibid., Communist Party of Canada,' August 1979. Emphasis is in original.

75 McDonald Commission, vol. 300: 125; NA, RG 146, vol. 56, Report of Corporal C. Guyer, 29 April 1971; ibid., vol. 2763, file 96-A-00045, 'O' Division to headquarters, 20 July 1971; ibid., vol. 30, file 93-A-00069, pt 3, D.D.G. to officer i/c Security Service, Vancouver, 9 August 1972; CSIS, Access request 117-1999-14, Barrette to Officer i/c 'C' Division, 25 November 1969.

76 CSIS, Access request 117-2000-22, 'The Role, Tasks and Methods of the RCMP Security Service,' Director-General Maurice Dare to Gordon Robertson, 30 December 1976; C/Superintendent D.G. Cobb to director-general, 2 February 1977; Normand Lester, *Enquêtes sur les Services Secrets* (Montreal 1998), 146–67. Cobb's suggestion of using 'communications interceptions' to monitor the PQ government supports similar allegations made by Mike Frost about the Communications Security Establishment. See Frost, with Michel Gratton, *Spyworld: Inside the Canadian and American Intelligence Establishments* (Toronto 1994).

77 CSIS, Access request 117-2000-22, D.W. Hall to Dare, 26 January 1977; ibid., Draft letter from the prime minister to Mr Fox, January 1977; ibid., Letter from Trudeau to solicitor general, second draft, no date.

78 Ibid., Aide-mémoire, 3 February 1977.

79 Ibid., Tassé to Hall, 22 February 1977.

80 NA, RG 146, vol. 4263, file AH-2000-00096, 'National Unity,' Ted Finn to Commissioner Robert Simmonds, 11 Sept 1979.

81 CSIS, Access request 117-1999-14, C/Superintendent Yule to deputy director-general, Ops, 31 January 1980; ibid., officer i/c 'D' Ops to officers i/c 'A,' 'B,' and 'H' Ops, 8 February 1980. The 'VIP program' targets in 1978 were 335 members of Parliament, senators, and civil servants, 120 provincial representatives and employees, 25 municipal officials, and 107 individuals who had left government; see ibid., VIP files, December 1979.

82 NA, RG 146, vol. 59, file 96-A-00169, pt 2, Inspector E. Boyd to [deleted: name of Mountie], 15 April 1980; ibid., vol. 28, file 93-A-00038, pt 2, Sergeant N.R. McAllister to O/C 'E' Division, 6 October 1971; ibid., vol. 59, file 96-A-00169, pt 2, A/Commissioner J.G. Giroux to areas commanders, 6 February 1981; CSIS, Access request 117-99-14, C/Superintendent C. Yule to area Commanders, 4 June 1980.

83 Confidential source.

84 NA, RG 146, vol. 2727, file 96-A-00045, pt 7, Revolutionary Workers League, 10 November 1977; ibid., 'Actions Subversives et la Mobilisation des Étudiants de Première Année au Département de Sociologie de l'Université Laval,' 12 October 1977; ibid., vol. 2733, file 96-A-00045, pt 19, 'Université du Québec,' 28 July 1977.

85 Ibid., vol. 74, file 96-A-00045, pt 60, Report of Ham, 26 October 1977.

86 Ibid., vol. 2769, file 97-A-00139, pt 1, 'Communist Party of Canada (M/L), 9 November 1983.

87 Ibid., vol. 2728, file 96-A-00045, pt 9, 'Groupe Socialiste des Travailleurs (GST),' 8 January 1980; ibid., vol. 2733, file 96-A-00045, pt 19, 'Reagan's Visit to Ottawa,' March 1981; ibid., vol. 2764, file 96-A-00045, pt 41, 'Revolutionary Workers League,' 18 February 1982. For more on the RCMP and

Operation Dismantle, see James T. Stark, *Cold War Blues: The Operation Dismantle Story* (Hull, QC, 1991).

9: Conclusion: From CSIS to APEC

1 Richard Cleroux, *Official Secrets: The Story behind the Canadian Security Intelligence Service* (Toronto 1990), 88–91.
2 For more on the Litton bombing and the RCMP investigation, see Ann Hansen, *Direct Action: Memoirs of an Urban Guerilla* (Toronto 2001).
3 CSIS, Access request 117-1999-14, 'Instructions re: Subversive Investigation and Correspondence,' 'Revised Chapter II.5–Counter Subversion Operations,' no date; ibid., Memorandum from A/Director-general, Countersubversion, to Comprehensive Management Services, 24 March 1987.
4 NA, RG 146, vol. 2951, file 98-A-00030, pt 2, Report of Kitchener, Security Service, re: Communist Party of Canada (M/L), 8 November 1984.
5 Cleroux, *Official Secrets*, 194–5.
6 SIRC, *Annual Report*, 1987–8, 14; CSIS, Access request 117-1999-14, Reid Morden to Solicitor General James Kelleher, 19 February 1988; ibid., 'Monitoring of Section 2(d) Targets by Analysis and Production Branch,' 16 March 1988.
7 CSIS, Access request 117-2000-22, Annual report of the RCMP Security Service, 1983–4; Normand Sirois, 'Access to Information: The CSIS Experience,' unpublished paper presented at the Canadian Historical Association annual meetings, 29 May 2000; NA, RG 146, vol. 76, file 96-A-00045, McGill University, pt 76, CSIS Transit slip, 11 May 1988.
8 Department of the Solicitor General, Access request 1336-SEC-98067, Ministerial directive of June 8, 1984; ibid., 'CSIS Security Investigations on University Campuses,' 12 August 1985; Robert Kaplan to author, 28 December 1998.
9 Department of the Solicitor General, Access request 1336-SEC-98067, Fred Gibson, to Solicitor General Perrin Beatty, 12 November 1985; ibid., Perrin Beatty to T.D. Finn, 12 November 1985.
10 Ibid., Memorandum of director-general, Security Policy and Operations Directorate, 26 February 1986; ibid., SIRC, Annual report, 1986–7.
11 Ibid., Deputy solicitor general to solicitor general, 4 February 1987.
12 SIRC, 'Security Investigations on University Campuses (Expurgated Version),' Document no. 2800-20; SIRC, Annual report for 1991; Department of the Solicitor General, Access request 1336-SEC-99002, Ward Elcock to Herb Gray, 27 October 1994.
13 Colin Leys and Elizabeth Grace in 'The Concept of Subversion and Its

Implications,' in C.E.S. Franks, ed., *Dissent and the State* (Toronto 1989), make
the point that one of the main changes between CSIS and the earlier
Security Service is that previously illegal or questionable activities, such as
mail openings and wiretaps, were made legal for the new agency, albeit
after convincing a judge to grant a warrant. One example of this shift
relates to access to private records. In 1971 John Starnes had to write to
Solicitor General Jean-Pierre Goyer to ask that the force be granted access
to the records of other departments. CSIS, on the other hand, enjoys a
special relationship with nineteen federal government departments that
gives it access private information about Canadians. McDonald Commission, exhibit M39, Starnes to Goyer, 3 June 1971; Andrew Mitrovica, 'RCMP,
CSIS Can Access Computer Files on Citizens,' *Globe and Mail*, 19 May 2000.

14 Department of the Solicitor General, Access request 1336-SEC-99002,
Memorandum from Raffaele Fasiolo to Allan Bartley, 24 January 1995.

15 Ibid., Paul Dubrule to Horst Intscher, 23 November 1995, 26 May 1996;
J.-L. Gagnon to Intscher, 8 July 1996; ibid., deputy solicitor general to
solicitor general, 17 September 1996; ibid., Intscher to Gagnon, 16 December 1996; ibid., Jean T. Fournier to Herb Gray, 5 February 1997; ibid.,
Fournier to Gray, 19 February 1997; ibid., Gray to Ward Elcock, 26 February 1997; SIRC, Access request 2800-82, 'CSIS Investigations on University
Campuses (SIRC Study 1998-14).'

16 SIRC, Annual report for 1998–9, 41.

17 Stewart Bell, 'Last Stand Against Terrorism,' *National Post*, 21 May 2001;
'Threat to Canadians?' *National Post*, 6 June 2001; 'Canada Grows as Target
for Terrorists: CSIS,' *National Post*, 13 June 2001; Stewart Bell, 'Cyber-
Attacks Threaten Canada: CSIS,' *National Post*, 18 July 2001.

18 Roy Greenslade, '"I Arrest You for Emailing,"' *Guardian*, 31 July 2000. The
broad definition of terrorism under the United Kingdom's Terrorism
Act 2000 can be read by searching in http://www.hmso.gov.uk/; Tony G.
Poveda, 'Controversies and Issues,' in Athan Theoharis, ed., *The FBI: A
Comprehensive Reference Guide* (New York 2000), 133–5.

19 David Pugliese and Jim Bronskill, 'Military Spies Target Dissenters,' *Ottawa
Citizen*, 19 August 2001.

20 Interview with anonymous, 29 May 2000; Comments of former SIRC
director Ron Atkey on *CBC Sunday Report*, 31 May 1998; Doug Beazley,
'Kurdish Student Sees Spies "Paranoia": We Don't Operate That Way, Says
the Canadian Security Service,' *Edmonton Sun*, 12 May 2000; Andrew Duffy,
'Chinese Spy Wins Reprieve; Judge Rules Concordia Student Doesn't Pose
Threat to Democracy,' *Ottawa Citizen*, 29 April 2000; David Pugliese and Jim
Bronskill, 'Military Spies Target Dissenters,' *Ottawa Citizen*, 19 August 2001;

Andrew Mitrovica, 'The Case of the Campus Rock Doctors,' *Globe and Mail*, 20 October 2001; Andrew Mitrovica, 'Spy Says University Kept Her out of Fear,' *Globe and Mail*, 22 October 2001; Jacques Steinberg, 'In Sweeping Campus Canvasses, U.S. Checks on Mideast Students,' *New York Times*, 21 November 2001.

21 CSIS, Access request 117-2000-22, A/Commissioner J.B. Giroux to Senior, 5 May 1980.

22 CSIS, '1999 Public Report'; Heather Hamilton, 'The Hands of Terror: Is Canada Safe from the Grasp of Terrorists?' RCMP Online, http://www.rcmp-grc.gc.ca/frames/rcmp-grc1.htm, 27 June 2000; Grant LaFleche, 'Jim Moses, Who Says He Was a CSIS Spy, Said Someone Tried to Kill Him in a House Fire,' *St. Catharines Standard*, 3 January 2000; Cleroux, *Official Secrets*, 259; George Oake, 'Secret Service Lifts the Lid on Its Calls to Universities,' *Toronto Star*, 6 May 1991; House of Commons, *Debates*, 3 April 2001, 1425; Hall to author, 11 April 2001.

23 For more on the meetings, the clash between demonstrators and the police, and broader legal questions surrounding the entire matter, see Wesley Pue, ed., *Pepper in Our Eyes: The APEC Affair* (Vancouver 2000); Karen Pearlston, 'APEC Days at UBC: Student Protests and National Security in an Era of Trade Liberalization,' in Gary Kinsman, Dieter K. Buse, and Mercedes Steedman, eds., *Whose National Security? Canadian State Surveillance and the Creation of Enemies* (Toronto 2000).

24 Reg Whitaker, 'The Politics of Security Intelligence Policy-Making in Canada: II, 1984–91,' *Intelligence and National Security* 7, no. 2 (1992), 57.

25 PCO, Records of the RCMP Public Complaints Commission, Exhibit V-010, Threat assessments/UBC, APEC Operational Plan, National Security Investigations Section, 4 November 1997; Hamilton, 'The Hands of Terror.'

26 SIRC, Annual report, 1986–7, 27; Cleroux, *Official Secrets*, 165–80; Stuart Farson, 'Sidewinder and the Minivan: Some Questions for Parliament to Ponder,' *CASIS Intelligence* 36 (spring 2000), 4–6.

27 Jean-Paul Brodeur, 'Countering Terrorism in Canada,' in A. Stuart Farson, David Stafford, and Wesley K. Wark, eds., *Security and Intelligence in a Changing World: New Perspectives for the 1990s* (London 1990), 193–4.

28 Records of the RCMP Public Complaints Commission, Exhibit V-016, Threat assessments/UBC, APEC, Report of Constable Donna Smith, 16 January 1997; ibid., Report of Constable S.P. Poirier, 23 June 1997; ibid., Report of Detective Constable J. Boyle, 9 August 1997; ibid., Constable Eldon J. Dueck to APEC Threat Assessment Group, Anti-APEC Functions, 30 October 1997.

29 Ibid., Report of Constable Rasche, 4 November 1997; David Pugliese and

Jim Bronskill, Undercover RCMP Actions Raise Questions about Police Role,' *Ottawa Citizen*, 22 August 2001.

30 Steve Hewitt, '"The Force Asked Too Much of Me": After 125 Years of the Mounted Police We Need More Contemplation and Less Celebration,' *Beaver* 78, no. 3 (1998), 49–50.

31 Bob Weber, 'Oil Vandal Jailed for 28 Months,' *Toronto Star*, 27 April 2000.

32 Reg Whitaker, *End of Privacy: How Total Surveillance Is Becoming a Reality* (New York 1999), 26–9.

33 Daniel Bell, *The End of Ideology: On the Exhaustion of Political Ideas in the Fifties* (Glencoe, IL, 1960).

34 Abby Scher, 'Crackdown on Dissent,' *Nation*, 5 February 2001; '15 Anti-missile Protesters Face Felony Charges,' *New York Times*, 12 August 2001; David Pugliese and Jim Bronskill, 'Caught in the Crossfire: Peaceful Protest a Right under Siege, Critics Say,' *Ottawa Citizen*, 18 August 2001; RCMP, Access request 01ATIP-26314, 'Public Order Program – Presentation to RCMP Senior Executive Committee,' 2 January 2001.

Illustration Credits

Every effort has been made to secure permissions for the use of illustrations in this book. Any omissions or errors pointed out to us will be corrected in future reprints.

L'Action Quotidien Catholique: André Marsan with camera, 14 November 1963.

Canadian Security Intelligence Service: Slides from a September 1971 RCMP presentation on security threats, Access request 117-1991-102.

The Carleton: Cartoon mocking the RCMP, from the Carleton University student newspaper, 25 January 1963.

Daniel Goldstick: RCMP report describing surveillance of Professor Goldstick.

Donald J. Inch: 1958 RCMP recruitment brochure.

National Archives of Canada: A. Bowen Perry, PA-201242; S.T. Wood, PA-203199; Historian Frank Underhill's Personal History File, RG 146, file 1027-97-A-00044, pt 1, 13 August 1940; Senior members of the RCMP's intelligence operations at a 1944 conference; Crowd gathered in front of a Montreal courthouse, PA-129626; Terry Guernsey, PA-202110; Combined Universities Campaign, December 1959, photograph by Ted Grant, PA-211304; Combined Universities Campaign, Thanksgiving, 1961, C146270; Another informant photograph, 1961, C146271; Mario Bachand, C140106; Jean-Pierre Goyer, PA-128172.

Index